SWAT Madness and the Militarization of the American Police

SWAT Madness and the Militarization of the American Police

A National Dilemma

Jim Fisher

PRAEGER

AN IMPRINT OF ABC-CLIO, LLC
Santa Barbara, California • Denver, Colorado • Oxford, England

Library of Congress Cataloging-in-Publication Data

Fisher, Jim (A. James)
  SWAT madness and the militarization of the American police : a national dilemma / Jim Fisher.
     p. cm.
  Includes bibliographical references and index.
  ISBN 978-0-313-39191-0 (alk. paper) — ISBN 978-0-313-39192-7 (e-book)
1. Police brutality—United States.   2. Police—United States.
3. Law enforcement—United States.   I. Title.
  HV8141.F54   2010
  363.2'32—dc22   2010018845

ISBN: 978-0-313-39191-0
EISBN: 978-0-313-39192-7

14 13 12 11 10 1 2 3 4 5

This book is also available on the World Wide Web as an eBook.
Visit www.abc-clio.com for details.

Praeger
An Imprint of ABC-CLIO, LLC

ABC-CLIO, LLC
130 Cremona Drive, P.O. Box 1911
Santa Barbara, California 93116-1911

This book is printed on acid-free paper ∞

Manufactured in the United States of America

*The crooks? Where are the crooks? It's the police
who give me all my trouble.*

—Charles Bukowski

CONTENTS

PREFACE

American law enforcement has become zero tolerant, more violent, and militarized. Local, state, and federal teams of elite paramilitary special weapons and tactics (SWAT) teams regularly patrol big-city streets and break into homes unannounced. Officers on routine patrol carry high-powered semi- and fully automatic weapons. Virtually every law enforcement agency in the country either has its own SWAT unit or has officers who are members of a multijurisdictional force. The barrier between the U.S. military and domestic law enforcement has broken down. The police have become soldiers and military personnel now function as civilian law enforcers. Paramilitary police officers wear combat gear, are transported in army-surplus armored personnel carriers, receive special-forces training, and view criminal suspects as enemy combatants. Federal, state, and local law enforcement agencies field teams of military-trained snipers. In many jurisdictions, the "public servant" concept of policing has been replaced by the "occupying force" model. The idea of community policing has become outmoded. If one didn't know any better, one would think that the nation was in the grip of a historic crime wave. However, compared with the 1930s and the late 1960s through the 1970s, the current rate of violent crime is much lower.

Every year SWAT teams conduct forced entry, no-knock raids into 40,000 to 50,000 homes in search of illegal drugs and drug paraphernalia. In many jurisdictions all drug-related search warrant executions involve SWAT team entries. Once a law enforcement agency forms a paramilitary unit, the officers on the team must be kept busy to stay sharp. For this reason, the great majority of SWAT raids in this country involve low-risk police work and are therefore unnecessary. The predawn, no-knock SWAT raid into a private home has become the signature of the government's escalating war on drugs. Even when the raids are not in some way botched, as when officers break into the wrong house, innocent bystanders, including children, are injured, manhandled, and/or traumatized. Following these raids, residents are left with broken doors, windows, and furniture and ransacked rooms. Occasionally the "flashbang" grenades the raiders use to disorient occupants cause injuries and start fires. It is not uncommon for subjects of these raids, thinking that their homes are being invaded by criminals, to pick up guns in self-defense. These people are often shot and killed. If they shoot and kill a police officer, they go to prison. In these cases it doesn't matter that the defendants didn't know who they were shooting at. Some of them end up on death row.

Because deranged and disturbed people do take hostages, barricade themselves in their homes, and on rare occasion vent their rage through killing sprees, metropolitan and regional SWAT operations have become a necessary component of law enforcement. And although the need to protect the country against acts of terrorism may justify cooperation between police and military, including the equipping and training of elite commando units, these paramilitary forces should not be used to search homes for drugs, pornography, evidence of white-collar crime, or nonviolent fugitives. Moreover, SWAT teams should not be employed to sweep high schools for drugs, raid home poker games and brothels, break up raucous musical events, or patrol subways, airports, and high-crime neighborhoods. Turning police officers into combat warriors and criminal suspects into enemy forces is not the way laws should be enforced in a country where citizens expect law and order without having to sacrifice their civil rights.

Police administrators, aware that Americans tend to be wary of governmental authority, have never been above fear mongering. The "thin blue line" metaphor—the notion that a fragile barrier of uniformed cops stands between civilized society and hordes of rapists and looters—is a good example of scaring citizens into accepting and appreciating excessive police authority. Those skeptical of the "thin blue line" concept were proven right in the early 1970s following a series of experiments in Kansas City, Missouri, that showed no correlation between police patrols and crime prevention. Government fear mongering, from the "reefer madness" era through the "thin blue line" period, continues. Now, in addition to the specter of a society collapsing under the weight of drug addiction and crime, the fear of terrorism propels the move toward a more militarized, heavy-handed form of law enforcement. If this trend isn't reversed, the day may come when the fear of crime and terrorism will be matched by the fear of the police. As Winston Churchill once said, "Democracy means that when there's a knock at the door at three in the morning, it's probably the milkman." Today, in America, it's certainly not the milkman, and if it's a SWAT team at your door, forget the knock.

—Jim Fisher
March 25, 2010

ACKNOWLEDGMENTS

I would like to acknowledge the research into police militarism conducted by professors Victor Kappeler and Peter B. Kraska of Eastern Kentucky University. Radley Balko, formerly of the Cato Institute and now senior editor at *Reason Magazine,* has reported brilliantly on SWAT team abuses. Balko is also the author of *Overkill: The Rise of Paramilitary Police Raids in America,* a white paper published by the Cato Institute in 2006. Dr. Doreen Valentine made valuable suggestions that significantly improved the manuscript. I also thank Praeger acquisitions editor Michael Wilt, whose support for the book led to its publication.

Chapter 1

THE NATURE AND SCOPE OF MILITARIZED POLICING

The U.S. Constitution represents the Founding Fathers' intent to protect Americans against heavy-handed government. Citizens have rights, which include the right to assemble peacefully, the right to speak freely, and the freedom to worship as they please. The Constitution protects against intrusive law enforcement by protecting individual privacy, granting the right against self-incrimination, and providing the right to legal representation. The presumption of innocence, the concept of due process, and limited law enforcement authority protect Americans from tyranny.

The Founding Fathers also placed limits on the military arm of government. Only Congress can fund and declare war, and the president, a civilian officeholder, is commander in chief. By placing military control in the hands of civilians, the Founding Fathers intended to at least discourage military personnel from meddling in civilian governance. Notwithstanding the existence of a wide range of procedural civil rights, military involvement in law enforcement, either directly or through highly militarized policing, is counter to the concept of limited government and is a threat to personal freedom.

THE INSURRECTION AND POSSE COMITATUS ACTS

In 1807, Congress passed a set of laws called the Insurrection Act, which restricted the president's power to deploy federal troops within U.S. borders. Under this act, the federal military could be used only to quell such lawlessness, insurrection, or rebellion as local governments could not or would not put down. Congress intended the act as a limitation on the president's ability to employ federal troops to enforce the law and maintain domestic order.

At the conclusion of the Civil War, Congress imposed martial law in the southern states. During this period, the army enforced reconstruction policies and interfered in local politics. Eventually, outrage stemming from military intervention in civilian affairs prompted Congress, in 1878, to pass the Posse Comitatus Act, which prohibited the military from playing any role in the enforcement of civil law. However, situations covered by the Insurrection Act of 1807 were exempt from this law. The Posse Comitatus Act, a federal statute one sentence long, in combination with the various constitutional restrictions on domestic military intervention, protected Americans against the tyranny of a nationwide force of military police.

With rare exception, until the 1980s and 1990s, military forces were not used to enforce civilian law. On a few occasions, the president, without congressional approval, used federal troops to maintain civil order and enforce federal law. These incidents were short-lived, last-resort measures, and once the federal objectives were achieved, the military troops were quickly withdrawn.

In 2006, as part of the 2008 Defense Authorization Bill, Congress amended the Insurrection Act of 1807. Entitled "Enforcement of the Laws to Restore Public Order," the act allowed the president to deploy military troops as a domestic force in response to natural disasters, disease outbreak, terrorist attacks, and any "other condition" the chief executive deemed threatening enough to warrant this action. The law allowed the president to declare a public emergency and to station the military anywhere in the country. It also allowed the commander in chief to take control of state-based National Guard units without the consent of the governor and other local authorities. Congress created this broadening of domestic military power to maintain law and order without hearings or public debate. The bill received bipartisan support in both houses.

Senator Patrick Leahy of Vermont, one of a handful in Congress who opposed the weakening of the Insurrection Act, said the following in September 2006: "We certainly do not need to make it easier for presidents to declare martial law. Invoking the Insurrection Act and using the military for law enforcement activities goes against some of the central tenets of our democracy. It creates needless tension among the various levels of government—one can easily envision governors and mayors in charge of an emergency having to constantly look over their shoulders while someone who has never visited their communities gives the orders."[1]

In 2008, in anticipation of the Defense Authorization Bill of the following year, Senators Leahy and Christopher Bond introduced a bill, backed by the nation's governors, to repeal the 2006 amendments to the Insurrection

Act. Congress, in 2008, repealed all of its 2006 amendments to the 1807 law. Since governments tend to expand rather than limit their powers, this action marked a small but important victory for those fighting for more individual freedom.

LOS ANGELES AND THE BIRTH OF SWAT POLICING

In 1967, amid a period of civil unrest in the form of anti–Vietnam War protests and race riots, the Los Angeles Police Department formed 15 four-man paramilitary units to protect the department's facilities. Members of these Station Defense Teams possessed street-patrol backgrounds and prior military service. These were not, however, full-time assignments. The concept of combat-trained paramilitary police units came from an officer named John Nelson, who passed the idea on to Inspector Darryl Gates, who presented it to the top brass. Gates wanted to call these units Special Weapons and Attack Teams, but this was considered a bit too militaristic for a civilian agency. In 1969, these units became known as Special Weapons and Tactical (SWAT) teams.

On December 9, 1969, when police officers tried to serve search warrants for illegal weapons at the Black Panther headquarters at 41st Street and Central in Los Angeles, the occupants fired on the officers with shotguns and automatic rifles. SWAT teams from around the city were called to the scene. Following a four-hour gun battle between six Black Panthers and 200 officers, the shooters in the house surrendered. Three SWAT team members and three Black Panthers had been wounded.

Following the Black Panther shoot-out, police administrators concluded that SWAT team response times would be improved by reassigning the 15 teams dispersed throughout the county to police headquarters in downtown Los Angeles. In 1971, SWAT team assignments became full-time positions. The Los Angeles Police Department, for several years, was the only law enforcement agency in the country with a paramilitary capability.

Four years after the Black Panther violence, the Los Angeles SWAT force consisted of 10 six-man teams. Each team had two five-man units called "elements," with a leader, two "assaulters," a scout, and a rearguard officer. SWAT team weapons included a .245-caliber bolt-action sniper rifle, two .223-caliber semiautomatic rifles, and a pair of shotguns. Officers were also equipped with service revolvers and gas masks. In their helmets, gloves, and body armor, they could not be distinguished from combat troops.

On May 17, 1974, six members of the Symbionese Liberation Army (SLA) barricaded themselves inside a house on East 54th Street at Compton Avenue, ignored orders from the police to surrender peacefully. The domestic terrorists responded to tear gas canisters lobbed into the premises by opening fire on the three SWAT teams and hundreds of regular police who had gathered at the scene. The police returned fire, eventually wounding all six occupants. The gun battle involved 3,772 bullets fired by SLA members and thousands of shots from the police. The shoot-out ended when a fire broke out inside the house, burning the structure to the ground. The occupants either died of their wounds or of the blaze. Investigators speculated that the fire started when a bullet hit a Molotov cocktail or a tear gas grenade. People around the country watched as the battle unfolded on live television.

Although there was little sympathy for terrorists who had fired on the police, the Los Angeles Police Department was criticized for allowing the situation to evolve into a scene of urban warfare. The department responded by tightening SWAT unit admission standards and upgrading the paramilitary training to reduce the occurrence of such spectacular violence.

BOMBS AWAY IN PHILADELPHIA

In 1979, nine members of MOVE (not an acronym), a small society of discontents who preached a back-to-nature lifestyle, were convicted of murdering a Philadelphia police officer. The group, made up of blacks all with the same adopted last name—Africa—resided as a community in a building located in a west Philadelphia neighborhood. A year earlier the MOVE site had been declared a public nuisance and its occupants ordered to leave the premises. The eviction deadline had passed and the place was still inhabited. When the police came to the vacate the house, they came under fire, which led to an officer's death and nine murder convictions.

Seven years later, the MOVE people were occupying a row house on Osage Avenue that had been declared a public nuisance. The police arrived on May 13, 1985, to enforce the court's eviction order. Officers were met with gunfire from behind a barrier on the roof of the house. After a 24-hour standoff, the mayor approved a plan to destroy the rooftop bunker. From a helicopter, the police dropped a homemade bomb on the dwelling. The device, comprising the explosives C-4 and TOVEX, set the structure on fire. The blaze ignited the houses next door, and by the time the fire was put out, 50 structures had burned to the ground. The firestorm killed four children and seven adults, including one member of the MOVE clan. In 1996, a jury in a federal civil rights case found that the Philadelphia police had used excessive force in their reaction to the armed MOVE assault.

THE COLUMBINE EFFECT

SWAT team use is no longer a backup, last-resort law enforcement measure. Since the mid-1980s, police administrators have significantly increased the number of paramilitary units and have incorporated SWAT-like methods and a militaristic philosophy into routine patrol duty, order maintenance, and crowd control. The expanding role of SWAT team policing parallels the recent history of American spree killing. For example, after a deranged shooter massacred 21 people inside a San Diego McDonald's in July 1984, the police department began putting more SWAT-trained officers on routine patrol. (The mass murderer was killed by a SWAT team sniper.) A pair of heavily armed men, during a February 1997 bank robbery and shootout, wounded 10 Los Angeles police officers and 7 civilians before they were killed by SWAT bullets. Following this event in North Hollywood, the police department issued 600 high-powered rifles to officers on regular patrol.

The Columbine High School killing spree on April 20, 1999, has been the single greatest catalyst to the militarization of routine policing in America. The Littleton, Colorado, killing of 12 and wounding of 24 other students by a pair of their bullied schoolmates has provided the rationale for arming and training "front line" patrol officers for SWAT operations. Critics of the police response to the mass murder point out that SWAT teams didn't enter the school until 1:09 P.M., almost 30 minutes after the killers had taken their own lives and almost 2 hours after the shooting had started. Had the first responders been trained in SWAT policing techniques and appropriately armed, they wouldn't have waited for the SWAT units while people inside the building were being shot.

Prior to the Columbine shootings, law enforcement's approach to killing sprees of this nature involved a contain-and-wait strategy designed to prevent officers and bystanders from being killed and wounded in the crossfire. Under this policy, responding patrol officers set up perimeters to contain the situations until the arrival of SWAT teams. Following the Columbine tragedy, police agencies across the country developed "active shooter" programs in which responding patrol officers are trained to rush toward the gunfire. Rather than wait for a paramilitary unit, many police departments now employ "contact teams" comprising heavily armed patrol officers who band together to enter the buildings and confront the shooter or shooters as soon as possible.

Northwestern University mass-murder expert Jack Levin doesn't believe that this more aggressive militaristic approach has reduced the likelihood of these kinds of deadly outbursts. Notwithstanding police assault training, more police officers in the schools, metal detectors, and the like, there have been, in the decade after Columbine, more than eighty school-site shootings. High-powered weapons and SWAT unit tactics have not kept young psychopaths and lone-wolf depressives from unleashing their fury on vulnerable students and teachers.

In February 2010, less than three miles from Columbine High School, a 32-year-old gunman in the parking lot outside a Littleton middle school shot and wounded two students. Math teacher David Benke ended the spree by physically subduing the shooter as he reloaded his bolt-action rifle. Despite the availability of nearby SWAT teams, it was an alert and brave civilian who saved the lives of children that afternoon.

In 2009, some $4 million of the $787 billion stimulus package went to local law enforcement. Although most of the money has gone into the hiring of new officers and the purchase of police vehicles and computers, agencies have spent a lot of the money on weaponry. As reported by Patrik Johnson of the *Christian Science Monitor,* the police department in Jeffersonville, Indiana, used $63,000 of its grant to buy 75 assault rifles. In Arlington, Texas, the authorities spent $56,000 on military-grade carbines. The police department in Barre, Vermont, used its share to acquire 6 handguns, 21 tasers, and 5 new shotguns. In Johnson's article, gun culture expert Brian Anse Patrick is quoted as noting that citizens who are concerned about police militarism are wondering if there will ever be enough guns to satisfy law enforcement needs.

Bucking the Trend in Boston

In May 2009, a proposal under consideration within the Boston Police Department to arm as many as 200 patrol officers with M-16 assault rifles became public after being leaked to the *Boston Globe.* According to the plan, officers who would carry the military surplus weapons (obtained free of charge) would receive up to 40 hours of training and shoot 2,000 practice range rounds. A departmental spokesperson responded to this story by saying that police commissioner Edward Davis was still mulling over the idea.

The idea of upgrading the department's firepower had been floated a year earlier but gained wider support after terrorists attacked the luxury hotels in Mumbai, India, in November 2008. Heavily armed terrorists in that city killed 166 and wounded 234 before being killed or arrested. Police administrators within the Boston Police Department used the Mumbai attacks as an additional rationale for the enhanced weaponry.

The arms proposal had sparked a debate within the department regarding issues of safety. At that time, high-powered weapons were kept locked in special vehicles that transported them to the sites of SWAT team activity. Opponents of the plan, including a number of police union officials, expressed concern that the M-16s were too powerful for city streets and could fall into the hands of the wrong people. Proponents noted that patrol officers in Denver, after the Columbine massacre, started carrying assault rifles. Regular patrol officers in Chicago, Miami, Las Vegas, Cincinnati, and Phoenix also patrolled with military-grade weapons.

After the Boston arms plan became public, community leaders in minority neighborhoods voiced their disapproval, noting that this form of police militarism contradicted Commissioner Davis's plan to revitalize community policing. The commissioner had promised to reduce inner-city crime by fostering trust and cooperation between minorities and the police. Quoted in the *Boston Globe*, Jorge Martinez, executive director of RIGHT, a violence prevention program in Roxbury, said: "It seems like people [the police] wanted to get their free toys, and now they have to make up the rhyme and reason for what to do with them. They come up with these ridiculous ideas. What's wrong with this commissioner? This guy is supposed to be a national leader in community policing."[2]

Commissioner Davis, asserting that the M-16s would give his patrol officers a more level playing field against heavily armed criminals, cited the Columbine shootings. Noting that it takes 30 to 40 minutes for SWAT teams to arrive at Columbine-like emergencies, his regular, quicker-responding officers have been trained to confront active shooters immediately. "To protect them," he said, "They need to have some type of equipment [M-16s] readily available to them." The commissioner pointed out that other police departments in Massachusetts, such as the one in Brookline, have issued M-16s to patrol officers.

Shortly after the M-16 debate became public, Boston mayor Thomas M. Menino announced that he would not approve of the plan. Expressing concern regarding these high-powered weapons being carried on Boston's streets, he said, "Other cities have done it . . . but I would not want them on regular patrol." The mayor said that possession of semiautomatic rifles should be limited to members of elite, specially trained SWAT units. A few politicians in the city and certain members of the police department criticized what they believed to be the mayor's soft stand on crime and terrorism.

A more recent shooting spree, one involving the deaths of four police officers and the man who shot them, will probably help prolong the Columbine effect for several more years until the next burst of homicidal violence. In east Oakland, California, on Saturday, March 21, 2009, Lovelle Mixon, a 26-year-old parolee, shot two motorcycle officers to death after they had pulled him over for a traffic violation. Mixon fled the scene to his home a block away in a 10-unit, three-story apartment building. A few hours later, members of the Oakland Police Department's SWAT team, without notifying or evacuating residents of the building, kicked in Mixon's door, tossed in flashbang grenades, and stormed into the apartment. From a bedroom closet, Mixon open fired with an assault rifle, killing two SWAT officers

before being killed by other members of the raiding unit. The police injured Mixon's 16-year-old sister when they tossed in the flashbang devices.
Although patrol officers armed with assault rifles won't eliminate the in-
herent dangers of random police stops, the murder of the four Oakland
police officers will lead some police administrators and politicians to call
for the issuance of more high-powered, automatic police weaponry to officers on routine patrol.

More Firepower in Western Pennsylvania

In April 2009, four weeks after a heavily armed man wearing a bulletproof vest killed three uniformed Pittsburgh police officers responding to a
domestic disturbance call, the deputy chief announced that members of the
entire patrol force were being issued semiautomatic assault rifles. Although
the city's rates of violent crime had been in steady decline, the deputy chief
cited the need for longer-range, more accurate firepower. Patrol officers,
like members of the department's 39-man SWAT unit (transported in a
20-ton armored truck with a rotating turret and gun ports), would carry
M&P 15s, the .223-caliber, 30-round version of the military's M-16.

A week later, in McKeesport, Pennsylvania, just outside of Pittsburgh,
the chief of police told members of the city council that the deaths of the
Pittsburgh officers demonstrated the need for a SWAT team in their town.
Unwilling to rely on SWAT teams already in place with the Pittsburgh Police Department, the Allegheny County Sheriff's Office, and the local state
police unit, the city council approved a federal grant.

Six weeks after the McKeesport revelation, a township superintendent
in rural Lawrence County, an hour's drive north of Pittsburgh, announced
the formation of the Lawrence County Emergency Response Team. The
new 15-officer unit would cost the financially strapped county $100,000 to
equip and thousands of dollars more a year in training and overtime costs.
The superintendent didn't say exactly why this county needed a SWAT team
or how it would be used. In Pittsburgh, a major city, the SWAT team is called
out about 80 times a year. In Lawrence County, a sparsely populated region with relatively low crime rates, the new paramilitary unit, if limited to
high-risk assignments, will have virtually nothing to do. If these part-time
SWAT officers are to be kept raid-ready, the unit will have to be called out
on routine, low-risk jobs.

SATURATION PATROLS AND CROWD CONTROL

The rate of violent crime in American cities peaked in the 1970s and 1980s.
Then, during the 1990s, it declined sharply. In the 21st century, violent

crime, while gradually on the increase, has not come close to what it was 20 and 30 years ago. However, if one had to guess the level of inner-city crime by the number and aggressiveness of militarized police, one would reasonably assume that the country was in the middle of a serious crime wave. This disconnect between inner-city policing and the level of violent crime has caused a rift between the police and the minority citizens they are paid to serve in these neighborhoods. New York professor of law Paul Chevigny, quoted in an article about militarized policing in 2000, said: "The police think of themselves as an occupying army, and the public comes to think the same. The police lose the connection with the public which is the principal advantage to local policing, and their job becomes progressively more difficult, while they become more unpopular."[3]

In the summer of 2008, several big-city mayors backed militarized police programs with names like "Operation Safe Streets," designed to "take back neighborhoods," as though they had been invaded by enemy forces. Throughout the summer in Washington, D.C.; Oakland, California; Philadelphia; Cleveland; and Chicago, mayors and chiefs of police could be seen on local television news standing behind or in front of tables laden with guns, drugs, and cash liberated from the enemy.

The main feature of these intense anticrime programs involves saturating the target areas—minority neighborhoods—with SWAT teams and regular patrol officers dressed and equipped for combat. At night the air is filled with the sounds of helicopters hovering above as armored personnel carriers (APCs) rumble along the streets amid flashing lights and patrol car sirens. Police set up checkpoints along the perimeters of cordoned-off neighborhoods where they check identification before allowing residents to enter the occupied area. Random vehicle stops, curfew arrests, and pedestrian "stop and frisk" detentions based on profiles of people likely to be armed produces the contraband that will be seen on television as evidence of the programs' success. In some cities, police officers go around the neighborhood asking parents for consent to search their children's bedrooms for guns and drugs.

Chicago's "Summer Safety" Plan

What the police do or don't do has little effect on the rate of serious crime. The idea that police prevent violence is largely a myth. Criminal homicide, aggravated assault, and rape are offenses usually committed behind closed doors or otherwise out of public view. More officers on the street with higher-powered guns and broader authority has more effect on law-abiding citizens than on criminals. Nevertheless, when violent crime in a neighborhood becomes a media event, the chief of police, in an effort to show that he or she means business, responds with a show of force. And in law enforcement, nothing represents force more than the presence of combat-ready SWAT officers.

In Chicago, following an April 2008 weekend during which 36 people were shot, 9 fatally, SWAT teams were added to the late-night patrols of the violent, predominantly inner-city neighborhoods. Tio Hardiman, the director of a Chicago violence prevention group called CeaseFire, voiced his objection to this escalation of police firepower this way: "Sending SWAT teams into the community is doing nothing but suppressing the community." Six weeks later, the police department launched what had become an annual anticrime initiative called the Summer Safety Plan.[4]

Components of Chicago's 2008 crime suppression program included transferring 80 desk jockeys to patrol duties in "challenged districts" and deploying SWAT teams to designated "violent zones." The plan also involved random vehicle inspections called "roadside safety checks," outdoor "roll calls" consisting of the coordinated flashing of patrol car emergency lights and the activation of sirens (a show of force initiated by the New York Police Department), and helicopter surveillances of parks and beaches. Despite the increased police presence in the targeted communities, the number of Chicago homicides by the end of June (229), had risen above the previous year's six-month total (203).

That fall, the Chicago police superintendent announced that the department planned to purchase an unspecified number of M4 carbine assault rifles for SWAT and street gang units. If regular beat officers wanted to increase their firepower—the rifle had a range double that of a sidearm—they could purchase the $1,200-weapon with their own money. Several community activists interpreted this decision as evidence that the superintendent was more interested in combat than cooperation with the citizenry. According to Logan Square, a south side community group protestor, arming patrol officers with high-powered rifles was "Almost like putting military might into the neighborhoods."[5] To those who questioned the wisdom of increased police militarization, the superintendent responded with a bit of fear mongering. The assault rifles were necessary, he said, because criminals had become better armed. However, the superintendent offered no statistics or empirical analysis to bolster this contention. It's hard to imagine how more assault rifles on Chicago's streets will make the city a safer place to live.

Across the country, these militarized police operations, and the drastic measures that go with them, have put the police at odds with the residents of these predominantly minority communities. Reverend Ricky Burgess of Pittsburgh's Homewood Nazarene Baptist Church said this about the militarized approach to crime control: "I do believe the police think they are helping, but they're causing trauma to the neighborhood. At some point they have to realize that to make a difference, they can give us a constant, community-oriented police presence without giving us a paramilitary force and without turning our community into downtown Beirut."[6]

Leaders in black and Hispanic communities warn that saturation patrols and other forms of paramilitary policing have created a lack of trust in the police, which has reduced the likelihood of witnesses coming forward to help detectives solve urban crimes. Jeremy Kahn, a writer based in Washington, D.C., wrote in the April 2007 issue of the *Atlantic* that the police in minority communities are encountering a culture of silence among the citizenry, a code of silence not unlike *omerta* from organized crime. By fighting crime the wrong way, the police are making things difficult for the law-abiding residents of these neighborhoods.

Making Chattanooga Safer

In July 2008, the police department in Chattanooga, Tennessee, purchased a hundred .223-caliber "urban rifles" that can fire a bullet more than 400 yards. These Bushmaster-brand sniper weapons, costing $700 each, were issued to officers on routine patrol. In 2006, according to Federal Bureau of Investigation (FBI) crime statistics, Chattanooga, a city of 155,000, was the site of 17 murders and 532 robberies. In justifying the purchase of these long-range rifles as well as a forthcoming batch of 150 more, Lieutenant David Roddy told a local newspaper reporter that they were needed to level the playing field between his officers and the criminals. Roddy said that revolvers, pistols, and shotguns were no longer adequate patrol weapons.

THE WAR ON DRUGS

The Drug Enforcement Agency (DEA), the primary drug-control arm of the federal government, became operational in 1973, a year after President Richard Nixon declared war on illegal drugs. At this time, one in four servicemen who returned from Vietnam came home with a drug problem. *High Times Magazine,* in 1974, reported that 30 million Americans smoked pot. In 1981, the year after President Ronald Reagan escalated the government's war on drugs by making drug enforcement a police priority, Congress passed The Military Cooperation with Law Enforcement Act, which allowed military forces to "assist" civilian police in drug enforcement.

Through this sweeping piece of federal legislation, Congress destroyed the barrier that for more than a hundred years had kept the military from enforcing civilian law. Under this act, the military could now sell assault rifles, handguns, flashbang grenades, tear-gas dispensers, armored vehicles, and even helicopters to law enforcement agencies. Across the country, federal, state, and local SWAT teams—equipped with helmets, combat boots, goggles, and flack jackets—would be trained on military bases by elite special forces personnel. The military assistance law also authorized the sharing of military intelligence as part of the mission to restrict the flow of drugs coming into the country from Mexico and abroad.

In 1986, as First Lady Nancy Reagan asked young Americans to "just say no to drugs," President Ronald Reagan, in an effort to promote an even closer relationship between the military and civilian law enforcement, issued a National Security Directive designating drugs as an official threat to "national security." The next year, Congress created a toll-free number to be used by civilian police administrators to request military assistance in the battle against the sellers and users of these illegal substances. Dissatisfied with civilian progress in the drug war, Congress, in 1989, enlisted the help of the National Guard. Today, National Guard helicopters patrol the skies over 50 states looking for pot farms and patches of marijuana.

President George H. Bush's contribution to the militarization of American law enforcement came in 1989, with the creation of six regional joint task forces (JTFs) within the Department of Defense. JTFs were formed to coordinate the drug enforcement operations of the police and military. Whenever police administrators feel the need for advice and more firepower, all they have to do is call upon their regional JTFs. That's what the locals did in 1993 prior to the horribly botched raid on the Davidian Compound in Waco, Texas.

In 1994, pursuant to a memorandum of understanding between the Departments of Justice and Defense, the military was granted the right to transfer, free of charge, tons of surplus military hardware to civilian law enforcement agencies. Between 1995 and 1997, police agencies across the country received 1.2 million pieces of military equipment. Everywhere, units within federal, state, and local law enforcement agencies were transformed, in mindset and mission, into combat troops.

In case there was any doubt that the military was assuming a larger role in the enforcement of civilian drug laws, President Bill Clinton, in 1996, appointed General Barry R. McCaffrey director of the Office of National Drug Control Policy. The year after the McCaffrey appointment, people concerned about the ramifications of the military's involvement in drug enforcement were alarmed when a U.S. Marine, assigned to an antidrug patrol unit on the Mexican border, shot 18-year-old Esequiel Hernandez as he tended goats on private land. The Justice Department settled a wrongful death suit filed by the Hernandez family for $1.9 million.

THE SWAT TEAM EXPLOSION

About half of the nation's SWAT officers are trained by active-duty commandos from Navy Seal and Army Ranger units. Police officers with special operations backgrounds in the military train the rest. When fully outfitted in Kevlar helmets, goggles, "ninja" style hoods, combat boots, body armor, and black or camouflage fatigues, and carrying fully automatic rifles and machine guns, these police officers not only look like military troops geared for battle but also feel that way. These elite paramilitary teams—composed of commanders, tactical team leaders, scouts, rearguards, snipers, flashbang grenade officers, and paramedics—are organized like combat units and are just as lethal. But unlike troops in Iraq, SWAT police don't encounter mortar fire, rockets, homemade bombs, or heavily armed enemy soldiers. A vast majority of SWAT raids, conducted after midnight, involve private homes inhabited by unarmed people who are either asleep or watching television. When a SWAT team encounters resistance, it's usually from a family dog, who often gets shot. Given the hair-trigger intensity of these operations, unarmed civilians who move furtively or are slow to comply with orders get manhandled and sometimes shot.

In a landmark study of police paramilitary units published in February 1997, Eastern Kentucky University professors Peter B. Kraska and Victor Kappeler found that by 1990 every state police agency and half the country's sheriff's offices (about 1,500 agencies) had SWAT units. Thirty-eight percent of the nation's police departments were also SWAT team–ready. Five years later, in cities with populations of more than 50,000—about 700 municipalities—90 percent of the police departments were deploying SWAT teams. At the dawn of the 21st century, according to Kraska and Kappeler, federal, state, and local police were making 50,000 SWAT raids a year. Twenty-five years earlier, there were 3,000 SWAT callouts annually. According to the best estimates of experts in the field—counting federal, regional, state, county, and municipal law enforcement agencies—there are now at least 3,500 paramilitary police units operating throughout the country.

The 1,300 percent jump in SWAT team deployment in less than twenty years does not reflect a concomitant increase in armed hostage taking, sniper cases, or other high-risk incidents requiring heavily armed, combat-trained units. Scholars like Kraska and Kappeler, who have studied the SWAT team phenomenon, estimate that 75 percent of the nation's drug raids involve no-knock, forced-entry drug searches. William Bratton, the former commissioner of New York City's Police Department, in response to an interviewer's question regarding the overuse of SWAT teams to conduct drug raids, reportedly said that "where the suspect might be armed, we would call in a special tactics unit. Over time, though, it became common [practice] to always use the tactical unit no matter what or who the warrant was for. They used stun grenades each time and looked at it [the raids] as practice."[7]

According to professors Kraska and Kappeler, 20 percent of police departments in cities with populations exceeding 50,000 regularly employ paramilitary units on routine street patrol. Ironically, funds supporting such deployments often come from federal "community policing" grants intended to foster a friendlier, more cooperative relationship between citizens and the police. The community policing model where law enforcement is practiced as a form of social work has lost ground to the role and image of the police officer as a warrior in the war on crime. Although the motto might be "to serve and protect," the goal is to break in and arrest.

In justifying the common use of SWAT teams in the execution of warrants in drug cases, the police cite officer safety. Nationwide, in 2006, the police made 2 million drug arrests resulting in the deaths of two police officers. This low officer death rate is due to the overwhelming military-like force of these raids. During 2006, drug-raiding police officers killed five people and seriously wounded seven. Another man who had barricaded himself in his house was shot to death by a SWAT team sniper. According to a SWAT team study conducted by the Cato Institute's Radley Balko, 62 civilians were killed by the police in drug raids from 1992 through 2005, and 42 of these deaths involved "innocent" [Balko's term] people. During the same period, 15 law enforcement officers were killed. It seems that living in a neighborhood where drugs are bought and sold is at least as dangerous as routine police work and a lot safer than being on a SWAT team. In 2007, according to FBI statistics, 57 law enforcement officers were feloniously killed in the line of duty, and 48 lost their lives the preceding year. Of the 55 officers shoot to death in 2007, a total of 38 were killed by handguns, 9 with shotguns, and 8 with rifles. Two officers were run over by vehicles. Since the government doesn't keep track of civilian deaths, no one knows how many people the police may have killed in any given year.

Since the war on drugs is so heavily fought in inner-city neighborhoods, minorities are common targets of SWAT-led drug raids. According to the *Source Book of Criminal Justice Statistics*, whereas African Americans are 20 percent more likely than whites to use illegal drugs, they are 13 more times more likely to be imprisoned for drug crimes. Representing 13 percent of the population, blacks make up 35 percent of drug arrests, 55 percent of drug convictions, and 74 percent of those in prison for drug-related offenses.

In 2002, University of Florida law professor Kenneth B. Nunn, in the *Journal of Gender, Race and Justice,* wrote: "The war on drugs has had a devastating effect on African American communities nationwide. Throughout the drug war, African Americans have been disproportionately investigated, detained, searched, arrested and charged with the use, possession and the sale of illegal drugs. Vast numbers of African Americans have been jailed and imprisoned pursuant to the nation's toughest drug trafficking laws, implemented as part of the war on drugs."

In Syracuse, New York, drug reformer Nicolas Eyle and city auditor Minchin Lewis conducted a study to determine the impact of the drug war on the city's minority population. They found that in 2004, the Syracuse police made 28,800 arrests, of which 22 percent involved drug-related offenses. That year the police arrested 2,000 suspects for possession or sale of marijuana. The authors of the study also determined that the typical drug raid targeted public housing units located in the city's six black neighborhoods. Because federal regulations call for the eviction of drug users from government housing, the war on drugs in Syracuse, and presumably other places, causes the splitting up of families.

SHOCK-AND-AWE POLICING

Stunning the enemy with overpowering, high-tech ordinance as a prelude to a full-scale military invasion, while effective as a combat strategy, is not a suitable approach for ordinary, everyday law enforcement. But in Aspen, Colorado, in December 2005, shock and awe was exactly the approach when a 53-man raiding party of DEA and Immigration and Customs Enforcement (ICE) agents—along with officers from the Colorado Department of Revenue and police from Aspen and Snowgrass Village—stormed two downtown restaurants. SWAT-attired officers with guns drawn invaded the establishments at 4 o'clock in the afternoon, stunning the customers, who were relaxing with drinks following a day on the slopes.

The restaurant raids drew the ire of Pitkin County sheriff Bob Brandis, who had been given no advance notice of the operation. The chief of the Aspen Police Department admitted that the sheriff's well-known disapproval of the drug war and the militaristic way in which it is waged was a factor in keeping him in the dark. The raids netted two ounces of cocaine and $3,000 in cash; in addition, 9 people were taken into custody for drug possession and 11 others for immigration-related violations.

SWAT teams in Buffalo, New York, over a 3-day period in mid-April 2008, raided 38 suspected drug houses in the Niagara district of the city. Lest the public think that politicians in Buffalo were soft on crime, police leaders invited members of the media to accompany the drug raiders to publicize the mission they had code-named "Operation Shock and Awe." Police arrested

76 people; they seized only a pound of marijuana and seven ounces of crack cocaine. In comparison, a single police officer during a routine traffic stop in the middle of "Operation Shock and Awe" confiscated 3½ pounds of pot. Of the 76 suspects taken into custody, 32 were out of jail within 24 hours of their arrest; 16 arrestees had their cases immediately dismissed for lack of evidence. A month after the raids, just 20 suspects still faced felony charges. The Buffalo version of the invasion of Iraq amounted to a lot of sound and fury signifying another example of law enforcement nothing.

On the night of May 30, 2008, at the La Familia Motorcycle Club on the northwest side of Chicago, members of this private organization, while celebrating a friend's birthday, heard a commotion at the front door. A few seconds later more that a dozen heavily armed SWAT police burst into the room. Several of the panicked patrons fled to the rear of the building, where they were met by a contingent of officers who, amid exploding flash-bang grenades, herded them back into the main room.

After the police had rounded up the patrons and restrained them with plastic strips, a female officer, in view of the others, strip-searched five of the women. A search team combing the premises for drugs and weapons seized $1,000 in cash from the club safe and $1,500 from a couple of video poker machines. The police arrested two people, one for reckless conduct and the other on an outstanding bond forfeiture warrant. The officers recovered a small quantity of drugs and one handgun. An informant's tip that a shipment of drugs had been sent to the club produced the search warrant that legally justified the intrusion and arrests.

Four of the club's surveillance cameras were recording the raid until the police, realizing that they were being taped, redirected the devices. A month after the raid, club members filed a $10 million lawsuit against the Chicago Police Department. When asked by a reporter to comment on the suit and the raid, a police spokesperson assured the public that the officers had acted appropriately within departmental guidelines, noting that the raid had been based on a valid search warrant.

The humiliation of the women in the La Familia raid is not an uncommon aspect of shock-and-awe policing by all-male SWAT teams. Whether this behavior is prurient, misogynistic, or reflects the warrior's disdain for the enemy, it's highly inappropriate. Such behavior can inflict serious psychological damage on the victimized women.

ZERO-TOLERANCE POLICING

One foreseeable byproduct of a more militarized approach to law enforcement is the overly officious, thin-skinned police officer who reacts to citizen disrespect as though it were a crime and a breakdown of law and order. This hard-nosed approach toward dealing with the public goes hand in hand with the theory of policing where "quality of life" violations— graffiti, panhandling, moderate disorderly conduct, loitering, and public alcohol consumption—are not tolerated. This "broken windows" theory of order maintenance holds that once a neighborhood is allowed to deteriorate in this way, the real criminals will move in and take over. There seem to be an increasing number of police officers who treat all offenders the same, regardless of how minor the crime. This form of "no discretion law enforcement" defeats the purpose of community policing.

On September 2, 2008, La Tanya Williams-Green, a 31-year-old manager of an information technology firm operating a state healthcare service, ran into a pair of zero-tolerant police officers in Trenton, New Jersey. On Monday evening, while attending a family get-together, La Tanya received a call from her cousin, who had been stopped for not wearing his seat belt. Because of a previous ticket, he was afraid the police would take him into custody and tow his car. To avoid the towing fee, he asked La Tanya to retrieve the vehicle.

The two police officers who had stopped La Tanya's cousin were assigned to a special patrol operation called Selective Area Field Enforcement (SAFE). Officers in this aggressive, high-crime patrol unit maintained order and "quality of life" with a zero-tolerance approach to crime, which included arresting people for minor offenses. It's not clear how not wearing one's seat belt threatened the quality of life in Trenton, New Jersey.

When La Tanya pulled up to the traffic stop at 7:15 in the evening, one of the officers instructed her to remain in the car. Later, a second officer approached her car and asked her a series of questions. La Tanya objected to these inquiries, which led to an argument. The angry police officer asked to see La Tanya's driver's license, which was in her purse in the trunk of the vehicle. When she climbed out of the car to comply with this officer's order, his partner, who had told her to remain in the car, pushed her over the hood of the vehicle and handcuffed her behind her back. When asked what she was being arrested for, the officer identified her crime as obstructing the law and improper behavior toward a police officer. The police did not articulate exactly how La Tanya had obstructed justice other than by expressing her anger and frustration over how the officers had treated her. In essence, these officers hauled her off to the police station for failing to exercise what they believed constituted proper citizen–police etiquette. They also ordered that her car be towed away, which would cost her $100.

At the police station, the officers humiliated La Tanya further by making fun of her weight and refusing her request to use the restroom. When she threatened to have an accident if she couldn't use the bathroom, one officer said, "We have a mop." That night, La Tanya, who had tried to help her cousin, was arrested, had her car towed, and spent an hour in custody. The SAFE patrol had not enhanced La Tanya's quality of life in the city of Trenton.

In Pittsburgh, Pennsylvania, citizens who show disrespect for the police by swearing at them or flipping their middle fingers receive disorderly conduct citations. In 2002, a police officer cited John Neidig, who, after being told he had a bad attitude, accused the officer of having an [expletive] attitude himself. Mr. Neidig sued the police department for malicious prosecution. The civil jury awarded him $3,000. Apparently no one had told this police officer that profanity and nothing more directed at a law enforcement official is a form of speech protected by the First Amendment.

Pittsburgh resident David Hackbart, on April 10, 2006, was unable to parallel park his car after a motorist pulled up behind him, blocking his path. Mr. Hackbart lost his temper and gave the other driver the finger. When a third person told him he shouldn't do that, Hackbart flipped him off as well. Unfortunately for Mr. Hackbart, that person turned out to be a Pittsburgh police officer. Sergeant Brian Elledge spun his patrol car around and wrote Hackbart a ticket for disorderly conduct. In response to Hackbart's civil suit against the police department, the city attorney asserted that the ticket was not for the obscene gesture but because Mr. Hackbart had been blocking traffic on a busy street. Mr. Hackbart's lawyer, curious to know if the sergeant's disorderly conduct citation reflected standard operating procedure at the Pittsburgh Police Department, filed a right-to-know request with the municipal court. This request produced startling information. Pittsburgh police officers, from March 1, 2005 to October 31, 2007, a period of 20 months, had issued 188 disorderly conduct citations for public swearing, loud talking, and disrespectful behavior toward a police officer. Initially, a spokesperson for the department had said there were no other cases in which citizens who had behaved as Mr. Hackbart had done had been cited for disorderly conduct. It seemed that police administrators in Pittsburgh either didn't know that their officers were abusing citizens in this way or didn't care.

On March 23, 2009, U.S. District Court Judge David Cerone ruled that Sergeant Elledge, by citing Mr. Hackbart, had in fact violated his civil rights. In explaining his decision, the judge wrote: "Elledge's response to Hackbart's exercise of his First Amendment right was to initiate a traffic stop and issue a citation for disorderly conduct. Clearly, Elledge's conduct was an adverse action in response to Hackbart flipping him off."[8]

Welcome Home Maurice White

Maurice White, a month after returning to his home on the Muscogee (Creek) Nation reservation in Gore, Oklahoma, following a tour in Iraq, became a well-publicized victim of zero-tolerance policing. On May 24, 2009, as an emergency medical technician (EMT) with the Creek Nation Emergency Medical Service, Maurice was in the back of his ambulance attending a heart patient on her way from Boley to the hospital in Prague. They were passing through the town of Paden, 40 miles east of Oklahoma City, when the ambulance driver, Paul Franks, noticed an Oklahoma Highway Patrol (OHP) car, its emergency lights flashing, coming up behind them at high speed. The police vehicle cut in between the ambulance and the car following it, which contained members of the patient's family. OHP Trooper Daniel Martin, angry that Franks had not pulled off the highway to let him pass, contacted the ambulance driver by radio and admonished him for not being observant and more accommodating. As Martin pulled up alongside the ambulance, Franks raised his hands as if to ask, "What did I do wrong?" (In his police report, officer Martin accused Franks of giving him the finger.)

The trooper continued to his destination which, according to his report, was a traffic stop that possibly involved a stolen vehicle. Before White and Franks reached the hospital, the ambulance passed Martin's patrol car at the police barracks. A few minutes later, Trooper Martin caught up to them and drove up alongside the ambulance. He signaled Franks to pull the vehicle over.

White, unaware of what was going on between the officer and the operator of the ambulance, thought they had been ordered to stop because the woman seated in the patrol car next to the trooper needed emergency medical treatment. White and Franks alighted from the ambulance and Martin climbed out of the police vehicle. Officer Martin, obviously furious, approached Franks and yelled, "I'm going to give you a ticket for failure to yield, and when I go by [you] you're saying 'What's going on?' You don't need to give me no hand gestures now. I ain't going to put up with that [expletive]."[9]

White, in an effort to protect his ambulance driver, inserted himself between the two men. Calmly speaking to the trooper, he said, "I'm in charge of this unit, sir. And I won't put up with your talking to my driver like that."[10] White then informed Martin that they had a patient in the ambulance whom they were taking to the hospital in Prague. Family members of the patient, who were witnessing the confrontation, were also alerting the officer of this important fact. Instead of acknowledging this information, Trooper Martin ordered White back into the ambulance. When the EMT mentioned the patient again, the officer became even more belligerent. He ordered White to wait in the ambulance while he wrote out the traffic ticket for failure to yield. Again, White pleaded on behalf of the patient. Trooper Martin informed White that he was under arrest for obstructing a police officer. He grabbed White by the arm and started to put on the handcuffs, but the EMT pulled away and reminded Martin that it was a felony to assault a paramedic in the line of duty. Meanwhile, a small crowd of citizens, all sympathetic to the ambulance men, had gathered at the scene. Members of the patient's family couldn't believe that a police officer was keeping a sick woman from receiving hospital treatment. White climbed back into the van to check on his patient. Trooper Martin banged on the ambulance door before climbing into the vehicle and pulling White out. This, of course, terrified the patient, who had no idea what was going on. Outside the ambulance, the two men scuffled until the officer, with White pressed up against the ambulance, grabbed hold of his trachea with a claw-like grip. After holding him this way for 10 to 15 seconds, the officer released White, who did not fight back. Martin, having gained some control of the situation, told White and the ambulance driver that they could proceed to the hospital with their patient. But before the vehicle pulled back onto the highway, Martin opened the back door and informed White that he would be taken into custody at the hospital. This led to another altercation outside the ambulance, which ended with the trooper subduing the EMT by holding him in a headlock. Eventually, both men settled down and the ambulance got under way, with the trooper following.

After the patient had been delivered and admitted, hospital personnel informed Trooper Martin that if he arrested Maurice, who did not have a replacement, he would shut down the emergency medical service for Okfuskee County. Martin then called the district attorney's office and was told not to make the arrest.

On June 1, after placing Trooper Martin on paid administrative leave, the Oklahoma Department of Safety—after amateur videos of the confrontation became public—released the official dash cam video. The patient's family promptly uploaded the video onto the video-sharing YouTube site. Officials looking into the incident were hampered by eyewitnesses, including members of the patient's family, who were so angry at the police that they refused to give the investigators any statements. Investigators did learn, however, that the woman in the trooper's car was his wife, whom he had picked up between his first encounter with the ambulance and his second, when he pulled Franks over to give him the failure-to-yield ticket. When Trooper Martin admonished Franks for not yielding to a police cruiser, was he responding to a police call or was he on his way to pick up his wife?

Clara Harper, the patient's sister, who had witnessed the confrontation, told a *Tulsa World* reporter on June 13 that White "never once became aggressive to that trooper." Regarding her sister, Harper said, "She was scared, and I was trying to calm her down and telling her that everything was going to be all right."[11] As it happened, medically speaking, everything did turn out all right. That day, on KOKI-TV, White said, referring to his run-in with Trooper Martin, "It was surrealistic because I've never had such an experience. My biggest concern was for the patient. If there's any nightmare from this, it's because of what that mother [the patient] had to go through."[12]

SHOCKING OLDER WOMEN: WHATEVER HAPPENED TO HELPING THEM CROSS THE STREET?

Tasers, which have been around since the 1970s, are handheld devices that deliver an electrical shock that temporarily stuns and disables suspects who resist authority or pose serious physical threats to arresting officers. The original five-watt stun gun, which produced a minor jolt, was followed in 1994 by a seven-watt version called the Air-Taser, a product manufactured and sold by Taser International. In 1998, the company developed a higher-powered taser designed to stop the more combative, dangerous suspect likely to fight through the lighter applications. A year or so later, Taser International came out with the M 26, a 26-watt device that stunned subjects with 50,000 volts. The company began selling the X 26 in 2003, a lighter, more portable version of the M 26.

While representatives of Taser International insist that their nonlethal device is safe, critics of the stun gun, such as Amnesty International, claim that tasers have killed more than a hundred people. In cases where citizens have died after being shocked by the police, forensic pathologists have found preexisting illnesses or the presence of drugs and other toxic substances. The safety debate continues in forensic medicine and in the courts. But among those who recognize and appreciate that tasers provide a nonlethal alternative to billy clubs and guns, there is concern over the indiscriminant use of the device on people whose behavior doesn't call for such force. Over the past few years, police officers have tasered (or tased) children as young as six years of age; people who were mentally ill or physically disabled; and elderly women. Police officers have also stunned peaceful protestors and citizens stopped for traffic violations and other minor offenses whose actions did not justify the unpleasant experience of being jolted by 50,000 volts.

At present, officers in 11,000 police agencies carry taser guns. Although there is no governmental agency that keeps a record of the frequency and consequences of taser use, groups like Amnesty International assert that the frequency of taser use is on the rise. The increasing number of outrageous examples of taser use reported in the news provide anecdotal evidence that officers are becoming less reluctant to deploy this nonlethal but extremely unpleasant type of force. Below are some of the more outlandish examples of zero-tolerance policing bordering on police brutality.

In June 2003, in Portland, Oregon, 71-year-old Eunice Crowder objected when a city employee came to her house to clean up her yard. The official called the police, who ordered Crowder to stop trying to retrieve items from her yard, which had already been loaded onto a city truck. Hard of hearing, she ignored the commands. To gain control of the situation, a police officer pepper-sprayed and tasered Crowder when she tried to kick him. The city, claiming no wrongdoing on the officer's part, settled Crowder's lawsuit for $145,000.

A pair of police officers in Kansas City, Missouri, in June 2004, approached a car occupied by 71-year-old Louise Jones. The officers were responding to a disturbance call that had originated from the house across the street, but they were drawn to Louise when she accidentally honked her horn. According to the officers, Jones became verbally hostile. (She claimed that her anger had been directed at the people across the street.) Because the officers didn't like being talked to that way, they threatened to give Louise a ticket for improper horn honking and demanded to see her driver's license. Instead of complying with the order, Louise climbed out of her car and headed for the house. One of the officers wrestled her to the ground and had a knee in the middle of her back and his handcuffs out when Fred Jones, Louise's husband, came to her aid by pushing the arresting officer away. This caused the arresting officer's partner to shock Louise with his taser device. Neither of the Joneses had criminal records or histories of violence. Both officers were disciplined, and the horn-honking charge was dropped. However, Louise and her husband received a year's probation for "sparking quarrels" with the police officers.

In October 2007, an anonymous caller to Chicago's Department of the Aging reported that 82-year-old Lillian Fletcher, a resident of the west side, was alone and needed assistance. In response to the "well-being check," Fletcher, a schizophrenic suffering from dementia, refused to let the social workers into her apartment. The department's employees then called the police, who—after getting Ms. Fletcher to crack the door open a few inches—forced their way into the apartment, where they encountered a confused and terrified old woman holding the hammer she kept by her bed for protection. One of the officers shot her in the abdomen with his taser. The shock didn't kill her but did send her to the hospital for five days. The police, describing the hammer as a deadly weapon and noting that Ms. Fletcher didn't look that old, insisted that they had not used excessive force. Because of her mental condition, the authorities did not charge Fletcher with assault with a deadly weapon or any lesser offense.

At 2 P.M. one day in May 2009, just outside of Austin, Texas, a Travis County sheriff's deputy pulled Kathern Winkfein over for driving her pickup 60 miles per hour in a 45-mile zone. The deputy filled out the speeding ticket and asked Winkfein to sign it. She refused. What happened next was recorded on the police officer's dashboard video camera.

Deputy Chris Bieze informed Winkfein that if she didn't sign the ticket, he would have to arrest her. In profane and vulgar language, the 72-year-old driver said she still wouldn't sign the ticket. Deputy Bieze opened the truck door and ordered Winkfein out of the vehicle. "Take me to jail. Go on and take me to jail," she said.

"Step on out," he replied.

Winkfein got out of the truck, and as she was walking along the highway close to the traffic line, said, "Give me the [expletive] thing and I'll sign it." At this point, the officer could have ended the confrontation by allowing her to sign the ticket. Instead, he pushed her away from the highway to a safer place on the shoulder. "You're gonna shove a 72-year-old woman?" she yelled.

"If you don't step back, you're gonna be tased," he said.

"Go ahead, tase me."

The deputy grabbed Winkfein but she twisted out of his grip. "Step back or you're gonna be tased, ma'am," he warned in a high-pitched, loud, almost hysterical voice.

"I dare you," she said. "I'm getting back in my car."

"You're gonna be tased," he said, blocking her path.

"I'm getting back in my car."

"No, ma'am," he says just before zapping her with 50,000 volts of low-amperage electricity. Winkfein dropped to the ground screaming. "Now put your hands behind your back, or you're gonna be tased again!"[13] Winkfein complied and was taken into custody and charged with resisting arrest.

The Travis County deputy's superiors insisted that Bieze, the department's taser instructor, had acted appropriately within departmental use-of-force guidelines. Indeed, one could argue that tasers were made for situations just like this—controlling harmless jerks who show no respect for the law. While for some there may be a degree of satisfaction seeing disrespectful people being put in their places, a 4-foot, 11-inch, 72-year-old woman who posed no physical threat to the police officer should not have been shocked. In this case the matter would have been resolved if the deputy had allowed her to sign the ticket. If taking this woman into custody was so important, this officer could have taken her car keys and called for backup. But tasers are just too easy. A harmless person acts up and zap—down he or she goes. It's not surprising that a nonlethal method of subduing people—which requires little discretion and saves the effort of figuring out ways of dealing with difficult subjects in the least forceful ways—is a law enforcement measure destined to be overused.

Winkfein sued Travis County for $135,000 for medical expenses, humiliation, and pain and suffering. Because it would cost more than $40,000 to defend the lawsuit, Travis County commissioners offered to settle the suit for $40,000. Plaintiff Wikfein, on October 6, 2009, accepted the offer.

A federal appeals court decision (*Bryan v. McPherson et al.,* 551 F. Supp. 2d. 1149) in December 2009 may have set the stage for the establishment of more restrictive guidelines regarding law enforcement's use of taser devices. In 2005, an officer with the Coronado, California, Police Department tasered a motorist he had pulled over for not wearing a seat belt. The unarmed arrestee, who did not threaten the officer in any way (he alighted from the car after being told not to), fell to the pavement and smashed four front teeth. The lower court judge ruled that tasering a nonthreatening arrestee did not constitute excessive force, and that the city of Coronado, owing to the doctrine of qualified government immunity, could not be sued. The U.S. Ninth Circuit Court's three-judge panel unanimously disagreed, finding that tasering is a more serious use of force than pepper-spraying, a distinction not reflected in the use-of-force policies of most law enforcement agencies. Pursuant to this court's rationale, officers should taser only those arrestees who pose an immediate physical threat. This would not include arrestees who attempt to flee or simply refuse to obey commands.

CRACKING DOWN ON KIDS

Police heavy-handedness toward disrespectful people and minor offenders is reflected in the way law enforcement officials now deal with children. There was a time when the police rarely had occasion to enter a school building. Today, many high schools are protected by entrance-door metal detectors, closed-circuit television networks, alarm systems, and armed patrols. In the post-Columbine era, all school facilities are essentially inaccessible to the general public.

Even in the grade schools, teachers and administrators have relinquished to the police some of the authority they once found useful to maintain order in the classroom, on the playground, in the cafeteria, and on the school bus. Misbehaving children, instead of being sent to the principal's office, are now routinely hauled off in handcuffs by police officers. The criminalization of childhood unruliness constitutes a frightening broadening of police power.

Although there are no official nationwide statistics regarding how many children below age 12 are arrested every year, it seems that the practice of charging persons so young has been commonplace since the late 1990s. A *St. Petersburg Times* investigation of this trend resulted in a two-part article published in December 2000 called "Under 12, Under Arrest." According to the study, Florida police, during the period June 1999 to June 2000, arrested more than 4,500 children under the age of 12. These arrests, usually for behavior that once didn't warrant police action, took place in and out of school. Quite often, arrestees as young as 7 years of age were held overnight in detention centers. A St. Petersburg police officer charged a 6-year-old boy with battery after the kindergartener kicked and hit him while being hauled out of music class for throwing a tantrum. Both of the boy's wrists fit into a single restraining cuff. In a Florida elementary school, a sheriff's deputy arrested an 8-year-old boy who had kicked and scratched a teacher's aide. That child spent several hours in the county jail.

Following the expose in the *St. Petersburg Times,* police in the state continued to arrest children under age 12 for school-related behavior. In Ocala, officers arrested two boys, aged 9 and 10, for drawing a pair of primitive stick-figure scenes depicting the stabbing and hanging of a classmate. In January 2005, the police took the boys out of school in handcuffs and charged them with making written threats to kill or harm another person, a second-degree felony. The third-graders were suspended from school. The prosecutor dropped the charges after the boys and their parents agreed to counseling.

A police officer in Avon Park, Florida, in March 2007, arrested a kindergartener who disrupted class with a temper tantrum and wouldn't calm down. Before being taken away in handcuffs and charged with a felony and two misdemeanors, the 6-year-old girl threw chairs at a teacher. The child's mother had to pick her daughter up at the police station. The authorities eventually dropped the charges but the student, afraid to return to that class, had to be enrolled at another school.

The police in 2003 arrested a girl in Toledo, Ohio, for violating the school's dress code. They hauled her off in handcuffs to a juvenile detention center. Of the 1,727 school-related arrests made in Lucas County, Ohio, in 2002, only a few were for serious crimes. The police had, for example, arrested students for such things as being loud and disruptive and for cursing at school officials and fellow classmates. Grade school misbehavior, instead of leading to the principal's office, had led to criminal incarceration.

In December 2004, the commissioner of the Philadelphia Police Department expressed concern when he learned that one of his officers had handcuffed a 9-year-old girl for bringing a pair of scissors to school. But three months later, another Philadelphia officer cuffed three third-graders and drove them to the police station after they were found playing with a can of mace they had found on the playground.

A deputy with the Tuscaloosa County, Alabama, sheriff's office, who worked as a "resource officer" for several schools, handcuffed a 9-year-old girl for refusing to do her jumping-jacks in physical education class. (The officer had interfered over the teacher's objections.) After slapping on the metal cuffs, the deputy tightened them down so that the little girl would know how it feels to disrespect the law. In 2003, the student's mother filed a civil suit and won in federal court.

In Brooklyn, New York, the mother of a 10-year-old girl filed suit in federal court claiming that a police officer, in January 2008, had falsely arrested and assaulted her daughter on a Bedford-Stuyvesant school bus. The plaintiff, represented by a prominent New York civil rights attorney, sought $500,000 in compensatory and $500,000 in punitive damages as a result of her daughter's mental anguish and trauma. According to the complaint, the police officer, after ordering the students to take their seats, told the plaintiff that if she didn't move faster, he'd arrest her. When she didn't comply, he put his knee in her back, grabbed the girl's arms, and handcuffed her. At a news conference outside the federal courthouse, the plaintiff's attorney said that he hoped the lawsuit would cause the police department to create guidelines regarding the treatment of misbehaving children who have not engaged in criminal acts.

Although the New York City Police Department doesn't have guidelines regarding the handling of misbehaving children, New York State law, under the Family Court Act, states that police officers cannot arrest schoolchildren under the age of 16 for minor noncriminal offenses, such as loitering, loud behavior, and disobedience. In October 2008, the New York Civil Liberties Union, under the Freedom of Information Act, obtained data revealing that between 2005 and 2007, the New York City Police had illegally arrested 309 students 15 years old and younger, hauling them off to police stations in handcuffs. Since 1998, mayors Rudy Giuliani and Michael Bloomberg have assigned more than 5,000 "school safety agents" and at least 200 armed police officers to the city's schools.

In February 2010, a middle school principal in Queens, New York, called the New York City Police after 12-year-old Alexa Gonzales scribbled on her desk with a lime-green marker. Officers came to the school, placed the terrified girl in handcuffs, and hauled her off to the police station. The arrest cost the traumatized student three days of school. Education officials, facing public outrage, admitted that the arrest was inappropriate. The prosecutor decided not to charge the girl with criminal vandalism. In big and not-so-big municipalities, this form of aggressive, zero-tolerance policing mostly stigmatizes and humiliates minority youths and students with special needs.

Besides the inability to distinguish childhood misbehavior from crime, police officers, in dealing with children who have committed criminal acts, often treat them as though they were violent adult offenders. The apprehension in southwestern Pennsylvania of an 11-year-old boy who had taken his foster mother's car reflects this ham-fisted, zero-tolerance law enforcement mentality. On Sunday evening, September 21, 2008, the foster mother called the state police to report that the boy, who had just joined the family a few days earlier, had driven off in her car. She believed he was headed toward his parent's house in a town about 50 miles away. An hour or so later, a state trooper on patrol spotted a white Toyota being driven by a child who could barely see over the steering wheel. The officer signaled the child to pull over but was ignored. A few miles from his parent's home, the young driver pulled onto Interstate 70 and, pursued by the state patrol car, hit speeds up to 85 miles per hour. After traveling 10 miles, shortly after the fleeing 11-year-old exited the interstate, the trooper rammed the Toyota, causing it to spin out of control and crash into a utility pole. The officer then apprehended the boy, who tried to escape on foot. After taking the child to the emergency room, where he was treated for minor injuries, the trooper drove him to the juvenile probation office. The authorities charged the boy with car theft, reckless endangerment, and aggravated assault and kept him at the juvenile facility. The officer based the assault charge on the boy's attempt, just prior to being forced off the road into the pole, to ram the police cruiser.

Geoffrey Alpert, a criminal justice professor at the University of South Carolina who studies police pursuit policies, called the 11-year-old's chase and arrest "absolutely ridiculous." Speaking to a *Pittsburgh Post-Gazette* reporter, the professor said, "Eleven years old—I don't know how he can see over the steering wheel. Should he be chased? I don't think so. You can just go [to his] home and pick him up in a few hours. An eleven-year-old, you could probably assume he's going home at some point."[14]

When Kelly King couldn't force her 10-year-old daughter, Kiara, to prepare for bed on November 11, 2009, she treated her resistance as a crime and called the police. The single mother and her daughter lived in Ozark, Arkansas, a river town of 3,500 in the northwest region of the state. Officer Dustin Bradshaw responded to the scene; what happened next is based upon his report of the incident.

Officer Bradshaw entered the house to find Kiara crying and lying in a ball on the living room floor. As he and Kelly carried the kicking and screaming child into the bathroom for a shower, Kelly informed the officer that if he wished he could taser Kiara to bring her under control—a fact the mother did not deny. After struggling without success to get Kiara into the bathtub, officer Bradshaw carried her back to the living room, where he threatened her with arrest and jail. The girl did not calm down and became, according to Bradshaw, "verbally combative." As a result, he placed her under arrest. As he tried to get her into handcuffs, she kicked him in the groin. To settle her down, the officer gave Kiara a shot in the back with his taser gun. She fell limp. Officer Bradshaw applied the handcuffs, carried the flaccid arrestee to the police car, and drove her to a youth detention center.

Sixteen days after Kiara's arrest, Ozark mayor Vernon McDaniel suspended Officer Bradshaw. Supporting Bradshaw's use of the taser on a 10-year-old girl, Chief of Police Jim Noggle and the mayor told reporters they had suspended Bradshaw because he had failed to activate the tiny video camera attached to his taser device. The officer had not violated the department's rules regarding taser use because there was no policy regarding the use of the device on children. (There was, however, a rule against tasering pregnant women.)

On November 30, three days after suspending Officer Bradshaw, Mayor McDaniels fired him for violating the video camera rule. By now, agents from the Little Rock FBI office were looking into the case. The mayor, in announcing the officer's discharge, reminded reporters that Bradshaw had not been fired for tasering the girl. Moreover, the officer was entitled to his unpaid vacation and holiday compensation.

The issue of whether officers should taser unarmed children came up in 2004 after citizens criticized the Miami, Florida, police for using a stun gun on an unruly 6-year-old boy. The next year, the Chicago police accidentally killed a 14-year-old with the device. In April 2009, a 16-year-old boy died after being tasered by the police in Detroit. His family filed an excessive force suit against the officers and the department in federal court. Less than a month after officer Bradshaw tasered Kiara in Ozark, Arkansas, a Pueblo County, Colorado, deputy sheriff used the device on an "out of control" 10-year-old boy. Despite public concern over these and dozens of similar cases, only a handful of law enforcement agencies have developed policies restricting the use of these devices on children. One such agency, the Vallejo, California, Police Department, prohibits the use of tasers on "young juveniles" unless they present an "actual threat of violence." Taser International, the manufacturer of some of the most popular models, recommends that tasers not be used on anyone weighing less than 60 pounds. According to the American Civil Liberties Union (ACLU), absent "exigent circumstances," the police should not use tasers on "vulnerable populations," including children, the elderly, frail or injured people, the mentally ill, and pregnant women.

In March 2009, the district attorney of Lawrence County in western Pennsylvania, an hour's drive north of Pittsburgh, charged an 11-year-old boy as an adult with two counts of criminal homicide on suspicion that he had intentionally killed (with a shotgun) his father's eight-months-pregnant girlfriend. If convicted, the boy could be sentenced to life without parole or even death. Pennsylvania, a state with 400 offenders who have been sentenced to life without parole as juveniles, is one of 14 states that allow a minor, no matter how young, to be tried as an adult. Nationwide, the number of juveniles who have committed murder dropped 55 percent between 1990 and 2000. During that period, however, the percentage of juveniles receiving sentences of life without parole increased by 216 percent. Police officers no longer make allowances for youth, and in many states, neither does the law.

THE EMERGENCE OF "DIRTY HARRY" POLICING

In modern law enforcement, the threat and use of deadly force has become commonplace. It hasn't always been that way. In the 1950s, 1960s, and 1970s, it was not unusual for a police officer to have been on the job 30 years without ever having to pull his gun. In those days, firing a shot in the line of duty was a rare occurrence. FBI agents didn't carry guns until 1936 (the agency was formed in 1908), and under director J. Edgar Hoover's policy, an agent could use deadly force only if threatened with imminent death or serious bodily injury. This did not allow firing at fleeing suspects either in cars or on foot or at suspects making furtive moves. Hoover didn't want his men pointing their revolvers at arrestees as means of intimidation. The bureau's rule was "if you pull your gun, you better use it." That rule wasn't always obeyed, but it reminded agents that they were armed solely for self-protection and the protection of others.

FBI agents in the Hoover era (1924–1972) dressed like businessmen. Hoover would have considered the now common FBI lettered jackets, ball caps, and quasi-military wear unprofessional. If agents needed more firepower for a high-risk arrest or a raid, they called on the local police for assistance. But this was rare. Most of the time FBI agents used patience, stealth, intelligence, and timing to arrest fugitives believed to be armed and dangerous. During Hoover's tenure, only a handful of agents lost their lives on duty, and very few civilians died at the hands of his agents. Although Director Hoover had his faults and excesses, he did not believe in a national police force, and he did not want his beloved agency overly militarized. He preferred the image of the professional, scientific criminal investigator to the crime-fighting warrior. Today, the FBI has at least 56 SWAT teams attached to its field offices around the country. Mr. Hoover must be turning in his grave.

There are many in the law enforcement community who do not approve of the militarized version of policing. Joseph McNamara, the former chief of police in San Jose, California, and Kansas City, Missouri, in reacting to an incident involving plainclothes officers in New York City who fired 50 shots at a car, wounding two men and killing a third, wrote the following in a November 29, 2006. *Wall Street Journal* column:

> Simply put, the police culture in our country has changed. An emphasis on "officer safety" and paramilitary training pervades today's policing, in contrast to the older culture, which held that cops didn't shoot until they were about to be shot or stabbed. Police in large cities carried revolvers holding six .38-caliber rounds. Nowadays, police carry semi-automatic pistols with sixteen high-caliber rounds, shotguns and military assault rifles, weapons once relegated to SWAT teams facing extraordinary circumstances. Concern about such firepower in densely populated areas hitting innocent citizens has given way to an attitude that police are fighting a war against drugs and crime and must be heavily armed.[15]

Criminal justice professors Peter Kraska and Victor Kappeler believe that militarized policing attracts job candidates who view law enforcement more like combat duty than community service. In their 1997 article about police militarization, they wrote: "The SWAT teams have this stuff. It's exciting to train. They use simulations—like the paint balls and play warrior games. This stuff is a rush."[16]

Aware of the public relations advantages of community policing over the more aggressive and antisocial militarized approach, former New Haven Police Chief Nicholas Pastore, in a 1999 article in the *Nation,* was quoted as follows: "Community policing broke down the anonymity between the people and the police. That creates accountability and cuts down on brutality. Brutality thrives on anonymity. Why do you think the SWAT teams wear those ninja suits, cover their badges and wear executioner masks?"[17]

POLICE SNIPERS

In the 1980s, the larger police agencies began beefing up their SWAT units with officers trained as military-type snipers. Ten years later, military marksmen were training members of small-town SWAT units. In 1999, a military sharpshooter trained the SWAT team of the University of Colorado at Boulder on how to use the AR-15 (the semiautomatic version of the M-16) as a sniper rifle. The fact that universities were fielding their own

SWAT teams is in itself indicative of the more militarized approach to the use of force in policing. The city of Boulder, a low-crime municipality with a police department and a university SWAT team, was sniper-ready.

Men who take hostages are either robbers trying to escape arrest or mentally disturbed, suicidal people holding the police at bay by threatening to kill their spouses, children, or lovers. The question then becomes at what point should the hostage negotiation be terminated in favor of the hostage being shot to death by the sniper? There is no way to know how many sniper-killed hostages would have eventually surrendered had the police been a little more patient.

In the military, when a sniper misses his target, an innocent bystander doesn't get shot. This is not true with police snipers. Military snipers seek long-range (500 to 600 yards) targets of opportunity, while police marksmen fire at specific targets much closer to them. Quite often police snipers have to hit tiny moving targets from 75 to 100 yards away. Over the years, more than a few hostages have taken the bullet instead of the intended target. In 2001, Clint Smith, the director of a private sniper school in Mountain Home, Texas, told *60-Minutes II* correspondent Jim Stewart that the civilian sniper is to law enforcement what the air force is to ground troops. "They [snipers] stand off a little bit," he said. "They get to hit stuff. They don't really kind of have to get dirty, and I don't mean that ugly. But there's a detachment from it a little bit."[18]

Although police snipers are trained at a few big-city police academies and a handful of private schools run by former special forces personnel, most are trained at the U.S. Army base at Fort Benning, Georgia. Every year instructors at the base host a seven-day event called the International Sniper Competition, in which sniper teams from police departments and military units around the world compete. The "countersniper" competitive event consists of a 10 minute "urban warfare" simulation in which sniper teams—amid machine-gun bursts, smoke, and explosions—scale a building and smash through second-story windows to eliminate the bad guy. This simulation, as a form of law enforcement action, is a good example of life imitating a police action movie. A television producer with the Military Channel's program *Top Sniper* featured the 2008 edition of the International Sniper Competition. Nothing represents the cross-fertilization of military culture and civilian law enforcement more than the police sniper.

THE FEDERALIZATION OF LAW ENFORCEMENT

Police authority has become increasingly centralized through the federalization of criminal law. In the 1960s, there were fewer than 1,000 federal crimes. Today there are 4,450 federal offenses and dozens of federal law enforcement agencies staffed by thousands of armed officers. The FBI alone fields 56 SWAT teams. Several other federal agencies have SWAT-type units, such as the Special Response Team of the Bureau of Alcohol Tax and Firearms (ATF), the Special Operations Group of the U.S. Marshal's Office, and the Special Response Team of the U.S. Immigration and Customs Enforcement (ICE) office. The Drug Enforcement Administration (DEA)— except for its Clan Lab Enforcement Teams, which raid clandestine drug laboratories—does not field specialized tactical units, since all DEA agents are trained and equipped for military-style drug operations. Even the U.S. Fish & Wildlife Service has its own SWAT team.

This form of centralized and expanded governmental power is in large measure a by-product of the escalating war on drugs, a law enforcement endeavor favored by conservative politicians and their supporters. The ideology of conservatism, however, is based on the idea of smaller, decentralized, less oppressive government. The support of the drug war by conservatives therefore presents a glaring ideological contradiction.

In 1998, former U.S. Attorney General Edwin Meese III, in the *Criminal Law & Procedure Practice Newsletter,* wrote:

> In the 1950s . . . there was virtually no federal involvement in the kinds of criminal justice functions that normally and traditionally had been, up to that time, left to state and local governments . . . In 1965, [President] Lyndon B. Johnson appointed a crime commission which made a number of recommendations for a much larger role for the federal government. This led to what became known as the Omnibus Safe Streets and Crime Control Act of 1968 . . . In the '80s and now in the '90s, it seems like almost every election year we have a crime bill which incorporates in it whatever might have been more or less horrendous or front page news during the past few years, giving the impression that somehow Congress is doing something about the crime problem . . . If there is a carjacking or a rash of carjackings, we suddenly have a federal carjacking law. If there are churches being burned, we suddenly have a federal church burning law . . . Very few people have looked into whether these offenses are actually prosecuted very much, but the statutes are on the books, and therefore, they can be prosecuted, usually dependent upon the whim of a United States Attorney.

Through the passage of the so-called hate and bias crime legislation, the federal government has expanded its power into areas of criminal justice traditionally handled by counties and states. In 1969, Congress made criminal homicide, aggravated assault, rape, and the destruction of property federal crimes if the offender's motivation was hatred of the victim's race, ethnicity, religion, or national origin. The law applied to victims attending federally funded public schools or participating in other federally protected activities. Critics of the legislation consider it redundant and excessive. Moreover, it creates a preferred class of victim and criminalizes motive or thought. Others criticize the legislation for not going far enough and for not including gay people.

The House of Representatives, in 2007, passed the Matthew Shepard Act, legislation named after the gay Wyoming college student murdered in 1998. The act expanded hate crime protection to gender, sexual orientation, gender identification, and disability bias. It also dropped the prerequisite that victims be engaged in federally protected activity. The U.S. Senate passed a similar bill, but it did not become law.

In October 2009, the House of Representatives passed another measure, this one attached to the $681-billion military policy bill of 2010, which mirrored the Matthew Shepard Act. The military appropriation and the attached hate crime legislation was taken up by the Senate, which passed its own version of the bill. Under this new legislation, signed by President Obama, the U.S. Department of Justice will allocate $5 million a year to help local authorities prosecute hate crimes.

The federalization of law enforcement has contributed significantly to militaristic policing. This is true in the war on drugs and even in the enforcement of arcane federal offenses against suspects without histories of violence who are not professional criminals. The following case is a good example of this.

FBI Agents on the Warpath

Although it has long been a federal crime to steal property owned by the U.S. government, Congress, in 1979, passed the Archaeological Resources Protection Act (ARPA), which specifically outlaws the theft of (and trafficking in) Native American artifacts from public lands. Violators of this law can be fined and sentenced to prison for up to 10 years. In 1990, Congress passed the Native American Graves Protection and Repatriation Act (NAGPRA), making it a federal crime to steal or traffic in artifacts from Indian burial sites. It is also a crime to remove Indian relics from state-owned land. But until recently, none of these laws have been strictly enforced.

Collectors of Native American artifacts and dealers in the Four Corners region (Utah, Colorado, Arizona, and New Mexico), an area rich in cave and cliff-house relics from the Pueblo and Anasazi cultures, have been gathering pottery, stone tools, flint projectile points, baskets, rugs, and even sandals (preserved by the arid climate) from these sites for decades. In the 1920s, archeologists with the University of Utah paid artifact hunters $2 for every ceramic pot they brought in. Today, if there is a ground zero for Indian artifact hunting, collecting, and dealing in the Four Corners region, it's in Blanding, Utah, a San Juan County town of 3,000 in the southeastern part of the state.

FBI agents and officers with the U.S. Bureau of Land Management, in October 2006, began working with an informant on artifacts dealing—a "Confidential Human Source" (CHS)—who wore a hidden audiovisual transmitter to record artifact hunting excursions on prohibited lands as well as the sales transactions involving relics taken from these sites. The CHS spent $335,000 of the government's money buying 256 relics allegedly stolen from public lands. The federal investigation came to a head on June 10, 2009, when seven- to ten-member FBI SWAT teams—accompanied by agents from the Bureau of Land Management as well as government archeologists and photographers—stormed the homes of ARPA and NAGPRA suspects in the Four Corners region. Most of the simultaneous 6 A.M. raids by FBI agents in full combat gear took place in and around Blanding, Utah. That morning, FBI agents hauled 19 San Juan County residents off to jail in handcuffs while searchers photographed and removed boxes of artifacts from their homes. Also arrested that morning were four suspects from New Mexico and Colorado. Later in the day, all of the arrestees, after making bail, returned to their ransacked houses. Most of the suspects, including the three women arrested, were either in their 50s, 60s, or 70s. The oldest was 78. None of these people possessed serious criminal records or histories of violence. Many of them had guns in their dwellings, but everyone in that part of the country kept guns in their houses. Several of those arrested claimed to have been manhandled and/or held at gunpoint. In one of the raids, after 10 hours of searching through a suspect's artifact collection, the agents left the house with one Indian relic.

Another of the homes raided that morning in Blanding belonged to Dr. James Redd and his wife, Jeanne. Dr. Redd, age 60, was the town's only physician. He and his 59-year-old wife had been collecting artifacts for years. In 2003, after being convicted in state court for taking relics from burial sites, the Redds had paid a $10,000 fine. As a result of the federal crackdown, they faced multiple counts of ARPA and NAGPRA violations that could send them to prison for several years. From their house, agents had taken several pieces of pottery, a couple of Indian necklaces, a pair of sandals, a stone axe, and two pendants.

Two days after FBI agents hauled Dr. and Mrs. Redd to jail in handcuffs, while searchers were taking suspected contraband from their house,

Dr. Redd committed suicide. He had driven his car to a pond at the edge of his property, where he died of carbon monoxide poisoning. The physician's death shocked a community already upset over the gratuitous violence of the artifact raids. Grayson Redd, one of the doctor's cousins and the chief deputy sheriff of San Juan County, expressed his disapproval of the FBI's methods to a reporter with the *Los Angeles Times:* "The heavy-handed tactics and the picture show the feds put on here was wrong. People need to obey the law, [but] two or three agents could have come in and done the [arrests]."[19] County commissioner Bruce Adams, as reported by the Associated Press, said, "These people would have surrendered peacefully."[20] Republican members of the U.S. Senate from Utah, Orrin Hatch and Bob Bennett, condemned the raids and called for a congressional investigation into the case. Senator Hatch issued a statement in which he said, "[The raids] have destroyed good feelings toward the government in that whole community. I felt like it was a dog and pony show, and I know one when I see it."[21]

On June 19, a week after Dr. Redd's suicide, 56-year-old Steven L. Shrader of Sante Fe, New Mexico, an artifact collector on the periphery of the ARPA/NAGPRA investigation, took his own life while visiting his mother in Shabbona, Illinois. Under federal indictment on counts of theft of government property for allegedly trafficking in stolen artifacts—a pair of sandals and a woven basket—Shrader had, two days after the house raids, turned himself in to the FBI in Santa Fe. According to court documents, Shrader, in 2008, had accompanied ARPA/NAGPRA suspects Vern and Marie Crites, ages 74 and 68, on an "arrowhead hunt" in Disappointment Valley near Dove Creek, Colorado. In speaking to the media after the suicide—Mr. Shrader had shot himself in the chest behind an elementary school—Mr. Crites said he didn't understand why the feds had charged him with theft of government property.

In August 2009, Dr. Redd's wife, Jeanne, and his daughter, Jerrica, pleaded guilty to five counts each of illegal artifact trafficking. The Redds also forfeited to the federal government their artifact collections. A federal judge, the following month, fined Jeanne $2,000 and sentenced her to 36 months' probation. Jerrica received a sentence of 24 months' probation and a fine of $300.

In October 2009, media outlets in the region identified the FBI's undercover operative—the "confidential human source"—as Ted C. Gardiner, a former antiques dealer and artifact collector from Farmington, Utah, a town located a few miles north of Salt Lake City. Prior to dealing in antiques and prehistoric Native American artifacts, Gardiner had owned and operated a Utah-based grocery store chain founded by his grandfather. He sold the company in the year 2000. Six years later, Gardiner approached the FBI with an offer to use his online antiquities business, Gardiner Antiquities, to gather evidence about collectors and dealers he said were trafficking in artifacts illegally acquired from federal lands.

Three months after Gardiner's initial exposure by the media, the U.S. attorney for Utah, in documents filed in connection with one of the artifact-trading defendants, revealed that the FBI had paid the sting informant an initial fee of $10,000, followed by monthly payments of $7,500. In addition to the $335,000 in government money Gardiner had spent on artifacts, the undercover operative received $162,000 in expense money.

Unemployed and living in a suburban Salt Lake City rental house with three roommates, Gardiner, with a history of mental illness and substance abuse, became anxious and fearful of some of the people he had informed on. He started sleeping with a gun under his pillow. After Dr. Redd killed himself, Gardiner started drinking again. Following Shrader's suicide, he became even more depressed. On the Saturday night of January 30, 2010, one of Gardiner's roommates called 911 and reported that Gardiner had become mentally unbalanced and was threatening to kill himself. Police officers came to the house, seized his handgun, and transported Gardiner to the hospital for observation. The next day Gardiner returned home.

At 6 P.M. the following Monday, a roommate called 911 again. Gardiner had acquired another gun and was holed up in his bedroom threatening suicide. The police entered the house, and as the officers approached the bedroom, Gardiner fired a shot. (It is unclear whether or not he fired at the officers.) One of the officers returned fire but missed the target. Gardiner fired again, this time fatally shooting himself in the head.

The local U.S. attorney told reporters on March 8, 2010, that despite Gardiner's death, the Four Corners artifact case would go forward. Attorneys for the 22 remaining defendants weren't so sure that the government, without its principal witness, had a case. The defense attorneys said they planned to challenge thousands of hours of conversations taped by Gardiner under the U.S. Constitution's Sixth Amendment, which gives the criminally accused the right to confront their accusers. This right includes subjecting prosecution accusers to the rigors of in-court cross-examinations by defense attorneys. At the time of Gardiner's death, the FBI had been paying him the $7,500 a month as a case consultant.

One would think that in post–9/11 America, the FBI should be focused on catching terrorists and violent criminals. But aside from the issue of law enforcement priority, why did the government deploy FBI SWAT teams to execute these low-risk search warrants? It seems that the government had used shock-and-awe policing to teach artifact collectors and dealers a lesson. This law enforcement tactic contributed to the deaths of two men who were not dangerous criminals and the suicide of a government informant who felt responsible for the consequences of the government's heavy-handedness.

BOTCHED DRUG RAIDS

Many believe that law enforcement's war on drugs has been more harmful to the country than the drugs themselves. In addition to the cost—$50 billion a year—and the effect on drug users—turning them into government informants or sending them to prison—the resultant police militarization has made drug enforcement dangerous and oppressive.

SWAT teams storming unannounced into occupied homes under circumstances that are not high-risk, while excessive and unnecessary, are not considered by the police as botched or inappropriate raids. As long as the officers break into the house listed on the search warrant, even when a citizen ends up injured or even killed, the authorities will classify the raid as a proper police operation. Moreover, the police do not apologize for breaking into a dwelling that hasn't housed the fugitive for years. They don't say they're sorry when a raid produces no evidence of crime. Instead, they blame the informant and insist that the intrusion, because it was based on a legal search warrant, was not a bungled operation. And in cases where the SWAT police have actually entered a house other than the one listed on the warrant, a truly botched raid, they rarely apologize. This is true in wrong-house invasions involving unarmed citizens shot by officers who felt threatened by a furtive move or an item wrongfully identified as a weapon. No one knows how many of the 40,000 or so SWAT raids conducted every year are not necessary or in some way botched. The government doesn't keep track of this form of police malfeasance.

In 2006, public policy analyst Radley Balko of the Cato Institute in Washington, D.C., a nonprofit libertarian think tank, published a report called *Overkill: The Rise of Paramilitary Police Raids in America.* According to Balko's research, updated in 2008, there have been, between January 1992 and January 2008, a total of 319 SWAT team raids that were excessive enough to make the news. During the period March 2005 to January 2008, some 38 badly bungled raids—wrong-house intrusions, questionable shootings, unnecessary manhandling, and the infliction of major property damage—were reported on television and in the press. Researchers at the Web site http://stopthedrugwar.org reported, during this time span, 44 bungled SWAT team raids not included in Balko's white paper. That makes, in a two-year period, 82 SWAT team fiascos. These figures do not include thousands of low-risk raids that were simply not necessary. Those who have investigated the overuse of SWAT teams believe that 75 percent of paramilitary drug raids do not warrant the militarized approach. Under that criterion, there are more than 30,000 SWAT home intrusions every year that represent excessive force.

A handful of jurisdictions have by law or administration restricted SWAT team use to high-risk situations. Police administrators in the smaller law enforcement agencies tend to resist such callout limitations because their SWAT officers would have nothing to do, which might lead to the dismantling of these units. Once a SWAT team is formed, getting rid of it is extremely difficult and rare. A chief of police who advocates disbanding a SWAT team will immediately lose the support of his officers. Moreover, the move will be challenged by the local police union.

POP CULTURE AND SWAT TEAM ACCEPTANCE

Organizations and departments outside of law enforcement commonly give themselves titles or missions that fit the letters SWAT. The acronym, symbolizing esprit de corps and a no-holds-barred methodology, is regularly used a verb, as in "Let's SWAT the problem." Despite the trauma and danger of having one's home invaded in the middle of the night by heavily armed men, and what this says about modern-day policing, middle-class Americans seem to embrace the concept. Indeed, SWAT team members have become crime-fighting heroes.

In feature films and television, SWAT teams represent the triumph of good over evil; in video games, they are the protagonists. College criminal justice programs are crammed with students who dream of future SWAT unit assignments. All across the country, teens can attend "SWAT camps," where they learn how to use battering rams and take down hostage takers. In 2006, a director of music videos made a 10-minute recruiting film for the Los Angeles Police Department depicting SWAT teams carrying out a variety of missions. And SWAT team members, in full combat gear, regularly visit grade schools. From grade school through college, students are exposed to favorable images of SWAT teams in action.

The idea that growing police militarism within a democratic society founded on the principles of limited government and civil liberty constitutes a dangerous trend has not gained much public support or political momentum. Decades of law enforcement fear mongering and the fact that more and more citizens are in need of government assistance has perhaps contributed to the acceptance, and even celebration, of this form of governmental intrusion. In an era of terrorism fears and rising crime, for those wary of police power and its militarism, the situation will probably get worse.

Part One

LOW-RISK SHOCK-AND-AWE POLICING

The first part of this book is about the use of excessive military-style force against criminal suspects without histories of violence who are not likely threats to the police. The cases in these chapters, in various degrees, ended badly for the citizens involved. In each instance, the police could have achieved their law enforcement objectives without traumatizing, injuring, or killing suspects and innocent bystanders. The wrong-house raids could have been avoided with prior investigation to confirm the suspected criminal activity, the identities of the occupants, and the fact that the officers were actually targeting the right place.

Chapter 2 begins with the botched Bureau of Alcohol Tax and Firearms (ATF) and FBI raids at the Davidian compound in Waco, Texas, in February and April 1993, a military-style assault that led to the deaths of 80 civilians. In it, military-trained FBI agents drove M-60 tanks and Bradley Fighting Vehicles, shooting 400 canisters of CS gas through the walls of the building; this accelerated the fire that burned the structure to the ground.

In April 2008, state and local SWAT teams raided the Latter Day Saints compound in Eldorado, Texas, on suspicion that adult males in the polygamist sect were sexually abusing under-age girls. Child Protection Services (CPS) workers seized and warehoused hundreds of children until they were placed in foster homes. Eight weeks after the assault, the Texas Supreme Court ordered the return of all of the children. The raid and massive uprooting of families had been predicated on a hoax perpetrated by a hotline caller claiming to be an under-age sexually violated compound wife.

Chapter 2 also covers the deployment of federal, state, and local SWAT teams to maintain order at political protest rallies and to break up rock concerts and other musical events. Discussions and examples include out-of-control police behavior at the 1999 World Trade Organization (WTO) protests in Seattle as well as the preemptive SWAT raids of protest headquarters on the eve of the 2008 Republican National Convention in Minneapolis–St. Paul. The chapter includes a discussion and description of the heavily armed police raids of "rave" concerts in Wisconsin and Utah, and a SWAT-like raid of a FUNK music celebrations at an art gallery in Detroit. Chapter 2 concludes with examples of excessive SWAT-style raids of workplaces for the purpose of rounding up illegal immigrants.

Chapter 3 focuses on the use of SWAT force in the arrest of nonviolent suspects of minor crimes; botched low-risk raids; the high-risk-case invasions of wrong houses; and SWAT team killings of unarmed people in stand-off situations. Botched low-risk cases include "flashbang" grenade injuries and fires and the killing of an unarmed suspect. In Minneapolis, in a potentially high-risk case, the SWAT team raided the wrong home—occupied by a family of eight—with disastrous results. The cases involving a deadly stand-off feature mentally disturbed people who posed little danger to the police.

Chapter 4 concerns the deployment of SWAT teams to enforce state laws prohibiting prostitution, possession of child pornography, home poker tournaments, and unauthorized sports betting. All of these raids, for one reason or another, were either unnecessary or badly botched. One of the raids resulted in the death of a gambler who posed no threat to the police.

Chapter 5 concerns SWAT-team use in smaller towns and less populated regions where they aren't really needed. Over the years, the federal government has provided law enforcement agencies with more than a billion dollars' worth of surplus military hardware at little or no cost. Much of this material has ended up in small police departments and sheriffs' offices in sparsely populated counties. This chapter explores the problems of inadequate SWAT training and supervision in many of the smaller law enforcement agencies, which has led to botched raids and excessive-force lawsuits. Chapter 5 features several examples of small-town SWAT abuse, including the infamous drug raid of a high school in Goose Creek, South Carolina, which led to nationwide outrage.

Chapter 2

STRONG-ARMING GROUPS: GUILT-BY-ASSOCIATION RAIDS

SAVING THE CHILDREN

Disaster at Waco

The April 19, 1993 raid of the Mount Carmel Branch Davidian compound in Waco, Texas, which resulted in the deaths of 80 cult members, is a worst-case example of how the militaristic approach to law enforcement can lead to disaster. Fifty-one days before the FBI assault, agents of the Bureau of Alcohol, Tax, and Firearms (ATF), at the conclusion of a seven-month investigation, had raided the compound to arrest cult leader David Koresh and search for a cache of guns that ATF agents suspected had been illegally converted to fully automatic weapons. That raid ended after a brief shootout in which 4 ATF agents were killed and 16 wounded. The officers retreated, leaving an unknown number of Branch Davidians dead and wounded.

The ATF agents, prior to the raid, had several opportunities to arrest David Koresh outside the Mount Carmel compound. These chances were missed because Koresh had not been under 24-hour surveillance. Had the ATF taken Koresh into custody when the opportunity presented itself, the raid might not have been necessary. The ATF had also lost the element of surprise, and they knew it when two National Guard helicopters, circling above the compound with agency supervisors aboard, took gunfire from below. The supervisors launched the invasion anyway. Although several ATF agents had been trained at Fort Hood by Green Beret personnel (the unsupported suspicion that the compound housed a methamphetamine lab served to justify the military's role in the operation), most of the agents

participating in the 9:30 A.M. attack had not been appropriately trained
or armed. Many of the 76 agents who charged the compound carried semiautomatic handguns.

Following the ATF fiasco, the FBI took charge of the stand-off. Following the 51-day siege and a series of failed negotiations, several FBI hostage
rescue teams, in full battle gear, armed with shortened variants of the standard M-16 assault rifle, and supported by Bradley Fighting Vehicles and
M-60 tanks, stormed the compound. Forty minutes after 400 canisters of
CS gas had been shot inside the building through holes punched in the
walls by the armored vehicles, the structure burst into flames and burned
to the ground. David Koresh and 17 children were among the 80 dead. Attorney General Janet Reno, operating on unreliable evidence that the Davidian children were being sexually mistreated, had authorized the assault,
which turned out to be the deadliest police action in American history.

Attorney General Reno, in the wake of the tragedy, asked former Missouri senator John C. Danforth to investigate the government's role in the
Waco raids. In 2000, following a 14-month investigation, Danforth found
that although an FBI agent had fired tear gas rounds at a concrete pit
75 feet from the Davidian living quarters, a fact the FBI had tried to suppress, agents had not started the fire. The former senator also concluded
that FBI agents had not fired bullets into the compound, and that the military's role in the raids had been lawful. Several months later, Thomas Lynch,
the director of the Cato Institute's Project on Criminal Justice, published
a report characterizing the Branch Davidian raids as "criminally reckless,"
and Danforth's investigation "soft and incomplete."[1] According to the Cato
investigation, FBI agents in National Guard helicopters had fired rifle
shots into the compound, a finding that contradicted the FBI's claim that
the helicopters had been deployed merely to distract the Davidians.

At a news conference, Senator Danforth defended the integrity of his investigation and attacked the Cato report. The debate over who started the
fire at the Davidian compound continues. Regardless of what FBI agents did
or didn't do on April 19, 1993, many believe the military-supported ATF
and FBI raids should not have been launched in the first place.

In Iraq, the military are criticized whenever they inadvertently kill a large
number of civilians who happened to be in proximity to enemy targets.
"Collateral damage" is, unfortunately, an aspect of war. It will also be a part
of law enforcement whenever the military, or the police functioning as
combat troops, are used to enforce domestic law.

The Eldorado Raid

Fifteen years after the ATF and FBI raids on the Branch Davidian compound in Waco, state, county, and city SWAT teams stormed the Yearning

for Zion (YFZ) Ranch, a 1,700-acre complex housing 700 members of a polygamist sect located in west central Texas outside the town of Eldorado. The self-sufficient ranch, owned by the Fundamentalist Church of Latter Day Saints (FLDS), had been built in 2003 by FLDS members who had fled polygamist enclaves in Utah and Arizona which had become targets of law enforcement, the media, and antipolygamy activist groups. In 2007, a jury in Utah had convicted the sect's leader, Warren Jeffs, of being an accomplice to the rape of a church member's under-age "wife."

The trouble began on March 29, 2008, when a Texas child protection service agency received a hotline call from a person named Sarah who claimed to be a 16-year-old resident of the YFZ Ranch married to a 50-year-old member of the sect who forced her to "have sex with lots of men" and who "beat and hurt her whenever he got angry."[2] Sarah said she was using someone else's cell phone to avoid being detected and punished. The following day, Sarah called again with more details of abuse. State and local law enforcement took over the case. Using unverified information supplied by an unidentified informant, the police acquired a warrant to enter and search every YFZ building. The authorities decided to act before confirming, through investigation, that the girl who had called was who she said she was and that there was a good chance she was telling the truth.

As it turned out, "Sarah" was not 16, not a resident of the ranch, and not a member of the FLDS. She was 33-year-old Rozita Swinton, a resident of Colorado Springs, Colorado, who had a history of calling hotlines with fictitious stories of abuse. Six weeks after the FLDS raid, which produced nothing but fear, heartbreak, family disruption, the recruitment of a swarm of lawyers, and taxpayer debt, a Texas child protection service (CPS) official praised Swinton for exposing child abuse at the YFZ.

On April 3, 2008, a force consisting of Texas Rangers, SWAT teams from the Department of Public Safety (DPS)—the Texas state police—and sheriff's deputies from six counties, with helicopters whirling overhead, police snipers in place, and a rolling armored personnel carrier providing cover, advanced toward the YFZ Ranch. Once again a religious compound in Texas was being invaded by a militarized force of law enforcement officers. But the residents of the YFZ Ranch were not Branch Davidians. They did not possess a cache of assault weapons, nor had they given law enforcement authorities any reason to anticipate armed resistance. It was like the Marines invading the Santa Barbara Tennis Club.

Police officers, in search of evidence that men over the age of 17 had engaged in sexual activity with under-age girls, rummaged through safes, vaults, drawers, closets, pantries, trunks, file cabinets, and desks. During the seven-day siege, 533 women and children were removed from the ranch and taken to a large shelter in Fort Concho, where police officers interrogated the children and health care workers examined their bodies for evidence of sexual abuse. The physical examinations included X-rays to reveal healed broken bones, and, where appropriate, pregnancy tests. The living conditions in the shelter—bad food, military cots, cribs, playpens, limited bathroom facilities, and 20 cases of chickenpox—made life there a nightmare. After these women and children had endured these conditions for a week, the authorities bussed them to a coliseum in San Angelo. A few days after that, CPS officials dispersed the children into 16 group shelters, and from these places to foster homes throughout the state.

Tom Green County judge Barbara Walther, on April 18, 2008, following two days of testimony in a custody hearing attended by hundreds of lawyers, ruled that the government had the authority to maintain custody of the 416 children seized in the raid. She also ordered DNA tests to establish family relationships. Following the DNA work, the state would hold a hearing for each minor to determine if that child would be placed into permanent foster care or returned to the ranch.

On May 22, 2008, the Texas Court of Appeals in Austin ruled that Judge Walther had abused her discretion and ordered the 416 children returned to their families within 10 days. The appeals court judges found that the state had not produced enough evidence of abuse to warrant the seizures. CPS lawyers appealed this decision to the Texas Supreme Court, which affirmed the ruling. The children would be returning to their families.

Although no one had been shot to death or seriously injured in this ill-advised paramilitary police action, it caused significant emotional trauma and a big expense for the state. As of November 2008, the state had spent $12.7 million, which included $9 million to house the children and their mothers for more than two weeks in the San Angelo Coliseum. These figures did not encompass the costs of the civil litigation that would arise from the operation.

In March 2008, almost a year after the YFZ raid, reporters with *People Magazine* visited the FLDS complex and spoke with three families whose children were among those returned to the ranch. Bob Barlow, whose children were back with him and his wife Mary, told a reporter that the experience has "been like a natural disaster. Like a hurricane hit us."[3] According to the couple, the raid had left their children, who had lived in a group foster home for two months, frightened and confused. During their absence from the ranch, they had been exposed to television, video games, clothing, and other aspects of modern society that conflicted with their upbringing and religious culture. Their foster parents had been intent on giving them a taste of what they had been missing growing up at the YFZ Ranch.

Although the raid had uprooted hundreds of people who have not been charged with any crimes (12 men have been indicted for sexual assault and conducting unlawful marriages), Patrick Crimmins, a spokesman for the

Texas Department of Family Protection (TDFP), told a *People* reporter that "We had what we thought was a credible allegation of abuse. And when we got there [at the ranch], we realized we needed to do a complete investigation."[4] Perhaps the TDFP should have conducted the complete investigation *before* the SWAT raid.

Found guilty of sexually assaulting a girl under the age of 17, Raymond Jessop, on November 5, 2009, was the first resident of the Yearning for Zion Ranch to be convicted of a crime. The judge sentenced the polygamist sect member to 10 years in prison.

A WAR ON TERROR OR A WAR ON DISSENT?

In their role as the keepers of the peace, nothing threatens police authority more that the "ugly mob." The history of American law enforcement reveals that when large numbers of civilian protesters gather in one place and some of them are loud and unruly, the police tend to overreact with excessive force.

Seattle WTO Protests

As members of the World Trade Organization (WTO) met inside the Seattle Convention Center from November 30 to December 2, 1999, some 40,000 to 50,000 people were outside protesting. When demonstrators moved into "no protest zones" or spilled onto the streets and blocked traffic, riot and SWAT police shot pain-inducing pepper spray into the eyes of hundreds of protestors and several journalists covering the demonstrations. Riot-clad officers also lobbed tear-gas canisters and percussion grenades into crowds and fired rubber and plastic-jacketed bullets at the protestors. All of this was caught on television, including one SWAT officer kicking a demonstrator in the groin, then shooting him in the back at point-blank range with a "beanbag" gun. (This officer was suspended for a week.) The police also used armored vehicles to disperse groups and intimidate demonstrators.

The Seattle police arrested hundreds of protestors for failure to disperse and for trespassing outside the "no protest zones." Years after the tear gas cleared and the protestors went home, the city of Seattle, and King County, were still settling civil rights and personal injury lawsuits that had been filed by protestors and journalists. As reported in the *Seattle Weekly,* 10 days after the disturbance, the U.S. Army Delta Force from Fort Hood, Texas, under the pretext that terrorists might exploit the occasion to launch a bio-chemical attack, had provided the police with surveillance support. According to the article, Delta Force personnel used high-tech equipment to map out potential problem areas and identify possibly violent demonstrators. Some of these special forces officers wore lapel cameras that continuously transmitted pictures of protestors to a master video unit in the command center. These images were used by law enforcement agencies to identify and track suspects. Critics of Delta Force participation in a domestic law enforcement operation considered this military spying on U.S. citizens. They viewed the government's handling of the WTO protest as the imposition of martial law in downtown Seattle.[5]

The Preemptive Raid

Rather than wait until protesters actually assemble for that purpose, the police have taken to raiding an organization's headquarters *before* the demonstration. On the weekend before the 2008 Republican National Convention (RNC) in Minneapolis, police raiding parties conducted preemptive strikes on three locations housing groups planning RNC demonstrations. Officers from the Ramsey County Sheriff's Office and the St. Paul Police Department stormed the first building at 8:30 P.M. on Friday, August 30. The place, located in St. Paul, was being used by the RNC Welcoming Committee, an umbrella organization of dozens of activist groups from around the country who had come to the twin cities to protest. The police handcuffed sixty to seventy activists and ordered them to lie on the floor while heavily armed officers executed a search warrant listing such items as Molotov cocktails, brake fluid, photographs, maps, computers, camera equipment, and protest-related documents. The raiders questioned and photographed the protest organizers and then left the premises without seizing anything dangerous. They did take laptop computers, cameras, protest schedules, sign-making supplies, and 7,000 "Welcoming Guides" organizers had planned to hand out to protestors as they arrived at the convention area.

The next morning, 30 police officers raided a St. Paul house where members of a New York City–based collective, called I-Witness Video, had come to record police and protest activities outside the convention hall. The officers handcuffed everyone, checked their identification, then corralled them in the backyard while the police searched the house. The searchers found nothing of interest and left without hauling anyone off to jail. The raid seemed to have no purpose other than to show force and to intimidate the protestors.

The second raid that Saturday morning took place at a house in Minneapolis being used by a group called Food Not Bombs (FNB). Ten or so officers from the Ramsey County Sheriff's Office and the Minneapolis Police Department, accompanied by a team of FBI agents, all dressed in riot gear and camouflage flack jackets, stormed into the house behind a flashbang grenade explosion. At one point during the siege, an officer escorted a five-year-old boy from the premises. The police arrested the principal FNB organizer on charges of conspiracy to riot.

On Monday, riot police, using pepper spray and firing rubber bullets, arrested 250 protestors including Amy Goodman, the host of the TV program *Democracy Now!* Officers manhandled Goodman when she came to the aid of her two producers, who were arrested and taken to jail on suspicion of rioting. That day, 2,000 law enforcement officers lined the street as 10,000 demonstrators marched peacefully to the Minnesota state capitol.

In defending the preemptive raids, a spokesperson for the St. Paul Police Department said, "We had probable cause. We had obtained information in advance that some of these people, maybe ten or twelve of them, were planning to cause disruption and destruction. For us not to act on that would have been irresponsible."[6]

OPERATION STOP THE MUSIC

If the police raided any high school, college dormitory, or National Football League football game, they could expect to find illegal drugs and, at least at the football game, a few guns and several people being sought by the law. Public intoxication, under-age drinking, and disorderly conduct at professional football games has become so commonplace that many fans are reluctant to take their children and grandchildren to the events. Yet the police don't raid professional athletic gatherings because the public wouldn't stand for it. Any police chief who would try such a stunt would be ridden out of town on a rail. That doesn't mean, however, that these events aren't policed or that fans who are disorderly aren't arrested. Before they closed Philadelphia's Veterans Stadium in 2003, officials had built an on-site jail cell and had a judge on duty to process unruly football fans taken into custody for disorderly conduct and other offenses. In this form of policing, individuals are targeted, not the event.

The approach of culling the bad apple is not how some police agencies deal with people assembled to enjoy certain kinds of music. Officers raid these events and arrest people for being present at a place where crimes are being committed by a few. Over the years, the police have conducted numerous raids of all-night parties where hundreds of young people have gathered to dance to "rave" music. Rave concerts feature a musical genre dating back to the 1980s, consisting of electronic dance music typically accompanied by laser lights, projected images, and stage fog. The police know that some of the rave attendees will be in possession of either ecstasy,

LSD, cocaine, or amphetamines, often referred to as club drugs. Since the authorities don't know who possesses what, the police raid these gatherings on legal pretexts, such as the organizers not having the proper licenses to hold the events; then they search everyone in attendance. SWAT teams control the crowds and maintain order, and in so doing they manhandle a lot of innocent people. This is not how the law should be enforced in a free society. As a method of evidence gathering, this is law enforcement's picking of the lowest-hanging fruit.

Raiding a "Disorderly House" in Racine

To raise money for the renovation of the Uptown Theater in Racine, Wisconsin, Gary Thompson, the executive director of the Uptown Theater Group, decided to host a rave Halloween party at the Tradewinds Village Banquet Hall just down the street from the theater. Prior to the scheduled event, the Racine Police Department received a tip from the U.S. Customs office that a dealer would be selling club drugs at the gathering. The fundraising party, featuring 16 DJs and all the trappings of a rave event, got under way on Saturday night, November 2, 2002.

Shortly after midnight, a 21-year-old attendee from Illinois sold a bag of ketamine (an animal tranquilizer widely used by young people to get high) and ecstasy pills to an undercover officer for $20. The police officer arrested this man and hauled him out of the building. The matter could have ended there, but it didn't. Thirty minutes later, 20 officers from the Racine Police Department, accompanied by U.S. Customs agents, stormed the banquet hall, creating chaos and fear among hundreds of law-abiding citizens.

The police raiders ordered everyone to the floor and told them to stay there until advised otherwise. Officers rushed into the restrooms with their guns drawn, kicking stall doors open. One woman, hit on the knee by a flying door, was yanked out of the stall and thrown to the floor before she could pull up her clothing. The police looked on as another woman was obliged to urinate in their presence. In the men's room, a police officer held one of the DJs at gunpoint for 30 minutes. Officers handcuffed another person who happened to be in men's room when the police burst in. They placed him in a police van, where he sat for three hours wondering what law he had broken. Out in the banquet hall, a man with a bad knee stood up to relieve his pain. An officer handcuffed this man, dragged him outside, and shoved him into the back of a van where he was held 30 minutes before being released. In the meantime, police identified, questioned, and searched everybody inside the building.

The raid and three-hour siege of the banquet hall, for all of its ferocity, produced more citizen misery and anger than contraband. The police arrested three suspects on drug charges and took four others into custody under an antiquated ordinance making it a crime to operate a "disorderly house." Everyone else, 445 people, was charged with being an "inmate of a disorderly house," the penalty for which involved a $968 fine. People who had gone to the rave party to have fun and raise money for the Uptown Theater ended up victims of heavy-handed law enforcement, which scared them, humiliated them, and cost them a hefty fine.

A spokesperson for the Racine Police Department defended the raid and mass issuance of disorderly house citations by calling the action "proactive law enforcement."[7] Others in the community also saw the raid as a good thing because no one in their right mind would ever again host a rave party in Racine. Public opinion, however, did not run in favor of the police. Most citizens were appalled that the authorities had wasted law enforcement resources on a group of civic-minded partygoers. And as stories of police manhandling surfaced, city politicians started feeling the heat. The city attorney, anxious to close the book on this public relations disaster, asked to meet with the 455 suspected disorderly house inmates. Only 100 showed up at City Hall to hear his deal: plead guilty and receive a reduced fine of $100. Only a handful of the raid victims accepted his offer. The rest decided to force the city attorney's hand by pleading not guilty and demanding a trial in which he would have to prove they knew that drugs were being sold at the Uptown Theater benefit. In January 2003, the city attorney dropped all of the disorderly house charges and promised to update the antiquated city ordinance.

An Illegal Assembly in Utah County

On July 16, 2005, in an area south of Provo, Utah, state and local police broke up a rave party on a ranch owned by Trudy Childs in the Diamond Park section of Spanish Fork Canyon. Although sheriff's deputies charged several partygoers with drug violations, most of the attendees were arrested for under-age drinking and disorderly conduct. The organizers of the event were fined for failing to acquire the proper "big event" permits from Utah County.

Rave promoter Brandon Fullmer, the manager of Uprock Records in Salt Lake City, and his partner Nick Mari, were more than a little concerned about the police raid in Spanish Fork Canyon because they were organizing a rave party scheduled for August 20. That event, entitled Versus II, would be held on the same site, 350 acres leased from ranch owner Trudy Childs. The promoters had already sold 700 advance tickets at $15 apiece ($10 off the gate price) and expected up to 3,000 attendees. Complying with the conditions of their "mass gathering" permit from the Utah County

Health Department, the organizers had arranged for a suitable number of portable restrooms as well as the proper water and trash facilities. They had also hired a licensed security company to provide officers to search attendees for contraband as they entered the concert grounds. Emergency medical technicians would also be on site. And finally, to protect their $20,000 investment, Fullmer had insured the event for $2 million.

Two weeks before the concert, promoters Fullmer and Mari petitioned federal court judge Dale Kimball to enjoin—to prevent—Utah County sheriff Jim Tracy, Jr., from raiding and closing down the event. Fullmer, an entrepreneur who had promoted more than a hundred rave concerts, had been working on Versus II since April. His attorney, noting that Sheriff Tracy had made it clear he didn't want rave parties in his county, argued that the sheriff didn't have the authority to shut down a lawful assembly. Judge Kimball, sitting on the district court bench in Salt Lake City, denied Fullmer's request.

On Saturday night, August 20, 2005, following months of preparation, the music in Spanish Fork Canyon started at 9:30 P.M. as hundreds of rave fans, many carrying sleeping bags and tents, moved slowly into the concert grounds through the security-posted gates. A few miles away, Sheriff Tracy had assembled 90 police officers, a number of police trucks and vans, and a helicopter. Officers from Utah County Metro SWAT, Provo-Drem SWAT, the Department of Public Safety SWAT, and the Department of Corrections Special Operations Unit were poised for action and awaiting word from the Utah County undercover officers mingling with the concertgoers. Although the sheriff expected his undercover agents to witness some drug use and under-age drinking, he didn't need any of that to justify shutting down the event. Promoters Brandon Fullmer and Nick Mari had failed to secure the $100 "legal gathering license" from the county commissioner's office, a permit that must be obtained 30 days in advance of any gathering of more than 250 people scheduled for longer than 12 hours. Versus II, therefore, was not a legal assembly.

The sheriff could have asked the promoters to pay the fee, or he could have shut down the concert before it started on the grounds that 700 tickets had been sold in advance. Instead, he waited until 1,500 concert fans had gathered in the canyon, then moved in with more than enough men and firepower to capture a nest of Hell's Angels. Of the dozens of firsthand raid accounts posted on the Internet, several, including the one below, appeared initially on the Apostate MySpace Web site:

At about 11:30 or so, I [Knick Evol] was standing behind the stage talking with someone when I noticed a helicopter pulling over one of the mountaintops. I jokingly said, "Oh look, here comes big brother" to the person I was with. I wasn't far off.

The helicopter dipped lower and lower and started shining its lights on the crowd. I was kind of in awe and just sat and watched this thing circle us for a minute. As I looked towards the crowd I saw a guy dressed in camouflage walking by, toting an assault rife. At this point, everyone was fully aware of what was going on. A few "troops" rushed the stage and cut the sound off and started yelling that everyone "get [expletive] out of here or go to jail." This is where it got really sticky.

No one resisted. That's for sure. They had police dogs raiding the crowd of people and I saw a dog signal out a guy who obviously had some drugs on him. The soldiers attacked the guy (four of them on one), and kicked him a few times in the ribs and had their knees in his back and sides. As they were cuffing him, there was about one-thousand kids trying to leave the backdrop, peacefully. Next thing I knew, a can of [expletive] tear gas is launched into the crowd. People are running and screaming at this point. Girls are crying, guys are cussing. Bad scene.[8]

Brandon Fullmer's girlfriend, Ashley Hawker, provided this e-mail description of how the raid affected her:

It gets to be about eleven-thirty and we see this light coming from over the mountains and it gets closer and closer. Then it starts shinning its light on the entire crowd. That's when I looked to my right and . . . I see a guy dressed in all green camo [camouflauge] and carrying a gun and wearing a helmet. I thought my eyes had deceived me but following right behind him are more big men carrying fully automatic guns. My whole body starts shaking uncontrollably.[9]

According to other accounts of the raid, the police knocked cameras, camcorders, and cell phones out of people's hands (a two-minute video showing officers throwing kids to the ground and kicking them surfaced on the Internet) and arrested anyone who didn't head for the exits immediately, including those who tried to retrieve their camping gear. Those who didn't flee the scene fast enough were charged with resisting arrest or disobeying a police officer and hauled off to jail in police vans. As another MySpace blogger described it: "The police in full riot gear came in, big trucks . . . next thing you know they are throwing tear gas at people, setting dogs on people, arresting kids . . . Making kids sit in the dirt with their hands tied all in a line, now you must remember in this whole thing *no one* was resisting arrest or making a big deal."[10]

Ranch owner Trudy Childs, when she learned of the raid, rushed to the scene to confront the police. Shortly after her arrival, officers handcuffed this 52-year-old woman, a sufferer from rheumatoid arthritis, behind her back. When Childs complained of the pain, they laughed it off as play-acting. Of the 60 people arrested that night, the police charged only a handful with drug offenses. Security guards who were holding drugs they had confiscated from concert attendees were among those charged. The SWAT officers had handcuffed and jailed several others for resisting arrest and disorderly conduct.

The next day, Sergeant Spencer Cannon of the Utah County Sheriff's Office assured the media that officers, in shutting down the rave party, had not employed excessive force. He denied that officers had dispensed tear gas, used tasers, or employed attack dogs. According to the official version of the raid, police officers had rescued a 17-year-old girl who had over-dosed on ecstasy. After paramedics treated her at the scene, the police took her home. In explaining the legal justification for sending SWAT forces into the canyon, Sergeant Cannon said, "We went in because it was an ille-gal gathering. They needed a permit for 250-plus people—they didn't have that permit. Illegal drug activity was discovered secondary to the closing down of the large gathering."[11] A few days later, Sheriff Tracy, Jr., revealed the real reason for the raid: "From several previous experiences with rave parties of this size, a large amount of drug use and under-age consump-tion of alcohol occur. In addition [there are] reports of sexual assaults, overdoses, firearm violations, vehicle burglaries, and numerous individu-als drive from the party under the influence of alcohol and/or drugs."[12] Based upon this statement, it appears that Sheriff Tracy's approach to law enforcement involves arresting and dispersing people *before* they have a chance to break the law.

Promoters Brandon Fullmer and Nick Mari, along with ranch owner Trudy Childs, filed suit in federal court on September 20, 2005, alleging that Sheriff Tracy and other Utah County officials had denied them their constitutional rights of privacy, due process, freedom of expression, and right lawful assembly. Two days later, the American Civil Liberties Union of Utah joined in the civil rights action. ACLU attorney Margret Plane, in announcing this decision, said, "Utah County's actions strike at the heart of First Amendment freedoms. The ACLU is joining this fight to help protect our fundamental rights from this kind of unjust law enforcement action."[13]

U.S. District Judge Dale Kimball, in June 2006, dismissed the case with prejudice. This meant that the suit could not be refiled. The sheriff had won; there would be no more rave concerts in Utah County, with or with-out all of the permits.

A Public Nuisance in Detroit

Every month, members of the Contemporary Art Institute of Detroit, a nonprofit organization that for 29 years has promoted art and education in the city, get together and dance to the music of James Brown, Aretha Franklin, and other singers in the "funk" music genre. Funk nights, beginning at midnight and running to 5 A.M., are heavily attended by college and graduate students from the suburbs. They are, compared with rave concerts, laid back and sophisticated. At these late-Friday-night/early-Saturday-morning events, employees of the institute serve beer and wine to members old enough to consume these beverages legally. Selling these drinks after 2 A.M., however, violated the city's after-hours alcohol sales prohibition. Aaron Timlin, the institute's director, had been informed of the ordinance, but the director had chosen to ignore it.

Some official, either in the Detroit Police Department or a person higher up in city government, authorized a raid of the Funk Night event held at the institute's facility on Rosa Parks Boulevard. At 2:30 A.M., Saturday morning, May 31, 2008, a squad of helmeted police officers dressed in black, wearing ski masks, and carrying semiautomatic weapons, burst into the building. At gunpoint, they ordered everyone to hit the floor. Officers who encountered partygoers slow to comply with their orders threw them to the floor and held them down with their boots planted in the middle of their backs. The violence and suddenness of the raid frightened and confused the Funk Night attendees—young people whose only experience with the police had involved traffic tickets.

That night the Detroit police cited 130 members of the Contemporary Art Institute with the offense of loitering in a place of illegal occupation, the occupation being the after-hours sale of beer and wine. Since the Funk Nighters had been charged with a public nuisance type of violation, the police, applying drug-case forfeiture powers, confiscated 44 of their vehicles. To get them back, each of the owners had to pay the Wayne County prosecutor's office $900. People who didn't ransom their vehicles out of the impound lot would be charged daily storage rent. One of the partygoers, after coughing up the $900, went to the impound lot to find that his car had been stolen. The car thief had driven the vehicle through the fence. Before officials returned this man's impound fee, the car owner had to run through a nightmarish bureaucratic maze. That night, the police, to their surprise and certain dismay, didn't find any illegal drugs, under-age drinking, or guns. As busts go, the Funk Night raid was a bust.

The citizens of Detroit, where violent crime was on the rise, criticized the mayor and the chief of police for this heavy-handed misuse of law enforcement resources. Instead of raiding the place, citing members with a ridiculous offense, and confiscating vehicles that had merely brought them to the party, why hadn't the authorities simply fined the events organizer? Was there more behind this police action than just poor judgment? Did it reflect anger toward Aaron Timlin, the flamboyant, disrespectful director of the institute? Many critics of the raid believed that the police chief and mayor had orchestrated the action to show Mr. Timlin who was boss.

Most of the Funk Nighters pleaded not guilty and demanded jury trials. Kary Moss, the lawyer representing the local ACLU office, weighed in on the controversy, asserting that the ordinance regarding "loitering in a place of illegal occupation" was unconstitutionally vague and overbroad and that in confiscating the vehicles the police had abused their vice forfeiture authority. In his motion to dismiss the loitering charges, Moss wrote: "Is Comerica Park during a [baseball] game . . . suddenly, and unbeknownst to the defendant, transformed into a place of illegal occupation simply because someone on the premises smokes marijuana? Such a result would be clearly absurd."[14]

On September 22, 2008, the Wayne County prosecutor, squirming under the heat of extremely bad publicity, dropped the charges against the 116 Art Institute members who had not pleaded guilty. The authorities, however, refused to return the money paid by the 44 partygoers whose vehicles had been impounded. For these people, Funk Night in Detroit had been traumatic—and expensive.

ROUNDING UP ILLEGAL IMMIGRANTS

In 2007, the Department of Homeland Security deported 300,000 people, some of whom were either U.S. citizens or lawful residents. On any given day, 30,000 illegal immigration suspects are being held in American jails and detention centers. Every year, illegal immigration raids, the detention of prisoners, and deportation hearings cost taxpayers more that a billion dollars. Advocates for illegal immigrants argue that in lieu of a coherent and integrated national immigration policy, the current system lacks due process, is inhumane, and is a huge waste of money. These critics believe that Immigration and Custom Enforcement (ICE) raids are alarmingly unfocused, terrifying, and disruptive of family and community life. They also describe conditions in the detention centers as squalid.

Over the past few years, raids by ICE agents on businesses employing illegal immigrants have become increasingly frequent and massive in scope. Between October l, 2007, and August 31, 2008, ICE special operations units working alongside U.S. Marshal's Office agents, rounded up 4,956 illegal immigrants working at food processing plants and other businesses across the country. About a fifth of the arrestees, with deportation orders already against them, were immediately sent back to Mexico. The authorities charged a few of the arrestees with identify theft and social security fraud. Assistant U.S. attorneys charged less than 200 business owners, managers, supervisors, and human resource people with offenses related to hiring illegal aliens. These worksite raids cost about $66 million, a sum offset by $30 million in business fines. Owing to the scope and sweep of these unfocused raids, ICE agents arrested, working alongside the illegals, an undisclosed number of U.S. citizens and other employees living and working lawfully in the United States.

During a single month, September 2008, a total of 95 ICE units working in 34 California counties made 1,157 workplace arrests. The following month, 100 ICE agents raided a chicken and turkey processing plant in Greenville, South Carolina. The agents rounded up, among the 300 taken into custody, several legal residents. The South Carolina raid alone cost $6.1 million. In 2008, ICE agents made thousands of worksite apprehensions in, among other states, Arkansas, New Jersey, Iowa, and North Carolina.

U.S. Senators Edward Kennedy of Massachusetts and Robert Menendez of New Jersey, in September 2008, introduced a bill intended to protect citizens and residents from unlawful raids and detention. The proposed legislation requires the employment of the same due process procedures that apply to regular criminal suspects. This would include the Fourth Amendment right to privacy, the Fifth Amendment right to remain silent, and the Sixth Amendment right to legal representation. Because so many Americans believe that illegal immigrants threaten national security and hurt the economy, Senators Kennedy and Menendez had no illusions that their bill would become law anytime soon. Congress also seems unable to find enough political support to control the Mexican border.

On June 18, 2009, the National Commission on ICE Misconduct and Violations of Fourth Amendment Rights, a body made up of labor leaders, former holders of public office, academic researchers, and legal experts, released the results of its two-year investigation of ICE's December 12, 2006, simultaneous raids of six meat processing plants. The 70-page report, called "Raids on Workers: Destroying Our Lives," involved the "military-style" raids of six Swift Company plants that employed a total of 12,000 workers. That day, ICE agents, in possession of just 133 warrants, arrested 1,300 Swift employees. Out of this group, the immigration authorities charged 274 with federal crimes that went beyond citizen status violations.

Darrell Harrington, a 22-year employee of the Swift plant in Greeley, Colorado, where shots were actually fired, described the raid to a reporter with the *Greeley Tribune,* saying that the gun-wielding agents who had stormed into his work area "didn't give the Mexicans a chance to get their green cards or notify their families to get their papers . . . Even as [legal] citizens, we were held for four to five hours without any bathroom privileges or without water or food or anything."[15] Commission member Bill Ong Hong, a University of California–Davis law professor, as quoted in the

Greeley Tribune, said, "I was totally shocked at the level of abuse that ICE visited upon the victims of the various sites we went to."[16]

Sheriff Joe's War on Illegal Immigration

City police chiefs and county sheriffs around the country are often at odds regarding how they should deal with illegal immigration. Should they defer to the federal authorities such as ICE, or enforce immigration laws on their own? Should this local enforcement include raiding workplaces to roundup undocumented workers? City and town police chiefs, appointed by mayors or city managers, are a little less affected by immigration politics that county sheriffs, who are elected to office and therefore are more sensitive to the political views of their constituents. Rural, suburban, and small-town voters who put sheriffs into office tend to be less tolerant of illegal immigrants than people who live in the bigger cities. As a result, sheriffs in the less populated areas are often more likely to raid businesses and round up their illegal employees. Police chiefs, on the other hand, tend to be less aggressive, only arresting illegal immigrants when they commit crimes that are not related to immigration.

The round-them-up versus let-the-feds-handle-it debate erupted into all-out war in Maricopa County, Arizona, where fourth-term sheriff Joe Arpaio, the "toughest sheriff in America," hell-bent on ridding his county of illegal aliens, shocked and offended a lot of citizens with what his critics considered strong-arm tactics. Whereas Sheriff Arpaio's supporters label him an independent, hard-nosed crime fighter, his detractors believe him to be a headline-grabbing bully who will do whatever it takes to gain attention and remain in office. No one disputes that Arpaio is flamboyant, outspoken, and controversial. He's the kind of person you either love or hate; if you're an illegal alien, you fear him.

In the spring and summer of 2008, Sheriff Arpaio, pursuant to his investigation of illegal hiring practices and the crimes of identify theft and document falsification that go with them, directed SWAT team raids of a door factory, a landscaping company, an amusement park, and several other Maricopa County workplaces. These military-style raids led to the arrests of hundreds of undocumented workers and the people who had hired them. The sheriff's crackdown on illegal immigration angered many in the business community, created political controversy, and garnered a lot of publicity. The raids had also strained the sheriff's relationships with other police leaders in the county.

On May 8, 2008, a security guard employed by the city of Mesa, Arizona, called the sheriff's illegal immigration hotline with a tip. According the this city employee, illegal aliens, hired by Management Cleaning Controls, a janitorial service based in Louisville, Kentucky, under contract with the municipality, were working in City Hall, the public library, and other city buildings. At the time of the immigration tip, Mesa officials were investigating the security guard on suspicion that he had used a city computer to send an offensive e-mail to a female coworker.

On May 21, a lieutenant with the Mesa Police Department, who had gotten wind of the whistleblower's call, voiced his concern at a meeting with personnel of the janitorial service. The company's manager said that since October 2007, the firm had been using a computer program called E-Verifying System to check job applicant citizenship. He promised to check into the matter. On June 4, the Mesa Police Department lieutenant followed up his talk with the janitorial company manager with an e-mail urging the company to resolve the matter quickly.

The security guard who had called Sheriff Arpaio's immigration hotline, following an internal investigation by Mesa officials, admitted to having sent the offensive e-mail. Although he said he regretted the incident, his supervisor fired him on September 22, 2008. In the meantime, Sheriff Arpaio, acting on the whistleblower's tip, had dispatched an Hispanic undercover officer to the Management Cleaning Controls Company where, after presenting himself as an illegal immigrant, he applied for a janitorial job. According to the sheriff's undercover operative, an official with the contract cleaning service tutored him on how to acquire fake citizenship identification. Sheriff Arpaio, armed with evidence that the city of Mesa used contract maintenance personnel who were not in the country legally, took his investigation to the next level—a SWAT raid of City Hall.

A Mesa police officer, on patrol 30 minutes past midnight on October 16, 2008, spotted a cluster of Joe Arpaio's deputies gathered in the city park near the Mormon Temple. Because these men were outfitted for a SWAT raid and were accompanied by police dogs, the patrol officer asked what was going on. After one of the K-9 deputies said they weren't supposed to reveal what they were up to, another SWAT team member informed the city officer that they were in the park training their dogs.

At 2:30 A.M., 30 deputies and as many volunteer citizen deputies with the Maricopa County Sheriff's Posse, all dressed for battle, stormed the eight-story Mesa City Plaza Building to round up illegal aliens cleaning the offices of the mayor, members of city council, and other city officials. Finding City Hall devoid of maintenance personnel, the 60-man force stormed into the public library on Main Street, where they apprehended three janitors. In the predawn hours following the library raid, Sheriff Arpaio's SWAT teams raided several homes, resulting in the arrests of six Management Cleaning Controls managers and as many illegal employees of the firm. Later that morning, deputies bearing warrants returned to City Hall to search for documents that would reveal the nature of the city's contractual relations with the maintenance firm. The search warrants were unnecessary because these documents were available to the public upon request. Sheriff Arpaio's critics considered his investigation audacious to say the least and his SWAT raids nothing more than publicity stunts intended to embarrass the mayor and other city officials.

At a news conference the following afternoon in Mesa, the mayor, Scott Smith, played a surveillance camera videotape depicting county SWAT officers pouring into the public library. Clearly upset by Sheriff Arpaio's tactics, Mayor Smith said, "I believe the safety of our citizens was gravely compromised . . . That crosses the line as what law enforcement can and should do." The mayor noted that the raid had terrified citizens who had been working in City Hall and in the library. "What could have happened was a simple phone call to the city of Mesa. I'm not hard to find. Anyone in Maricopa County can call me and again, we are more than willing to work [together]."[17]

Sergeant Fabian Cota, representing the Mesa Police Association—a police labor union—labeled the raid "unprofessional" and called Sheriff Arpaio a "loose cannon" who functions as a "one-man show." Speaking at the news conference, Cota said, "It could have been handled with a lot more tact. But the sheriff has demonstrated that he's more interested in trying to cause embarrassment and controversy than working with agencies to get a handle on the problem."[18] Ronald Reinstein, the former chief criminal court judge of Maricopa County, agreed. "I just can't remember anything like it,"[19] he said.

In Phoenix that afternoon, Sheriff Arpaio held his own news conference to defend the SWAT raids. One reporter, noting that the sheriff was up for reelection in less than a month, asked if the raids had been politically motivated. Another correspondent wanted to know if Arpaio's eye-popping tactics had been a ploy to divert the media's attention from the brutal death of a county jail inmate the day before his SWAT raids. Referring to the city of Mesa, Arpaio said, "It's my jurisdiction, too. I'm the sheriff of the whole county . . . Everybody's after me. Why?" After puzzling over the fact he and his deputies weren't receiving medals for their efforts to rid the county of illegals, the sheriff said, "This [the indignation] is all hype put out by the police and the mayor to cover up their embarrassment that we went in there and we took care of business when their own police department avoided it. The raid took place at night because that was when the janitors were working and the city buildings would be otherwise empty. Very simple."[20]

The citizens of the state's most populous county put Joe Arpaio into office for the fifth time on November 4, 2008. He defeated his opponent, a credible candidate, by getting 56 percent of the vote. The election results gave Sheriff Arpaio a mandate to continue his countywide war on illegal immigration.

Sheriff Arpaio's aggressive enforcement of the federal immigration laws, however controversial, is not beyond the scope of his legal authority. In 2002, Congress added, to the Immigration and Naturalization Act of 1996, section 287 (g) entitled, the "Delegation of Immigration Authority." Pursuant to this addendum, simply referred to as 287 g, the Immigration and Customs Enforcement agency has the authority to deputize local law enforcement officers as federal immigration cops. This allows the local police to round up illegal aliens who have not otherwise broken the law. Police officers and sheriff's deputies, under 287 g, are eligible for five weeks of immigration enforcement training at the ICE Academy in Charleston, South Carolina. Several of Sheriff Arpaio's deputies have gone through the program.

Since its inception, 287 g has come under severe criticism. Opponents of the law believe it encourages, on the part of local law enforcement, racial profiling and other civil rights violations. These critics cite Sheriff Joe Arpaio as an example of why 287 g is a bad idea. President Obama's new Secretary of Homeland Security, former Arizona Governor Janet Napolitano, shortly after taking office, announced her intention to review 287 g to make certain local authorities weren't abusing their mandate under this provision. As the former governor of Arizona, Secretary Napolitano was quite familiar with the controversy surrounding Sheriff Joe Arpaio's illegal alien roundup in the city of Mesa.

On February 4, 2009, Arpaio, the target of 2,700 civil rights complaints and with a backlog of 40,000 felony arrest warrants yet to be served, promoted his upcoming Fox Reality Channel television show *Smile, You're Under Arrest!* by marching 200 shackled illegal aliens from the Durango jail to Tent City, his illegal-alien holding complex. The spectacle of the black-and-white striped prisoners being led down the street in chains offended many, including U.S. Senator Richard Miranda. At a news conference on February 17, the senator said, "What's happening . . . is the parading of human beings who are incarcerated, some of whom many not be convicted al all. They are not trophies on a mantel to be paraded around and shown as conquests. We're not going to tolerate any more civil rights violations."[21]

Late in 2008, attorneys with the U.S. Department of Justice began looking into Sheriff Arpaio's immigration sweeps and raids for evidence of civil rights violations. In June 2009, in response to the justice department's expanded investigation into Arpaio's management of county money, the sheriff accused his political enemies in Arizona of pushing federal investigators into what he called a witch hunt. The sheriff, quoted in the *Phoenix*

Business Journal, said, "I have nothing to hide. Let them look. The [FBI agents] are just coming down here hoping to find something."[22]

The Department of Homeland Security, in October 2009, stripped Sheriff Arpaio's 160 federally trained deputies of their 287 g authority to make immigration arrests. The Sheriff responded to this action with a public statement that he would not bow to the authorities in Washington. Arpaio made it clear that because people who crossed the border illegally were criminals, he would not stop rounding them up.

Joe Arpaio, in March 2010, announced that he was considering a run for the office of governor of Arizona. This was the fourth time Arpaio had contemplated such a move. According to the 77-year-old sheriff, if he did run for governor, he would win because the people of Arizona support his politics. Arpaio has been a good example of why police administrators with SWAT teams and a political agendas are not good for law enforcement or, for that matter, democracy.

Chapter 3

BOOTS IN THE HOUSE: BROKEN-DOOR RAIDS

HIGH-RISK TACTICS IN LOW-RISK CASES

In communities where police administrators have woven SWAT tactics into the fabric of everyday law enforcement, people have grown accustomed to scenes on the nightly news featuring combat-like raids into the residences of burglars, check passers, nonviolent parole violators, petty thieves, and people suspected of minor assault. In July 2008, a SWAT team showed up at a motel in Moraine, Ohio, to arrest a suspected purse snatcher. In Miami Beach, Florida, a SWAT team, in January 2005, dropped a police dog down the hatch of a yacht to corner a 49-year-old female intruder. Officers cordoned off the streets around the Fontainebleau Hilton Resort as the operation unfolded. A police spokesperson told reporters that officers feared the woman possessed a flare gun. They arrested her without a struggle. In Indiana, the Allen County SWAT team, in September 2008, raided a house in Fort Wayne to arrest a man charged with driving with a suspended license and violating his probation in a drug case. Finding cocaine and marijuana in his house, they charged him with the sale and possession of drugs and placed him in jail, where he was held without bail.

Many police administrators admit that SWAT team officers have to be kept busy to keep them motivated and sharp. For this reason, SWAT teams are used to make relatively low-risk arrests and to execute search warrants associated with these nonviolent cases. This type of deployment should not be justified simply because the police entered the correct premises, didn't break anything, hurt anyone, or rough anyone up. John Gnagey, executive director of the National Tactical Officers Association in Doylestown, Pennsylvania, as reported in a 2006 BBC article, said, "I have no problem with using these paramilitary style squads to go after known, violent, armed criminals, but it is an extreme tactic to use them against other sorts of suspects."

Sheriff Joe's White-Collar Bust: The SWAT Raid as Political Theater

In 1989, one year after being elected to the office of Maricopa County Superintendent of Schools, Sandra Dowling founded education facilities for homeless children called the Thomas J. Pappas Schools. Over the next 15 years, Dowling, considered arrogant and incompetent by her critics, made more than her share of political enemies. Notwithstanding budget shortfalls at the Pappas Schools, Dowling refused to cut costs, which put her at odds with the county board of supervisors. By 2005, she and the board were locked in battle. Rumors that Dowling had been stealing education funds from the county arose from this heated political dispute. When members of the board of supervisors demanded an investigation, Maricopa Sheriff Joe Arpaio stepped into the limelight.

In a move highly uncharacteristic of a white-collar investigation of a public official, the sheriff ordered a SWAT team raid of Dowling's home in West Valley, Arizona. With a pair of helicopters overhead spotlighting the house and television crews filming the raid for the nightly news, a dozen or so heavily armed Maricopa County SWAT officers stormed the residence. Dowling's husband Dennis stood by in shock as detectives arrested his wife and searched the dwelling top to bottom, seizing computers and boxes of documents.

Following an 11-month investigation by the Arizona attorney general's office, a Maricopa grand jury, in November 2006, indicted Dowling on 25 counts of felony theft involving $1.9 million that she had allegedly stolen from public school funds. Dowling denied any wrongdoing and, as the investigation moved forward through 2007, the case started falling apart. By 2008, judges had dismissed all 25 of the felony charges. That spring, Dowling pleaded guilty to the class 2 misdemeanor offense of hiring a relative. (In 1999, she had given her daughter a summer job at $5 per hour.) At her sentencing proceeding in July, the judge denied the prosecutor's request for a $10,000 fine and a year's probation. Noting that the defendant hadn't stolen a dime from the county, the judge fined Dowling $750 and placed her on four months' probation.

Michael Manning, Dowling's attorney and long-time nemesis of Joe Arpaio, in September 2008, filed a notice of his client's intent to sue the sheriff and the Maricopa Board of Supervisors for malicious prosecution. Claiming that the vengeful and politically motivated case had cost his client $200,000 in legal fees and thousands of dollars in medical bills associated with stress-related illnesses, he sought $1.75 million in damages for the plaintiff. Attorney Manning, in his 11-page notice of suit, cited Arpaio's SWAT raid as evidence of the sheriff's malicious intent:

> The SWAT squad was not in search of a meth lab, Islamic terrorists or even brown-skinned aliens. They were there to execute one or two of the 40,000 felony warrants that languished back at the Maricopa County Sheriff's Office headquarters. It was the home of Dr. Sandra Dowling and her husband, Dennis.
>
> Never willing to pass on an opportunity to puff his tough-cop façade for the press, the sheriff had conveniently alerted the press to be "camera ready" for his over-the-top paramilitary incursion, so that this would ensure a splash on the nightly news . . . His pretense as a tough crime fighter, just as any deflating balloon, requires frequent bursts of hot air to maintain its appearance.[1]

Claiming that Sheriff Arpaio had lied to the magistrate in order to acquire the warrant to search her house, Dowling filed her suit in the Maricopa Superior Court on June 3, 2009. According to her claim, the Maricopa Board of Supervisors, in cahoots with the sheriff, had abused their powers by trying to intimidate her with the highly publicized SWAT raid. If she won the case, she would ask the jury to determine the amount of the award. To a journalist with the *Arizona Republic,* Dowling, in referring to her ordeal, said, "To say it has been traumatic is an understatement. I don't know if I'll ever be able to work in education again."[2]

On November 20, 2009, Sandra Dowling settled her lawsuit against the County Board of Supervisors for $25,000 and lawyers fees.

Paramilitary Presence in New Hampshire

New Hampshire, not one of the more populated states or a place known for its high crime rates, has six regional paramilitary law enforcement units that operate independently of the state police, which has its own SWAT team. One of these regional squads, the Central New Hampshire Special Operations Unit, has 85 members from 40 police agencies in the upper valley section of the state. New Hampshire is SWAT-ready.

On August 2, 2006, 16 officers assigned to the Central New Hampshire Special Operations Unit raided the home of Thomas and Tina Mldozinski in Bristol. The SWAT team had come to arrest Mr. and Mrs. Mldozinski's son,

17-year-old Michael Rothman. The boy had been charged with second-degree assault. According to the affidavit in support of the warrant, the suspect, three days earlier, had struck an acquaintance with an expandable police baton. The police also had information that Rothman carried a gun.

The Special Operations Unit broke into the Mldozinski home just before dawn. Within a matter of minutes the entire family, still in their nightclothes, were handcuffed and on the floor. The raid terrorized Michael's 15-year-old sister who, while the police interrogated the family at gunpoint, kept asking what they had done wrong.

The police didn't find the baton or a firearm, but they did seize drug paraphernalia and a small quantity of marijuana. In October 2007, Rothman pleaded guilty to the lesser offense of reckless conduct. The judge sentenced him to probation. After the Mldozinski family filed suit against the Central New Hampshire Unit, the question of who would pay in the event the state lost the case became an issue. This led to the revelation that the regional SWAT units possessed limited liability insurance. This meant that the burden of civil suit judgments would fall upon the law enforcement agencies employing the special operations officers.

Lawsuits filed by victims of unnecessary paramilitary raids have become common and cost taxpayers money that could be better spent elsewhere. In the era before the SWAT team craze, a pair of detectives would have approached Michael Rothman in broad daylight someplace outside his house. Shortly thereafter, two other officers would have gone to the home, introduced themselves to his parents, and then executed the search warrant. When there are 85 police officers in one special operations unit, every police action in New Hampshire is in danger of becoming a special operation.

Friendly Persuasion versus Show of Force

Arden Troyer, an old-order Amish man, left his wife, Wilma, and their two daughters after Sam Mullet, his wife's father and the bishop of the Amish settlement near the village of Bergholz, Ohio, excommunicated him. Located just west of the Pennsylvania line in the central part of the state, Bergholz has a population of 800. Mr. Troyer had accused members of the Amish community of sexually molesting children in the enclave. He wanted to move his children and his wife out of that settlement, but she had refused to leave her family.

In May 2007, Fred Abdalla, the sheriff of Jefferson County, picked up Wilma Troyer in his car and drove to her in-laws' house, where she met with Arden, her estranged husband. From there, as prearranged, Arden took Wilma and the children to Indiana, where they lived for a short while before moving to

Genesee, Pennsylvania. A few days after arriving in Pennsylvania, Wilma's parents hired a driver, who brought her and the girls back to Bergholz.

On the morning of September 14, 2007, Sheriff Abdalla, in possession of a court order authorizing the seizure of Wilma Troyer's children, rolled up to her place of employment, a one-room Amish schoolhouse. It's not clear why the sheriff chose the school as the place to serve the court order or why he brought along several of his deputies and the regional SWAT team. The sheriff and a deputy approached the building and tried the door, which was locked. "Open up," he yelled, "I want to talk to Wilma Troyer. Open that door; I have a court order." Inside the structure, the sheriff heard many of the 29 children crying. Some of them were screaming "They're going to shoot us!"[3]

The school door opened and Wilma, amid her panicked students, walked out. The sheriff handed her the court order, which she threw to the ground. She then ran to her parents' house, where she and her two daughters resided. The sheriff, after warning the Amish onlookers who had gathered at the scene that he would arrest anyone who interfered with his seizure of the Troyer children, gathered up his deputies and the SWAT team and proceeded to the farmhouse. A short time later, with the dwelling surrounded by the police, a member of Wilma's family came out of the house with the two girls and handed them over to the sheriff. That ended the siege.

In a press release issued a week after the sheriff's show of force and seizure of the Amish children, Bryan Felmet, the Steubenville, Ohio, attorney representing Wilma Troyer and others in the Amish community, criticized the way Sheriff Abdalla had executed the court order. Pointing out that the police were armed with automatic assault rifles and a battering ram, he wrote that the Amish community "has been on edge since the invasion of [the Troyer] farm by law enforcement officials. Adults as well as children are afraid to go to school, to work in the fields, and especially to leave Wilma alone. It is unreal that you can do things like this and get away with it in a free country. We can't figure out who they think they are."[4] The attorney told reporters that he didn't understand why the sheriff hadn't arranged the transfer of the children through him.

Sheriff Abdalla, claiming that the local Amish bishop, Sam Mullet, had threatened his life on more than one occasion, spoke to a local television correspondent: "If it wasn't for all the allegations being made, for all the statements being made and the threats being made, we would have handled it differently. I don't care if it's a school or a church. I'm going to take whatever action is necessary. Based on threats to my life and on my deputies' lives, based on the threats [Sam Mullet] has made on his own family, surely Mr. Bryan Felmet doesn't think I should approach the situation with sticks in my hand."[5] The attorney, to the same reporter, said, "Machine guns, and bulletproof vests, and camouflage—what is that about? There's no explanation. I don't care.

There's no explanation unless he thought these children were armed and dangerous."[6]

The Troyer custody hearing in the Jefferson County juvenile court, over the course of several weeks, produced testimony that Bishop Sam Mullet and his 28-year-old son Chris had allegedly been sexually molesting Amish women and children. This testimony came from the sheriff as well as from members of the Amish community. The judge, basing his decision on this evidence, granted custody of the girls to their father. He also ruled that Sheriff Abdalla had not abused his authority by executing the court order in the way that he did.

In September 2008, Chris Mullet pleaded guilty to three counts of unlawful sexual conduct with two minors in 2003 and 2004. His victims, now of age, had forgiven him and asked the judge for no punishment. The judge, instead of sending Mullet to prison, sentenced him to probation.

Thirty-five members of the Bergholz Amish community, in September 2008, filed a $35 million lawsuit in federal court against the Jefferson County Sheriff's Office. According to the plaintiffs, the sheriff had used excessive force in the execution of a routine civil law court order and in so doing, violated the civil rights of those in the schoolhouse that day. The paramilitary-style action, according to the plaintiffs, induced fear and panic among the children, who fled the scene in fear for their lives. Sheriff Abdalla, responding to these claims, said this to a local newspaper reporter: "What about the rights of the children who were sexually abused for years and the adults who knew about it?" By that statement, it didn't appear that Sheriff Abdalla understands the distinction between his motives and his tactics.

Excessive Force in Colorado:
The SWAT Seizure of John Shiflett

Eleven-year-old John Shiflett, while playing at his home near Glenwood Springs, Colorado, fell and sustained a black eye. His father, Tom Shiflett, a medic during the Vietnam War, examined his son and decided he didn't require hospital care. That Thursday morning, January 3, 2008, a neighbor, concerned about the boy, called an ambulance. Paramedics arrived at the mobile home and entered the premises without Tom Shiflett's permission. One of the paramedics called the Garfield County sheriff's office when Mr. Shiflett refused to allow the crew to take his son to the hospital.

The next morning, a pair of social workers came to the Shiflett house and spoke to the boy in private. That afternoon, Tom, his wife, John, and five of John's siblings went shopping. The family didn't know it, but in the meantime the social workers had acquired a court order allowing the seizure of the boy for purposes of a medical examination.

Sheriff Lou Vallario, to carry out this assignment, decided to deploy the Garfield County SWAT team. Later, when reporters asked him why he had made this decision, the sheriff pointed out that Mr. Shiflett was a "self-proclaimed constitutionalist" who had made threats and "comments" over the years. The sheriff also noted that Mr. Shiflett had been "rude and confrontational" when the paramedics entered his home.[7]

At eleven o'clock on Friday evening, January 4, 2008, the Garfield County SWAT team broke down the front door to the Shiflett residence and entered with their guns drawn. They first encountered the Shiflett's 18-year-old daughter, whom they threw to the floor. She was held in that position with a knee pressed into her back. Once they had the rest of the family on the ground, a SWAT officer grabbed the terrified 11-year-old and hauled him to the hospital.

The physician took John Shiflett's blood pressure and had X-rays taken of his head. After offering pain medication, refused by the boy, and suggesting the application on an ice pack, the doctor declared him in good health. The SWAT team officer drove the boy home. Sheriff Vallario, confident that his decision to deploy the SWAT team had been the correct way to proceed, offered no apology to the family. His actions, however, outraged many in the community.

In the Name of Property: Busting Burglars

In Maryland, detectives with the 2nd District Burglary Unit of the Montgomery County Police Department suspected that six members of the 54 Mob, a gang affiliated with the Bloods, had committed a burglary in the Scotland neighborhood of Potomac. The intruders, on August 29, 2008, had stolen a pair of expensive leather jackets, a high-end watch, and a Dior purse. The police estimated the total value of the loot at $15,000. During the predawn hours of September 24, 2008, Montgomery County SWAT teams, armed with no-knock search and arrest warrants, stormed six homes in the mostly African American communities of Cabin John, Potomac, and Germantown. That morning the police arrested six young black men but didn't find the stolen merchandise. A magistrate released five of the suspected burglars on unsecured personal bonds, a move suggesting the judge didn't consider them dangerous. The magistrate held the sixth suspect on $1,000 bail.

In the wake of the burglary raids, residents of the invaded homes complained of unnecessary manhandling of innocent bystanders, excessive property damage—doors ripped off their frames and furniture destroyed—threats of violence, and foul language. Residents of the Scotland neighborhood formed a community action group that included representatives of the American Civil Liberties Union and the NAACP.

Several of the raid complainants, on October 13, 2008, told their stories at a public meeting sponsored by Roger Berliner, a Montgomery County councilman. Standing before the group of concerned citizens who had gathered at the Scotland Community Center, Leo Thompson, the father of one of the suspected burglars, gave his account of what took place at his house that night. Just before dawn, when he awoke and stepped outside his residence in Potomac to investigate a noise, he encountered SWAT officers, who ordered him to the ground before they "splattered his brains all over the place." As a SWAT-team member approached a shed on the property, Mr. Thompson offered to give him the door key. The officer, as he smashed the door with a battering ram, said he had one. Throughout the ordeal, Mr. Thomson said officers continuously threatened and cursed him. His 21-year-old son was not at home, but the police took the son's bandanas and a pair of his sneakers.

Other accounts of the raids included a suspect's aunt, who said the police pulled her out of bed and threw her to the floor. At another house, officers photographed a teenage girl as she lay naked on the carpet. Another woman reported that the police pulled her out of the bathtub, then placed her in handcuffs. In all of the incidents, the complainants described police officers who were foul-mouthed, extremely threatening, and destructive.

Critics of the raids accused the Montgomery County police of using the no-knock burglary warrants as an excuse to break into the homes of suspected gang members. Others called the operation a law enforcement witch hunt. Following the sweep, police spokesman Lieutenant Paul Starks announced that officers had seized, from the targeted homes, clothing, address books, photographs, and other gang-related paraphernalia. In response to critics who challenged the use of SWAT teams in the pursuit of suspected burglars, Starks admitted that the Montgomery County Police Department operated under no formal guidelines regarding the deployment of such a force. Because of the community uproar over the SWAT raids, the matter was turned over to internal affairs for an investigation. As for the property damaged by the police, Lieutenant Starks, noting that the raids were based upon lawfully acquired search warrants, said the department was not responsible for repairing broken doors and locks or fixing smashed furniture.

At a preliminary hearing in November 2008, a judge, citing lack of evidence, dismissed the charges against two of the burglary suspects. Two weeks later, the state's attorney assigned to the county gang prosecution unit dropped the charges against the other suspects after the burglary victim stopped cooperating with his office. According to the authorities, the internal investigation into the raids produced no evidence of racial harassment or excessive force. (In June 2009, bad publicity continued to haunt the Montgomery County SWAT operation. Nancy Njoroge, the victim of a botched drug raid in Gaithersburg, sued the county. In 2005, the SWAT team had burst into her apartment at

4 A.M., handcuffing the Kenyan immigrant and her two teenage daughters. Dressed in a revealing night garment, Njoroge lay on the floor for 30 minutes with her hands bound behind her back before the police realized they were in the wrong dwelling. According to the search warrant, they were supposed to raid the apartment next door.)

Knuckle Under or Be Raided

John and Jacqueline Stowers and their nine children live in a sprawling house on 26 acres along State Route 303 in Pittsfield Township outside of La Grange, Ohio, a rural town of 2,000 on the western edge of metropolitan Cleveland. In 2002, the Stowers started Manna Storehouse, an organic food cooperative that, by 2008, supplied wheat, flour, sugar, grass-fed beef, lamb, turkey, and eggs from free-range chickens to 100 members of their buying club. They obtained the meat and produce from local Amish farmers as well as from a national distributor of organic foods.

The Stowers refused to acquire a retail food license because they weren't retailers, and this had angered the bureaucrats in Lorain County who oversaw this type of enterprise. On November 30, 2007, in an effort to prove that the Stowers were in fact retailing food without a license, a third-degree misdemeanor, three agents with the Lorain County Health District showed up unannounced at their house. The officials were unable to inspect the facility because the Stowers denied them entrance to their home. Without a search warrant, they had no choice but to leave. However, by exercising their constitutional rights, the Stowers had made themselves targets of governmental agents, who tend to equate this form of independence with belligerent disrespect for the law.

Desperate for evidence that the Stowers were operating a grocery store out of their home, officials with the Ohio Department of Agriculture (ODA) sent an undercover agent to the house to buy eggs. The undercover operative feigned interest in joining the co-op. The Stowers, explaining that membership was limited to family and friends, turned him down. The next day, the ODA man returned with a different approach. He asked if he could purchase a dozen eggs produced by range-fed chickens for his ailing mother. The agent hung around the house for two hours. In an effort to get him to leave, Mrs. Stowers gave him the eggs. As he left, the agent laid money on the kitchen counter so he could report a retail buy. In law, this ODA agent's actions defined classic entrapment.

On November 26, 2008, ODA Agent William Lesho obtained a warrant to search the Stowers' house and outbuildings for evidence of a retail enterprise and income derived from that illegal activity. Although the affidavit in support of the warrant made no mention of guns or other weapons or the

possibility of evidence being destroyed, the ODA and Health District personnel who would conduct the search waited outside until the house had been secured by a squad of Lorain County sheriff's deputies. Several of these officers, including Ed Gawlik, the deputy in charge of the Stowers case, were members of the Northern Ohio Violent Fugitive Task Force. On the day of the raid, December 1, 2008, these deputies showed up in their paramilitary garb. The Lorain County bureaucrats were about to get their pound of flesh.

At 11:30 A.M. that Monday morning, Katie, one of the Stowers' daughters, answered the door and came face to face with Deputy Gawlik. Frightened by the sight of a man in combat dress, she tried to shut the door, but it was too late, he was already in the house. Five other men followed him into the house. Jacqueline Stowers, on the second floor, home-schooling the other eight children, heard the ruckus and rushed down the stairs to investigate. Ignoring her demands for the police to leave the house, Deputy Gawlik handed Jacqueline the search warrant and asked if her husband John was on the premises. She replied that he wasn't. Following a brief but heated exchange with Jacqueline, Deputy Gawlik told her and Katie to remain in the room. Two officers had already climbed the stairs to herd the children down to the first-floor room with their mother and sister. The family was not allowed to leave this room while agent Lesho and the Health District inspectors were rummaging through the house and outbuildings.

Once word got out about the raid, civil libertarians across the country expressed their outrage in blogs, chat rooms, Web sites, and other online venues. The use of SWAT-like force to search for evidence of a crime no more serious than a traffic ticket in a house occupied by a woman and nine children had struck a nerve. The ODA, on flimsy evidence at best, had shut this family operation down for the better part of a day. Apparently tone-deaf on the issue of overreaching, militarized law enforcement, Captain Richard Resendez of the Lorain County Sheriff's Office assured the media that the Stowers case involved nothing more than an "uneventful execution of a search warrant." Although Captain Resendez considered the raid routine and "uneventful," the family, which had been traumatized by it, had a different perspective.[8]

On December 17, 2008, attorney Maurice A. Thompson of the Center of Constitutional Law, the legal arm of the Buckeye Institute in Columbus, filed suit on behalf of the Stowers family against the ODA, the Ohio Attorney General's Office, and Lorain County. Attorney Thompson asked the court to enjoin (stop) the defendant agencies from further raids and to declare the execution of the ODA search warrant—which had caused the Stowers children unnecessary shock and fright and their parents embarrassment and indignity—unconstitutional.

In the press release announcing this legal action, David Hansen, the president of the Buckeye Institute, said, "The use of these police state

tactics on a peaceful family is simply unacceptable. Officers rushed into the Stowers' home with guns drawn and held the family—including nine young children—captive for six hours. This outrageous case of bureaucratic overreach must be addressed."[9] Maurice Thompson, the family's attorney and the Buckeye Institute's law director, said, "Ohioans do not need a government permission slip to run a family farm and co-op, and should not be subjected to raids when they do not have one. This legal action will ensure the ODA understands and respects Ohioan's rights."[10] Although John and Jacqueline Stowers had not been charged with any crime as of June 2009, Thompson said the law center would defend them if the occasion arose.

The Frat House Sweep

At 8:30 P.M. on the night of January 21, 2009, when a sergeant with the Pullman Police Department shone his flashlight into a parked red Honda, he spotted a bong and what he suspected was a packet of marijuana. The officer quickly acquired a search warrant and recovered the contraband. The car belonged to a Washington State University student who lived in the Phi Kappa Sigma fraternity house on North East Colorado Street. The Honda had been sitting in its parking lot.

There had been complaints that minors had been served alcohol at Phi Kappa Sigma parties. Three months earlier, officials with the national fraternal organization had placed the Washington State chapter on probation. Following the Honda search, instead of questioning its owner and taking the case from there, the police obtained a warrant to search the three-story fraternity house for drugs and evidence of under-age drinking. The police searched the place at 1 A.M. on the same night the officer had recovered the evidence from the red Honda.

Although armed drug dealers, fugitives from the law, and deranged people with guns rarely inhabit fraternity houses, Commander Chris Tennant of the Pullman Police Department decided to activate the regional SWAT team. Fifteen officers from three agencies—the Whitman County Sheriff's Office, the Washington State University Police Department, and the Pullman force—stormed into the house that night. Fortunately no one got manhandled or shot. The results of the search, small amounts of marijuana and some paraphernalia, were pitiful. The police didn't take any of the fraternity house residents into custody.

Because the police didn't hurt or kill anyone, the use of 15 SWAT officers to raid a frat house for marijuana didn't create much of a fuss other than a few Internet protests from a handful of civil libertarians. However, 10 days after the raid, Commander Tennant felt criticized enough to downplay the SWAT aspect of the police action. "No one was dressed up in battle dress uniforms or riot gear," he said. "They were all in police uniforms . . . We have misdemeanor levels of marijuana and paraphernalia issues we have to deal with on several house members that we'll be following up on."[11] The commander said that because the frat house was so large, he needed the 15-man force to search the place. The commander, apparently, in weighing the drug war payoff against the danger of sending 15 armed officers into a fraternity house, had come down on the side of marijuana enforcement. It wasn't as though he were taking guns off the street, arresting violent criminals, or even shutting down a drug dealer. In this commander's mind, the fact that these SWAT officers didn't carry automatic rifles, knock down doors, or roll in flashbang grenades made this frat house invasion appropriate and routine.

BOTCHED LOW-RISK RAIDS

The SWAT raid of the Shiflett house to seize the 11-year-old boy with the black eye was, from a tactical point of view, a successful law enforcement mission in that no one was injured or killed. The police had invaded the right house and had seized the person listed in the court order. It was all quite legal. Still, many people criticized the sheriff for having ordered an unnecessary raid which had traumatized a family. The Shifletts were not criminals and were not charged with any crimes. Nevertheless, the sheriff, believing his actions appropriate, didn't feel the need to apologize.

Although some people object to the use of SWAT teams to arrest suspects who are not known to be violent, the criticism intensifies when the police in some way *bungle* a low-risk raid. All arrests are potentially dangerous, but whenever a SWAT team is involved, the chance of a civilian getting hurt or killed increases. The question becomes, where is the balance point between officer and citizen safety? Have the American people become so dangerous that most police agencies in the country can field, and regularly use, SWAT teams?

FLASHBANG GRENADE FIRES

Flashbang grenades, also known as stun grenades, are routinely detonated in SWAT raids to confuse, disorient, distract, and momentarily blind people inside the targeted premises. The device, unlike a fragmentation grenade, remains intact after it goes off. The explosion does produce intense heat which can cause serious burns, ignite flammable liquids, and set fire to furniture.

A SWAT team in Topeka, Kansas, in June 2002, detonated a flashbang grenade in a drug raid that injured a two-year-old boy. Although it is standard policy not to throw a stun device into a room occupied by children, the police in this case didn't know the boy was in the house. Peter Christ, co-founder of an anti–drug war organization called Law Enforcement Against Prohibition, when interviewed by a reporter covering an incident involving a flashbang injury, said, "These are like military devices. When you use [flashband grenades], you're putting people in danger."[12]

Niagara Falls, New York

In Niagara Falls, the police department's Quick Entry Team, accompanied by ICE officers, launched a predawn raid in January 2005 into an apartment occupied by a suspected 23-year-old marijuana smuggler. While the police arrested Michael Johnson and seized a 9-mm handgun and a small amount of pot, the flashbang grenade set the bed on fire and burned an 18-year-old woman who happened to be staying with Johnson that night. Johnson's companion suffered second- and third-degree burns on her chest and stomach. There was no evidence that this woman had anything to do with the drug trade.

San Bernadino County, California

At 5 A.M. on January 16, 2008, the San Bernadino County SWAT team and officers with the Barstow, California Police Department conducted a raid into an one-room apartment inhabited by 42-year-old Charles Sherman. The police were looking for evidence related to an attempted murder in the neighborhood, and they used a flashbang grenade. Sherman's bed caught fire from the grenade, burning him in the chest and groin areas. According to reported accounts of the arrest, police dragged him out of the room and kicked him while he was still burning.

Charles Sherman did not have an arrest record in the county but years earlier had been convicted elsewhere of robbery with a weapon. Four days before the SWAT team invasion, officers had found four boxes of ammunition in the ex-felon's apartment. This had led to a criminal charge, which justified the raid. A spokesperson for the San Bernadino County SWAT team, in explaining to the press why the sheriff had deployed a SWAT team in this case said, "If somebody hasn't been arrested for a long time, it does not mean that such person cannot be dangerous."[13]

Gary, Indiana

Police in Gary acquired a warrant to search Darrell Newbern's house for cocaine after an undercover officer made three buys there. The 31-year-old had never been convicted of any crime and was not known to be dangerous. On January 22, 2007, nevertheless, 25 police officers with the narcotics–vice unit and the Gary SWAT team raided his house. The first flashbang grenade didn't go off, so they tossed another into the room. Newbern saw the second device and ran toward it. This grenade detonated, burning him on the head, back, and arms. The police seized a handgun, but it had been locked inside a safe. Although he could have been put in prison for 50 years for dealing in cocaine, the judge sentenced Newbern to 6 years, half of this time to be served on probation.

Corvallis, Oregon

On October 10, 1997, two men robbed a Corvallis jewelry store, taking jewelry, cash, and two guns (an assault rifle and a .357 magnum revolver). Then they drove off in a blue Geo Metro with the store owner shooting at them. One of the bullets hit the car, shattering a window. Four days later, as the police staked out an apartment identified by a snitch as the suspects' residence, two men came out of the complex and got into a blue Geo Metro. One of the men met the general description of one of the jewelry store robbers. Following a brief chase, the police stopped the men, searched the car, found a gun, and arrested them both.

Just before dawn the next day, officers with the Corvallis Police Department and the Benson County SWAT team raided the apartment in search of the jewelry and the two stolen guns. Aware that several people were inside the place, the team made sure the flashbang grenade went off near the front door, an unlikely place for someone to be sleeping. As it turned out, Kristianne Boyd happened to be sleeping on the floor near the front entry. A medic treated her the scene and then rushed her to the hospital with severe burns on her arms.

Kristianne Boyd sued the city of Corvallis and the Benson County SWAT team for injuring her with the flashbang grenade and violating her Fourth Amendment right to privacy. The federal district court judge dismissed the suit. The federal court of appeals for the Ninth Circuit, in ruling that the deployment of the flashbang grenade did not amount to excessive force or result in an unreasonable search, upheld the lower court decision.

Burlington Township, New Jersey

In 2003, a total of 29 police officers, led by a New Jersey State Police SWAT unit, raided a home in Burlington Township. The local officer who had obtained the warrant to search for drugs described the homeowners as armed and dangerous, even though he had no factual basis for this characterization. At 5 A.M., the drug war warriors broke down the door and tossed two flashbang grenades into the house, burning a hole in the carpet and setting fire to a television set and a pair of speakers. The homeowner's 17-year-old son, asleep in his bed, was the only person at home.

An hour after the raid, the boy's father, Michael R. Fanelle, came home to find his ransacked house filled with cops in battle dress. They had not found any drugs or weapons. Mr. Fanelle opened his safe and handed over a small quantity of methamphetamine. A few months later he pleaded guilty to possession of meth with the intent to distribute. The judge sentenced him to probation.

In 2006, an appeals judge ordered an unusual hearing to determine whether such a massive raid, involving the detonation of flashbang grenades, was justified in this case. At the hearing, the judge learned that the police had no credible information that Mr. Fanelle posed any threat to law enforcement. Based upon the evidence disclosed at this proceeding, Superior Court Judge James Morley, in a landmark decision with major law enforcement implications, ruled that the use of flashbang grenades in this case made the search unreasonable, therefore rendering the evidence seized inadmissible against defendant Fanelle. In overturning Mr. Fanelle's conviction, Judge Morley said, "This was a commando raid–like scenario . . . and my decision was based on the overall way [the police] approached the case—at five A.M. with twenty-nine police officers in commando gear and pointing weapons at a sleeping seventeen-year-old."[14]

In speaking to the media after the ruling, deputy public defender Kevin Walker said, "The ruling tells the law enforcement community that these devices [flashbang grenades] will be subject to judicial review. They [the police] can't descend on a house and blindly toss these devices."[15] Michael Luciano, the assistant county prosecutor, said he would consider filing an appeal but agreed that as it stood, Judge Morley's decision would affect the way the police enforced the law. "This is a matter of some import and could have some impact on how search warrants are executed throughout the state."[16]

Sheriff Joe Arpaio's Incendiary Raid

Sheriff Arpaio's detectives in Maricopa County, Arizona, suspected that Gabrial Gordon, a 28-year-old ex-felon on probation for armed robbery, had stolen a cache of automatic weapons and armor-piercing bullets from a gun dealer in Las Vegas. Gordon lived with 26-year-old Eric Kush and 22-year-old Andrea Barber in a house in Ahwatukee, an upscale bedroom community that had been annexed by the city of Phoenix. Barber's daughter and Kush's 10-month-old puppy also lived in this $250,000 home nestled in the quiet, gated neighborhood called Fairway Hills. Neither Barber nor Kush had criminal records.

Maricopa County detectives arranged to have Gordon's probation officer lure him to his office, where, on July 23, 2004, they took him into custody. According to Gordon, Kush was the one who possessed the weapons cache. The police would also claim that Gordon warned them that Kush had been acting in an erratic way and carried a gun.

Just before noon on the day of Gordon's arrest, a SWAT tank and an unmarked white GMC Suburban van full of county SWAT officers rolled into the neighborhood and parked on the street in front of the house rented by Gordon and the others. Outfitted in full battle gear, five officers approached the front of the house while another contingent took positions at its rear. Andrea Barber, at the sound of loud banging coming from the main entrance, started down the stairway to answer the door. But before she got there, officers kicked it open. As they rushed inside, other SWAT officers launched canisters of white tear gas through second-story windows in the front and rear of the house. A few minutes later, a fire broke out in the master bedroom, which quickly enveloped the place.

Eric Kush, who had fled to the attic at the inception of the raid, ran out of the house to escape the fire. A police officer threw him to the ground and another officer sprayed a fire extinguisher into the face of his dog, driving it back into the house. The puppy perished in the fire, which completely destroyed the structure. An officer, in pulling the SWAT tank away from the blaze, lost control when the electric brakes disengaged. The massive vehicle then rolled down an incline and smashed into a parked car.

Investigators with the Phoenix Fire Department concluded that a lit candle knocked over in the confusion of the raid had caused the fire. Andrea Barber, however, insisted that a tear gas canister had set the bed ablaze. Either way, had there not been a raid, there would not have been a fire, and Kush's dog would not have suffered an agonizing death.

The Maricopa County SWAT team raid that destroyed an expensive home, killed a dog, and traumatized a quiet neighborhood resulted in the seizure of an antique shotgun and a 9-mm pistol. The police arrested Kush on a misdemeanor warrant for failure to appear in a Tempe municipal court on two traffic tickets. He paid the $1,000 bond and was released from custody. In the week following the raid, the neighborhood, stank of fire debris and the rotting puppy.

San Antonio, Texas

Narcotics officers with the San Antonio Police Department suspected that two men were selling heroin out of a house in the 100 block of Belmont Street on the east side of the city. At 9:30 P.M. on the night of February 3, 2009, these officers and 15 members of the department's SWAT team were at the house to execute a no-knock search warrant. According to the informant, the suspects had guns in the house.

Before destroying the front door, a SWAT officer, following standard operating procedure, heaved a flashbang grenade through window glass. The device landed and exploded on a mattress, setting it on fire. As SWAT officers filed into the house over the battered door, they encountered one of the suspects anxious to get out of the place before it burned to the ground. SWAT officers arrested the second man as he tried to escape out the back door. Suddenly searching for drugs became secondary to knocking down the flames. After exhausting a pair of fire extinguishers, the police had to clear out of the house. By the time fire trucks rolled up to the blaze, the place was a total loss. Thanks to the firefighters, the conflagration didn't spread to neighboring dwellings. Fortunately, no one was hurt.

The next morning, in searching through the debris, narcotics officers found evidence of heroin dealing in the form of syringes, baggies, balloons, and spoons. They also recovered a small amount of the drug. The officers did not find any guns. A sergeant with the San Antonio Police Department, in referring to the flashbang grenades, told a local television correspondent that, "We have used these things hundreds and hundreds of times in the past and this hasn't happened. But it's always possible that it could. And what we saw tonight, is an example of how that could happen."[17]

The fact that the police, instead of entering that house after they had arrested the suspects somewhere else, had burned the place down before they could even search it, amounted to a one-day news blurb in the local media. No one bothered to ask this police sergeant if the flashbang house fire had sparked a reevaluation of how and when the police should deploy these devices. Based on this officer's comments to the television reporter, a rethinking of flashbang use seemed unlikely. Someone would have to be killed in one of these fires before such an inquiry took place.

THE KILLING OF PEYTON STRICKLAND

Shortly before midnight on December 1, 2006, 18-year-old Peyton Strickland, a welding student at Cape Fear Community College, was at home playing a video game with his roommate, a student at the University of North Carolina at Wilmington. When Strickland heard knocking at his front door, he got up with the game controller in his hand to answer it. Outside the house, 16 police officers—9 SWAT team members from the New Hanover Sheriff's Office, 3 with the Wilmington Police Department, and 4 members of the University of North Carolina Police—were poised to charge into the dwelling. Strickland and a University of North Carolina student who lived elsewhere had allegedly hit a third student with a blunt object and had stolen two of his Playstation 3 game consoles. The police were at his door to arrest him for armed robbery, assault with a deadly weapon, and breaking and entering.

Police officers at the front entrance saw Strickland approaching them through the door glass. For some reason, Strickland stopped, turned, and walked back into the house. That caused an officer to strike the door with a battering ram. As Strickland turned in response to that noise, a deputy sheriff fired five shots, two of which passed through the door hitting Strickland in the head and chest, killing him on the spot. The officer had discharged his weapon because he had confused the sound of the battering ram for gun shots coming from inside the house. Another deputy shot and killed Strickland's two dogs.

The sheriff placed three deputies on paid leave pending the results of an internal investigation of the shooting. He fired the deputy who had fired the fatal shot. A grand jury indicted the former officer in December 2006 for second-degree murder, but a judge set aside the indictment because the jury foreman, on the indictment document, had checked the wrong criminal charge box. In July 2007, the county prosecutor presented the case to a second grand jury, but only 12 of the 18 jurors voted to indict the ex-deputy for involuntary manslaughter. The grand jury vote fell four short of the 16 needed for a true bill.

Peyton Strickland's parents sued New Hanover County for the wrongful death of their son. In February 2008, pursuant to an out-of-court settlement, the county paid them $2.45 million. Nine months later, the family sued the University of North Carolina at Wilmington and their police department for leading the heavily armed deputies to Peyton's door on the word of an unreliable informant. That case is pending.

THE DEADLY USE OF A NONLETHAL WEAPON

In the Bedford-Stuyvesant section of Brooklyn, on September 24, 2008, Inman Morales, a mentally disturbed 34-year-old man, told his mother he was going to kill himself. Her 911 call brought members of the New York Police Department's Emergency Service Unit (ESU) to the third-floor apartment. Cross-trained for rescue and high-risk law enforcement assignments, ESU officers are part of a citywide contingent comprising 400 special operations police organized into 10 squads.

When the ESU officers arrived at the apartment early that afternoon, a totally nude Morales crawled out onto the fire escape and climbed to the apartment above but was unable to enter that place through a window. As a result, he descended and stepped out onto the two-foot-wide metal ledge on a roll-down security gate above a vacant store front. "You're gonna kill me!" he yelled as he ripped an eight-foot fluorescent light bulb from the sign above the abandoned store and used it to poke at a police officer trying to reach him from the fire escape.[18]

Inman had been on the ledge about 30 minutes when ESU Lieutenant Michael Pigott, a 21-year veteran, ordered another officer to stun the distraught man with 5,000 volts from a conducted energy device popularly known as a taser. For some reason, officer Pigott decided not to wait for the arrival of an inflatable airbag to break the man's fall. From the sidewalk 10 feet below, officer Nicholas Marchesona, with a cluster of neighborhood residents looking on, shot Inman with the taser gun. The nude man froze, then pitched forward off his perch, landing on his head 10 feet below. Paramedics rushed him to the hospital, where he was pronounced dead.

Based upon a statement issued by the police department the next day, it seems that the lieutenant, in ordering the tasering of Mr. Inman, had violated departmental guidelines regarding the use of this nonlethal weapon. A police commander, pending an investigation by the district attorney's office, placed Lieutenant Pigott and officer Marchesona on desk duty.

Lieutenant Michael Pigott, distraught over Inman Morales's death and worried that he would be charged with criminal homicide, committed suicide on October 2, 2008, at ESU headquarters in Brooklyn. He was 46 years old. The day before, he had attended an ESU refresher course on how to handle mentally ill subjects. In a note found in his locker, the lieutenant wrote that he didn't want his children to see him hauled off to jail in handcuffs. According to newspaper reports, an ESU supervisor had been taunting Pigott with the possibility of arrest. Following the suicide, a spokesperson from the Brooklyn District Attorney's Office advised the media that a negligent homicide indictment would have been unlikely. A few days before he shot himself in the head with his service pistol, Lieutenant Pigott told a *Newsday* reporter that he felt "Terrible about what happened to that man."

Dealing with distraught and irrational people in a way that protects the police, the public, and the disturbed individuals themselves is often difficult. Officers in charge have to make split-second decisions of a life and death nature. But in this case, no one was in danger but Mr. Inman. Of the limited options available to the police in this situation, the one chosen by Lieutenant Pigott was the least appropriate. Understanding the rationale behind this decision would require knowing more about the officer who made it. Because Lieutenant Pigott obviously didn't intend to have Mr. Inman killed, the outcome was a tragedy for him as well.

THE HIGH COST OF POLICE MISTAKES IN HIGH-RISK RAIDS

SWAT raids of places where members of street gangs live or hang out is definitely high-risk law enforcement. Dealing with armed hostage takers, while more risky than routine police work, is more dangerous for the hostage and the person holding the victim at gunpoint. Standoffs with armed and deranged people hell bent on suicide are a lot less dangerous for SWAT police than for the holed-up mental cases waving their guns around. All of these police–citizen encounters involve high emotion and life and death, hair-trigger situations. If these heavily armed, adrenaline-hyped police officers make a mistake—raid the wrong address, base their actions on unreliable information, or misinterpret the words or body language of a person they encounter—there is no margin for error. Whenever this happens, it's usually a citizen who is seriously injured or killed. Because these special forces operations are so risky to suspects, victims, and innocent bystanders, they should only be deployed, even in potentially high-risk cases, as a measure of last resort.

Dodging Bullets in Minneapolis: The Vang Khang Case

This high-risk situation involved 34-year-old Vang Khang, his 29-year-old wife, Yee Moua, and their six children, ages 3 to 15. They were hill people from Laos who spoke little English, living in a high-crime neighborhood in northeast Minneapolis. Just before midnight on December 16, 2007, Yee Moua, while watching television, heard window glass shatter. Thinking that criminals were breaking into the house, she bolted up the stairs to where her husband and children were sleeping.

Awakened by the commotion, Mr. Khang grabbed his shotgun from the closet and, hearing heavy footsteps advancing up the stairs, fired a warning shot through his bedroom door. Khang didn't know it, but he had opened fire on officers with the Minneapolis Police Department's Violent Offender Task Force (VOTF). The paramilitary unit had broken into the wrong house in search of street-gang guns and drugs. The exchange of gunfire that erupted after Khang's warning shot included 22 bullets from the VOTF officers and two more blasts from Khang's shotgun, the pellets harmlessly striking the body armor of two of the officers. The moment he heard his children yelling, "It's the police!" Khang, who miraculously had not been shot, dropped the shotgun and raised his arms. A few seconds later, he was lying on the floor with a boot planted firmly in the middle of his back.

The police, quickly realizing that their informant had directed them to the wrong house, did not take Vang Khang into custody. (Had he injured or killed one of the officers, Khang would have been arrested and hauled before a grand jury.) VOTF officers, leaving behind broken windows and bullet holes in the bedroom wall, left the house without apologizing to the family they had endangered and traumatized.

The botched raid, while not a major news story, did receive one-day coverage in the local media. The next day, an unapologetic spokesperson for the Minneapolis Police Department said this to a local newspaper reporter:

"It was bad information that came on the informant's end . . . The first two addresses were very good. . . . We did everything in good faith."[19] One wonders if the police would have been so forgiving if Mr. Khang, *in good faith,* had killed a VOTF officer. That this police spokesperson didn't think raiding the wrong house and almost killing an innocent citizen wasn't police malpractice reveals why, in law enforcement, lessons such as double-checking informant information before conducting an armed home invasion are rarely learned. If, by now, police officers don't know that informants regularly produce flawed information, they will never be aware of this reality.

Seven months after the bungled raid, long after the public's memory of the fiasco had faded, the police chief in Minneapolis did something really stupid and callous. Chief Tim Dolan awarded the VOTF officers who had invaded the wrong house medals of valor for "bravery in action under fire." By so doing, Dolan reminded the public of the mistake, offended the Khang family, and rewarded these officers for good luck and bad police work. Outraged by this slap in the face, Mr. Khang announced his plan to file a lawsuit against the city.

Minneapolis mayor R. T. Rybak, who had been on hand for the medal ceremony, later issued a statement acknowledging that in awarding officers who had participated in a botched raid that had nearly killed innocent people, the chief was sending a bad message. The issuance of these medals of valor had not only been astonishingly inappropriate but had turned the botched raid into a much bigger news story. The raid had become, for the Minneapolis Police Department, a national embarrassment.

In December 2008, the Minneapolis City Council approved a $600,000 settlement for the Khang family. At the news conference, Tom Heffefinger, the attorney who had negotiated the settlement for the Khangs, said, "This [search] warrant was the result of a flawed investigation done by the Violent Offender Task Force. Shots missed Lee and Vang by less than a foot."[20] Chief Dolan finally apologized to the Khangs. He said that while no members of the VOTF raiding party had been subjected to an internal inquiry, he had asked an unnamed outside agency to investigate the matter. The Khangs, plagued by traumatic memories of the home invasion, had moved out of the house. Lee Moua, Vang's wife, told those assembled at the news conference that "There are no excuses for what they have done to my family, there is no amount of money or anything that can fix what the police put us through."[21]

No Bullets, No Story

Wrong-house raids by remorseless SWAT officers that do not feature blazing guns, while they seriously traumatize the people they encounter, do not result in much media coverage. Indeed, rather than cause public fear and loathing, these raids, although botched, may actually reassure citizens that the police are on the job. In any war, including the one against crime, there will be collateral damage.

A botched raid in Orlando, Florida, that garnered scant media attention is a good example of how excessive police force coupled with incompetence doesn't necessarily make a compelling news story. On October 17, 2008, SWAT officers tossed a smoke bomb through Henry Marshall's window and then entered his house by breaking through his front and back doors. In handcuffs with a gun pointed at his head, Marshall, a man with no criminal history, had no idea what he might have done to deserve this much police attention. The officers were looking for Quinton, Marshall's 21-year-old grandson, who hadn't lived in the house for six years. What dastardly act had Quinton committed? He had used a cell phone that, unbeknownst to him, had been stolen in a robbery. Marshall, in an effort to clear things up, called Quinton, who rushed to the house to turn the stolen phone over to the police. After that, he was free to leave. The police didn't know it, but a three-month-old child had been in the raided house. Much to everyone's relief, the baby escaped injury. The officers left the grandfather with a broken window and a pair of ruined doors. They also left him rattled, and without an apology. The event, an ephemeral one-night story on local television, failed to ignite public outrage or journalistic curiosity. Like a lot of small stories comprising tiny pieces of a larger problem, Mr. Marshall's experience barely registered on the newsworthiness meter.

Sudden Death: Fatal Endings to Standoff Dramas

Miami SWAT team officer Alejandro Macias, in March 1999, killed 25-year-old Jesse Runnels by shooting him in the face as he stood in his girlfriend's kitchen yelling out the window at the police. Obviously intoxicated, Runnels had been saying things like, "Suicide by cop!" and "I'm going to kill a police officer."[22] He also said he had a shotgun, which the police never saw. Just prior to the standoff, Runnels had cut his wrists, but the wounds were superficial. Runnels had not injured his girlfriend and appeared more of a danger to himself than anyone else. There was no shotgun or any other weapon in the house.

After the shooting, officer Macias told investigators that he had fired three shots when Runnels rushed forward and stuck his right hand and what looked like a handgun through the open window. The SWAT police had found, on the ground beneath that window, a toy pistol. Dade County prosecutors, however, believed that Runnels, at the time Macias shot him, had been holding a cell phone. They also suspected that the toy gun had been planted.

The Dade County prosecutors, following numerous delays, tried officer Macias in May 2004 on two counts of obstruction of justice. The jury had to decide whether Macias, fearing that the shooting wouldn't be ruled justified, had planted that toy gun beneath the window and lied to investigators. Several members of the SWAT team testified that they had not seen a toy gun at the scene immediately after the shooting. The jury, on July 8, 2004, acquitted the defendant on both counts. The dead man's parents, however, received a $1.25 million settlement from the city.

A year before the Jesse Runnels case, another jury had acquitted officer Macias and two other Miami SWAT team members of obstructing justice in connection with the March 1996 death of a 73-year-old man named Richard Brown. The SWAT police, on an informant's tip that earlier in the day he had seen the former salesman selling drugs out of his two-room apartment, knocked on his door and demanded entry. According to the police, Brown refused to let them in, so they broke down the door. As they entered the apartment, the suspect fired two shots at them. In response, SWAT officers fired back with 123 bullets, 8 of which went into Mr. Brown. His 14-year-old granddaughter, in the room with him, miraculously survived the barrage unharmed. There weren't any drugs in the apartment, but outside, beneath a window, the police did find narcotics. Prosecutors believed that this evidence had been planted.

Richard Brown's granddaughter received a $2.5 million settlement from the city. For the citizens of Miami, the police department's SWAT team had become an expensive public service—and also a dangerous one.

Killing Cheri Lyn Moore

On the anniversary of her son's suicide, Cheri Lyn Moore drew a SWAT team to her apartment in Eureka, California, when she brandished a flare gun and threw clothing out of her second-story window. During the two-hour standoff in April 2006, the disturbed 48-year-old woman threatened to burn down the building. Moore put the flare gun down, then suddenly picked it up again. When she did, SWAT officers stormed the apartment and shot her to death.

The county prosecutor did not charge the officers who had fired the fatal shots with any crime. Instead, he sought and acquired, in December 2007, an indictment against the chief of police and the commander of the SWAT team. The Humboldt County grand jury indicted these men even though they were not at the scene of the shooting. They were indicted for involuntary manslaughter because they had failed to adequately supervise or properly direct a SWAT raid that had led to the death of an unarmed woman. The prosecution's highly unusual attempt to hold off-site police administrators criminally responsible for a botched operation sent shock waves throughout the law enforcement community.

On August 26, 2008, a Humboldt County judge dismissed the involuntary manslaughter charges against the two Eureka police administrators. The superior court judge's decision, made before a courtroom jammed with police officers, drew loud applause. Had the chief and the commander been tried and convicted and this measure adopted throughout the country, SWAT teams would virtually cease to exist as a law enforcement technique.

SWAT Raid Consequences: The Killing of Anthony Jarvis

Based upon the number of combat-ready police officers who took up positions around a house, barn, horse trailer, and camper on Summer Street in Charlestown, New Hampshire, one would think that an armed and dangerous felon with a history of violence was about to be arrested. On that Saturday evening, July 26, 2008, members of the Western New Hampshire Special Operations Unit, the New Hampshire State Police SWAT team, and officers from the Claremont and Charlestown Police Departments had come to arrest 26-year-old Jesse Jarvis. The police also had a warrant to search the dwelling and outbuildings on the property for guns.

According to police reports, Jesse Jarvis, out of prison two months following a three-year stretch for simple assault, had stolen two Nazi flags from a residence, escaped arrest by wrestling with a police officer, and—in an incident unrelated to the house theft—had punched a man. Jarvis also had a history of drug and alcohol abuse. He was not a very good citizen, but he was not John Dillinger.

In order to secure the area before executing the search warrant, the police directed the occupants of the house and outbuildings to exit the premises and be accounted for. Immediately a young woman walked out of the house and a man emerged from the camper. The other occupant of the camper, Jesse Jarvis's 53-year-old father Anthony, an ex-felon with his own history of drug and alcohol abuse, refused to come out. An officer with the state police gave Anthony a warning: "State Police Canine. Come out now or I will send in the dog."[23] Another officer informed Jarvis that they had a warrant to search the camper. Insisting that he had done nothing wrong, Anthony threatened to shoot the dog. While all of this was going on, Anthony's son Jesse surrendered himself to the police. Having arrested the man they had come for, the police turned their attention to clearing Anthony out of that camper.

The police kicked off the raid by detonating a flashbang grenade followed by the entry of a state trooper, who attempted to incapacitate Jarvis with a taser gun. Undistracted by the flashbang explosion, Jarvis fired a shot at the officer. The state trooper, after returning fire with the taser gun, took a bullet in the leg. He fell to the floor and, as he crawled for cover, was hit again in the finger and upper thigh. The state officer returned fire with his .45-caliber pistol. A second member of the raiding party fired three shots at Jarvis with his .223-caliber semiautomatic rifle. Before being hit by 15 bullets, Jarvis got off 16 shots. The police found him dead at the rear of the camper, his 9-mm Ruger lying next to his body. The autopsy revealed that Jarvis had been killed by the slugs from the state trooper's firearm. A blood alcohol analysis showed that the dead man had been heavily intoxicated.

The New Hampshire Attorney General's office investigated Anthony Jarvis's death and labeled it a justifiable homicide. Based upon the testimony of the officers involved, the state trooper had killed Jarvis in self-defense. But for Colonel Frederick Booth, the director of the New Hampshire State Police, the incident raised broader issues regarding the deployment and training of New Hampshire's six regional Special Operations Units made up of 200 officers under the control of six independent boards of directors. Colonel Booth said, to a reporter with a local newspaper, "You have six different units operating around the state under a different set of standards. And the question that may come out of that is should there be a standard set of training that each SOU [Special Operations Units] member needs to meet in order to be a team member? I think that's a positive first step."[24] The director called for an independent review of the regional system of special operation units.

The state trooper who killed Anthony Jarvis was neither a member of the state's 25-member SWAT team nor an officer assigned to the Western New Hampshire Special Operations Unit. He had simply responded to the scene on his own. Sending this officer into the camper with a taser device and handgun raised questions about the competence of the raid commander. The attorney general's inquiry produced evidence that the wounded officer had not been told that Jarvis was an ex-felon who might be armed. The 16-member Western New Hampshire unit was placed in stand-down status pending further review.

Beyond tactical and administrative questions, the Jarvis case raises an important issue regarding the role SWAT teams play in American law enforcement. Although Anthony Jarvis had no right to resist the police as he did, he was in his home minding his own business when the officers arrived to arrest his son, a relatively minor offender who offered no resistance at all. Perhaps a lower-keyed approach whereby a couple of police officers could have sent Jesse Jarvis into the camper to retrieve his father would have saved Anthony's life and kept a police officer from being shot. Instead of spending so much effort organizing paramilitary raids, the police should spend more of that energy thinking of alternative, less violent ways to get the job done.

Chapter 4

STOMPING ON SIN:
PROSTITUTION, PORNOGRAPHY,
AND GAMBLING RAIDS

While criminologists, criminal justice professors, and politicians argue over whether vice offenses are victimless crimes or if they should be legalized or decriminalized, there isn't much discussion about the overaggressive tactics used by the police to enforce laws regarding prostitution, possession of pornography, and illegal gambling. The arrest of vice suspects and the search for evidence of these crimes normally does not involve high-risk police work. Nevertheless, SWAT teams routinely raid brothels, massage parlors, escort services, and strip clubs as well as the homes of people believed to be in possession of pornography and those suspected of running home poker tournaments and other types of gambling operations. Critics of these militaristic raids, in rejecting the officer safety rationale, accuse police administrators of media grandstanding and politicking.

Applying shock-and-awe policing to vice enforcement makes the enforcers look like bullies, and when judges, prosecutors, and police officers are rounded up in some of these sweeps, the whole thing smacks of hypocrisy. When vice cops raid the wrong house, it's even worse. But fortunately for the police, even in wrong-house vice raids, unless someone is seriously hurt, the media aren't particularly interested.

PROSTITUTION RAIDS

Cat House or Wrong House? Ask Philip Petronella

In the summer of 2004, following the death of his wife, 63-year-old Philip Petronella, a retiree living in Woodbridge, New Jersey, rented a house in another part of town. His daughter, who had recently suffered a stroke, had moved in with him. She and her husband resided on the first floor of the newly remodeled dwelling.

On May 9, 2005, at 11 A.M., Mr. Petronella, alone in the house and dozing in bed with the television on, heard a loud bang followed by another. Suddenly intruders were in his house and coming up the stairs "like a herd of elephants."[1] In a matter of seconds, four police officers, wearing helmets, goggles, and masks, were aiming rifles at him. One officer told Mr. Petronella not to move while another ordered him to raise his hands. After they searched the room for weapons, an officer ordered Mr. Petronella to put on his pants and sneakers. Once he was dressed, they handcuffed him behind his back, escorted him to the living room, and sat him on the sofa. From where he sat, Mr. Petronella looked out his window and saw a small army of cops carrying rifles moving about his front yard.

The stunned retiree repeatedly asked his captors why they were there. Had he done something wrong? After an hour on the couch, his arms and back began to ache. Finally, an officer removed the restraints and rehandcuffed him in front. When one of the New Jersey State Police SWAT team officers informed Mr. Petronella that they suspected he was using his house as a place of prostitution, he said, "You gotta be kidding. I ain't getting any. Nobody else is getting any out of here."[2]

Once the house had been secured by the SWAT team, members of the state's Special Crimes Unit conducted a search, which included rummaging through drawers, closets, and Mr. Petronella's safe. The vice officers were looking for client lists, credit card numbers, personal phone directories, employee rosters, cash, and drugs. This raid on the wrong house was part of a statewide crackdown on prostitution called Operation Risky Business. During the previous several months, 40 people, mostly Russian and Chinese immigrant prostitutes and their johns, had been swept up in 14 raids.

At 4 P.M. that afternoon, five hours after the invasion, Mr. Petronella found himself alone again in his ransacked house. The police had left the place a mess. They had ruined his front door, which had been unlocked, knocked over family photographs, and torn up all of the floor molding. Clothing, personal items, and documents were strewn about the place. Handcuffed for five hours in his own home, watching the police tear the place apart, Mr. Petronella was left without an explanation or an apology. He was thankful for one thing: at least his daughter had been spared the ordeal.

The next day, state police spokesperson Della Fave admitted that it had been more than a year since the previous tenants had used Mr. Petronella's house as a place of prostitution. "We just got there too late," she said. "They were there, and they moved on. It happens."[3] Della Fave was right, it does happen, and all too often. But in the war on vice, collateral damage like that experienced by Philip Petronella is to be expected, and in the overall scheme of things, accepted. Operation Risky Business—how appropriate.

Rounding Up the Lap Dancers

There are nightclubs and bars, commonly called gentlemen's clubs, featuring striptease and lap dancing, in every state, with high concentrations in California, Texas, Florida, Nevada, and West Virginia. It's a $5-billion-a-year industry that is highly regulated by state law and local ordinances. In some states, the women can be topless; in others, full nudity is permitted. Only a few jurisdictions allow physical contact between the dancers and the patrons. As one can imagine, these places are common venues for prostitution and are regularly raided by federal—usually the FBI—and local law enforcement agencies. State and local governments allow these obvious sources of prostitution to exist because of the demand as well as the tax revenues. Then they use up a good portion of the tax money to investigate and raid these places.

In Broward County, Florida, local police and officers with the Department of Business and Professional Regulation had spent two years investigating possible prostitution at the Cheetah Nightclub on Ansin Boulevard in Hallandale Beach. On Saturday, March 7, 2009, at 12:30 A.M., local vice cops and various state agents, following behind the Hallandale Beach SWAT team, rushed the club. They served an order to suspend operations and arrested the two managers for running a house of prostitution. Under the law, the Cheetah Club had become a threat to the state's public safety, health, and welfare. The police also arrested 16 women for offering customers more than a lap dance. The raid didn't produce any weapons or drugs.

The Cheetah Club SWAT raid and prostitution arrests made the local news, but only for a day. The media reported the basic facts of the operation, and that was it. Raids of this nature had become so routine that no one bothered to ask why a town of 37,000 even had a SWAT team, and why they were using it to raid strip clubs where the lap dancers were suspected of doing more than just dancing.

WRONG-HOUSE PORNOGRAPHY POSSESSION RAIDS

It seems that Americans enjoy perusing adult pornography even more than smoking marijuana. As a result, they don't like it when the police interfere with this activity. Child pornography, however, is another story. Because a vast majority of citizens consider child pornography vile and taboo, politicians and police administrators get away with employing aggressive enforcement tactics against those who possess this material. Possessors of child pornography are not particularly dangerous to the police, therefore treating them like armed and violent criminals for publicity or other reasons is not good law enforcement. And the more militaristic the raid, the bigger the mistake when the police raid the wrong house.

Deputy Shaquille O'Neal:
The Missed Slam Dunk in Gretna, Virginia

In 2006, Michael Harmony, a lieutenant with the Bedford County Sheriff's office, commanded the battle against child pornography in south central Virginia. Lieutenant Harmony headed a high-profile regional task force called Blue Ridge Thunder. Shaquille O'Neal, the seven-foot-one, 325-pound center for the Miami Heat professional basketball team, an off-season reserve deputy with the Bedford County Sheriff's Office, was a member of the regional task force. The sheriff had enlisted the famous basketball player, also a gun-carrying reserve officer in Miami Beach, as the public face of the area's anti–child pornography campaign. O'Neal had accompanied the Blue Ridge Thunder team on several military-style child pornography raids.

In September 2006, a cyberspace undercover investigator assigned to the task force downloaded child pornography via an Internet Provider (IP) address. Based on this information, a local magistrate subpoenaed Fairpoint Communications, the source IP, requiring the company to identify the person or persons at this IP site. The IP complied, providing the authorities with the name of A. J. Nuckols, a resident of Gretna, Virginia. The police didn't know it, but someone at Fairpoint Communications had misread the subpoena. Therefore the identification of the Nuckols family in connection with the IP address was a mistake. Without further investigation into the identity of Mr. Nuckols and his family, the police used this faulty information to acquire a warrant to search his house.

Mr. Nuckols, a 45-year-old tobacco and cattle farmer, lived with his wife, Lisa, an elementary school teacher, on a farm near Gretna. Two of their children, ages 12 and 16, lived at home. Their 21-year-old daughter attended a nearby college. The family kept their one computer, used mostly by the children for homework, in their living room. The parents didn't know their own e-mail address and rarely shopped online or downloaded information from the Internet. There was nothing in their histories, lifestyle, or associations that suggested any connection to child pornography.

Saturday morning at 10:30 A.M., September 23, 2006, two officers from the Blue Thunder Task Force knocked on the Nuckols's front door. Invited into the house by Lisa, they informed her of the warrant allowing them to search the dwelling for child pornography. "I was in shock," Lisa later told a newspaper reporter. "At first it was not just disbelief. I told them, 'We don't live that way.'"[4]

As the police officers spoke to Lisa Nuckols, a fleet of police cruisers from Bedford and Pittsylvania Counties rolled up to the house. Suddenly 10 officers, dressed in black and camouflage and wearing flak jackets, were moving about the yard carrying semiautomatic weapons. Mr. Nuckols, working near the barn, looked across the field and saw all the police vehicles. Fearing that something awful had happened to his wife or one of his children, he jumped into his truck and sped to the house. "What's going on?"[5] he asked, climbing out of the pickup. Instead of getting an answer, one of the officers dropped into a shooting position, aimed his pistol at the farmer, and said, "Turn around and put your hands on the truck." Another member of the team handcuffed Mr. Nuckols behind his back. As they led him toward the house, Lieutenant Michael Harmony reportedly said, "Had a rough day? It's about to get a whole lot worse."[6]

Lieutenant Harmony informed Mr. Nuckols that he or someone in his family was suspected of having downloaded child pornography from 150 Web sites. The police were there to search the house for evidence of this crime. Later, in a letter to the editor of the local newspaper, Mr. Nuckols expressed how he felt at that moment: "When it finally became clear what they were there for, I was just flat-out mad. They came and assaulted my family for something we had nothing to do with."[7]

The children came home at 2 P.M. from a high school cross-country meet. The police, still in the house, asked them if they had downloaded child pornography. The children were as stunned by the accusation as their parents. Ninety minutes later, the officers departed, taking with them the family computer, DVDs, videotapes, and other personal belongings. Before he left, Lieutenant Harmony told Mr. Nuckols that the child pornography investigation would take between six and nine months to wrap up, noting that the state crime lab was backed up.

At one point during the siege, Mr. Nuckols recognized the famous basketball player. "You're Shaquille O'Neal,"[8] he said. The big man, dressed like the others and armed, replied that his name was Tony. Nine days later, when the Nuckols family learned that the search and seizure had been based on an erroneous IP address identification, O'Neal denied involvement in the raid. However, after the Bedford County Sheriff's Office confirmed his participation, he admitted his role.

After the raid, before they were aware of the mistake, Lisa Nuckols told neighbors and friends what had happened. Worried that she might lose her job, she advised the principal and school superintendent as well. In his letter to the newspaper editor, Mr. Nuckols wrote: "When you come into someone's home, that's an intrusion. I feel the same about the raid as I would about any assault on our home and family. A robber would be wrong, and these officers were wrong. No matter what the spin the police put on it, the public will always believe it's wrong. People can't believe this happens in this country."[9]

In response to the criticism following the revelation that the Blue Ridge Thunder team had raided the wrong house, Lieutenant Harmony blamed the Fairpoint Company. According to him, the IP had made the mistake, not the police. Lieutenant Mike Taylor with the Pittsylvania County Sheriff's Office, though not a participant in the raid, apologized to the Nuckols family. Shaquille O'Neal, however, took another approach by accusing Mr. Nuckols of exaggerating his account of the raid to make the police look bad. When members of the media questioned him about his role in the raid, the basketball player reportedly said, "We did everything right, went to the judge, got a warrant. You know, they [the Nuckols] made it seem like we beat them up, and that never happened. We went in, talked to them, took some stuff, returned it—bada bam, bada bing."[10]

If there is one thing in law enforcement rarer than a slam dunk case, it's an apology for shoddy police work.

Milwaukee SWAT: A Dollar Short and Six Weeks Late

Denise Berndsen, her father, Jerry, and a man she had been dating had just sat down for dinner when the door flew open and heavily armed men entered the room. Denise lived in West Allis, Wisconsin, just outside Milwaukee. She and her guests had been invaded by the Milwaukee SWAT team accompanied by the West Allis police and detectives assigned to a state task force investigating Internet crimes against children.

Earlier that day, the 43-year-old AT&T employee, who was on disability, had returned from the hospital following back surgery. For that reason, when the police stormed into her apartment and ordered her to "hit the floor," she begged them not to handcuff her behind her back. The officers, to their credit, saw that she was infirm and granted her request. Her 74-year-old father and the man she was dating, who was probably wondering what he had gotten into, were cuffed and laid out on the floor. The next day, in describing the ordeal to a newspaper reporter, Denise said, "My apartment was wall-to-wall cops. They proceeded to destroy my apartment. They not only told me the detective would explain all in time, they also had the nerve to tell me I should be lucky not to be in handcuffs."[11]

The searchers, in typical SWAT raid fashion, showed contempt for the suspect's home, furniture, fixtures, decorative pieces, documents, photographs, and items of clothing. They seemed to relish pulling out drawers, emptying closets, tearing apart beds, cracking mirrors, ripping up carpets, breaking plates, and knocking things over. Trashed and damaged search sites have become SWAT team calling cards. The more severe the destruction, the better the search.

Forty-five minutes into the siege, after trashing the place and attaching a device to Denise's laptop computer, the detectives realized that the suspect they were after no longer lived there. Had they checked with the landlord before launching the invasion, they would have learned that the suspect had been evicted six weeks earlier. Suddenly aware that they had traumatized a woman who was not well, the officers offered to call an ambulance. Denise, not wanting to incur a medical bill she couldn't afford to pay, declined the offer.

As the shock troops filed out of the apartment, one of the detectives, in a lame attempt to shift the blame, said, "I guess you're just one more of his [the suspect's] victims." Denise replied, "No, we're *your* victims."[12]

The next day, a spokesperson for the Milwaukee police, in a statement combining insensitivity and a denial of reality, said, "We had very reasonable belief the suspect was still there."[13] Statements like this, following raids like that, are not reassuring.

In February 2008, four months after the raid, Denise Berndsen filed a $10,600 claim against the city of Milwaukee. The city attorney, on the ground that the search warrant had been "based upon reasonably reliable and current information,"[14] recommended that the claim be denied. A month later, the five-member Judiciary and Legislation Committee voted unanimously to disallow Denise's claim. In Milwaukee, no one in a position of power had the courage to condemn sloppy investigative work, destructive search practices, and the use of SWAT teams for low-risk law enforcement.

RUSH TO JUDGMENT: THE WALMART "PORN" CASES

Charles Town, West Virginia

Sam Bellotte had driven from Charles Town, a village located in West Virginia's eastern panhandle, to the Walmart store in Winchester, Virginia. He had made the trip to use the store's self-service photograph printer to develop photographs he had taken with his digital camera. When Bellotte approached the counter to pay for the service, the clerk took the envelope and surprised him by asking if any of the photographs depicted people who were nude. Embarrassed, Bellotte said yes, there were nude pictures in the envelope. This brought the assistant manager, who said he would have to confiscate the pictures. Still shaken by this unexpected turn of events, Bellotte did not object to the seizure. He did, however, remind the assistant manager that the contents of the envelope were private. Before Bellotte left the store, the assistant manager assured him that the photographs would be shredded, sight unseen.

The photographs were destroyed, but not before employees of the store looked at them. And what they saw, or thought they saw—pornographic photographs of a young Asian girl—caused them to acquire Mr. Bellotte's identity through his debit and credit card number. Following this bit of detective work, they called the Winchester police, who verified Mr. Bellotte's identity, then alerted the authorities in Jefferson County, West Virginia.

Based upon the characterization of the photographs by the Walmart employees, the police in Jefferson County obtained a warrant to search the Bellotte house in Charles Town for evidence of child pornography. Although Mr. Bellotte had no criminal record and there was no reason to believe he owned a gun, 10 police officers, including the regional SWAT team and federal agents from the Immigration and Naturalization Service, raided his home in the middle of the night.

The raiding party broke into the house on May 31, 2007, terrifying Bellotte, his wife, and their son and daughter. Mrs. Bellotte, an Asian woman who didn't speak fluent English, had no idea who the intruders were or what they were going to do to the family. Terrified, she couldn't stop screaming. After the police handcuffed everyone, an officer, in front of Mrs. Bellotte and the children, called Mr. Bellotte a sick person and a child pornographer. Another cop informed Mrs. Bellotte that she could lose custody of her children.

The police ransacked the house and found no evidence of child pornography. They left the dwelling with Bellotte's computer but without him. The next day, details of the Charles Town child pornography raid appeared in the *Martinsburg Journal.* Bellotte was not mentioned by name, but people in town could figure out whose house had been raided.

The child pornography case against Bellotte evaporated after the authorities realized that the woman in the photographs was an adult. In May 2008, a year after the raid, Bellotte and his wife filed defamation and invasion of privacy suits in state and federal court against Walmart and the police. The cases are pending.

Gridley, Indiana

In Gridley, Indiana, Jeffrey L. Shoemaker photographed a group of five nude boys at his son's birthday party. An employee of the Walmart store where Shoemaker had taken the film to be developed called the police. The McLean County prosecutor, in June 2006, charged the 51-year-old with creating child pornography. Ten months later, with both sides stipulating that the defendant had not directed or posed the boys, the case was tried without a jury. The judge found Shoemaker guilty and sentenced him to four years in prison. Shoemaker appealed the conviction. The justices on the state appeals court held that the trial judge had made a mistake by interpreting the photographs as pornographic. The county prosecutor appealed the conviction to the Indiana Supreme Court, which declined to hear the case. That meant that the conviction reversal stood. Mr. Shoemaker, after a year behind bars, walked free.

In jurisdictions where the sheriff has promised voters that child pornography will not be tolerated in his or her county, in places where regional SWAT teams are itching for missions, a person charged with creating or possessing child pornography stands a good chance of being awakened in the middle of the night by a flashbang grenade. In Gridley, Indiana, after the Walmart employee called the police and Shoemaker was charged, a single detective arrested Shoemaker when he arrived at the store to pick up his pictures. Although he had been wrongfully convicted and had to spend a year in prison, at least he hadn't been victimized by overzealous police storming into his house and traumatizing his family.

GAMING YES, GAMBLING NO: RAIDING THE BAD BETTORS

If the act of gambling is a crime that harms the bettor as well as society, why is it legal in so many forms and so many places? What is the difference, in terms of behavior, between legal and illegal gambling? Why are the laws outlawing gambling still on the books, even in states where legislatures have sanctioned lotteries and gambling casinos? If there is so much violent crime and terrorism is such a serious threat, why are the police using their limited resources to shut down home poker games and confiscate video poker machines? (In 2007, FBI agents took a break from catching spies and looking for terrorists to investigate and arrest 12,161 gamblers. There are no statistics regarding how many gamblers are arrested every year by state and local police.) And finally, why do law enforcement agencies, in waging the war against the bad gamblers, employ SWAT teams?

A lot of gambling enforcement involves politics and money. Politicians, fearing retribution from certain elements of the religious and business communities, are reluctant to legalize all forms of gambling. Many sheriffs, eager to impress voters, and police chiefs, following the politics of their mayors, come down hard on illegal gambling operations, which are easy enforcement targets. Although it is unnecessary and inappropriate, police administrators often use SWAT teams to show how serious they are about stomping out vice. While the image of full-combat cops raiding a house where poker enthusiasts are having a good time may reassure some, others find this use of police power disturbing and un-American.

The Charleston County Poker Wars

In Mount Pleasant, South Carolina, a suburb of Charleston, police and sheriff's deputies were watching a house on Glencoe Street where low-country Texas hold'em poker enthusiasts gathered regularly for small-stakes games. In writing about the popularity of this game, Paul Myerscough, in the *London Review of Books,* explained how it is played:

> In hold'em, each player is dealt two cards which no else sees (their "hole cards"). The two players to the left of the dealer make small forced bets ("blinds"), and each player in turn must decide whether to fold their hand, match ("call") those bets or raise them. Next, three cards are dealt face up in the middle of the table (the "flop"), then another card (the "turn") and a final one (the "river"); there is a round of betting at each stage. Players must make the best five-card hand they can from their two hole cards and the ones in the middle, which they all share; the quality of your hand can change dramatically as the flop, turn and river are dealt. A hand doesn't always reach the river—if every player but one has folded by then, the last player standing takes all the money in the pot without showing his cards—but if it does, the remaining players turn their hole cards face up and the one with the best hand wins.[15]

A South Carolina law enacted in 1802 made it a crime in the state to play any game that involves cards or dice. That makes playing Texas hold'em poker a criminal act. In the Mount Pleasant game under surveillance, the host had collected $20 buy-in fee from each player. The police watched as poker lovers drove into the quiet neighborhood, parked their vehicles along Glencoe Street, and entered the house.

On the night of April 14, 2006, a team of combat dressed and equipped officers from the Mount Pleasant Police Department and the Charleston County Sheriff's Office, their faces hidden behind ski masks, raided the game. Following a single knock, the officers rushed in through the front and patio doors. Bob Chiminto, one of the players, would later describe the intrusion to a local reporter this way: "All of a sudden it was like a commando SWAT team raiding a bunch of crack dealers. It's all like the SWAT team you see on TV busting into your home, guns drawn, ski masks on, full protective gear, and demanding that we put our hands on our heads. . . . Someone could have been killed that night."[16]

Another player, 78-year-old Midge Chesebrough, thought the intrusion was a joke; "Then we realized it was real when we saw guns and masked faces."[17] An officer placed Midge in handcuffs but, according to her, he didn't tighten them down. She said they were so loose she had to keep them from slipping off her hands. That night, Midge lost the $20 in chips she had on the table, plus $85 seized from her purse. She later pleaded guilty to illegal gambling to avoid the fine, but she still had to pay the $50 in court costs. The arrest, however, did not discourage Midge from enjoying Texas hold'em. After the raid, she continued playing the game at another house.

The police cited 22 poker players, 8 of whom were from Mount Pleasant. The rest had come from Charleston, North Charleston, Summerville, James Island, and Hanahan. That night, the police confiscated $6,000 in cash as well as a small quantity of drugs. They didn't find any guns in the house. Of the money the police seized, only $250 had been taken off the two poker tables. They had seized the rest from the players' pockets, wallets, handbags, and cars.

The use of SWAT methods to arrest people assembled at a middle-class home to play low-stakes poker generated an angry newspaper editorial and a couple of days of radio talk-show criticism of the police. The SWAT raid also added fuel to the debate over whether this activity should be legalized. Proponents of legalization argued that poker is more a game of skill than chance and therefore is not gambling. Televised tournaments have made this form of poker a national craze, creating pressure on state legislators to make organized poker events legal. Poker advocates often compare their get-togethers to chess tournaments, where participants win trophies, prizes, and cash. Many even consider poker a sport.

Following the Mount Pleasant SWAT raid, state representative Wallace Scarborough, a Republican from James Island, introduced a bill that made poker, Monopoly, and Yahtzee legal as long as the house didn't take a cut. The bill also allowed churches to hold raffles. (The proposed legislation died in committee in March 2008.) To a local reporter, Bob Chimento, one of the low-country poker enthusiasts cited in the Mount Pleasant raid, argued against South Carolina's ban on card and dice games this way: "In reality, there are few games which may be played by any individual that does not include cards or dice. These are rudimentary elements to the vast majority of games citizens play."[18]

The mayor of Mount Pleasant, also quoted in the local press, made it clear where he stood on the issue: "I am proud of our nationally certified [police] force and satisfied with the clear message they [the police] are sending to lawbreakers. We will not tolerate this type of activity in our town."[19] The mayor apparently had no problem using SWAT-team tactics to send this message: if you play poker in this town, you might find yourself in handcuffs looking down the barrel of a semiautomatic rifle held by a man wearing a ski mask. The police will take the money you had on the poker table and the cash you were carrying in your pocket, wallet, or purse. Besides a fine, the judge will also order you to pay a fee covering the cost of adjudicating your bad behavior.

During the months following the raid, all but five of the Mount Pleasant poker players pleaded guilty to the misdemeanor charges and paid their fines and court costs. For the holdouts, the case dragged on. Attorneys for these defendants, on the grounds that the South Carolina law banning card and dice games was vague and therefore unconstitutional, filed motions to have the charges against them dismissed. In August 2008, municipal judge J. Lawrence Duffy, stating the state legislature had reviewed the 1802 law nine times and had found it suitably specific, denied the motions to dismiss.

Charleston County sheriff Al Cannon, unfazed by constituents who considered his gambling raids heavy-handed, authorized a dinnertime raid of a popular restaurant in Hanahan. The county SWAT team, in December 2007, stormed into the restaurant and seized a number of video gambling machines while the restaurant's patrons, thinking they were being robbed by masked bandits, looked on in terror. The sheriff's critics questioned the timing of the raid, the excessive show of force, and the ski masks.

On April 4, 2008, the Charleston County SWAT team broke up four home poker games in Hanahan. At one of the houses, the police arrested Martin Reyes and 26 others. They were all hauled off to jail, booked and forced to post bond. The police seized $20,000 from Reyes's safe and $30,000 worth of his furniture, electronics, artwork, and other household belongings as "fruits of an illicit enterprise." The officers also reached into the pockets of the players, grabbing another $12,000. In the other three houses, the masked raiders arrested 38, including a public school teacher, a police officer, and an attorney.

Nineteen of the Hanahan poker players pleaded guilty shortly after the raids, each paying fines of $154 to $257. Several others hired attorneys and filed claims in civil court to get back the money the police had taken out of their pockets—cash they had not intended as wagering funds.

The Hanahan raids generated additional negative publicity for the sheriff's office. A radio talk-show host ridiculed the officers for wearing ski masks. Jeff Phillips, the Greenville, South Carolina, attorney representing Bob Chimento in the Mount Pleasant raids, referring to the SWAT gear, called these raids "costume parties." Those who remembered the restaurant raid six months earlier also questioned the necessity of those ski masks. Sheriff Al Cannon, however, was not apologetic and not about to change his aggressive gambling enforcement policy.

Because Bob Chimento and the four other Mount Pleasant poker defendants had challenged South Carolina's 1802 gambling law, Judge J. Lawrence Duffy would decide whether Texas hold'em was a game of chance or skill. If he declared it primarily a game of skill, he would be in agreement with judges in 38 states. A jury in Greeley, Colorado, in January 2009, acquitted the founder of a local poker league who had been charged with illegal gambling. In arriving at that verdict, the jurors relied on the testimony of Robert Hannum, professor of statistics at the University of Denver, who testified that poker is more skill than chance. In Pennsylvania that month, a judge held that poker playing did not constitute gambling under the state's wagering prohibition. In Texas, where the game is extremely popular, several legislators had recently sponsored a bill that would legalize playing card games for money. In 2006, the police in Dallas had raided 10 poker rooms, arrested 270 players, and seized $113,000 in cash. Those raids, and others like them throughout the state, had driven poker playing further underground, which in turn had exposed players to dangerous home-invasion robberies. Under the proposed Texas legislation, the state lottery commission would issue poker licenses to authorized establishments and would limit the number of poker tables a licensee could run. Operators would be taxed on their revenues and pay application and licensing fees.

The Associated Press in South Carolina ran a story in January 2009 about the Mount Pleasant poker raid and the debate over whether the game should be legalized. Entitled, "Poker Aficionados Watch South Carolina's Texas Hold'em Case," the article included a quote from Jeff Phillips, the attorney representing Bob Chimento and the other four defendants. According to attorney Phillips, "The typical police raid of these games . . . is to literally burst into a home in SWAT gear with guns drawn and treat poker players like a bunch of high-level drug dealers. Using taxpayers' resources for such useless Gestapo-like tactics is more of a crime than is playing the game."[20]

Bob Chimento and the other Mount Pleasant defendants went to trial before Judge Duffy on February 13, 2009. The judge, after listening to the testimony of several poker experts, agreed that the game—based on calculations, timing, and the ability to read the faces and body language of opposing players—was more one of skill than of chance. But, under South Carolina's 207-year-old dice and card game prohibition, the skill factor was irrelevant. The judge therefore found Bob Chimento and the other poker players guilty as charged. The defendants said they would appeal their convictions.

In March 2009, State Senator Glenn McConnell introduced a bill to legalize home and charity poker games in South Carolina. The law would also permit religious, fraternal, and other nonprofit organizations to hold "casino nights" as fund-raising events. The bill did not allow slots, video-gambling machines, horse race wagering, or sports betting. The senator scheduled public hearings around the state in order that citizens could discuss and debate the issue.

Crashing the Party in San Mateo, California

Cutberto "Bert" Cardenas loved to play poker and associate with people who shared his enthusiasm for the game. The 42-year-old resident of San Mateo County had organized, through MeetUp.com, a poker group that gathered Saturday afternoons at his home in Eichler Highlands. The Texas hold'em players, mostly professional types in their thirties and forties, paid a buy-in fee of between $25 and $55, the proceeds of which paid for tournament prizes. Cardenas also charged the six to twenty people who showed up each week a $5 refreshment fee to cover the cost of pizza and beer. Patricia McCoy, a friend of Cardenas, helped him host the small-stakes, socially oriented poker group. McCoy occasionally allowed her 13-year-old son to participate in the games. Cardenas' daughter, who was also 13, did not participate although she was in the house while the games were being played.

During the last three months of 2007, undercover operatives with the San Mateo Sheriff's Office played in the Saturday tournaments. Under California law, home poker games are legal as long as the house doesn't take a cut out of the action. Although Cardenas hosted a small-stakes poker group that was more about socializing than gambling, the police secured warrants accusing him of taking money under false pretenses—skimming some of the buy-in money—and corrupting the morals of his daughter. Because Patricia McCoy's son had actually played in some of the tournaments, the police swore out a warrant for her arrest as well. By charging his guests a $5 refreshment fee, Cardenas had also broken the state law prohibiting the unauthorized sale of alcohol.

In what can only be described as a parody of law enforcement, the San Mateo sheriff ordered a SWAT-style raid—helmets, flak jackets, a battering ram (which wasn't needed because the front door was unlocked), and semiautomatic rifles—of Cardenas's Saturday afternoon poker group. On January 12, 2008, about 30 minutes into the tournament, the players heard someone pounding on the front door. "It's probably the cops," a player joked. A few seconds later, a dozen or so sheriff's deputies, accompanied by gambling control agents with the California Department of Justice, rushed into the house. The card players sat in stunned silence after being ordered to keep their hands on the poker tables. "Does anyone have a weapon?" one of the officers asked. No, they all said, truthfully. Officers handcuffed Bert Cardenas and Patricia McCoy and hauled them away. A child protection services person took custody of the 13-year-olds. (They were taken to relatives until their parents posted bail later that day.)

The police didn't charge any of the poker players but detained them long enough to photograph and question them. The interviewers asked the players if Cardenas had been skimming from the buy-in fund and if he had been using marked cards. None of the players accused Cardenas of skimming or cheating. As far as they knew, their host had not organized the group as a money-making venture. As a poker player himself, Cardenas usually lost money.

The next day, the sheriff's office, perhaps anticipating that a lot of people would question the wisdom and appropriateness of a three-month investigation followed up by the raid of a weekly, low-stakes poker group, issued a press release that bordered on the bizarre: "A background check on the house's residents led officers to a Web site advertising weekly poker games. The Web site was used to *lure unwitting* [italics added] participants to the tournaments which required a $25 to $55 buy-in with an extra $5 refreshment fee."[21]

It's hard to imagine citizens of San Mateo County, after reading that press release, breathing a sigh of relief over the demise of Cardenas's Saturday afternoon poker tournament. Although it suggested that crime in San Mateo County was virtually nonexistent, the Cardenas case carried the disturbing notion that the police in that jurisdiction were either ignoring the real criminals or simply keeping busy by overenforcing the law.

The Fight against Poker in North Carolina

In 2006, the North Carolina Supreme Court ruled that poker was a game of chance. The state law prohibiting gambling therefore applied to the playing of poker for money. This was not good news for poker enthusiasts living in a state where the game is popular.

At 9:15 on the night of October 3, 2008, SWAT teams in Fayetteville raided Christian Lusardi's home and his business, the Yadkin Road Poker House. They arrested the 36-year-old organizer of "free roll" poker tournaments at his home on the misdemeanor charges of gambling and violations of state alcohol laws. The police also took, as proceeds of an illicit enterprise, $3,000 in cash from his safe.

In the simultaneous raid of Lusardi's business, the other SWAT unit, comprising a dozen or so men in helmets and face masks, cited 39 free-roll tournament players who were gathered inside the building on Yadkin Road. In free-roll poker, players are given a number of free chips to begin the game. If they need more, they have to pay. The police seized $1,000 from the players, many of whom were soldiers from Fort Bragg, and $6,000 from Christian

Lusardi's business safe. The police also took away three poker tables, four large televisions sets, a pair of pool tables, video surveillance cameras, and poker playing paraphernalia. Outside the building, police officers searched players' vehicles and found a small quantity of marijuana, 57 oxycodone pills, some crack cocaine, and three firearms. The next day, as is the custom following such police operations, the chief of the Fayetteville Police Department appeared on television with a display of the seized contraband. The chief took this media photo-op to assure his antigambling supporters that this form of illegal behavior would not be tolerated in his town.

The Atlanta Area Crackdown

In Georgia, where organizing or hosting a poker-for-profit enterprise is a felony, the players are usually charged with misdemeanor gambling. Within the Atlanta metropolitan area, residents have reason to be concerned about violent crime. The police, on the other hand, seem very worried about the region's growing underground poker scene. Over the past few years, law enforcement agencies have been cracking down on high- and low-stakes Texas hold'em games held regularly in commercial venues and in private homes.

In February 2005, the Gwinnett County SWAT team raided a house in Duluth, Georgia, a town of 22,000 a few miles northeast of Atlanta. None of the 23 Texas hold'em players rounded up by the police that night—a diverse group that included a software consultant, a paralegal worker, a truck driver, a college student, and a guy who assembled playground swing sets—possessed drugs or a gun. No one had a criminal record or a warrant outstanding against him. The police took $17,000 of their money and charged them all with misdemeanor gambling.

Officers with the Fulton County SWAT unit, shortly after midnight on April 9, 2007, broke into the basement of an eight-room house at the end of a suburban cul-de-sac in Roswell, Georgia, a bedroom community of 88,000 just north of Atlanta. The raiders broke up a high-stakes, three-table Texas hold'em assemblage organized by Dan Tyre, the owner of a car wash, and his wife Angela, who worked for a local wine distributor. The weekly invitation-only gathering had evolved from a Monday Night Football get-together into a $10,000-to-play poker event. The police hauled the 27 arrestees off to jail in three police vans and towed their vehicles to the impound lot. They charged Dan and Angela Tyre with commercial gambling and the rest with the misdemeanor version of the crime. One player was also charged with drug possession and another with carrying a firearm. Because the Tyres ran a "safe game," where winnings and losses were tallied on paper, the police didn't seize much cash that night.

In Jonesboro, a town on the southern edge of the Atlanta area in Clayton County, people had been playing Texas hold'em for two years at the Poker Palace, an establishment just down the street from the sheriff's office. Given the big sign over the door that read "Poker Palace," this was hardly a clandestine business. On April 10, 2007, one day after the raid in Roswell, officers with the Clayton County Joint Task Force raided the Jonesboro card hall. The police arrested 53 players, including a Clayton County magistrate.

On Super Bowl Sunday, February 1, 2009, a dozen police vehicles containing SWAT officers with the Sandy Springs Police Department and the Fulton County force rolled up to an eight-bedroom house in the Sandy Springs enclave called Huntcliff. The SWAT officers broke into the spacious dwelling, where they arrested Texas hold'em players sitting around a pair of poker tables in the basement. Tow trucks came for the players' vehicles, which were parked out of public view behind a fenced area. The raiders confiscated the two poker tables, 5,000 poker chips, and several flat-screen television sets. Depending on the night, the buy-in at this house ranged from $150 to $1,000. The police didn't reveal how much cash they had recovered.

The Fulton County prosecutor charged the homeowner, a man from Sandy Springs, and two others, with commercial gambling. Twelve players faced comparable misdemeanor charges. The police didn't arrest the two food-and-drink servers, the armed security guard, or the valet parking employee. All of the arrestees were men in their mid-twenties.

Ruthless in Virginia: The Death of a Sports Bettor

In Virginia, as in many states, the government, while aggressively enforcing laws against sports betting, spends $20 million a year promoting its lottery. In the lottery states, wagering on the outcome of a football game is bad, but paying money to win a state lottery (where the chance of winning is ridiculously remote), is not only good, it's encouraged. In other words, it's okay to gamble as long as the government gets its cut.

Salvatore J. Culosi, Jr., a 37-year-old optometrist with Walmart offices in Manassas and Warrenton, Virginia, enjoyed betting on college and professional football games with friends who gathered on weekends at a local sports bar. Culosi, unmarried and prosperous, could afford to wager up to $100 on the outcome of a game. The amicable University of Virginia graduate resided in a town house off Lee Highway in Fairfax. He didn't own a gun, use illegal drugs, or associate with people who did. He had never been accused of a crime or arrested. Salvatore Culosi was a hard-working, taxpaying citizen who enjoyed betting on sports.

In October 2005, Culosi met a man in the sports bar who wanted to bet more than Culosi's standard $100-a-game wager. As the football season progressed, Culosi began wagering large sums of money with this person, a man he considered a friend. They wagered, over a period of three months, $30,000. Culosi's betting companion, undercover Detective David J. Baucom with the Fairfax County Police Department, had been betting large sums of county money on the games so that he could charge Culosi with the more serious crime of conducting an illegal gambling operation, the threshold of which involved having bet more than $2,000 on a single day. Having achieved that goal, Detective Baucom was ready to arrest the optometrist and search his home for evidence that he was a sports bookmaker.

In law enforcement, there is a fine but distinct line between a police officer providing a suspect with the *opportunity* to commit a crime and the legal doctrine of entrapment, which involves the act of *encouraging* a person to break the law. Detective Baucom, if not legally, had at least ethically crossed that line. He had, in essence, spent county time and money engineering a case against a productive citizen who had no ties to organized crime.

Detective Baucom telephoned Culosi on the night of January 24, 2006, to tell him he was coming by to collect the $1,500 Culosi owed him on a recent bet. He'd park his SUV outside the town house and wait for Culosi to come out with the money. Culosi, of course, had no idea he was being set up for an arrest by a couple of Fairfax County SWAT officers waiting nearby in a second vehicle.

Culosi, dressed in jeans and a T-shirt, came out of his house at 9:30 P.M. and walked to the passenger side of his "friend's" car. As the cash exchanged hands, Detective Baucom gave the signal for the SWAT officers to move in. As Deval Bullock, a 17-year veteran of the force, climbed out the passenger side of the SWAT car, which had pulled up behind Baucom, he accidentally fired his semiautomatic Heckler & Koch pistol. As he yelled "Police!" the .45-caliber bullet entered Culosi's left side, collapsing him to the ground. A SWAT medic worked on Culosi at the scene, to no avail. An ambulance rushed Culosi to Fair Oaks Hospital, where he was pronounced dead.

Forty minutes after the shooting, police officers searched the dead man's townhouse, where they found betting slips and $38,000 in cash. Fairfax County police chief David M. Rohrer placed officer Bullock on paid administrative leave for two days, then assigned him to a desk job. In responding to media inquiries, Chief Rohrer acknowledged that in Fairfax County, SWAT teams were deployed in all searches, including white-collar and gambling investigations. The chief did not reveal the identity of the SWAT officer who had shot Culosi. He said the incident was being investigated by detectives with the internal affairs unit.

Three days after Salvatore Culosi's death, the *Washington Post* published a front-page story on the killing, featuring quotes from experts on law enforcement policy on the use of force. David Yates, a firearms instructor, described officer Bullock's sidearm as a reliable weapon that did not have a hair trigger. According to Yates, if the suspect had not been intentionally shot, he had been killed out of the officer's "ignorance and carelessness."[22] John Gnagey, the executive director of the National Tactical Officer's Association, opined that SWAT teams should not be used in low-risk operations. He also said that police officers should not be pointing their guns at suspects who are not threatening.

Salvatore Culosi had been dead for two months when Robert F. Horan, Jr., Fairfax County's veteran prosecutor, at a news conference held at the police department, announced he would not seek a grand jury indictment of the still unnamed officer who had killed the gambling suspect. Although the shooting had obviously occurred out of a degree of carelessness, the officer, in the prosecutor's opinion, had not acted in a manner reckless enough to warrant a charge of involuntary manslaughter. Asked if Culosi had been running a sports betting operation, the prosecutor said, "He wasn't a kingpin," noting that Culosi had associated with at least one "layoff man,"[23] a person who made bets for him. No one from the police department was on hand to identify the shooter or explain why SWAT officers were involved in Culosi's arrest.

In May 2006, Culosi's parents, Salvatore and Anita, held their own news conference. They expressed anger over the fact the police department, four months after the tragedy, still hadn't released the name of the police officer who had killed their son. They also accused Detective Baucom of calling their son's friends and acquaintances, after his death, to inquire about his gambling habits. The parents had written letters to the FBI field office in Washington, D.C., and the U.S. Attorney's Office, requesting federal investigations into their son's death. They had also sent a letter to the Fairfax Board of Supervisors asking for a review of the county's SWAT team deployment policy.

Police internal affairs investigators, in the course of looking into the fatal shooting, filed an interim report in November 2006. The *Washington Post* got hold of this document, and on November 25, 2006, published its findings and the name of the officer who had fired the fatal shot. Mayor Thomas Ryan, commenting on the internal affairs report, said the shooting occurred when the car door flung open and then bounced back, striking Officer Bullock's left side as he alighted from the vehicle. The impact caused the pistol in his right hand to discharge. According to Mayor Ryan, "This hurried movement caused [Officer Bullock] to lose sight of his surroundings and compromised the safety of his weapon while the muzzle was pointed in the direction of Mr. Culosi."[24] As to why the officer had pulled his gun before getting completely out of the car, Bullock had told the internal affairs investigators that Culosi "began to exhibit the characteristics of someone who was going to run." This begs the question: assuming that the unarmed sports bettor had fled, would officer Bullock have shot him?

Chief of Police Rohrer, in accordance with the internal affairs report's recommendation, suspended officer Bullock for three weeks without pay and transferred him out of the SWAT unit. Bullock's fellow officers, believing this punishment to be extremely harsh, had expected nothing more than an official reprimand. Marshall Thielen, the attorney for the police union, called the suspension "way off the charts."[25] Culosi's parents, on the other hand, were stunned by what they considered a slap on the wrist. They had expected Bullock to be fired, banned from police work, and perhaps tried for negligent homicide. This wildly divergent view of reality between the police and the people they victimize is a common factor in law enforcement.

At a news conference a year after Culosi's death, Chief David Rohrer released the final report on the shooting, officially identifying the officer involved. Chief Rohrer acknowledged that SWAT officers should not have been used to arrest Culosi and advised that the department would be revising its risk-assessment policy. According to the chief, officer Bullock had himself questioned the decision to use SWAT officers to arrest a sports gambler. Based upon their investigation, the internal affairs detectives had concluded that the car door had caused officer Bullock's finger to slip down onto the trigger. The resultant "involuntary muscle contraction" caused the pistol to discharge. As far as they were concerned, the case was closed.

For the Culosi family, no one had been sufficiently held responsible for Salvatore's death. In March 2007, they filed a $12-million federal civil rights lawsuit against the Fairfax County Police Department and former SWAT officer Deval Bullock. Grounds for the action lay in the decision to utilize a SWAT force to arrest a gambler who obviously made his living as an optometrist. The police also knew that Culosi did not own, possess, or carry a firearm, had no criminal record, and had no reputation for violence. The Culosi family suit, owing to pretrial procedural appeals filed by lawyers on both sides, remained on hold for three years until, in February 2010, the U.S. of Appeals for the Fourth Circuit returned the action to the local court for disposition.

In the press release issued in June 2007, the FBI and the U.S. Department of Justice announced that the police killing of Salvatore Culosi did not constitute a federal crime. According to the release: "In order to prove a violation of the applicable federal civil rights laws, prosecutors must establish, beyond a reasonable doubt, that a law enforcement officer willfully deprived an individual of a constitutional right. Neither accident, mistake, fear, nor bad judgment is sufficient to establish such a criminal violation."[26]

If there is wrongdoing in this story, it's not the shooting itself. People shouldn't go to prison for accidents. It's not even Detective Baucom's ruthless pursuit of a suspected bookie. The evil here is a law enforcement policy that allowed the mindless, indiscriminate use of SWAT-style force. Although officer Bullock and Detective Baucom could not have reasonably foreseen Salvatore's death, it is reasonable to predict that the unrestricted use of militaristic force in low-risk law enforcement will lead to tragedies like this one.

In March 2009, New Jersey state senator Raymond Lesniak filed a federal lawsuit seeking to overturn the federal law that bans sports betting in 46 states. According to Lesniak, the law is unconstitutional because it treats four states differently than the rest. The law prohibits sports betting in all states except Nevada, Delaware, Montana, and Oregon. Of those, only Nevada and Montana currently allow sports wagering.

Chapter 5

PART-TIME WARRIORS: SMALL-TOWN SWAT

Nationwide, the vast majority of SWAT team duty is performed on a part-time basis. Except in the largest metropolitan areas, there aren't enough hostage situations, armed standoffs, or other high-risk assignments to justify full-time SWAT team positions. Although they are on call around the clock, most paramilitary team members, when they are not on SWAT calls, perform routine police work. The smaller the law enforcement agency, the less need there is for a SWAT unit. Therefore SWAT officers in the smaller agencies either grow stale from inactivity or are deployed in low-risk cases in order to keep sharp. Being busy also boosts officer morale. This form of SWAT utilization exacerbates the universal problem of small-town over-enforcement.

Forming and maintaining a SWAT team is expensive, and most law enforcement agencies are strapped for money. The National Tactical Police Officers Association's (NTOA) minimum personnel standard for the staffing of one SWAT unit is 17 officers. The equipment, ongoing training, and overtime necessary to support a single SWAT team can cost $200,000 a year, a figure that doesn't include the purchase and maintenance of a SWAT tank or an armored personnel carrier. Moreover, this sum doesn't take into consideration the insurance and legal costs associated with civil liability suits when things go wrong. To save money, some small departments field SWAT teams comprising ten officers, far below the NTOA recommendation.

Eastern Kentucky University professors Peter B. Kraska and Victor Kappeler, in their 1997 landmark study "Militarizing Mayberry and Beyond: Making Sense of American Paramilitary Policing," found that by 1996, some

70 percent of police departments in towns with populations between 25,000 and 50,000 had fully equipped SWAT units. Today, in towns without their own SWAT teams, select members of these departments belong to regional, multijurisdictional paramilitary units. Police chiefs and sheriffs in lightly populated, low-crime jurisdictions, in justifying the formation of SWAT teams, almost always cite self-sufficiency. Why should they have to humble themselves by having to request, a few times a year, help from neighboring agencies? The keeping-up-with-the-Joneses aspect of small-town SWAT proliferation reflects the competitiveness, professional jealously, and even hostility among law enforcement agencies that traditionally do not cooperate well with one another.

SWAT policing has become a part of small-town law enforcement. There are, for example, SWAT teams in places like Maryville, Tennessee; Medford, Oregon; Mansfield, Texas; Winchester, Virginia; and Harwich, Massachusetts. The campus police at the University of Central Florida employ SWAT officers even though the county has a paramilitary force. Combat-style policing is no longer an urban affair.

The police department in Mountain City, Tennessee, in October 2007, became combat-ready. In announcing the formation of a SWAT team, Chief of Police Jerry Proffitt said, "We're not going to stand by and wait for somebody else to take care of our problems."[1] It's not clear what problems the chief was referring to, since only one homicide and two rapes had been reported in the town of 24,000 during the previous five years. Since police departments don't form SWAT teams to let them die on the vine, the citizens of Mountain City were about to experience a more militarized approach to local law enforcement.

CALL TO ARMS

Since 1995, thousands of state and local police agencies of all sizes have acquired, through the Department of Defense's Law Enforcement Support Office (LESO), more than a billion dollars worth of military hardware at little or no cost. Today, everything from combat boots, helmets, rifles, pistols, shotguns (called "street sweepers"), gas masks, grenade launchers, and ammunition to bazookas, armored personnel carriers, and helicopters can be ordered online through the LESO Web site. In the beginning, a few local police administrators resisted this federal giveaway bonanza billed by the government as a recycling program of benefit to taxpayers.

Several years ago, in New Haven, Connecticut, Chief of Police Nick Pastore resisted the temptation to form a SWAT unit and to arm his department with army surplus hardware. The chief feared that his officers would start behaving more like combat troops than as public servants. Today, the New Haven Police Department, under new leadership, operates a

20-member paramilitary unit called the Special Emergency Response Team (SERT). Although this sounds less militaristic and perhaps more service-oriented, SERT is just another name for SWAT.

In March 2003, the *St. Petersburg Times* ran an article about the overarming of Florida law enforcement. Among others, the piece featured the police department in Jasper, a town with three stop lights, a population of 1,780, and seven police officers. A few years earlier, the department had acquired seven military surplus M-16 assault rifles. In Marion County in 1998, the sheriff's office purchased from military surplus warehouses, at a cost of $41 million, 23 helicopters and two turboprop aircraft to be used to combat the marijuana trade from the air. According to the authors of the *Times* article, the police weaponization of Florida was not accompanied by proper military instruction, training, or weapons-cache security. (Over the years, throughout the country, there have been hundreds of incidents regarding stolen SWAT team weaponry.)

In 2003, the Charleston, West Virginia, Police Department, at the cost of $2,500, purchased a .50-caliber BMG sniper rifle that fired a suppository-sized bullet 4.2 miles. In justifying the acquisition of the 33-inch-barreled weapon, the head of the SWAT team said he needed a gun that could fire through barricades and stop cars.

In northern New Jersey, a part of the state where gangs and violent crime are not serious problems, the Bergen County Police Department and the sheriff's office have SWAT teams staffed on a part-time basis. Officers with the police department's tactical unit are called out on an average of 10 times a year. In a county where officers from all of the police agencies together discharged only 13 bullets in two years, 10 of which were fired to dispatch sick or dangerous animals, six towns have SWAT teams. In Tenafly, a town of 15,000, SWAT team officers carry fully automatic rifles that fire armor-piercing bullets. According to a journalistic survey conducted in 2008 by *The Record,* half the county's police agencies, whether they have SWAT teams or not, either possess these high-powered assault weapons or plan to purchase them. In 2005 and 2006, in the Bergin County towns of Alpine, Closter, and Norwood, criminals committed eight violent offenses. Notwithstanding this absence of serious crime, in 2007 the Alpine Police Department acquired, at a cost of $1,300 apiece, two .40-caliber Heckler & Koch UMP assault rifles. Throughout the country, small-town police chiefs, rather than occasionally relying of regional tactical forces or SWAT units in larger, nearby municipalities, prefer to arm their own agencies with military-grade weaponry.

SWAT Vehicles

Since the mid-1990s, the country's largest police agencies have used armored personnel carriers (APCs) to patrol high-crime districts, transport

SWAT officers, and function as raid-site operations centers. In recent years, medium- and small-sized law enforcement agencies have been acquiring these military transporters. Although they come in various sizes and designs, APCs are full-tracked, armored, amphibious vehicles capable of traveling over rough terrain at relatively high speeds. Many are equipped with high-caliber, fully automatic turret weapons. APCs are not nearly as lethal as combat tanks, but in a civilian setting, particularly in small towns and rural areas, they are intimidating and out of place. These vehicles were designed for war, not law enforcement.

In February 2008, the Richland County, South Carolina, sheriff's office, for a mere $2,000, purchased a military surplus M11 3A2 APC. Called "the peacemaker," this 23,880-pound, 275-horsepower vehicle with enough room for 13 SWAT officers, came equipped with a turret-mounted, belt-fed, .50-caliber machine gun. In a press release announcing the new addition to the police arsenal, Sheriff Leon Lott assured the citizens of Richland County that his officers "don't look at this [vehicle] as a killing machine. It's going to keep the peace. We hope that the fact that we have this is going to save lives. When something like this rolls up, it's time to give up."[2] One can only hope that deranged, suicidal hostage takers, upon seeing the advance of that massive vehicle, will gather their thoughts and surrender peacefully.

In Georgia, the Cobb County Police Department, headquartered in Marietta, obtained, in September 2008, an APC that had been used by the Army in Panama. The six-wheel peacemaker model, big enough to transport nine SWAT officers and equipped with thermal sensors, computer tracking devices, and tear-gas launchers, had cost the military $500,000. Although the taxpayers of this affluent, low-crime county didn't pay for the vehicle, the sheriff's office spent $45,000 on a new engine and transmission. If the need ever arose in the fifty or so annual Cobb County SWAT calls, the peacemaker could rush the paramilitary team to the site at 60 miles per hour. When a newspaper reporter asked Chief George Hatfield why his department needed an army surplus APC, he replied, "In these times, you don't know what you are facing. We want the maximum safety for our officers and the public. We want to be prepared for whatever comes up. This is another tool that will allow us to be quicker and faster in our response."[3]

In Newman, Georgia, a Coweta County town of 27,000 just 40 miles southwest of Atlanta, the chief of police has the wherewithal to dispatch his own paramilitary unit, called the Special Response Team (SRT). In July 2008, chief Buster Meadows announced the acquisition of a military surplus APC that cost the department only $600 to adapt to police use. In his press release, Chief Meadows's rationale for the armored vehicle sounded a lot like Chief Hatfield's in Cobb County: "In today's time, we must be prepared for any given situation. With [the criminal's] access to weapons of any type now, our officers need the extra protection that this vehicle will give them. When approaching a barricaded structure, officers are exposed to danger zones for extended periods of time. This will help cut down on the danger zone and help get them closer to the target."[4]

Chief Meadows didn't indicate the last time an armed person in his jurisdiction had taken a hostage and held off the police. Nor did he reveal the frequency and nature of his recent SRT deployments. Just how dangerous was it to live in Newman? Assuming that the worst didn't come to his town, would the chief let the APC sit in the garage and rust? Or would he find other law enforcement uses for his big machine?

In July 2008, the safety director of Canton, Ohio, a town of 78,000 located in the northeastern section of the state, asked the city council for authorization to receive bids and enter into a contract to buy a 25-foot SWAT command vehicle. The $100,000 truck would replace the converted ambulance that had been used as the mobile command post in the ten to twenty SWAT raids conducted every year in the town. The Canton police already owned a military surplus APC. Money from drug-bust forfeitures, a fund of nearly $1 million, would pay for the new command vehicle. The council authorized the purchase.

In Colorado, the forfeiture board in charge of drug money confiscated by police departments in Grand Junction, Fruita, and Palisade, as well as the Colorado State Police and the Mesa County Sheriff's Office, authorized the purchase of a new $225,000 SWAT rescue vehicle. The 18,000-pound armored truck, purchased in July 2008, would be shared by SWAT units in the sheriff's office and the Grand Junction Police Department.

In times of economic stress, SWAT units can stay afloat by raiding the homes of suspected drug dealers. Without the war on drugs, most of the smaller agencies would lose their SWAT teams. It's the drug trade that keeps the APCs, mobile command centers, and rescue trucks rolling. So, in a way, it's drug users who are keeping America safe for the rest of us.

In Springfield, Ohio, the Supreme Specialty Vehicle Company (SSV) produces and sells custom-built prisoner transport buses, fire rescue units, bomb squad trucks, mobile crime labs, and a variety of casualty/disaster vehicles. SSV also offers a line of trucks adapted for paramilitary police use, such as the SWAT Rapid Deployment Vehicle, a 10-passenger, standing-height transporter featuring curb- and street-side exits and double-swing rear doors, allowing the officers to pour out of the vehicle quickly. According to company ad copy, "They [the crooks] won't know what hit them!"[5] The SSV-built SWAT Command Center is based on the chassis of a bus.

For the SWAT commander who wants it all, SSV offers the Avenger, a 19,000-pound tactical armored transport that is a cross between a Brink's truck and an Army tank and "has all the features you need in a hot counter-fire situation." Equipped with remote-controlled spotlights, a loudspeaker system, five rifle ports, a height-adjustable gun turret, and a roof hatch, the $250,000 vehicle can bring, at highway speeds, a dozen SWAT officers to the disturbance or raid.

Police departments and sheriff's offices, before making the decision to purchase an SSV product, are allowed to "test drive" the vehicles they're interested in. During the fall of 2008, the police in Cedar Rapids, Iowa, borrowed an Avenger for a month. Captain Steve O'Konek, in speaking to a local newspaper reporter, noted that "There are no armored car capabilities in eastern Iowa. The closest one is in Des Moines, a couple of hours away." Calling up the image of Cedar Rapids as a town under siege, Captain O'Konek reportedly said, "Something like this protects your officers and lets them get really close to someone who has large weapons. It's also good to drive up in between victims and the bad guys in dangerous situations so we can get people out safely who've been hurt. There are a lot of systems that could help us do our jobs better . . . A quarter million dollars is to me a drop in the bucket when it comes to saving somebody's life."[6] Captain O'Konek didn't get his Avenger. After a months on the streets of Cedar Rapids, it rumbled back to Springfield, Ohio. Perhaps the vehicle would find a home in a place with a more lucrative drug trade.

TRAINING AND SUPERVISION

Of the estimated 3,500 to 5,000 police paramilitary units in the United States, more than half are in law enforcement agencies with less than 100 officers. For part-time SWAT members, the National Tactical Officer's Association (NTOA) recommends, at a minimum, the following training regimen: a basic 40-hour introductory course followed up by 16 hours a month of critical skills maintenance training. In addition, SWAT officers, every year, should receive 40 hours of in-service training. Because initial and ongoing SWAT training is time-consuming and costly and the fact that no national standards are required or even state-mandated minimum SWAT training standards, many paramilitary units, particularly in the smaller departments, are insufficiently prepared and inadequately supervised. These small-agency SWAT units, many of which are also understaffed with 10-member teams instead of the NTOA-recommended 17, have been responsible for the wrongful deaths of civilians and police officers alike.

QUALIFIED POLICE IMMUNITY
IN WRONGFUL DEATH SUITS

Fatal SWAT operation shootings almost always lead to costly civil rights–based legal actions filed in federal court by the families of the deceased.

Plaintiffs accuse officers of excessive force which they blame on inadequate police training and supervision. Under the legal doctrine of qualified immunity, individual police officers, supervisors, and high-ranking administrators are generally shielded from personal liability for the acts and omissions associated with the performance of their law enforcement duties. Plaintiffs, to break through this legal barrier to personal liability, have the burden of proving that the shooters had acted recklessly *and* that their supervisors had *deliberately* or with *gross indifference* neglected to adequately train or supervise them. In order to sue a supervisor, the plaintiff must establish a direct, causal link between the lack of training or supervision and the negligent shooting. Otherwise, only the reckless police officer can be held personally liable for damages. Although proving officer recklessness caused by inadequate training or supervision constitutes a difficult barrier to breach, a few plaintiffs have managed to break through it.

Jensen v. City of Oxnard

Sergeant Daniel Christian, an officer with the Oxnard, California, Police Department, had been written up on two occasions for "poor judgment" and "unprofessional conduct." The internal affairs detectives who had investigated the complaints against the sergeant suspected that he was using mind-alerting prescription medicine. They recommended that officer Christian be taken off the department's SWAT team. That didn't happen.

On March 13, 1996, Sergeant Christian and his fellow SWAT officers conducted a predawn, no-knock drug raid on a two-story townhouse in Oxnard. Once inside, officer James Jensen, Sergeant Christian's friend and protégé, led the team up the stairway toward the second floor. Before reaching the top step, Jensen tossed a flashbang grenade onto the landing. Amid the smoke and the invasion turmoil, Sergeant Christian fired three 12-gauge shotgun rounds at what he thought was a gun-wielding resident of the house. As it turned out, the dwelling was unoccupied and the person he shot was officer Jensen, who died at the scene from wounds in his back.

A postraid analysis of the sergeant's blood showed traces of the prescription drug Vicodin. Officer Christian admitted that he had been taking eight extra-strength pills a day for headache relief. The chief of police didn't fire Sergeant Christian, demote him, or discipline him in any way. He simply removed the officer from the department's part-time SWAT team.

Officer Jensen's widow filed a civil suit, in federal court, against the chief of police, the assistant chief, Sergeant Christian, and others under Title 42 of the U.S. Code, Section 1983, in which the widow accused the defendants of violating her deceased husband's constitutional right to a safe workplace. In her complaint, the plaintiff alleged that the chief, his assistant, and the SWAT commander knew that Sergeant Christian not only used phenobarbital and other mind-altering prescription drugs but also had a propensity for unnecessary violence. She accused the defendants of a failure to provide adequate SWAT training and supervision, an omission that led directly to the killing of her husband. The fact the Oxnard SWAT team had raided an empty house did not help their case.

The attorneys representing the city, and the officers, argued that assuming the plaintiff's allegations were all true, the law did not recognize a constitutional right to a safe workplace. And even if it did, the defendants, as police officers performing their lawful duties, were protected from personal liability by the doctrine of qualified police immunity. On these grounds, the defense attorneys filed motions to dismiss the case before it went to trial. The district court judge denied this motion, and the defendants appealed this ruling to the Ninth Circuit Court of Appeals, which affirmed the lower court's decision.

Worried that a jury might award this plaintiff a large sum of money, the city of Oxnard agreed to settle the case for $3.5 million. Following the August 1999 settlement, the largest of its kind in the city's history, the chief of police announced that his officers would be required to report prescription drug use to their supervisors. (There is no such thing in police work as random drug testing.) The chief also made departmental SWAT team assignments full-time positions. Now that the SWAT team was a full-time operation, the unit's commander would undergo specialized training at a state-run SWAT academy.

Killing Troy Davis

In 1997, the North Richland Hills Police Department, serving a town of 55,000 not far from Fort Worth, Texas, formed a SWAT team staffed by officers also assigned to regular police duties. Because the SWAT team led every drug raid, its officers saw a lot of action. In a September 1998 memo to his supervisors, the SWAT team commander expressed concern that the department had not formulated a policy limiting SWAT team use to high-risk assignments. Moreover, the agency hadn't created written guidelines laying out appropriate operational tactics. They were, in other words, operating by the seats of their pants.

Upon completing sniper training at a nationally recognized school in 1998, a North Richland Hills officer wrote a memo criticizing the lack of standards in the selection of the department's SWAT personnel. He reminded the chief that candidates for the position, drawn from 109 officers on the force, did not have to pass any kind of written test, be physically fit, be psychologically sound, or even possess exceptional shooting skills. Regarding the latter, the officer wrote: "I personally do not want to be the one to have to explain in court that our tactical weapons proficiency standards were based on the state's minimum requirements."[7] The memo writer warned that if and when the SWAT team had to use deadly force, given the substandard quality of its personnel, there could be civil liability, even if the shooting were justified.

SWAT team member Allen L. Hill, although not mentioned specifically in the officer's memo, could have been cited as a case in point. In reviewing Hill's personnel file, one might wonder why he had been selected for SWAT duty. Hill had earned the nickname "Penie" for his habit of exposing himself to his fellow officers for laughs. Based upon citizen complaints following traffic ticket encounters with officer Hill, he had earned the reputation of "coming off too aggressive at times." A citizen whom officer Hill had pulled over for a traffic stop had reported that he had acted "like a psycho," and was "going to kill somebody."[8] On three occasions in SWAT training simulations, Hill had fired his pistol in situations that did not call for its discharge.

On December 14, 1999, an anonymous informant sent an e-mail to a North Richland Hills narcotics officer accusing 25-year-old Troy Davis of growing marijuana inside his mother's house. According to the snitch, the police would find "substantial amounts"[9] of marijuana in the dwelling. The e-mail sender also stated that Troy Davis had a habit of answering his door carrying a .9-mm pistol. Without any follow-up investigation such as confirming who lived in the house or watching the place for awhile to see if any suspected marijuana buyers were coming and going from the site, the narcotics cop asked a judge for a no-knock search warrant. This judge, unwilling to issue a warrant on such flimsy evidence, denied the search application. Instead of gathering more information, the narcotics officer found a judge in Fort Worth who was willing to authorize the no-knock entry.

The following morning at 9:30, a 17-member party made up of local narcotics officers and the North Richland Hills SWAT team rolled up to the target house. Officers popped the storm door with a pry bar they called their "hooligan tool" and then smashed open the inner door with a battering ram. Officer Hill, as the point man, led the squad into the house. Because Hill normally functioned as the SWAT team medic, this was the first time he had been the first man through the door. Two seconds into the dwelling, Hill fired his .45-caliber pistol, hitting Troy Davis in the chest and stomach. Davis dropped to the floor and gasped, "I didn't know. I didn't know."[10] He died where he fell.

According to Officer Hill's account of the shooting, the man he had shot had pointed a gun at him. SWAT team officers said they had found a pistol lying on the sofa near Davis's body. They also found three dead marijuana plants in the backyard and seized, from the refrigerator, pills that turned out to be the recently outlawed date rape drug GHB (gamma hydroxbu-tyrate). They also encountered Troy Davis's mother, Barbara Davis, the au-thor of paperback true-crime books. When asked about the GHB pills in the refrigerator, Barbara Davis said they were sleeping aids that belonged to her. Based on this admission, the police arrested her for possessing the contraband. Mrs. Davis learned of her son's death while being booked on the drug charge at the police station.

Barbara Davis's account of the shooting differed from Officer Hill's. Ac-cording to her, when the police burst into the house, Troy was standing in the living room with his arms outstretched, yelling, "Don't hurt us! Don't hurt us!" She denied that her son owned a firearm and accused the police of planting the pistol they said they had found on the couch.

Allen Hill resigned from the Richland Hills Police Department in May 2000. He told reporters that he had been pressured into quitting by his su-pervisors and the chief who believed he had either killed an unarmed man or had fired his gun before Davis had a chance to drop his. Hill accused his bosses of harassment and hoped he could land a job with another law enforcement agency. Shortly after his resignation, a Tarrant County grand jury voted not to indict him on the charge of voluntary manslaughter.

That spring, Barbara Davis filed a civil rights suit against Allen Hill for using excessive force in the killing of her son. She also sued the chief of police and three police supervisors for inadequate training and supervision. Attorneys for Hill and the others, claiming qualified police immunity, moved to have the suit dismissed on summary judgment. The federal district judge granted the motion but then reversed his decision when he learned that the police department had withheld evidence from the plaintiff. The defense appealed this ruling to the fifth Circuit Court of Appeals.

Barbara Davis, to avoid going to prison, had pleaded guilty to the posses-sion of GHB, the designer drug found in her refrigerator. But she had re-served the right to appeal, and on June 17, 2004, a three-judge panel sitting in Fort Worth found that the SWAT raid of her house had been based upon a search warrant that was defective because it was not supported by sufficient probable cause. As a result, the court overturned her drug conviction.

The chief of the North Richland Hills Police Department retired in Janu-ary 2005 after being arrested twice for driving under the influence. It was no secret that the chief, for years, had been taking prescription medicine to relieve pain in his back. There had been persistent rumors that he had become addicted to the drug.

The Fifth Circuit Court of Appeals, in April 2005, on the issue of whether the defendants could be sued in connection with Troy Davis's death, ruled that the plaintiff's excessive force claim against Officer Hill could go for-ward. On the issue of qualified police immunity, the appellate judges found that the chief and the police supervisors, on claims of inadequate SWAT training and supervision, were protected. The court, in justifying this decision, found that on the facts presented, Officer Hill's behavior, while perhaps reflecting poor judgment and unprofessional behavior, didn't create a *pattern* of excessive force. Moreover, his failures in SWAT training, as well as the substance of the civilian complaints, did not foreshadow the fatal shooting of Troy Davis. Because Hill's supervisors were not deliberately indifferent to his SWAT training and supervision, they were immune from civil liability.

In June 2006, Allen Hill told a reporter he was joining the army because he couldn't find work in law enforcement. As of May 2009, some 6½ years after Troy Davis's death, the civil case had not come to trial.

Amateur Night in Preble County, Ohio

On the evening of September 27, 2002, a total of 30 police officers assigned part time to the Preble County Emergency Services Unit (ESU), a multiagency tactical squad, stood poised to break into a red brick farmhouse outside of West Alexandria, a village 50 miles north of Cincinnati. Because only 42,000 people lived in the county, a quiet, peaceful place, the ragtag unit of sheriff's personnel and small-town cops didn't see much action. This particular raid had been organized by George Petitt, Jr., a sheriff's office detective who was present at the raid site along with his wife and son, both Preble County deputies.

On Thursday, the day before the raid, a recently convicted burglar awaiting sentence informed detective Petitt that less than a week earlier, he had purchased a small quantity of marijuana from an unidentified person living in that farmhouse. According to the snitch, besides the dozen or so people and the two dogs living in the rented house, the police would find 15 to 20 pounds of pot. Petitt had spent a few hours watching the place and had seen enough general activity around the house to convince him that marijuana was being sold out of the dwelling. He did not confirm this suspicion with an undercover buy or conduct any investigation to identify the people who lived in the house. Instead, he obtained a no-knock search warrant and organized the raid.

Before the Preble County ESU officers had completed their final preparations for the assault, a passing car caused Deputy Petitt to commence the operation prematurely. This resulted in the wrong group of officers arriving at the target door ahead of the others. At six minutes after seven, ESU officers tossed a flashbang grenade through a front window and then forced their way into the house. They ordered a young man named Ian Albert to the floor at the base of the stairway near the entrance. The commotion awoke

Clayton Helriggle, a 23-year-old local man who worked in his family's garage-door business. Helriggle had been napping in his second-floor bedroom. He grabbed what the police later described as a 9-mm Ruger, and descended the stairs, where he encountered Sergeant Kent S. Moore of the Lewisburg Police Department. For some reason, Sergeant Moore, thinking he had been shot, dropped to the floor, then jumped back up and fired his 12-gauge shotgun, hitting Helriggle in the chest. Helriggle then bled to death in his roommate's arms. (Albert would later insist that Helriggle had come down the stairway holding a blue plastic cup.) The police had been in the house about two minutes.

Preble County deputies didn't search the sealed-off house until the next day. Instead of 15 to 20 pounds of marijuana, they found less than an ounce and a few rolling papers. The police didn't arrest any of Helriggle's four roommates.

The dead man's family, as well as hundreds of others in the community, were shocked and outraged by what had happened to this hard-working young man who had never been in trouble with the law. The Preble County sheriff placed Sergeant Moore on paid administrative leave and asked the special investigations unit with the Montgomery County Sheriff's Office to investigate the shooting and the raid. The Preble County sheriff, citing financial constraints, also disbanded the ESU. Detective Petitt, instead of accepting a demotion to road patrol, retired on medical disability. He and his deputy wife separated. Sergeant Moore returned to work but was assigned a desk job.

The Montgomery County investigators discovered that members of the Preble County ESU had trained only four hours in the nine months preceding the raid. The investigation also revealed that 10 days before the raid, Detective Petitt's wife had flirted with Helriggle while both were drinking with friends at a local bar. The 54-year-old detective told investigators he learned of his wife's connection to the dead man *after* he had organized the marijuana raid. The Preble County prosecutor, having concluded that the farmhouse had not been a place where drugs were being sold, decided not to bring charges against Helriggle's housemates. In March 2003, a Preble County grand jury voted not to indict Sergeant Moore on charges of criminal homicide.

That September, the Helriggle family sued the Preble County Sheriff's Office and 20 former ESU officers for unconstitutionally entering the farmhouse without notice on a bogus warrant and, once inside, using excessive force. Had detective Petitt knocked on the farmhouse door, Ian Albert would have answered it and invited the police inside for the search. The case would have been resolved with a $100 fine, and Clayton Helriggle would not have been killed.

Hudson v. Michigan and the Helriggle Case

The Fourth Amendment requires that the police, before entering a home to execute a search warrant, knock and announce themselves. The so-called knock-and-announce doctrine protects citizens who, thinking they are being invaded by criminals, pick up guns for self-protection and are killed by raiding police officers who are forced to shoot back to protect their own lives. The U.S. Supreme Court, recognizing that people suspected of possessing drugs and other easily disposable evidence will try to destroy the contraband before the police get into the premises, created an exception to the knock-and-announce rule that essentially applies to every drug raid. As a result, the no-knock raid has become the rule in drug enforcement rather than the exception. In balancing citizen versus officer safety, the judicial system has come down in favor of the police.

In June 2006, the U.S. Supreme Court, in *Hudson* v. *Michigan,* ruled five to four that in cases where the police have violated the knock-and-announce doctrine, evidence seized pursuant to those searches can still be used against the defendants in court. By this decision, the Court, by removing the exclusionary rule (illegally acquired evidence cannot be used against the defendant) incentive against unconstitutional behavior, gave SWAT drug raiders the green light to enter homes without notice. Although the exclusionary rule didn't apply to the Helriggle raid because no one had been charged with a crime, attorneys for the family believed *Hudson* v. *Michigan* had made it more difficult for the plaintiffs to win the civil suit against the police. As a result, the family, relying on advice from their lawyers, accepted the county's offer to settle the case for $500,000. Believing that the police had wrongfully killed their son, the Helriggle family began lobbying for a state law requiring adequate training for all SWAT officers.

Did William Bing Have to Die?

At 6:30 P.M. on October 14, 2002, several police cars in Whitehall, Ohio, a town of 20,000 within the urban sprawl of Columbus, pulled up to a cluster of people standing in their yards and on the street near William Bing's house. Bing, the sole resident of the dwelling, retreated inside at the arrival of the police. The officers were met by a group of middle-school children who reported that Bing, in a state of intoxication, had shot at them with a handgun. Other witnesses said the boys had been taunting the man and he had fired a gun into the air and into the ground to scare them away. In either case, this was not the first time Bing had discharged a firearm outside his residence.

Bing didn't respond when an officer asked him over a loudspeaker to come out of the house. They called him on the telephone and got a busy signal.

Officers knew the subject was in the house because they saw him through his windows moving from room to room. After 45 minutes of watching and waiting, the officer in charge of the standoff called in the SWAT team.

Operating out of a command center set up inside a neighbor's house, the leader of the 11-man SWAT team, through his hostage negotiator, continued the effort to contact Bing by telephone. Thinking that Bing had taken his receiver off the hook, a SWAT officer, at 8:45, broke a window and tossed in a "bag phone," a communications system comprising a microphone and a line between a pair of hand receivers. The negotiator used the device to ring up Bing, but the subject didn't answer.

Although Bing was not holding a hostage inside the house at gunpoint and had not fired his weapon from inside the house, he was, if not an immediate danger to his neighbors or the police, a mentally disturbed, intoxicated man who had barricaded himself in his house with a firearm. At this point, the police had three options: wait him out, try to gas him out, or go in and bring him out, dead or alive. Ten minutes after inserting the bag phone into the house, a SWAT officer, in the event that the team would have to enter the premises, bashed the front door in with a battering ram. Other officers fired six canisters of pepper gas through Bing's windows. A few minutes later, officers heard, over the bag phone microphone, Bing coughing and gagging. The gassed environment forced Bing to step outside through a side door, take in a few breaths of fresh air, and then disappear back inside. At 9 P.M., SWAT officers fired 12 more canisters of pepper gas into the dwelling.

At 9:30, Bing's Alcoholics Anonymous sponsor arrived at the scene to talk his friend out of the house. According to the sponsor, Bing was in the throes of a four-day binge, which included huffing some kind of inhalant. The friend also informed the police that Bing owned several guns. After 15 minutes of pleading, the friend handed the loudspeaker back to a police officer.

At 10:20, a SWAT team member crept up to a broken window and tossed a flashbang grenade into the house. Seconds after the explosion, police officers heard gunfire coming from inside the structure. After tossing another phone bag into the house, the police officer who did this reported that he had seen a bullet hole near the window. From this, the SWAT commander concluded that Bing had not shot himself but had fired at his men. There were now two options: wait until Bing either passed out, fell asleep, or decided to come out on his own or go in and bring him out. Five hours after the trouble began, the SWAT commander ordered his men to put on their gas masks. They had waited long enough.

What took place inside the house between Bing and the police comes from the officers' account of the exchange of gunfire. Upon entering the dwelling, one of the men saw Bing peeking through a fist-sized opening in an inner door. Using that hole as a gun port, Bing fired a shot at the police, withdrew his weapon, then fired a second bullet. From about 15 feet, two SWAT team members returned fire with their 12-gauge shotguns. A third officer lobbed a flashbang grenade toward Bing. Within seconds of the explosion, flames broke out in the house. The SWAT team officers retreated from the burning structure without knowing if the subject was dead or alive. If Bing was alive and didn't follow them out of the house, he'd for certain be killed by the fire.

Members of the fire department arrived at the scene but were not allowed to put out the blaze until the police were certain that Bing was not a threat. After the house collapsed in flames, firefighters knocked down the blaze and pulled Bing's body from the debris.

The medical examiner reported that Bing had been fatally shot in the back by a shotgun. He had also broken his leg. A forensic scientist hired by Bing's family reported that the gun purportedly used by Bing against the police did not possess his latent fingerprints. This expert's reconstruction of the events surrounding the shooting, based upon an analysis of the physical evidence, suggests that at the time of his death, Bing had not been armed.

In 2003, Bing's family brought suit against the city of Whitehall and the SWAT officers for illegal entry and excessive force. The defendants filed a motion for summary judgment on the grounds that the exigent conditions made a search warrant unnecessary and that the force used, under the circumstances, was reasonable. Attorneys for the SWAT officers also claimed qualified police immunity. The federal district court judge denied the defendants' motion for summary judgment on the substantive issues of unconstitutional entry and excessive force. The judge found that until Bing started firing at the police through his window, the authorities were not in danger and had plenty of time to acquire a search warrant, which made their later entry invalid. The court also ruled in favor of the plaintiff on the issue of qualified police immunity. This judge believed that the police officers could be held personally liable. The defendants appealed these decisions to the Sixth Circuit Court of Appeals.

The appellate court justices, on the issue of qualified police immunity, disagreed in part with the district judge. The appeals panel ruled that, regarding the warrantless house entry, and the use of the pepper gas and flashbang grenades, police immunity applied because of the exigent circumstances that surrounded these actions. However, on the question of whether or not Bing had been armed at the time of his death, a factual issue that could be resolved only at trial, the justices denied the defendants qualified police immunity. The civil case has yet to be resolved.

On wonders if the Whitehall SWAT team could have restored order without killing Bing. Did they escalate the problem into an exigency that, in turn, justified their aggressive behavior? If this case had unfolded in the pre-SWAT era, would it have ended in a house fire and the killing of an intoxicated, distraught man? Although Bing's behavior had certainly contributed to and perhaps justified his death, the police were not obligated to kill him. In modern law enforcement, playing it by the book doesn't include exhausting all of alternatives to deadly force.

THE GOOSE CREEK FIASCO

The police department in Goose Creek, South Carolina, a bedroom community of 36,000 within the Charleston metropolitan region, does not have a SWAT team. With tactical units operating out of Charleston proper as well as the county sheriff's office, there's no need for one. But just because a small law enforcement agency doesn't field a SWAT team doesn't preclude its officers from participating in military-style operations. When this happens, the results are often disastrous.

On November 1, 2003, an informant told Lieutenant Dave Aarons of the Goose Creek Police Department that students were dealing drugs in the hallways of the 2,760-student Stratford High School. According to the snitch, the transactions took place in the morning before the bused-in students started class. Lieutenant Aarons viewed hallway surveillance tapes from the previous four mornings, and although he didn't see drugs exchanging hands, he believed that some of the students were acting as lookouts while those they were protecting conducted their business out of the cameras' view. The lieutenant played the tapes for the school principal, George McCrackin, who agreed that this activity looked suspicious. In his report, officer Aaron wrote that he had "observed constant, organized drug activity," and that "students were posing as lookouts and concealing themselves from the cameras."[11] At this point, the officer and the principal devised a plan whereby the police, before the arrival of the morning school buses, would hide in utility closets and under stairwells. When McCrackin gave the signal, the officers would come out of hiding and secure the area while faculty members sealed off hallways. Once order had been established, the police would bring in the drug-sniffing dog.

At 6:45 A.M. on November 5, a total of 14 Goose Creek police officers wearing bulletproof vests surprised 130 students who were mingling in the hallway after the school buses had dropped them off. With their pistols drawn, the police ordered the students to hit the ground and put their hands over their heads. Most of the students they encountered were 14- and 15-year-olds. The police, in dealing with students too startled or shocked to comply with their orders quickly, braced them up against the wall and put them in handcuffs. As officers rummaged through students' possessions, the agitated and barking drug dog, a large Czechoslovakian shepherd, nosed their backpacks. Although the dog responded to a dozen book bags, the police didn't find any drugs. They didn't find any weapons either. The unproductive and highly intrusive drug raid had been conducted without a judge-approved search warrant.

The next day, the CBS television affiliate in Charleston, having obtained a copy of the school surveillance tape, played it on the nightly news. It showed police officers yelling frantically at the stunned and frightened students as they waved their guns about amid the disconcerting sounds of the barking dog. Most of the students were either on their knees or lying on their stomachs with their wrists handcuffed behind their backs. Principal McCrackin, obviously aware that a lot of people disapproved of the raid, publicly defended his decision to authorize the sweep, stating that he would "utilize whatever forces that I deem necessary to keep drugs out of the school."[12] Lieutenant Aarons also stood behind the operation: "I don't think it [the raid] was an overreaction. I believe it was one tactical method by which we could safely approach the problem to ensure that everybody was safe."[13]

The Goose Creek drug-raid tape, shown on all of the cable news networks, led to a *Today Show* appearance by one of the ambushed students. In describing the experience, the 14-year-old said, "I thought one of the guns was going to go off and shoot and kill somebody, so I just got down to my knees and covered my head for protection."[14]

Within the school district, the incident outraged some parents, while others were either indifferent or actually relieved that the local police were on the job against drugs. A handful of Stratford teachers demonstrated in support of their principal, but most of them disapproved of the raid. Elijah Simpson, a member of the Charleston County SWAT team whose son was caught up in the drug sweep, criticized the operation. Quoted in *USA Today,* he said, "A school raid is not a SWAT situation, but that's how the Goose Creek police handled it . . . It was a crossfire just waiting to happen. If one door slammed, one student dropped a book or screamed, and then guns would have gone off all over the place. Did you see how they were swinging those guns around? That's not how you do it."[15] Experts in the handling of drug canines criticized the Goose Creek police for allowing the dog such close proximity to the students. Principal George McCrackin, with public opinion turning against him, resigned a few weeks after the raid.

A month after the fiasco, attorneys filed a class-action lawsuit on behalf of 150 students against the former principal, the chief of police, and others involved in the raid. The suit charged the defendants with assault, battery, false arrest, and violations of the plaintiffs' Fourth Amendment right to privacy. In August 2004, the U.S. Attorney's Office in South Carolina announced that Goose Creek police officers had not committed any federal crimes in connection with the raid. That month, the town of Goose Creek settled the class-action suit for $1.6 million. Students who had sought psychological counseling would each receive $11,000. The others would be awarded $6,000 apiece.

SMALL TOWN, WRONG ADDRESS

Valid Warrant, Wrong House in Pewaukee

The police department in Pewaukee, Wisconsin, a town of 12,000 in Waukesha County located in the southeastern part of the state, has a SWAT team. So does the local sheriff's office. In December 2005, the police department's SWAT unit had a warrant to search for marijuana in a second-story apartment on Park Avenue. H. Victor Buerosse, a 68-year-old retired attorney, lived in the one-story building attached to the address listed in the search warrant. Instead of raiding the apartment where the marijuana supposedly was, the police broke into Buerosse's house. "You guys are in the wrong place!"[16] Buerosse yelled as he was thrown to the floor and hit in the head with a riot shield.

The sergeant in charge of the raid, either unconcerned or unaware that the man on the floor didn't match the description of either of the suspects in the marijuana case, informed Buerosse that "We have a valid search warrant."[17] When one of the other SWAT officers recognized Buerosse as someone he knew, the SWAT-team members realized they were in the wrong house. They scrambled out of the dwelling without an apology and a few minutes later recovered a small quantity of marijuana and some drug paraphernalia from the second-story apartment.

Although Buerosse chose not to sue the police department, he expressed his displeasure with the police to the local media, referring to the raid as "law enforcement running amok." He also said this: "SWAT teams are not meant for single pot possession cases . . . This should not happen in America. To me, you can't justify carrying out simple, routine police work this way."[18]

You Weren't Home, So We Let Ourselves In

The police department in Sandpoint, Idaho, a town of 7,000 on the northern edge of the state, didn't have a SWAT team. But its officers did conduct, on a regular basis, paramilitary raids in petty drug cases. On May 2, 2007, five Sandpoint officers, dressed for combat, arrived at Debbie Bergman's trailer in the Ponderay Mobile Home Park. The search warrant they had with them, although listing Debbie's address, was really meant for a place two trailers down the street. According to police records, the drug suspects lived at Lot 23, the place where Debbie Bergman had resided for the preceding eight years. Had they checked with the mobile home park manager, they would have learned that their warrant stated the wrong address.

One of the Sandpoint officers knocked on Bergman's front door, and when no one answered, another member of the team picked up a shovel from the front stoop and pried it open. In the process of tearing the place apart in search of drugs, an officer came across pieces of mail addressed to Debbie Bergman at Lot 23. Realizing that they were ransacking the wrong place, an officer spoke with the park manager, who directed them to the correct trailer. It was there that they seized a small amount of marijuana.

The Sandpoint chief of police, Mark Lockwood, did two things that are rare in wrong-house raids: He replaced Bergman's front door and apologized for the blunder. "This is the first time this has happened," he said. "We made a mistake. We went to the wrong house with wrong information on the warrant."[19] Because the dwelling was not occupied, the raid didn't traumatize, injure, or kill anyone. Although the chief didn't have to apologize, this was a case where an admission of police wrongdoing wouldn't cost the town a civil court settlement. The chief could afford to apologize, and to his credit, he did.

Who Were Those Masked Men?

Sitting in her Durango West, Colorado, mobile home at 11 A.M. watching *The Price is Right,* 77-year-old Virginia Herrick had no reason to worry that armed men would break into her trailer. Even when she heard rustling sounds and looked out her window and saw a group of men wearing gas masks, she thought that there might have been a gas leak. The next thing she knew, her back door banged open and several men wearing black barged into her living room and ordered her to lie on the floor. As she lay sprawled on her carpet, one of the intruders, while his associates tore the place apart looking for drugs, asked if she knew a certain man. She replied that she had never heard of this person. A short time later, a SWAT officer helped her to her feet and removed the handcuffs. Virginia Herrick resided at 74 Hidden Lane. The address on the search warrant read 82 Hidden Lane, the mobile home next door.

Moments after realizing their mistake, the officers broke into the neighbor's house, where they arrested two men and seized 7.2 ounces of methamphetamine. Later that day, the La Plata County sheriff, on behalf of his SWAT team and the Southwest Drug Task Force, came to Mrs. Herrick's house and apologized. She appreciated the gesture and expressed relief that she no longer had neighbors who were dealing in drugs.

On June 15, 2007, a week after the wrong-house raid, Mrs. Herrick's son David was quoted in *The Durango Herald* as follows: "Why they thought it

was necessary to handcuff her and put her on the floor I don't know. And
then they had to ask her what the address was."[20] Sheriff Duke Schirard, in
justifying the way the police had manhandled Mrs. Herrick, said it was common practice in SWAT raids to make all occupants lie on the floor in handcuffs in the event that gunfire should erupt. "It's just safe for everybody if
they're controlled on the ground," he told the reporter. Mrs. Herrick, thinking she was lucky not to have been hurt, said, "For them to raid the wrong
trailer was not very smart."[21]

Part Two

DRUG-WAR RAIDS

The second half of this book reveals how paramilitary police units are used as shock troops in the war against drugs. Chapter 6 shows how the federal law, which prohibits all aspects of marijuana possession, clashes with the laws of 13 states that have legalized the use, sale, and cultivation of medical marijuana. Featured cases involve Drug Enforcement Administration (DEA) raids of the homes of medical marijuana growers and users as well as the clinics where the state-authorized marijuana is dispensed. The second part of the chapter features local sheriffs who raid medical marijuana facilities on the grounds that the growers, users, and dispensers are abusing the state laws that legalize this activity.

Chapter 7 contains case histories of nondeadly wrong-house SWAT raids based upon faulty information from unreliable confidential informants. The botched raid that generated the most publicity occurred in Berwyn Heights, Maryland, after a Prince George's County SWAT team wrongfully raided the mayor's house and killed his two dogs. This 2008 raid led to calls for more law enforcement transparency regarding the acquisition of no-knock search warrants and the use of SWAT teams to execute these drug warrants in the state of Maryland.

Chapter 8 concerns SWAT team raids of homes in which citizens, thinking that their dwellings were being invaded by criminals, shot at the police who fired back, killing them. Because these raids were not technically botched and were based on valid, no-knock search warrants, none of the officers were charged with criminal homicide. But the question remains whether these SWAT raids were necessary, and if not, who is at least morally responsible for the deaths of these citizens? This chapter features eight cases beginning in 2005 and ending in 2008 with the killing of Tarika Wilson. The Wilson shooting took place in Lima, Ohio, and shocked the community, causing a reevaluation of how the law should be enforced in that town.

Whereas the SWAT teams in Chapter 8 raided the houses they had intended to enter, the police in Chapter 9 killed citizens whose homes they had mistakenly broken into. Of the five no-knock SWAT raids featured in this chapter, four involved big-city law enforcement agencies. Although none of the police officers involved in these raids were convicted of criminal homicide, all of their deadly mistakes cost taxpayers millions of dollars in court settlements.

Chapter 10 features cases involving citizens who wounded or killed SWAT officers during drug raids. All of the assault and homicide defendants, in defending their actions, said they had thought their homes were being invaded by criminals. Although there was no evidence to dispute these claims, all of the defendants were convicted. Under the law in most jurisdictions, the prosecution does not have to prove that the defendant knew the person he or she fired at was a police officer. The cases in the first half of this chapter involve civilians who wounded SWAT officers. The remaining accounts are about citizens who took an officer's life. In these cases, despite the mitigating circumstance that the shooters were unaware that police officers had broken into their houses, the citizens were still eligible for the death penalty.

Chapter 6

LEGAL POT: THE WAR ON MEDICAL MARIJUANA

Since President Ronald Reagan's escalation of the war on drugs by making the problem a law enforcement priority, the battle has cost Americans $1 trillion. Today, the government spends $40 billion to $65 billion a year to enforce drug laws and another $60 billion in court and prison costs. This is 10 times what was spent on drug enforcement in 1981. If the continuing use of illegal drugs is the standard by which the effectiveness of this war is measured, the drug dealers have won. According to a national survey conducted in 2006, more than twenty-five million Americans smoked marijuana. Six million used cocaine, almost four million took hallucinogens, two million abused inhalants, another two million used methamphetamines, a million and a half had problems with crack, and more than half a million were addicted to heroin.

President Reagan would not have been pleased with these statistics or with the current status of the drug war. Politicians and government officials, rather than acknowledging the hard truth and scolding Americans for their weakness for drugs, tend to push for more drug enforcement, as though the problem were in the dealing rather than the using. In March 2009, while on a trip to Mexico, Secretary of State Hillary Clinton shocked a lot of people with her blunt analysis of the drug situation: "Our insatiable demand for illegal drugs fuels the drug trade. Our inability to prevent weapons from being illegally smuggled across the border to arm these criminals [Mexican drug lord thugs] causes the deaths of police officers, soldiers, and civilians. How could anyone conclude any differently? I feel very strongly we have co-responsibility."[1] Regarding the 30-year drug war, she said, "It's not working.

We have certainly been pursuing these strategies for a long time. I remember Mrs. Reagan's 'just say no [solution].' It's been very difficult."

August Vollmer, the progressive chief of the Berkeley, California, police department from 1909 to 1932, considered the father of modern American policing, would have agreed with Secretary of State Clinton. In 1937, the year Congress made marijuana possession and sale a federal crime, he wrote: "Repression has driven this vice underground and has produced the narcotic smugglers and supplying agents who have grown wealthy . . . Drug addiction is not a police problem, it never has and never will be solved by a policeman. It is first and last a medical problem."[2]

Today, despite the escalating, more militarized law enforcement crusade against the distribution and use of illegal substances and the fact that some 400,000 people are serving time for state and federal drug violations, these prohibited chemicals and narcotics are more abundant, purer, and cheaper than ever. In 2006, federal, state, and local police arrested 1,889,810 drug-offending suspects, which represented 13 percent of all arrests that year. About half of the drug arrests were for marijuana violations. About 80 percent of all drug arrests involved possession-only crimes committed by people without histories of drug sales or violence. In a country where one out of every 31 adults is in prison, in jail, or on supervised release, the war on drugs is swamping our correctional system.

A handful of federal and state legislators are considering new approaches to the war on drugs. In March 2009, New York governor David Paterson and state legislative leaders agreed to new legislation that would replace mandated minimum drug sentences with more sentencing leeway, including allowing judges to send low-level drug offenders into treatment instead of prison. Chief August Vollmer, who would not have liked the idea of sending SWAT teams into the homes of suspected drug users, would have applauded this first step to a new drug enforcement policy in the state of New York.

THE FEDERAL WAR ON LEGAL MARIJUANA

The California legislature, in November 1996, passed the Compassionate Use Act to carry out the mandate of Proposition 215, a grassroots initiative calling for the legal use of marijuana as a physician-sanctioned pain-killing and therapeutic medication. Although 56 percent of California voters supported Proposition 215, local officials in some of the state's rural areas declared the law null and void because it conflicted with the federal prohibition against the cultivation, marketing, and possession of marijuana. Following passage of the Compassionate Use Act, DEA agents raided numerous marijuana treatment centers. One of these raids took place in Santa Cruz on September 5, 2002. Flak-jacketed DEA agents, decked out in camouflage and carrying M-16s, hit the Wo/Men's Alliance for Medical Marijuana Treatment Center at 7 A.M. They encountered 42-year-old Susanne Pfeil, a patient disabled by polio who, when ordered to get out of bed, couldn't move. One of the agents handcuffed her to the bedpost and then began searching through her belongings. Allergic to pharmaceutical medication, Pfeil used cannabis for muscle and nerve pain. Critics of the DEA considered these raids disrespectful of the state's democratic process.

In 2005, this conflict of law issue reached the U.S. Supreme Court in the case of *Gonzales v. Raich* which arose out of a DEA raid similar to the one in Santa Cruz. In a six-to-three decision, the Court found that Congress had the authority, under the commerce clause, to regulate the illicit drug market. The court did not, however, declare the Compassionate Use Act, a law contradicting the federal prohibition of marijuana, null and void. California's conflict of laws problem therefore remained unresolved.

Following the *Raich* decision, DEA agents, in 2006, raided 30 marijuana treatment centers in Modesto, San Diego, Los Angeles, Grenada Hills, Oakland, Sacramento, and San Francisco. The feds seized cannabis plants, cash, and vehicles owned by the operators of these marijuana-dispensing clinics. They also arrested patients, physicians, and others associated with the operations. These military-style raids on places operating legally under California law outraged supporters of Proposition 215, which included the state's 200,000 legally qualified cannabis patients.

In Washington, one of the 13 states that allows the dispensing of medical marijuana, DEA agents, in a July 2008 raid of a Seattle treatment center, seized the medical files of hundreds of patients; they also confiscated 12 ounces of dried marijuana and several pounds of the less potent cannabis leaves. A month later, DEA agents raided a center in Culver City, California. Officers handcuffed patients, broke into a safe, uprooted a vegetable garden, and left the place in shambles. Shortly thereafter, federal agents raided four dispensaries in San Diego, confiscating 20 pounds of marijuana.

At a Washington, D.C., news conference held in February 2009, Eric Holder, Jr., President Obama's new attorney general, indicated that the DEA would not raid any more medical marijuana clinics. On the campaign trail in March 2008, candidate Obama had told an interviewer that his mother had died of cancer and that he saw no difference between doctor-prescribed morphine and marijuana as pain relievers. The presidential candidate considered it appropriate for states to legalize the medicinal use of marijuana. On February 2, 2009, White House spokesperson Nick Schapiro, in reference to the 13 states that have legalized medical marijuana, said, "The president believes that federal resources should not be used to circumvent state laws."[3] A month later, Attorney General Holder declared that the Justice Department would put a higher priority on white-collar financial crimes than on the investigation of medical marijuana cases, which had higher priority in the Bush administration. DEA spokesman Garrison Courtney made it clear, however, that the DEA would still go after medical marijuana subjects who broke state laws by selling to minors, selling excessive amounts, and/or distributing marijuana grown by unsanctioned cultivators.

In the summer of 2008, before Attorney General Eric Holder announced the change in the government's policy with regard to the enforcement of marijuana laws in states that allowed medical marijuana, a jury found Charles Lynch, the operator of a California dispensary in San Louis Obispo County, guilty of violating the federal prohibition against marijuana. In explaining why he had gone after the 47-year-old medical marijuana dispenser, the U.S. attorney cited the fact that Lynch was not his customers' (all under age 21) primary caregiver and that he provided no other medical treatment at his clinic.

Attorney General Holder's announcement came between Lynch's conviction and his sentencing, which gave advocates for a change in federal drug policy hope for a lenient sentence. In June 2009, Judge George H. Wu disappointed medical marijuana supporters by sentencing Lynch to a year and a day in prison. Judge Wu noted that the defendant, convicted of five counts, could have received five years. The judge had reduced the sentence because Lynch had no criminal record or history of violence. Moreover, the defendant did not fit the federal definition of a "leader" of a criminal enterprise.

Following Lynch's sentence, a Department of Justice spokesperson said that as a general proposition, federal prosecutors would not be going after medical marijuana dispensers in California or the other 12 states. However, U.S. attorneys would pursue cases involving clinic operators who, in addition to breaking the federal law, also violated state regulations. In other words, if a state didn't enforce its own medical marijuana policy to the letter of the law, the federal government would do that for it.

On October 16, 2009, in a memorandum directed at the 13 states that allow medical marijuana, the justice department announced that people who use marijuana for medical purposes and those who provide it for them would not be federally prosecuted. According to the directive, the federal government would not use its limited resources to prosecute patients and distributors who were in "clear and unambiguous compliance" with the state marijuana laws.

Although it was now less likely that the feds would raid state-authorized medical marijuana facilities, members of the medical cannabis community were not immune from locally launched law enforcement raids, arrests, and seizures. In 2004, the California State Assembly created the right of medical marijuana users to form collectives or cooperatives, or "cannabis clubs." Under this law, marijuana patients can form collectives to grow cannabis as a nonprofit operation so that members can purchase the product at safe and reliable storefronts. Pursuant to regulatory guidelines established by the California Attorney General's Office, cannabis club members cannot buy or sell marijuana outside the confines of their collective.

In the early morning hours of February 24, 2010, as part of a multiagency operation, the Santa Barbara Police Department SWAT team raided four cannabis clubs in Santa Barbara, Goleta, Summerland, and Ventura, arresting 12 people and seizing 12,000 plants, 100 pounds of herb, and thousands of dollars in cash and assets. The SWAT team also raided the home of Charles Restivo, a graduate of the University of California at Santa Barbara who was a practicing certified public accountant. Restivo owned three dispensaries and belonged to the Pacific Coast Collective. Restivo, his wife, and the other arrestees were charged with buying and selling marijuana outside the confines of the collective, thus breaking the attorney general's "closed-loop" restriction. Regardless of whether or not Restivo and the others had violated the closed-loop rule, SWAT teams should not be utilized in the ironing out of regulatory wrinkles in the application and enforcement of medical marijuana laws.

MEDICAL MARIJUANA: USE IT, SELL IT, BUT DON'T GROW IT IN COLORADO

Much to the disgust and dismay of the law enforcement establishment in Colorado and the citizens of the state who support the idea of sending pot smokers to prison, a majority of voters in 2000 approved an amendment to the state constitution allowing the use of medical marijuana. Pursuant to Amendment 20, people suffering from debilitating medical conditions, upon a doctor's recommendation, could acquire a state-issued certificate or card giving them the right to purchase and use the herb for medicinal purposes. The amendment protected registered patients, their physicians, and the proprietors of storefront dispensaries from criminal prosecution.

By 2008, a total of 3,302 patients in the state, upon the recommendation of 500 doctors, were registered marijuana users. Although there were 11 dispensaries operating openly in the urban centers, medical marijuana users in the rural areas of the state either grew their own pot or bought it from local cultivators. These patients, on their cannabis cards, could designate, under the category "caregiver," the person who grew their marijuana supply. As proof that they were cultivating state-sanctioned medical pot, these growers, most of whom were card-holding patients themselves, kept photocopies of their customers' marijuana patient certificates listing them as caregivers. These suppliers, believing that the law allowing the use and sale of medical cannabis also provided for its cultivation, considered the caregiver status a license to grow the crop.

Sheriffs and prosecutors in a handful of Colorado counties, however, noting that Amendment 20 did not expressly exempt pot growers from criminal
prosecution under the state's cannabis laws, did not recognize the caregiver
designation as a license to cultivate the prohibited crop. The sheriffs of Huerfano and Larimer Counties, taking a hard line on pot growing, had used
SWAT teams to confiscate marijuana crops and take growers into custody.

The DEA in Colorado, unlike its action in California, had not bothered
medical marijuana users, dispensers, or growers. But Jim Sweetin, the head
of Denver's DEA field office, was not shy about commenting on the intelligence of the majority of Colorado's voters. Referring to Amendment 20, he
reportedly said, "I think it was a mistake. It is bad public policy, and it put
cops in a terrible spot. The very term 'medical marijuana' doesn't hold much
water. I mean, really, what kind of medicine do you smoke?"[4] By putting
police officers in a terrible spot, Sweetin presumably meant requiring them
to use a little law enforcement discretion. In police work, black and white is
a lot easier to deal with than gray.

Don't Grow Pot in Huerfano County

For Mike Stetler, a resident of Huerfano County in the sparsely populated south central region of Colorado, Amendment 20 was a blessing. Following a serious car accident in 1990, he treated his chronic pain with
drugs—OxyContin and morphine—that put him in a perpetual fog. As
a certified user of medical cannabis, Stetler, in 2002, began growing his
own pot. According to his doctor, he needed to cultivate 15 plants to produce enough cannabis to alleviate his pain. Four years after the passage of
Amendment 20, Stetler, as the designated caregiver to 13 other card-holding
medical marijuana users, tended 44 plants on private land miles from a
paved road in a county with less than 8,000 residents. To publicize the fact
that he cultivated cannabis under the protection of Amendment 20, Stetler
prominently displayed copies of his customers' marijuana certificates on the
property.

Sheriff Bruce Newman didn't like Amendment 20 and didn't want anyone, including so-called medical marijuana caregivers, growing pot in his
county. In the fall of 2006, a helicopter loaded with heavily armed Huerfano
County sheriff's deputies landed on Stetler's property. The raiding team broke
open two padlocked gates, ripped a hole in the roof of a trailer, and made
off with Stetler's marijuana crop. Asked why his officers didn't take Stetler
into custody, the sheriff reportedly said, "We want to see what happens with
some of the other cases. There's a lot of legal stuff up in the air, and it's going
to take judges making decisions to figure it out."[5] In the meantime, Stetler

and the legal users of his marijuana would have to find a source of cannabis outside Huerfano country.

To a newspaper reporter covering the marijuana raid, Mike Stetler reportedly said, "The police are supposed to be protecting me from thieves and such, but they are making up their own laws ... They are mocking the voters they serve."[6] Regardless of how the courts would resolve the marijuana caregiver issue in Colorado, Mr. Stetler would not get his cannabis back. The sheriff had it destroyed.

Caregiver Troubles in Larimer County

In northern Colorado, Jim Alderden, the sheriff of Larimer County, had established himself as a hard-nosed, zero-tolerance kind of crime fighter in the style of Joe Arpaio in Maricopa County. Like his Arizona counterpart, Sheriff Alderden got as much mileage as he could out of his SWAT team. His aggressive law enforcement tactics, as is often the case, had created controversy and in some cases embarrassment.

On Saturday afternoon, June 19, 2006, Larimer County SWAT officers rushed a small Denver-based production company whose members were filming a hostage scene in the North Pines Campgrounds just west of Loveland. As the SWAT unit, armed with M-16 rifles, advanced toward the film crew, camera operators, actors, the director, assistant director, and other members of the group heard "Freeze! We're gonna shoot you! We're gonna send rounds your way!" A few moments later they were all on the ground. While lying in the park in handcuffs, the director kept yelling, "We're making a movie!"[7] One of the SWAT officers ordered the director to shut up until they had finished questioning the "hostage."

Film crew members lay on the ground for 30 minutes before the deputies sorted things out. As it turned out, the production company had a permit to use the park but had failed to acquire a special permit to film a movie in the park. The SWAT team leader, before withdrawing his men, cited the actor playing the hostage taker with disorderly conduct and charged the director for being an accessory to that crime. Perhaps this would deter other lawless film makers from shooting scenes in the park without securing the proper battery of permits.

Sheriff Alderden, in January 2007, decided to complement his SWAT team with another specialized, elite group of deputies called the Criminal Impact Unit. He created this squad to target gangs, drug dealers, and repeat offenders. The Larimer County commissioners, because none of their constituents had complained of gang activity, and the fact the police departments in Fort Collins and Loveland had active drug enforcement units, refused to provide extra money for another elite force. Undeterred, the sheriff financed the unit by reallocating deputies from other squads, such as officers previously assigned to investigate crimes against the elderly and children.

Calling Amendment 20 "ill-conceived," Sheriff Alderden did not approve of medical marijuana. Referring to designated caregivers, Alderden told a reporter that "these people are nothing more than dope dealers, and they are hiding under this thing, and we are not going to back off."[8]

Christopher Crumbliss, age 32, and his wife, Tiffany, both legal users of medical marijuana, lived in Loveland, where they grew medical marijuana for 40 other certified patients. A Larimer County judge, pursuant to Amendment 20's limit of five patients per caregiver and six plants per patient, authorized no-knock searches of the Crumbliss homes in Loveland and in Fort Collins. In Loveland, just before dawn on May 31, 2007, officers with Sheriff Alderden's Criminal Impact Unit and his SWAT team, pulled Christopher out of bed and dragged him out of the house in his underwear. The officers then confiscated 200 plants, and 20 pounds of dried marijuana. In Fort Collins, Alderden's deputies seized 5 pounds of packaged marijuana and six firearms. They arrested the couple on felony counts of growing and possessing marijuana for sale.

Sean McAllister, the Breckenridge attorney representing Christopher and Tiffany, referring to the militaristic raid as a Larimer county "smash and grab" operation, called these law enforcement tactics "The worst abuse I've ever seen [in medical marijuana enforcement] because they are arresting first and determining if it's legal later . . . You can make [cannabis]. You can dispense it. But how are they supposed to grow it? Unfortunately the Crumblisses are the guinea pigs who are going to have to test the legal status of Colorado's medical marijuana laws."[9]

In July, three months after the Crumbliss SWAT raids, a district judge presiding over a medical marijuana case in Denver ruled that the five-patient, six-plant limitation to Amendment 20 violated the state's constitution. Notwithstanding this decision, the authorities in Larimer County did not drop the charges against the Crumblisses.

Larimer County's Embarrassing SWAT Team Sugar Bust

In Loveland, 32-year-old Jeremy Myers lived in an apartment inside a building that was once a sugar factory. A hard-working young man with no history of crime, Jeremy ran his back-hoe business out of the old manufacturing plant. Local narcotics officers, acting on an anonymous tip that Jeremy Myers operated a methamphetamine lab in the building, had failed to find evidence of meth production by searching through his trash. The deputies had also installed a pair of surveillance cameras outside Myers's apartment to monitor his comings and goings. On September 6, absent solid evidence supporting the tipster's accusation, narcotics officers led by SWAT teams from the Loveland Police Department and the Larimer County Sheriff's Office, stormed the old building.

Once the SWAT teams took control of the former sugar factory, officers with the Larimer County Drug Task Force began their search. They didn't find any meth or evidence of its production in the suspect's apartment. They found no signs of its manufacture in the old plant, nor did they seize bundles of cash, incriminating paperwork, or guns. In a storage shed, they seized an old Mason jar containing an unknown substance that had crystallized. One of the officers, after exposing a sample of the contents to a crime scene test kit chemical, presumptively declared the questioned evidence methamphetamine. Without having this identification confirmed in a crime lab, narcotics officers arrested Jeremy Myers on felony drug charges. The arraigning magistrate set his bail at $75,000.

For sheriffs and police chiefs, meth lab busts, publicity wise, are right up there with recovering kidnapped children. The next day, the *Loveland Register-Herald* carried a photograph of an officer in an HAZMAT suit holding the Mason jar as though it were a trophy fish. According to the authorities, as reported in the newspaper, the jar contained enough crystal meth to get 1,800 people high.

Jeremy Myers had to sell off his business assets to make bail and to cover the expense of exonerating himself. He paid to have the Mason jar contents analyzed at the Colorado State Crime Lab, which found that the substance was not methamphetamine or any other form of contraband. He hired a Fort Collins environmental hygiene company to search for evidence of meth in his apartment, in the plant, and in the soil surrounding the facility. The experts found no signs of contamination. Myers also had samples of his hair analyzed for traces of meth ingested within the past 90 days. That test came back negative as well.

Myers's attorney, at the preliminary hearing on November 5, 2007, presented the exonerating evidence. The judge immediately dismissed the charges. Jeremy Myers was free, but the law enforcement fiasco had cost him his business and, worse, his reputation. Although the police in Larimer County had conducted a shoddy investigation, used SWAT troops to raid Myers's apartment, and then misidentified the contents of the Mason jar, they did not apologize for their incompetence and strong-arm tactics. Their law enforcement malpractice had cost them nothing.

Jeremy Myers, in November 2009, filed suit against the chief of the Loveland Police Department, the head of the Fort Collins Police Department,

Larimer County sheriff James Alderden, the cities of Loveland and Fort Collins, and Larimer County. In addition to the out-of-pocket expenses related to the destruction of his property, the plaintiff sought damages for the emotional stress, humiliation, and loss of his reputation caused by the informant-based SWAT raid that produced no evidence of criminal wrongdoing.

More Trouble for the Crumblisses

At 4 A.M. on August 14, 2008, Sheriff Alderden's Criminal Impact Unit and SWAT team, accompanied by SWAT officers from Summit and Boulder Counties, made simultaneous no-knock raids of the homes owned by Christopher Crumbliss in Loveland, Fort Collins, and Blue River. In Fort Collins, SWAT officers pulled Crumbliss out of bed and wrangled him to his front yard, where he stood with the beam of a laser-scoped assault rifle dotting his T-shirt. Fearing that they were going to shoot him on the spot, Crumbliss yelled, "I have a license to grow medical marijuana!"[10]

Officers confiscated a total of 200 plants and 25 pounds of finished product. Charged with felony counts of marijuana cultivation, possession with intent to distribute, and possession of more than eight ounces of cannabis, the police booked Crumbliss into the Larimer County Detention Center. If convicted of all charges, a judge could send him away for up to 10 years.

Sheriff Alderden grabbed his 15 minutes of national fame in October 2009 after a helium balloon resembling a flying saucer traveled 50 miles across Colorado and landed in Kansas. Until the contraption hit the ground in a cornfield, law enforcement authorities and millions watching the event on live television believed that a six-year-old boy might be aboard. What could have been a tragedy turned out to be a stunt that created a lot of publicity for the boy and his family as well as for Sheriff Alderden.

In Colorado, after a judge in 2007 set aside the five-patient-per-caregiver limit, the number of medical marijuana cards issued each year in the state jumped from 2,000 to 60,000. The "Green Rush," involving the explosion of taxpaying storefront medical marijuana dispensaries in Denver and other cities, created a new source of badly needed government revenue and thousands of new jobs. John Suthers, the state's attorney general and one of many law enforcement officials who consider Amendment 20 a license for drug abuse, believed that state legislators should more actively regulate the medical marijuana industry. The attorney general in part blames what he considers the unhealthy proliferation of medical marijuana dispensaries on the U.S. Department of Justice's October 2009 decision not to enforce the federal prohibition on marijuana.

Aside from the question of whether legalized medical marijuana is good public policy, sheriffs and chiefs of police who use SWAT teams to conduct no-knock raids on medical marijuana growers and the people and clinics they supply either have their crime-fighting priorities out of order or don't have enough serious crime in their jurisdictions to justify these paramilitary units. In either case, the showboating is not good policing, and these SWAT units should either be disbanded or limited to high-risk assignments.

Chapter 7

COLLATERAL DAMAGE: NONFATAL WRONG-HOUSE DRUG RAIDS

One would expect that before employing the tactic of breaking into someone's home in the middle of the night, the police would be certain that (1) the suspects involved were dangerous people; (2) there was no other, less violent way of executing the arrest and/or search; (3) children and other innocent people would not be traumatized and endangered; (4) the target or targets of the raid were inside the dwelling and were solid suspects; and (5) the officers were entering the dwelling they intended to raid. Although invading the home of an innocent person or breaking into the wrong dwelling by mistake can both be classified as wrong-house raids, the police recognize only the latter as such. As far as they are concerned, as long as the premises they have broken into is the one listed on the search warrant, regardless of the fact the warrant is based on faulty information from an unreliable snitch, the raid is valid. The police own up to wrongdoing only when they accidentally raid a house other than the one they intended to invade. And even then, unless someone is injured or killed, they do not seem to appreciate the seriousness of their mistake. It's like this: crime fighting is war, and in war there is collateral damage.

Regardless of whether or not a particular wrong-house raid can be blamed on an unreliable confidential informant, these botched operations reflect police incompetence. These bungled raids leave citizens with damaged doors, smashed windows, broken furniture, burned carpets, and ransacked belongings. In the worst of these nondeadly raids, SWAT officers injure people, burn down houses, and kill pets. These wrong-house, nonfatal police operations rarely generate more than one day's coverage in the media. Since there is no governmental data base that records wrong-house SWAT raids, no one knows how many of these there are every year. In 2006, based on the media coverage alone, Radley Balko, a senior editor at *Reason Magazine* and a former policy analyst for the CATO Institute, estimated that over the past 15 years, SWAT teams had been involved in about 200 "wrong door"[1] raids. The vast majority of these botched operations involved cases of drug enforcement. Since there is no way to know how many wrong-house raids didn't get reported in the media, this figure probably doesn't come close to representing the true scope of the problem.

SNITCH-BASED DRUG-RAID FIASCOS

The police know that confidential informants, whether they snitch on people for money or simply to stay out of jail, are notoriously unreliable. Nevertheless, informants play a vital role in drug enforcement. Narcotics officers routinely pressure users caught in possession of drugs to rat out their suppliers in return for reduced charges or even free passes. It is no wonder the information from these snitches is so untrustworthy.

Given the nature of how the authorities identify dope dealers, it is not surprising that the war on drugs has turned America into a nation of police informers. In 2008, capitalizing on the willingness of desperate people to inform on their fellow citizens, the Albuquerque Police Department started running newspaper ads soliciting criminal informants. The ad read: "Wanted: People who hang out with crooks to do part time work with the APD. Make some extra cash. Drug use and criminal record OK."[2] According to the captain of Albuquerque's Special Investigations Unit, a snitch who fingers a drug dealer can earn $50. And if the informants have their own troubles with the law, they can get off the hook by striking a deal with the district attorney.

Confidential informants rarely testify in court because their identities have to be kept secret. As a result, the information they provide usually goes unchallenged. They are principally used by narcotics officers to provide the probable cause they need to acquire search warrants. Whenever an informant's story is the sole evidence supporting a search warrant, there's a good chance the search will produce nothing. Conducting a no-knock, predawn SWAT raid solely on the word of an informant, without the supporting evidence of police surveillance and at least one undercover drug buy, is irresponsible and dangerous.

Louisville, Kentucky: Calvin Roach

Armed with a search warrant based solely on the word of an informant that crack cocaine was being sold at 1773 Wilson Avenue in Louisville, the

Metro Police SWAT team, in December 2004, broke into the house while the occupants slept. Had the police conducted a cursory investigation, they would have learned that Calvin Roach, the man who lived in the house with his wife and their six children, wasn't a dealer in dope. Moreover, they would have learned that the cocaine in question was being sold out of a house just down the street from the Roach residence.

A female SWAT officer (this is rare), calling Mr. Roach a motherfucker, told him if he didn't hit the floor, she'd blow his fucking brains out. Interviewed by a television correspondent, Mr. Roach said, "We were just blown away. We didn't know what was happening, it happened so fast. I was in shock."[3] Fortunately no one was hurt. Had Mr. Roach, believing that criminals were invading his home had picked up a gun, the police might have killed him.

The chief of police, eight months after the wrong-house raid, apologized to Mr. Roach and his family. Although it was a little late, it was still an unusual police gesture. In August 2007, a judge dismissed Mr. Roach's lawsuit against the city on the grounds that Kentucky's qualified official immunity doctrine protected the police from civil liability in cases of honest mistakes. In other words, as long as the police exhibit good-faith incompetence, they aren't liable for their actions.

North Little Rock, Arkansas: Tracy Ingle

A narcotics officer with the North Little Rock Police Department received information on December 20, 2007, that a woman known only as Kate was selling methamphetamine out of the house at 400 East 21 Street. The confidential informant, who said he'd purchased meth there, didn't know who owned the dwelling, if other people lived there, how much drug activity was going on at that location, or anything about Kate other than she usually carried a gun. A judge, relying entirely on this sketchy report from a confidential informant, issued a nighttime no-knock warrant to search the house.

At 7:40 P.M., 17 days after the judge issued the warrant, Tracy Ingle, a 40-year-old former stonemason with a bad back, was asleep in his first floor bedroom in the back of the house at 400 East 21 Street. Mr. Ingle awoke with a start at the sound of the SWAT battering ram breaking down his front door. He instinctively reached for his pistol, the unloaded and broken handgun he kept at his bedside to scare off intruders. This would not be the first time burglars had broken into his home. Suddenly, a flashbang grenade came though the window near his bed, filling the room with blinding light. The SWAT officer who climbed into the bedroom through the broken window yelled, "He's got a gun!"[4] That's when the shooting started. The first bullet, fired from a .223-caliber semiautomatic rifle, tore into Ingle's left leg just above the knee. As he dropped to the floor, SWAT officers outside the window fired 20 more shots, hitting Ingle in the arm, calf, hip, and chest. Moments later, several officers were in the room. One of the officers kept calling Ingle Michael and Mike. Before being rushed to the Baptist Health Hospital, Ingle said, "My name is not Mike."[5]

The police did not find methamphetamine or any other illegal drug at Tracy Ingle's house. They didn't find Kate, whoever she was, or any incriminating evidence in Ingle's car. They did seize a digital scale and a few baggies, common household items they designated as drug paraphernalia. Ingle's sister, a surgical nurse who made jewelry as a hobby, told the police the scale and baggies belonged to her.

Because the police had broken into Ingle's house and shot him five times, then failed to find the drugs they had raided the home for, they had to charge him with something. And they did: two counts of aggravated assault for picking up his handgun in self-defense and felony possession of drug paraphernalia. The North Little Rock police, in a botched drug SWAT raid, had almost killed a citizen who had never been convicted of a felony. Instead of apologizing for their shoddy work and overaggressive tactics, they wanted to send him to prison.

Ten days after the shooting, the hospital discharged Ingle from the intensive care unit. The police immediately picked him up and drove him to the police station. For the next six hours, detectives grilled Ingle without an attorney present. From the interrogation room, they hauled him to the Pulaski County Jail, where they booked him, still in his hospital scrubs. When they released Ingle four days later (he had sold his car to make bail), his wounds had become infected because he had been unable to change his bandages every six hours.

The internal affairs investigation of the shooting cleared the two SWAT officers of wrongdoing. Seeing the gun in Ingle's hand, they had responded appropriately. Responsibility for this drug enforcement fiasco rested on the shoulders of the case detective and the judge who had signed the no-knock search warrant. Ingle, who couldn't afford to hire a lawyer, finally caught a break in May when John Wesley Hall, a well-known Arkansas defense attorney, agreed to represent him.

In an April 2008 interview conducted by a reporter with the *Arkansas Times,* North Little Rock Chief of Police Danny Bradley spoke about the department's SWAT team, officer safety, and police militarism. Because North Little Rock is a small city of 50,000, the SWAT team is made up of 12 to 15 regular-duty patrolmen and detectives assigned to the squad part time. They train for the position twice a month. The chief said he deployed the unit only in high-risk situations. "If we have any doubts about detectives and uniformed officers being able to execute the warrant safely, we're going to use the SWAT team. I would rather spend the extra money that it takes to get the SWAT team together than risk someone getting injured."[6] Regarding nighttime no-knock home invasions such as the one that got Tracy Ingle shot and almost killed, Chief Bradley said, "How do you weigh a situation where executing a warrant safely means exploiting the element of surprise, versus the natural reaction of a person when someone is intruding into their house? It's a dangerous business." The chief allowed that he didn't like the term "war on drugs" because he didn't want his officers thinking they were soldiers, and drug suspects the enemy. In that regard, he had worked to eliminate some of the militaristic trappings of the force. For example, he had switched his regular patrol officers out of their "fatigue-looking" uniforms.

Tracy Ingle's attorney, on September 8, 2008, filed a motion to suppress the evidence against his client. John Wesley Hall argued that owing to the vagueness of the informant's report, the warrant authorizing the raid lacked sufficient probable cause, which rendered the evidence against Ingle inadmissible. Moreover, had there been sufficient probable cause in the first place, it had been severely attenuated by the 17-day delay in the warrant's execution. In other words, the evidence had grown stale. Under Arkansas law, search warrants must be served within a reasonable time but not more than 60 days after issue.

In March 2009, a jury found Ingle guilty of maintaining a drug house and of felony assault. The judge sentenced him to 18 years in prison and fined him $18,000. Tracy Ingle took his case to the Arkansas Court of Appeals, which, on May 12, 2010, affirmed his conviction.

Troy, New York: Ronita McColley

A confidential informant told an investigator with the Rensselaer County District Attorney's Office that a number of unidentified people were selling cocaine out of three houses and an apartment in Troy. On June 23, 2008, a member of the county drug task force sent an undercover operative into one of the houses, where he purchased cocaine from a known dealer. A few days later, a judge in Troy issued four no-knock nighttime warrants based on nothing more than the snitch's tip and the one controlled buy.

At 4 A.M., an explosion inside the house at 396 First Street awoke Ronita McColley and her five-year-old daughter. Seconds later, officers with the Troy Emergency Response Team (ERT) and county drug police poured into McColley's home past her splintered door. McColley would describe that moment to a local reporter this way: "The flash and then coming into my house and me not having any clothes [on] . . . Just a lot of men looking at [me] and no female in sight."[7]

After breaking down her front door, smashing a window with the flash-bang grenade—which burned a hole in her carpet and scorched a wall—and rummaging through her personal belongings, the police found no evidence of illegal drug activity. Some of the men thought they had accidentally raided the wrong house. But no, this was one of the addresses the snitch had identified. No one got hurt that night, including McColley's five-year-old daughter. The police didn't apologize for the destruction and terror, and no one offered to replace the door, the window glass, or the carpet. This wrong-house raid was just another case of collateral damage in the war on drugs.

In the other raids that night in Troy, the police didn't confiscate any cocaine. They found small quantities of marijuana but didn't take anyone into custody. Criticism of these fruitless, potentially dangerous no-knock intrusions prompted an internal police inquiry into the operation. On September 17, the *Troy Record* published excerpts of Assistant Chief of Police John Tedesco's report. According to Tedesco, "The bulk of this [drug] investigation was predicated upon the word of the CI [confidential informant] absent further investigation. Arguably, the reputation [of providing reliable information] of the CI was established. However, this fact alone does not negate the need to substantiate the CI's claims. Surveillance or controlled buys at the . . . locations is the seemingly appropriate investigative pursuit to accomplish this function."[8]

Ronita McColley's attorney, Terry Kindlon, gave notice of his intent to bring a lawsuit against the city. Interviewed by a *Troy Record* reporter, he said, "I sometimes think . . . that rather than doing thoughtful, thorough police work, they are phoning it in and they end up throwing bombs at one of the nicest, sweetest women I have ever met."[9] McColley's legal action has yet to be resolved.

BOOTS IN THE HOUSE—THE WRONG HOUSE

Neutralizing the Chidesters

At 10 P.M. on the night of May 25, 2005, the Utah County Metro SWAT team was about to break into a house on South State Street in Springville to confiscate methamphetamine, guns, and any other contraband they might find in the dwelling. The Sierra Team, one of the four Utah County SWAT groups involved in the raid, pulled into the neighborhood first. The six snipers in the unit took up positions 50 yards from the target house. The Sierra snipers were in place to watch the house and report any activity at or near the dwelling to the other SWAT units as they moved into their attack positions. From this point on, any bystander who happened onto the surveillance area would be viewed through the cross-hairs of rifle scopes.

The remaining 24 SWAT officers arrived at the scene. Alpha Team members, taking up positions 70 yards from the house, would break into the house through the front entrance. Team Charlie had the side door. The Bravo squad, setting up behind a wooden fence in the back, 50 yards from the target, would enter the house through the rear door.

At 10:30, the Alpha, Charlie, and Bravo teams were supposed to reach the target at the same time, tossing flashbang grenades into the front, side, and rear of the house. Because of some kind of miscommunication, the Bravo team entered the back door ahead of the other two units, which were moving toward the dwelling from 65 yards away.

Forty-year-old Larry Chidester lived in the basement quarters of his parents' place next door to the SWAT target. Awakened by the flashbang explosion coming from the other side of his house, Larry came out his side door to investigate what he thought was a car accident. Instead, he saw a group of SWAT officers charging toward his neighbor's house. Before he got back inside, Larry heard one of the officers yell, "There's one!" Alpha team member Jason Parker, a reserve sheriff's deputy, ran up to Larry and ordered him to the ground. Each time Larry lowered his arms to help himself down, Deputy Parker, his rifle pointed at Chidester's head, yelled, "Keep your hands up!"[10]

"I'm not resisting! I'm not resisting!"[11] Larry pleaded as Deputy Parker tackled him to the ground and kept him there a minute or so with his knee pressed into the middle of Chidester's back. Although not seriously injured, Chidester had the wind knocked out of him and suffered abrasions to his forehead, nose, shoulder, back, and knees.

As Larry lay pinned to the ground under Reserve Deputy Parker's knee, Sergeant Deke Taylor and another Alpha team officer stormed into the Chidester house. Deputy Taylor encountered Larry's mother, Emily, in the kitchen, and at gunpoint, ordered her to the floor. The other officer found Lawrence Chidester in the bedroom sitting on the edge of his bed putting on his trousers. This deputy grabbed Mr. Chidester by the shirt and threw him to the floor, ripping the garment off his back. Shortly after the two Alpha team officers left the Chidesters shaking and bruised, a third deputy entered the house and apologized for the intrusion.

Sheriff Jim Tracy insisted that the Chidester incident did not fall into the category of a wrong-house raid. His men were merely protecting themselves by taking control of the target area. From a law enforcement point of view, the only mistake involved the deputy's on-site apology, which suggested police wrongdoing.

The Chidesters filed suit against the Utah County Sheriff's Office and deputies Jason Parker and Deke Taylor individually for violating their Fourth Amendment rights of privacy. The deputies raised the issued of qualified police immunity, arguing that they had acted in good faith. A federal district court judge, in August 2006, ruled that the Chidesters had grounds to sue the officers as individuals. The deputies appealed this decision, and in March the Tenth Circuit Court of Appeals held that Deputy Parker's actions did protect him from personal liability under the immunity doctrine. However, the appeals court judges did not bar the plaintiffs from suing Utah County and Deputy Taylor as an individual. The lawsuit is pending.

Here We Come, Ready or Not

During the early morning hours of June 27, 2006, a total of 100 federal, state, and local drug enforcement agents and officers raided 23 homes in Decatur, Huntsville, Madison, and Hartsville, Alabama. The raids culminated a two-year investigation, by the High Intensity Drug Trafficking Area Task Force, of a Mexican-based cocaine, marijuana, and methamphetamine trafficking operation doing business in the northern part of the state. That morning, task force officers arrested 29 people, including 28-year-old Jerome Wallace, who lived with his father, James, at 13355 Honey Way, a dirt road in rural Limestone County. Officers arrested Jerome as he stood in his front yard after task force members, a couple of houses down the road, had raided the wrong place—his uncle's home—looking for him. That search warrant bore the wrong address, and the mistake almost killed Jerome's uncle, Kenneth Jamar.

Before daybreak, several vans rolled down Honey Way and parked across from Kenneth Jamar's house. Agents with the DEA, ATF, FBI, and ICE, and the Alabama Bureau of Investigation, along with Alabama state troopers and SWAT teams from Huntsville and Madison County, alighted from their vehicles. A few seconds after one of the officers yelled, "Open Up! Police!" they broke into the house through Kenneth Jamar's front door. They assumed that Mr. Jamar—a 51-year-old semi-invalid with severe gout and a pacemaker—had heard to police announce themselves, but even if he had, he could not have made it to the door in time to let them in. Had he tried, Jamar would have walked into a flashbang grenade explosion. He did pick up a pistol, and when one of the SWAT officers kicked open his bedroom door and four of them entered the room, they saw Mr. Jamar standing next to his bed pointing his weapon. The police then opened fire on him. Of the 16 bullets from their rifles, one hit Jamar in the hip, another in the groin, and a third in the foot. He went down without firing a shot.

Paramedics rushed Mr. Jamar, in critical condition, to a hospital in Huntsville, where he spent two weeks in the intensive care unit. After searching his house, the police confiscated Jamar's gun collection. Perhaps because the SWAT team had broken into the wrong house, the Limestone County prosecutor chose not to charge Mr. Jamar with attempted assault.

In the days and weeks following the shooting, newspaper accounts of the raid were sketchy because Mike Blakely, the sheriff of Limestone County, the man heading up the internal investigation, did not release much information to the media. According to the sheriff, the officers had to "neutralize" a man who was "aggressively resisting."[12] Regarding the fact the police had entered the wrong house, the sheriff reportedly said, "I guess you could call it a clerical error over the address, but I don't think Jamar's house even has a street address." This statement begs the question: if Mr. Jamar's dwelling didn't have a street address, what was on the search and arrest warrants that led the police to his house?

Because the SWAT officers who shot Kenneth Jamar were not personally responsible for the wrong-house raid and had fired their weapons in self-defense, they were cleared of wrongdoing. Kenneth Jamar, on June 26, 2008, filed a $7.5 million suit in federal court claiming that the city of Huntsville and others had violated his civil rights. He nephew, Jerome Wallace, the object of the raid, pleaded not guilty to charges of drug conspiracy. Mr. Jamar's lawsuit awaits adjudication.

Mindless and Trigger-Happy in Prince George's County

On July 28, 2008, drug traffickers in Los Angeles sent, by Federal Express, a box containing 32 pounds of marijuana to an address in Berwyn Heights, Maryland, a town of 3,000, 10 miles south of Washington, D.C. The residents at the shipment's point of destination had nothing to do with the delivery, the address being a drop where an accomplice would pick up the package before someone took it inside. Ideal drop locations were homes occupied by childless couples who worked during the day. It also helped if the house had a front porch and at least one of the conspirators worked for the delivery company.

This particular marijuana delivery operation fell apart when, at a FedEx facility in Arizona, a drug dog made a hit on the parcel. The authorities in Arizona, after notifying the Prince George's County Police Department, resealed the box and sent it on its way. In Maryland, at the FedEx station in Beltsville, narcotics officers with the county police department took possession of the contraband.

Instead of conducting a cursory investigation to determine the identities and backgrounds of the people who lived at the point of delivery and conferring with the chief of the Berwyn Heights Police Department to determine if there had been suspicious drug activity associated with this house, the officers in charge of the case decided to deliver the package and then raid the place after the resident took the box inside. Had they checked with Patrick Murphy, the Berwyn Heights chief of police, the Prince George's County officers would have leaned that 37-year-old Cheye Calvo, his wife Trinity, and her mother, Georgia Porter lived at that address. Mr. Calvo worked for a nonprofit organization that ran several public boarding schools for at-risk children. Trinity had a job as a state finance officer. These people were not only law-abiding citizens but Mr. Calvo himself was the mayor of Berwyn Heights. Had the Prince George's County police enlisted Mr. Calvo's cooperation, they could have caught the drug movers at the point of destination. Instead, the county officers obtained a search warrant to raid Calvo's house. (They failed to secure a no-knock warrant, which added to the mix of police incompetence.)

According to the plan, on the day after the package had been intercepted at Beltsville, a county officer, posing as a deliveryman, would bring it to the Calvo house at 6:30 P.M. The police department's SWAT team, however, wasn't available to lead the raid that day. Melvin High, Prince George's County's chief of police, called the department in Greenbelt and asked if he could borrow their SWAT unit. The chief in Greenbelt said he couldn't help because his unit was not authorized to operate outside the boundaries of the town. Chief High then turned to Michael Jackson, the sheriff of Prince George's County, who agreed to send his SWAT deputies into the house. Every police leader in the county knew of the impending raid but Patrick Murphy, the chief of police of Berwyn Heights. Not only were they planning a wrong-house intrusion but the SWAT team Chief High had recruited, a unit used mainly to intercede in domestic disturbances, had little experience conducting drug raids.

At 6 P.M. on the day of the raid, Calvo arrived home from work ahead of his wife, Trinity. He gathered up Payton and Chase, his two black lab retrievers, and took them for a walk. While he was away, a police officer approached the residence with the package of marijuana. Georgia, Calvo's mother-in-law, came to the door and instructed the "deliveryman" to leave the white box, addressed to her daughter, Trinity Tomsic, on the front porch. The drug trafficking accomplice, stationed at the point of delivery and realizing that the police had intercepted the package, then fled the scene. Mayor Calvo and the dogs returned from their walk a few minutes before 7 P.M. He picked up the box, set it on a small table near the front entrance, and then climbed the stairs to change out of his work clothes.

A few minutes later, Georgia, while preparing dinner, looked out the kitchen window and saw a SWAT officer pointing a rifle at her head. She screamed, and a few seconds later, SWAT officers broke down the front door. From the second floor, Calvo heard his mother-in-law scream, the front door cracking apart, loud voices, and gunfire. Several deputies entered Calvo's bedroom, grabbed him, and dragged the stunned mayor down the stairs in his boxer shorts. Payton, the seven-year-old lab, lay dead in the living room. The officers ordered Calvo to his knees and to remain there with his hands cupped on his head. No one would listen as he tried to tell them he was the mayor of the town and that they had made some kind of mistake. One of the SWAT officers, in speaking to another member of the unit, said he thought the subject who was kneeling in his own living room was crazy. In the meantime, officers were tearing the house apart looking for evidence of the drug trade. Finally, after an hour of this, an officer told Calvo they had intercepted a box of marijuana that had been sent to his house. He assured Calvo that the police had a search warrant and what they were doing was all quite legal.

With his hands bound behind his back, Calvo was led into the kitchen, where he saw Georgia lying face-down on the floor, her hands restrained behind her back and a rifle barrel pointed at her head. Near her body he saw his other dog Chase, lying in a pool of blood. An officer had shot the three-year-old retriever as the terrified dog fled into the kitchen.

Ninety minutes after the intrusion, about the time personnel from an animal control agency hauled away the dead pets, a member of the SWAT team removed Calvo's plastic hand restraints. A narcotics officer informed him that while the white box delivered to his house by the police was enough to arrest him and his wife on drug charges, they would give them both a break as long as they cooperated. When Trinity came home a little after eight, police questioned her in the front yard. Having found no evidence of drug trafficking in the house, the invading officers departed, leaving Mr. Calvo, his shaken mother-in-law, and his distraught wife with a smashed front door, a ransacked house, a dark cloud of suspicion hanging over their heads—and without their beloved pets.

That night, Calvo and his wife cleaned up the blood and tried to put their house back together. An officer from the Berwyn Heights Police Department came by at midnight to help the mayor secure the front door. The next morning, the couple's friends started calling, offering their support and sympathy. The local and national media took an immediate interest in the story. Much to the dismay of the law enforcement agencies involved, this case, unlike most wrong-house raids, was going to become quite newsworthy.

At a news conference held on August 5, 2008, Prince George's County Police Chief Melvin High announced that his officers had arrested two suspects allegedly involved in the interstate scheme to deliver marijuana by shipping packages to unsuspecting homes. The package addressed to the mayor's house in Berwyn Heights was one of six or so parcels intercepted by the authorities in northern Prince George's County. In all, the packages contained 417 pounds of marijuana worth $3.6 million. One of the suspects worked for FedEx.

Chief High and Sheriff Michael Jackson said they would not apologize for the Berwyn Heights raid, which they characterized as legal and responsibly conducted. The sheriff said his SWAT team had been deployed because guns and violence are often associated with drug rings. Chief High, to those assembled at the news conference, said, "In some quarters, this has been viewed as a flawed police operation and an attack on the mayor, which it is not. This was about an address, this was about a name on a package . . . and, in fact, our people did not know this was the home of the mayor and his family until after the fact." When asked by a reporter if the arrests of the FedEx deliveryman and his alleged accomplice had cleared Mayor Calvo and his wife, Chief High said, "From all the indications at the moment, they had an unlikely involvement, but we don't want to draw that definite conclusion at the moment. Most likely, they were innocent victims."[13]

Two days after the police news conference, a spokesperson for the FBI field division office in Baltimore announced that agents would be conducting a civil rights investigation into the Berwyn Heights SWAT raid. Standing in front of his house, surrounded by local politicians and friends, Mayor Calvo told a large media assemblage that "A shadow was cast over our good names. We were harmed by the very people who took an oath to protect us. We have witnessed a frightening law enforcement culture in which the law is disregarded, the rights of innocent occupants are ignored and the rights of innocent animals mean nothing."[14]

On August 8, 2008, Chief of Police Melvin High telephoned Calvo to inform him that Maryland's attorney general had cleared him and his wife of drug trafficking. While the chief didn't apologize for the SWAT raid, he expressed regret over the killing of the dogs. The chief told the mayor that he and Sheriff Jackson did not appreciate the fact the FBI had been called into the case. In an interview published in the *Washington Post*, Sheriff Jackson revealed that his deputies had been briefed on the layout of the house and knew there were dogs inside. The SWAT team had planned to gather at the front door and demand entry but had to break into the house when they heard a woman scream. "At that point, they see you, you don't see them, and you don't know where they are . . . That's dangerous. You really don't have time to deal with that person. You have to secure and go. It is unfortunate that those dogs were killed. That would be the case whether it was the mayor's house or anyone else's house. A loss of life is always unfortunate. That is not our goal."[15]

A month after the Berwyn Heights SWAT raid, Melvin High retired after 5½ years as police chief. Although he had spent most of his law enforcement career in Washington, D.C., before his Prince George's appointment he had been head of the police department in Norfolk, Virginia. He denied that the Calvo raid had anything to do with his decision to retire.

The internal affairs investigators, obviously aware that the killing of the dogs seemed unwarranted and made the SWAT team look like a squad of armed and vicious law enforcement zombies, did their best to make the killings appear justified. According to a preliminary report issued by the sheriff's office, the officer shot Payton because the dog had "engaged" a deputy. The police killed the other pet because it ran toward an officer. These vague justifications, this implausible denial, didn't make sense and didn't ring true. Americans take a lot from the police in the name of law enforcement, but they will not stand for the mindless killing of dogs. And the police know this.

A few days after the police made the September 4 preliminary report public, Calvo released the results of necropsies (animal autopsies) performed by a veterinarian with the Maryland Department of Agriculture. According to the findings of this expert, the police had shot Payton four times, twice in the chest/flank region, once in the jaw, and once in the neck. Chase had been shot twice, one of the bullets striking his chest, and the other his left rear leg, which suggested he'd been running away from the shooter when hit.

In conducting the internal inquiry, the investigators did not interview Mr. Calvo or his mother-in-law. Quoted in the *Washington Post,* Calvo said, "The fact they've done an internal review without contacting the victims of their raid, the people whose house they stormed through, shows they're not very interested in the facts." Calvo, in the piece, called the force used in the raid "unbelievably excessive."[16] The mayor expressed hope that FBI agents would determine why the officers didn't know whose house they were raiding and why they had broken in without having obtained a no-knock search warrant.

Law enforcement officers who feel misunderstood and unappreciated tend to be self-righteous and thin-skinned when it comes to criticism. They don't like admitting their mistakes and are loathe to apologize for anything. They are particularly sensitive to criticism from the media. Kent Corbett, a Milwaukee homicide detective and former SWAT team member, took exception to an article in the September 1, 2008, issue of the *National Review* in which the author was critical of the handling of the Calvo case. In a letter to the editor published on September 29, the detective wrote:

> I have personally been involved in the execution of no-knock search warrants, the killing of dogs during those executions, and the investigations of numerous drug-related homicides and officer-involved shootings. Yes, no-knock warrants are issued to avoid the destruction of evidence such as drugs, but they are also issued to protect the officers executing those warrants. In addition, each warrant requires a judge's authorization, and obviously the available evidence satisfied the judge in this case. [In this case the officer did not apply for a no-knock warrant.]
>
> Sorry if Calvo and his mother-in-law were "restrained" for "almost two hours." Would you rather have them be comfortable for those two hours, and risk officers' lives and safety? Calvo should be able to understand what the officers did and why they did it . . . Drug investigations

are inherently dangerous, and so is the Monday-morning quarterback-
ing you are doing.[17]

The *Washington Post*, on February 1, 2009, published a long article about
the SWAT raid entitled, "Deadly Force." April Witt's feature story, sympathetic to Mayor Calvo and his family, provided dramatic and graphic details
illustrating the violence of the intrusion and the killing of the two dogs. The
following excerpt, told from mother-in-law Georgia Porter's point of view,
contradicts the official account of the shootings:

> Georgia stood trembling in front of the kitchen stove. Payton, who had
> been stretched out in a corner of the living room farthest from the front
> door, his head resting near the threshold to the kitchen "turned toward
> the front door when I turned," Georgia recalled. "He didn't have time
> to do anything else." Almost immediately, men in black ran forward and
> shot Payton in the face," Georgia said. "They kept shooting," she re-
> called. "I don't know how many times they shot Payton because there
> was so much gunfire."
>   Chase, always timid even when there was nothing to fear, did what he
> did best—he ran. He ran away from the men in black, zipped past Geor-
> gia at the stove . . . The screaming, running men followed Chase, shoot-
> ing as he tried escaping into the dining room . . . Georgia watched in
> horror as men in black rushed the dining room from all directions. "I
> could hear Chase whimpering," Georgia said. Then she heard someone
> shoot at Chase again.
>   Men kept yelling at Georgia to get down, but she couldn't budge.
> "Somebody pushed me on the ground, and they put a gun to my head,"
> she said. Face down on the kitchen floor, Georgia felt someone yank her
> hands behind her, rip the spoon away and secure her hands. When she
> lifted her eyes, she could just see Payton's big head resting near the kitchen
> threshold. He wasn't moving.[18]

Mayor Calvo, after doing some research on the subject of SWAT raids and
the militarization of American law enforcement, decided to push for state
legislation requiring police agencies to maintain public records regarding
the number and nature of their SWAT raids. He hoped an informed public
would demand the cessation of no-knock entries in low-risk cases. In February 2009, he visited Annapolis, the state capital, to urge passage of a bill
requiring police agencies in Maryland to submit monthly reports detailing
their SWAT activities. State Senator C. Anthony Muse, in a letter to his legislative colleagues, wrote that the law would "shine some light on paramilitary

police operations that take place in our communities, and perhaps inform the broader worthwhile conversation on this issue."[19] At a news conference that day, Calvo said, "[Law enforcement's] job is to serve and protect. . . . SWAT teams are paramilitary operations. They are trained in military tactics and given military equipment. Collateral damage is part of the deal."[20]

Several victims of recent botched SWAT raids in Maryland, on March 4, 2009, testified before a committee of 11 state senators considering the SWAT bill. Major Sam Billotti with the Washington County Sheriff's Office also appeared before the committee. He apologized to those who had been traumatized by these raids but said he opposed the bill because "all it's going to do is collect numbers."[21] After the hearing, Calvo, in speaking to a gathering of reporters, said, "Reporting alone is not going to address the issue. It needs to be coupled with additional efforts. But without good data and oversight, we won't be able to understand the patterns and problems. As a result, we won't have that information at hand when we try to craft better police policy."[22] This was what the law enforcement community really feared, the crafting of "better police policy."

That month, the Maryland legislature passed the SWAT reporting bill. Calvo, in a press release a few days later, responded to the new legislation this way:

> Although the botched raid of my home and killing of our dogs, Payton and Chase, have received considerable attention in the media, it is important to underscore that this bill is about much more than an isolated, high-profile mistake. It is about a growing and troubling trend where law enforcement agencies are using SWAT teams to perform ordinary police work. Prince George's County police acknowledge deploying SWAT teams between 400 and 700 a year— that's twice a day—and other counties in the state have said that they also deploy their special tactical units hundreds of times a year . . . Although I applaud lawmakers for passing this bill over the objections of law enforcement, I was disappointed that state law enforcement groups decided to oppose this measure rather than embrace it as an opportunity to restore the public trust. I remain especially concerned with the argument put forward that only law enforcement should police itself, and that it is somehow inappropriate for elected leaders to legislate oversight and accountability.[23]

The police don't like to be policed. They never have and never will. In the late 1950s, law enforcement agencies across the country fought hard against the imposition of civilian review boards. A common feeling among police officers is that civilians don't know what it's really like to be on the front line in the war on crime. As a result, attempts by outsiders to impose rules and restrictions on the police will be misguided and counterproductive. And when these arguments fail to convince, police administrators play the officer safety card. Calvo has learned that nothing in government is more difficult to achieve than police reform.

The internal affairs investigators finished their review of the Berwyn Heights SWAT raid, and in June 2009, Sheriff Michael Jackson held a news conference to announce the findings. Although the results didn't surprise anyone—no wrongdoing on the part of the Prince George's County's narcotics officers and SWAT team members—the sheriff's arrogance and lack of perspective did. Jackson told those gathered at the news conference the findings were "consistent with what I've felt all along. My deputies did their jobs to the fullest extent of their abilities . . . I'm sorry for the loss of their family pets. But this is the unfortunate results of the scourge of drugs in our community. Lost in this whole incident was the criminal element . . . In the sense that we kept these drugs from reaching our streets, this operation was a success."[24]

Proving once again that government officials often seem incapable of learning from their mistakes, the sheriff obviously didn't realize that police militarism, botched SWAT raids, and traumatized citizens were the unfortunate results of the "scourge of drugs in our community." Mayor Calvo, responding to what he considered a whitewash, said, "It's outrageous. Not only is he not admitting any wrongdoing, he's saying this went down the way it was supposed to and he's actually commending his police officers for what they did."[25] Mayor Calvo was right to condemn Jackson's endorsement of his deputies in this instance, but because sheriffs and chiefs of police believe they can't survive without the full support of the rank-and-file force, they tend to be weak leaders. As a result, when it comes to reform, most of them are more talk than action.

Mayor Calvo, on June 22, 2009, filed a lawsuit in Prince George's County Circuit Court against the state of Maryland and the local sheriff's office. Claiming that the defendants, whom he characterized as members of a "rogue, paramilitary culture" within the sheriff's department, had acted "intentionally, with an evil and rancorous and improper motive, will ill will and actual malice,"[26] sought damages and a court order forcing the county to revise how law enforcement agencies executed their search and arrest warrants. Speaking to reporters at his news conference, Calvo said, "We had hoped the sheriff's office and county police department could exercise internal leadership to acknowledge wrongdoing and make these changes on their own. But their comments and actions over the last year make clear they lack the will and credibility to do so."[27] In March 2010, a local judge denied state and county motions to deny the lawsuit.

Michael Jackson, the unapologetic sheriff of Prince George's County who had been in office seven years, felt confident enough in his law enforcement record to run for higher office in 2010. Apparently convinced that the highly publicized SWAT raid of the Calvo home did not reflect poorly on his department and himself, he felt qualified to become the chief executive of Prince George's county.

The *Baltimore Sun,* pursuant to a public information act request to the Maryland Governor's Office of Crime Control and Prevention, discovered in February 2010 that in the previous six months of 2009, Prince George's County Police made more SWAT raids—an average of more than one a day—than any other police agency in the state. Statewide during that period, the police launched 804 SWAT raids, or 4.5 such deployments per day. Ninety-four percent of these raids involved the serving of warrants in drug cases. Mayor Calvo, in response to these revelations, said this to a *Baltimore Sun* reporter: "There are too many people in Prince George's County employed solely to dress up in military gear and kick in doors. How is this an efficient use of resources? They are creating situations where bad things can happen. Most of the time, things go fine, but sometimes the trigger goes off. Sometimes things go terribly wrong."

Keep Your Dogs out of Maryland

Two weeks before the *Washington Post* published April Witt's story of the Berwyn Heights raid, someone broke into a pair of marked police cars in Howard County, Maryland. The thief stole a Sig Sauer rifle, three ammunition magazines, a bag full of police gear, and a police field manual. Suspecting that 21-year-old Michael Leon Smith possessed the loot at his Elkridge, Maryland, home, officers with the Howard County Police Department obtained a no-knock warrant to search the dwelling. Elkridge is a town of 22,000 located a few miles west of the Baltimore–Washington International Airport. In the early evening of January 15, 2009, officers with the Howard County Police Department's SWAT unit raided Michael Smith's house. They came up empty.

Operating on the chance that Smith had stashed the stolen goods at his stepfather's house on the 6600 block of Deep Run Parkway in Elkridge, an officer acquired another no-knock warrant for that place. Smith's stepfather, 39-year-old Mike Hasenei, a computer analyst with Marriott International, had never been in trouble with the law. He lived on Deep Run Parkway with his wife, Phyllis, and their 12-year-old daughter. The police either didn't know or didn't care that Michael Smith hadn't lived in his stepfather's house for three years.

At 9 P.M. on January 15, a few hours after the Howard County Police Department's SWAT team had raided Michael Smith's residence, 25 men in black ninja outfits stormed his stepfather's house. Awakened by the sounds of his front door being bashed in, Hasenei jumped out of bed and ran into his living room, where his wife and daughter lay face-down on the carpet, guns trained on their heads. The next thing he knew, the police had him on the floor in handcuffs. When Hasenei asked what was going on, an officer informed him that they were all under arrest. The family pets, an Australian cattle dog and a smaller mixed breed, had fled to Hasenei's bedroom. As a SWAT officer entered the daughter's room by kicking her door off its hinges, another officer followed the pets into her father's room. This officer fired three shots at the Australian cattle dog, two of the bullets hitting the animal as it cowered on the bed. The third slug went into the mattress. The other dog, hiding under the bed, escaped being shot.

Mr. Hasenei kept asking the officers what they were looking for, and they kept telling him to shut up. Finally, once the police realized the stolen items were not in the house, someone mentioned the patrol car thefts. Before leaving the ransacked home, the two broken doors, and the dead dog, an officer assured the badly shaken Hasenei family that the raid, based upon a valid judge-issued no-knock warrant, had been perfectly legal. The police, therefore, had absolutely nothing to apologize for.

The Hasenei wrong-house SWAT raid didn't receive much media attention until after the publication of April Witt's story about the Berwyn Heights fiasco. Hasenei, in speaking to a reporter with the *Howard County Times* two weeks after the home intrusion and killing of the family pet, said, "They looked through everything. They didn't find a single thing. I knew they wouldn't because we don't commit crimes."[28] Hasenei told this reporter he had filed an official complaint with the Howard County Police Department and had spoken to a lawyer about a possible lawsuit. A police spokesperson, other than to say the matter was under internal investigation, refused to respond to Mr. Hasenei's complaint.

Gwinnett County Malfeasance

In Gwinnett County, Georgia, a suburban community of 700,000 within the Atlanta metropolitan area, narcotics officers had been watching a house in Lawrenceville for three months. Members of the county police department's Special Investigations Section suspected that the man living at 2934 Valley Spring Drive was selling methamphetamine. At 9:15 A.M. on December 9, 2008, a total of 20 officers with the department's 60-member SWAT unit began making final preparations for the no-knock raid. Thirty minutes later, after a detective with the Special Investigations Section pointed out the meth suspect's house, the SWAT team moved in on the target. The officers didn't know it, but the detective had sent them to the wrong house. The suspected drug dealer lived a few places down the street.

The day after the raid, John Louis, the 38-year-old whose house the police wrongfully entered, described the intrusion to a local television reporter: "They came in here and put guns on us. The house was full of police. I never had a gun in my face before. I've never even held a gun . . . All I see is a bunch of police, you know, guns drawn, yelling, 'Hands in the air! Hands in the air!'"[29]

When the SWAT officers broke open the front door, Heather James, John Louis's girlfriend who had been asleep with their three-month-old baby, stepped out of the bedroom in her nightgown. Police ordered her to the floor at gunpoint. The couple asked the police what they wanted and were told to shut up and remain still. The raid came to an abrupt halt when one of the officers, seeing the baby, realized they had broken into the wrong place. As the SWAT unit decamped to raid the suspect's house, one of the officers apologized for the intrusion and promised to have the front door fixed.

In an interview with a TV correspondent the next day, a Gwinnett Police Department spokesperson pointed out that the narcotics officers had been watching the meth suspect's house for three months. In response to this, John Louis said, "If you had this house under surveillance for three months, why did you come here? You broke in and put all our lives in danger, and all you can say is you're sorry?" In explaining what went wrong, the police spokesperson said, "Somehow there was an investigator that had been working closely with the case that . . . mistakenly pointed out the wrong house, the wrong location." When asked if the police department had any kind of policy regarding no-knock raids, the police representative replied, "We double check the address, there's a description of the location as well as an address of the house that we're looking at on the search warrant, and we always have someone double check that every time."[30]

On December 12, 2008, three days after the raid, the commander of the Special Investigations Section, in a news release, announced that the detective who had directed the SWAT team to the wrong house had been transferred to the uniform division. Without identifying this officer, the commander characterized the incident as "a case of human error and not deliberate malfeasance on the part of the investigator."

The dust had just started to settle on this wrong-house fiasco when, a week later, Gwinnett County police officers burst into the wrong garage to arrest a material witness in a street gang trial. Instead of taking someone into custody, they shot a two-year-old Dalmatian. The wounded dog ran off but turned up the next day at a neighbor's house. The pet survived, but its owners were not pleased, nor were they reassured by the fact this malfeasance had not been deliberate.

As long as the war on drugs rages on and officer safety trumps all other considerations, SWAT teams will be deployed in low-risk situations. Non-violent criminal suspects and innocent people will continue to be terrorized, injured, and in some cases, killed.

Chapter 8

UNJUSTIFIABLE HOMICIDE: AVOIDABLE DRUG-RAID FATALITIES

No one in their right mind would argue that no-knock SWAT raids, particularly of homes, don't put lives at risk. Because these raids are so hair-trigger sensitive and dangerous, they should be measures of last resort. In modern law enforcement, however, they are not. Police agencies large and small routinely employ paramilitary units to execute search warrants in minor drug cases. Most of the time the people targeted in these raids are unarmed. If there are guns in the house, the people most in danger are the occupants who think they are being invaded by criminals and try to defend themselves. Rather than finding alternative, less dangerous methods, such as arresting drug suspects outside their homes and then searching through their possessions under safer conditions, the police have gotten into the habit of going straight to the use of overwhelming, militaristic force. As a result, citizens are being killed needlessly.

The following nine cases involve drug suspects shot to death by members of paramilitary units in raids conducted during the period 2005 through 2008. These incidents feature local police, seizures of relatively small amounts of drugs, and questions regarding the civil and criminal justifications for the use of deadly force. None of the shootings in these cases resulted in the indictments of any of the officers directly responsible for the deaths of these citizens. In the opinions of many, all of these fatalities could have been avoided without sacrificing law and order.

LICENSE TO KILL IN BALTIMORE COUNTY

While searching trash cans behind row houses on Del Haven Road in Dundalk, a suburban community southeast of Baltimore, narcotics officers with the county police department found traces of drugs and drug paraphernalia from the dwelling occupied by Charles Noel, his wife, Cheryl, and their 23-year-old son, Matthew. Armed with evidence of drug use at 8192 Del Haven Road, the officer in charge of the case asked a magistrate for a no-knock search warrant. Although this appeared to be a rather ordinary, small-potatoes drug case, the judge issued the warrant because all three suspects had criminal histories and possessed lawfully registered handguns. This meant that for purposes of officer safety, the raiding party needed the element of surprise, which would require the deployment of the Baltimore County Police Department's SWAT team. Although that might have been advantageous for the officers involved, this operation was to put the suspects' lives in peril over a trifling drug case.

Charles Noel, a 55-year-old employee of the wastewater division at Fort Meade, had been convicted in 1973 of second-degree murder. His wife, Cheryl Lynn, a water technician at the Back River waste water treatment plant, had a pending (but unspecified) criminal complaint against her. Their son, Matthew, a month earlier, had been charged with attempted murder for allegedly shooting a man in the foot.

On January 21, 2005, at 4:30 A.M., camouflaged SWAT team members carrying ballistic shields and a battering ram took down the front door amid flashbang grenade explosions. Four of the SWAT officers advanced up the stairs to the master bedroom. Cheryl Lynn, thinking that her home was being invaded by criminals, grabbed her .357 revolver and was holding it at her side (according to Charles) as the officers kicked open the door and entered the room. Officer Carlos Artson, seeing the gun, fired two shots at Cheryl. She slumped to the floor at the foot of the bed. Officer Artson ordered the wounded woman to move away from the handgun, which had fallen onto the bed. When she didn't respond, he fired a third shot, hitting the 44-year-old in the chest and killing her on the spot. (According to the police version of the shooting, Artson fired the third shot when Cheryl moved toward her gun.)

The authorities charged Charles and Matthew with drug possession. A few weeks after the raid, the Baltimore County state's attorney's office, following an internal inquiry, cleared officer Artson and the SWAT team of wrongdoing and classified the fatal shooting as a justifiable homicide.

Members of the Noel family, in August 2006, filed a federal wrongful death lawsuit against Baltimore County, officer Artson, and three other members of the SWAT team. According to the plaintiffs, officer Artson had "made an unreasonable seizure of the person of Cheryl Lynn Noel by shooting and killing her, violating her rights under the Fourth and Fourteenth Amendments to the United States Constitution."[1] In the complaint, attorney Terrell Roberts III wrote, "The use of a SWAT team to execute a routine drug warrant was excessive and overkill. The woman never knew the police had entered her home. She was doing everything that could be expected of a law-abiding citizen to protect her own life. She was shot and killed without any warning that the police were present or to drop her gun." Alleging that Cheryl Lynn Noel, when the officers burst into her bedroom, was not pointing her gun at them, the attorney wrote, "Clearly, a third shot was wholly unnecessary and grossly excessive."[2]

The wrongful death trial got under way in March 2009, almost four years after Cheryl Lynn Noel's death. In his opening statement to the jury, Attorney Roberts said, "If the police had knocked-and-announced, this never would have happened. They were not going after Osama bin Laden . . . Cheryl Lynn Noel didn't have fair warning that her home was being invaded."[3]

Paul M. Mayhew, an assistant Baltimore County Attorney, represented the defendants. In his address to the jury, he said the SWAT team in the Noel case had followed departmental protocol. "We do the same thing every time," he said. "We tell the people [the targets of the raids] who we are and hope they listen to us . . . We do not apologize for one minute."[4] Two weeks later, the jurors found Baltimore County, officer Artson, and the three other SWAT officers not liable for Cheryl Lynn Noel's death. The plaintiffs and their supporters were shocked and devastated. In speaking to the media following the verdict, attorney Roberts, referring to no-knock SWAT raids, said, "There's no margin for error here. It really should be examined closely whether a SWAT team ought to be used in cases like this. This was more of a military raid than it was a police execution of a search warrant."[5]

EXCITABLE AND CONFRONTATIONAL IN PINELLAS COUNTY

After graduating from high school in 1991, Christopher Taylor served briefly in the Air Force, tended bar at Red Lobster, and worked as a fitness trainer. In 1996, he left Maryland for St. Petersburg, Florida, where he became a civilian paramedic attached to the Pinellas County SWAT team. Two years later, Sheriff Jim Coats hired the 26-year-old as a deputy and kept him on the SWAT team, but now as a gun-carrying member.

While on routine patrol in May 2000, deputy Taylor shot a man in Seminole, Florida. The nonfatal incident occurred on the parking lot of a Home Depot store, where the man allegedly had interfered with a shoplifting arrest. An internal review of the shooting cleared Taylor of wrongdoing. Four years later, Taylor and another deputy fired their guns at a truck driver who had snagged a sheriff's patrol car under his boat trailer. The civilian wasn't hit, and an intra-agency investigation proclaimed that shooting justified.

Although Deputy Taylor's supervisors considered him, overall, an above average law enforcement officer, one of his bosses recognized what he considered a dangerous flaw in his personality. According to this supervisor, when suspects do not quickly obey Taylor's orders, he "sometimes becomes excitable and confrontational."[6] This police administrator worried that Taylor's propensity to overreact under these circumstances might lead to trouble and that Taylor "may react without thinking through optional avenues of action or interview techniques which could produce his desired goals." In other words, Deputy Taylor, under the right circumstances, might shoot first and ask questions later. Despite this supervisor's expressed concerns and the fact that Taylor had been involved in two shooting incidents, Sheriff Coats did not remove him from the Pinellas County SWAT team.

On April 12, 2005, following a two-month narcotics investigation of suspected drug dealing out of a house on 16th Avenue South in St. Petersburg, the Pinellas County SWAT team launched a no-knock raid. Nineteen-year-old Jarrell Walker, his cousin Dorian Williams, and Walker's three-month-old son, Kamau, were in the dwelling as the eight-man SWAT unit, led by Deputy Taylor, broke through the door behind the flashbang explosion. Taylor encountered Jarrell Walker in the living room and ordered him to the floor. Unarmed, Walker complied, but as he lay on the carpet, Taylor, at a range of between two and three feet, shot him twice in the back with his Glock pistol. Walker died shortly thereafter.

In justifying his use of deadly force, Deputy Taylor said he thought the subject was reaching for a gun that was hidden under a nearby sofa. Police officers recovered a loaded 9-mm handgun from the house, but they didn't find it under the couch or within Walker's reach. Sheriff Coats placed Taylor on paid administrative leave and promised an internal investigation into the shooting. The FBI announced that it would conduct an investigation into the matter.

A few weeks later, after the Pinellas County investigators concluded that the fatal shooting had been justified, Sheriff Coats, perhaps worried that this could happen again, took Deputy Taylor off the SWAT team. Bernie McCabe, the state's attorney for Pinellas–Pasco Counties, while deciding not to charge Taylor with criminal homicide, lamented that another "young black male [had] met his death at the hands of law enforcement in Pinellas County."[7] In November 2006, the FBI, having completed its civil rights investigation, found that the deputy had not committed a federal crime. After a sheriff's review board spokesperson recommended a higher threshold in the use of deadly force, Sheriff Coats promised to study his office's policy regarding the use of deadly force. Nothing came of this promise. Jarrell Walker's mother, on April 2, 2007, filed a civil rights suit in the U.S. District Court in Tampa against Sheriff Coats and the SWAT officer who had killed her son.

The fact that an unarmed man can be shot in the back without consequences for the officer involved reveals how easy it has become to justify a police killing legally. Based upon the standard of acceptable deadly force in the Jarrell Walker case, law enforcement officers have a license to kill, particularly in the course of conducting no-knock SWAT raids.

THE PREDAWN RAID IN SUNRISE, FLORIDA

In Florida, where the war on drugs is intense, militarized law enforcement flourishes. There's no area within the state that is not covered by layers of federal, state, county, and regional narcotics enforcement agencies, each crime-fighting body with its own paramilitary muscle. Florida's lawmakers, by regularly increasing penalties for marijuana possession, have contributed to the drug enforcement frenzy. In 2008, the legislature mandated prison time for marijuana growers possessing more than 25 plants. If children live in the grow house, the violator can be sent away for up to 30 years. Roger Scott, an Orlando attorney and marijuana legalization advocate, has pointed out that in Florida, violent prisoners are being released early to make room for pot growers. With all the narcotics enforcement activity in the state and the guns on both sides of the struggle, the drug war in Florida, as in so many other places, has become a shooting war. During a four-day stretch in August 2005, narcotics officers in three south Florida jurisdictions killed three men, including 23-year-old Anthony Diotaiuto.

Diotaiuto and his mother, Marlene Whittier, lived in a house in a quiet neighborhood in Sunrise, a place once called Sunrise Golfing Village. Located in Broward County not far from Fort Lauderdale, the town of 90,000 had its own SWAT team. Anthony was a bartender at the Carolina Ale House in Weston; on the weekends he worked as a D.J. He got off work from his bartender job at 3 A.M., and because he didn't feel safe arriving home at that hour, had a permit to carry a concealed handgun. In south Florida, this was not unusual. Anthony also kept a shotgun in the house for personal safety against intruders.

Acting on a tip that Anthony sold marijuana and cocaine out of his mother's house on the 8500 block of Northwest 21st Street Court, narcotics officers with the Sunrise Police Department watched the house for two months. During this period, an undercover narcotics officer made one controlled buy. Based upon this evidence, a magistrate issued a search warrant. At 6:15 A.M. on Friday, August 5, 2005, a couple of hours after Anthony had come home from his bartending job, the Sunrise SWAT team, led by officer Daniel Kobayashi, knocked on his front door, tossed a flashbang grenade through a window, and then forced their way into the house. (Because the police have not released their reports on this raid, what happened next is a bit sketchy.) According to a police spokesperson, two people—Officer Sean Visners, a six-year SWAT veteran, and his partner Andre Bruna, a four-year member of the unit—encountered Anthony in the living room. They yelled "Freeze!" and "Get to the ground!" Instead of complying with these conflicting orders, Anthony ran into his bedroom. Officers followed him there and shot him ten times. Broward County's medical examiner, Dr. Joshua Perper, revealed to the media that Anthony had been shot in the head, chest, torso, arms, and legs. A search of the house produced two ounces of marijuana, a scale, and packaging materials. Neither of the officers who fired at Anthony Diotaiuto had shot anyone in the past.

A group of Anthony's friends and relatives gathered in protest outside his house that afternoon. Some of the protesters expressed disbelief that he had been selling drugs. One friend speculated that Anthony had panicked when the SWAT officers broke into the house.

Lieutenant Robert Voss, a Sunrise police spokesman, told a reporter with the *Fort Lauderdale Sun-Sentinel* that Anthony's concealed weapons permit had been a "major factor" in the decision to deploy the SWAT team. "He had a gun and he pointed it at our officers. Our SWAT team fired," the lieutenant said. Later that day, Lieutenant Voss modified his earlier statement regarding the pointed gun: "In all likelihood," he said, "that is what happened. I know there was a weapon found next to his body . . . The potential for violence was there." The lieutenant informed the reporter that when no one answers the door when the SWAT team knocks, the door goes down. "Unfortunately, this was one of those [raids] that's gone bad,"[8] he said.

On August 9, four days after the killing, 15 of Anthony Diotaiuto's friends and relatives showed up at a city commissioner's meeting demanding to know why the Sunrise Police Department, in such a minor narcotics case, had conducted a SWAT raid. Why hadn't narcotics officers simply arrested Anthony before he entered his house that morning? He had no police record, no history of violence. No wonder so many people were being killed by the police. The protestors left the meeting that night without receiving a satisfactory explanation of Anthony Diotaiuto's death.

Official inquiries into the fatal shooting by the Sunrise Police Department, the Broward County State's Attorney's office, and the FBI absolved the SWAT officers of using excessive force. A Broward County grand jury voted not to indict officers Visners and Bruna for criminal homicide. In

January, Anthony Diotaiuto's mother, after the police department refused to release documents pertaining to the raid, the shooting, and matters related to SWAT training, deployment policy, and tactical guidelines, sued the city for withholding information that should be open to the public. In defending the police department, the city attorney argued that the public had no right to view these documents. A judge agreed. Frustrated by what she considered official stonewalling on the issue of her son's killing, Marlene Whittier, in March 2007, filed a civil rights case against the city, the chief of police, and members of the Sunrise SWAT team.

A federal district judge dismissed the suit against the city, the chief of police, and the officers involved in the shooting. On September 1, 2009, the Federal Court of Appeals sitting in Atlanta, on the issue of whether officer Daniel Kobayashi had violated Diotaiuto's Fourth Amendment rights by failing to announce the SWAT team's presence before the entry, held that because the defendant had acted reasonably, he was protected from civil liability under the doctrine of qualified immunity.

JUSTIFIED KILLING, UNJUSTIFIED RAID

Cheryl Ann Stillwell lived alone in a cottage on Amelia Island in the Atlantic off the Florida coast near Jacksonville. The 41-year-old computer engineer had been prescribed OxyContin for pain relief. Concerned about the illegal drug activity in her neighborhood, she had purchased a 9-mm pistol for protection. Cheryl Ann had tried, but failed to entice police officers to move into two houses she owned by offering rental discounts. A private, almost reclusive person, Stillwell lived in fear of home invaders.

A narcotics officer with the Nassau County Sheriff's Office, acting on the word of an anonymous snitch who said he had purchased an unknown quantity of OxyContin from an "unknown white female" who lived in a white cottage on Midway Road, acquired a warrant to search Stillwell's dwelling. The officer had no idea who lived there, if the place was the site of drug trafficking activity, or if the person or persons living there was or were dangerous. And the deputy didn't bother to obtain any of this vital preraid information. This narcotics officer, in possession of nothing close to the amount of evidence constitutionally required for the search of a home, had found a rubber-stamp magistrate who had issued the warrant. Cheryl Ann Stillwell, completely innocent of drug trafficking, didn't know it, but her worst home invasion fears were about to come true.

At 5:15 A.M. on December 22, 2005, Nassau County deputies in full battle dress, armed with semiautomatic rifles and a week-old, baseless search warrant that listed a description of a house rather than an address and that contained no information regarding the occupant or occupants of the

place to be raided, approached the white cottage on Midway Road. An officer knocked on the front door but bashed it in before anyone inside had time
to open it. Deputy Dallas Palecek, on the force four years, charged into the
cottage, and with his Heckler & Koch UMP-40 submachine gun, shot Cheryl
Stillwell in the right leg, chest, and face. Flown by emergency helicopter to a
hospital in Jacksonville, she died 3½ hours later.

According to the sheriff's office's inventory of the items taken from Stillwell's home, searchers found an unspecified number of unidentified pill bot-
tles, and some empty blister packs. No actual drugs, legal or otherwise, were
listed in the document. The ill-conceived, legally deficient raid had achieved
nothing, and at the expense of a human life.

At a press conference the next day in Jacksonville, Nassau County Sheriff
Tommy Seagraves identified Dallas Palecek as the deputy who had shot
and killed Cheryl Ann Stillwell. While investigations into the incident were
under way, Palecek would remain on paid administrative leave. The deputy
had shot the woman, Seagraves said, after he "encountered gunfire"[9] inside
the house. The intrusion into Stillwell's cottage had been one of three unrelated drug raids that morning on the island.

At news conferences following drug raids, sheriffs and chiefs of police
like to stand behind tables laden with piles of drugs, stacks of cash, and rows
of automatic weapons. In this case, Sheriff Seagraves didn't display any evidence, and he refused to say if his men had found illegal drugs in the dead
woman's possession. He did say, however, that they had raided the place
after a confidential informant (an anonymous tipster), reported that he had
purchased OxyContin from the person who lived in the white cottage. When
asked how many officers had been involved in the raid and where in the
house Stillwell had been shot, the sheriff had no information for the media.

A ballistics analysis at the shooting site by a forensic firearms identification expert revealed that Cheryl Ann had fired her 9-mm pistol *after* deputy Palecek shot her. This caused Sheriff Seagraves to modify his account of
the confrontation by stating that his deputy had killed the woman because
she had *pointed* a gun at him. Officer Palecek, according to the sheriff, had
fired his H&K submachine gun when he saw Stillwell's trigger-finger twitch.

In April 2006, Nassau County State's Attorney Granville Burgess announced that based upon investigations by the FBI, the Florida Department
of Law Enforcement, and his office, Deputy Palecek's killing of Cheryl Stillwell constituted justifiable homicide. However, in a March 14 memorandum in which Burgess analyzes the circumstances surrounding her death,
he questions the rationale behind using SWAT measures in this case and
wonders why the police hadn't bothered to identify the resident of the cottage. Noting that Stillwell was not a drug dealer, Burgess wrote, "If they had
[acquired] background information I am sure they would have approached

[the search] differently."[10] Since the cottage was dark when the deputy entered, Burgess questioned how officer Palecek had seen Stillwell's finger twitch on the trigger. The FBI also criticized the handling of the case, implying that the sheriff's office had unwittingly set up Stillwell for death.

David Hunt, a reporter with the *Florida Times Union,* wrote a story on the case published on November 5, 2006. In that piece, Hunt quoted Stillwell's brother, J. Doyle Wright, as follows: "It was two [OxyContin] pills she gave to somebody. Somebody told her that they couldn't get their prescription filled for a couple of days and, when they did, they'd give the pills back. They [the police] knew she was protective [of her home] and they knew she had a gun, but somehow the sheriff's office said, 'Okay, send in the SWAT team and shoot to kill.'"[11] David Hunt also interviewed Sheriff Seagraves, who said, "I didn't want to see this happen, but I didn't want to see my officers get shot, either. That lady pointed a loaded gun at them. I'm a human being. I didn't want anybody to lose their life, but at the same time, we had a job to do."[12]

One could argue that if the police in this case had performed "the job they had to do" a little better, Cheryl Ann Stillwell would not have been killed.

THE PREDAWN RAID ON SUNSET STREET

The sun hadn't come up that Tuesday morning, February 13, 2007, when combat-ready police officers from three agencies gathered in front of the Castillo home on Sunset Street in Wharton, Texas. Wharton is a town of 10,000 not far from Houston. The raiding party, consisting of officers with the police department's Emergency Response Team (ERT), the sheriff's Tactical and Raid unit (STAR), and the Wharton County District Attorney's Narcotics Force, had gathered to execute a search warrant based upon an informant's report of seeing 17-year-old Daniel Castillo, Jr., sell cocaine and marijuana out of the house he shared with his parents, his sister, and her one-year-old child. Although the narcotics officer who had watched the place had seen a lot of people coming and going out of the dwelling, he had not engineered an undercover drug buy to verify the snitch's information.

Daniel shared a bedroom with his 21-year-old sister, Ashley, and her one-year-old baby. According to her account of what happened that morning, she had been awakened by the sounds of people breaking into the house. When the officers burst into the bedroom, Ashley met them holding the child in her arms. "Please don't shoot the baby!" she screamed. That woke up Daniel, who was shot in the face as he rose out of bed. The police officer who killed him then turned his gun on Ashley.

The next day, 100 protestors gathered outside the Wharton Police Station. At this point there had been no word about the incident from the chief of police or from the district attorney's office. Mr. Castillo, in the meantime, was telling newspaper and television reporters that his son was not a drug dealer. According to Castillo, his son had no criminal record and had been unarmed when the police shot him. Mr. Castillo had already asked the FBI to investigate the killing. That night, friends and relatives held a candlelight vigil in the young man's honor.

District Attorney Josh McCown, on Thursday, February 15, publicly identified the shooter as Wharton police sergeant Don Falks, who had joined the department six years earlier without previous law enforcement experience. Although he would not release details of the raid and fatal shooting, McCown said the police had recovered drugs from the Castillo house. Because the matter was being investigated by the Texas Ranger's Office, documents pertaining to the case would not be released to the media. The following day, in response to accusations of a news blackout, a police spokesperson reported that searchers had found $5,000 worth of crack and marijuana on the premises. (A friend of the family would claim the drugs were found in a car parked at the house that didn't belong to young Daniel.) The police spokesperson also revealed that officers had arrested the boy's uncle that morning and had charged him with possession of drug paraphernalia.

On March 15, 2007, a month after the deadly raid, a Wharton County grand jury, in the process of determining if Sergeant Falks should be charged with criminal homicide, heard the testimony of Angela Castillo, Officer Falks, the Texas Ranger assigned to the investigation, and a Texas Department of Public Safety expert on the use of police force.

In summarizing to the grand jurors the police version of what happened that morning, District Attorney McCown said, "He [Daniel Castillo] went into a defensive position and then an offensive posture. He was not asleep or just waking up when the officer entered the room. Officer Falks, in his statement, said Castillo reached into the waist of his pants and pulled a black object from his waistband. He [Falks] assumed it was actually a gun."[13]

That black object, found on the floor of a closet near the body, was a small knife. According to Officer Falk's testimony, Castillo had punched him in the nose and was about to attack him with the blade when he fired his gun in self-defense. Castillo dropped the knife, and it rolled under the closet door. Blood spatter patterns at the scene supported this account of what happened. Moreover, DNA and trace fiber analysis linked the knife to Daniel Castillo. Presented with this testimony, and the district attorney's version of the shooting, the grand jurors voted not to indict Sergeant Falks.

The family, disappointed with the grand jury verdict, filed suit in federal court, charging the police department, Sergeant Falk, and others with violating Daniel Castillo's civil rights. This case, viewed in the light most favorable to the police, begs the question of proportionality. Was the potential drug violation serious enough to warrant an armed invasion of a house occupied by the suspect's innocent parents, sister, and her one-year-old child? Was it worth the life of Daniel Castillo, Jr.?

ONE KILLING: TWO STORIES

On April 4, 2008, two SWAT team officers with the Denver Police Department shot and killed 26-year-old Nathan Aguillard. They shot him in his 600-square-foot apartment in a housing complex on the 4700 block of Peoria Street in Denver. What follows is the official version of the events leading up to and during the drug raid.

Toward the end of March, Aguillard's neighbors, suspecting drug dealing, complained to the police about all the people who came to his apartment, stayed briefly at the front door, then left. A narcotics officer spoke to a confidential informant who said Aguillard sold crack cocaine out of his place, and a police surveillance of the complex confirmed the foot traffic to and from his door. According to the snitch, Aguillard carried a firearm in his waistband, information backed up by a March 20 traffic stop in which the patrol officer had seen a handgun on the front seat of Aguillard's 1992 Jaguar. The officer didn't seize the weapon or take Aguillard into custody on a firearms charge. (It's not clear if the police, at this time, had Aguillard under investigation for drugs.) On April 12, four members of Denver's Street Crime Attack Team (SCAT) took up positions around Aguillard's apartment while a fifth SCAT officer approached the door to make an undercover buy. Following a $50 purchase of crack that went off without incident, the specialized paramilitary unit—created to combat street gang activity and major drug trafficking—left the scene without further action. The next day, a narcotics officer acquired an "immediate entry" (no-knock) warrant to search Aguillard's apartment for drugs.[14]

On April 4, 2008, at 10 A.M., officers with the Denver Metro SWAT and SCAT as well as Emergency Medical Services (EMS) personnel gathered for a preraid briefing. Thirty minutes later, a van transported the combat-equipped officers to the apartment complex. At 11 A.M., a SWAT officer hit the door to apartment 1–107 twice with a battering ram. As it flung open, another member of the raiding party rolled in a flashbang grenade. As two other officers rushed into the apartment behind the explosion, they yelled, "Police! Police! Police!"

Inside the smoked-fogged apartment, SWAT officers Thomas McKibben and Donald Fox, both 21-year veterans of the Metro SWAT team, opened a door and burst into Aguillard's bedroom shouting, "Police! Police! Police!" They spotted the subject standing against the far wall between his bed and dresser with his arms hanging at his sides. He stood at an angle that prevented the officers from seeing his right hand. "Show me your hands!" ordered one of the officers. Aguillard squared himself and raised a pistol with his right hand. McKibben fired his weapon, hitting Aguillard in the chest. Officer Fox's bullet struck him between the eyes. The dying man dropped his gun and collapsed. EMS officers came into the room three minutes later and worked over the fallen man until an ambulance crew rushed him to a Denver hospital. At 11:15 A.M., doctors pronounced Aguillard dead.

In the apartment, police searchers found three loaded handguns: the .25-caliber Lorcin pistol Aguillard had pointed at officers McKibbens and Fox, a .45-caliber semiautomatic firearm recovered from beneath the bedroom dresser, and a chrome five-shot .32-caliber pistol found lying on the kitchen counter. The police also discovered several boxes of ammunition, a 10-inch survival knife, and an army surplus bayonet. In terms of illegal drugs, the search results were a little less dramatic. Aguillard had been caught with four bags of crack cocaine and a marijuana pipe.

Immediately following Aguillard's sudden and violent death, several investigative bodies—the Denver Police Department's homicide unit, the Internal Affairs Bureau, the Use of Force Review Board, the local district attorney's office, and the Department of Safety for the City and County of Denver—launched inquiries into the killing. City homicide detectives spoke to Nina Aguillard, the dead man's 33-year-old sister who, according to the police report, portrayed her brother as a mentally unstable, uncontrollable person who could fly off the handle at the slightest provocation and become violent. At the time of his death, her brother had been too mentally unbalanced to hold down a job. Although Nina had no knowledge of drug dealing on his part, she didn't know how he paid his rent or otherwise supported himself.

On April 22, 2008, District Attorney Mitchell Morrissey announced that based upon the results of the various investigations into Aguillard's death, criminal charges would not be filed against officers Fox and McKibben. In October, the Department of Safety for the City and County of Denver released a lengthy report that supported the exoneration of the SWAT officers. According to these findings, the police officers had killed Aguillard in self-defense. As far as the authorities in Denver were concerned, this case was closed.

Pursuant to the narrative created by the authorities in Denver, Nathan Aguillard was an armed and dangerous crack cocaine dealer who had been shot and killed while pointing a loaded pistol at SWAT officers executing a lawful search warrant. Aguillard's friends and relatives, however, considered his death a good example of police overaggressiveness and excessive force. According to this interpretation of his death, Aguillard's severe mental disability had rendered him too fearful of people to engage in drug dealing or any other form of commerce in which he would have had to interact with the public. This aspect of Aguillard's history didn't exactly square with the police version of the shooting.

Through a series of newspaper interviews during the week following Aguillard's death, Nina Aguillard provided a background sketch of her brother and his life. A moody and reclusive kid plagued by numerous phobias, including the fear of birds, he dropped out of school in the sixth grade. A schizophrenic like his mother, he suffered from paranoia, which explained his fascination with and need for handguns. As a juvenile, the police in New Orleans had arrested him for disorderly conduct, after which they found that he possessed marijuana. In the wake of Katrina, the family moved to Arkansas, where Nathan got caught shoplifting a pair of trousers. From Arkansas the family moved to Denver.

Craig Skinner, a Denver attorney looking into the fatal shooting on behalf of the Aguillard family, said this to a reporter with the *Denver Post:* "They [the police] chose what seemed to be the most confrontational approach to arrest him."[15] Attorney Skinner said he couldn't understand why the SCAT officers didn't arrest Aguillard after the undercover cocaine buy two days before the raid. This would have been safer for everyone. The police would have gotten their drugs and Nathan would be alive. In July, the family gave notice of their intent to file a federal excessive force suit against the city and county of Denver for $5 million. They actually filed the action on October 24, 2008.

It's not easy to understand why the police in Denver didn't take Nathan into custody immediately after their undercover buy. They could have conducted a warrantless search of his apartment incidental to that arrest. Assuming there was, in fact, an undercover buy, the SWAT raid was as unnecessary as Nathan Aguillard's death.

DEATH BY ASSOCIATION

The police in Easton, Connecticut, a rural community of 8,000 in the southwest corner of the state, first became aware of Ronald Terebesi, Jr., on March 31, 2008. The 42-year-old former bank manager, who once worked for Virgin Airlines, lived by himself in a small gray house on Dogwood Drive. On the last day of March, Easton police officers and EMS personnel found Terebesi passed out on his living room sofa after he had called 911. After being revived and treated at the scene, Terebesi consented to a search of his house, which led to the seizure of three crack cocaine pipes and a .357 revolver. A week later, the authorities charged Terebesi with the possession of drug paraphernalia. He had no prior history of arrest.

On May 7, six weeks after the police search, someone drove up to Tere-besi's house at 4 A.M., got out of a car, and fired four shotgun blasts through his front windows. Terebesi was home but was not injured. He told the po-lice he had no idea who was behind the assault or why they had targeted him. Coming as it did after his drug paraphernalia arrest, the police suspected that it might have had something to do with the drug trade.

In Norwalk, Connecticut, a city of 84,000, 20 miles south of Easton, Ronald Terbesi's friend Gonzalo Guizan asked Chandra Parker, an exotic dancer who had just gotten off work, to drive him to Terbesi's house. Guizan, a 33-year-old graduate of Fairfield Prep and Fairfield University, had been talking to Terebisi about the two of them starting a contract employment agency. He and Parker, who didn't know Terebesi, arrived at his house at 7 A.M. on Sunday, May 18. After watching pornography that morning with the two men in Terebesi's living room, Shandra Parker drove to the Eas-ton Police Department, where she reported that Terebesi had been smok-ing something she described as a brown and white rock. A narcotics officer, at 11:30 that morning, used this information and Terebesi's recent arrest, plus the suspicious May 7 shotgun assault on Terebesi's house, to obtain a no-knock warrant to search his place for "two small clear glass smoking pipes" and "crack cocaine in a tin box."[16]

Although possession of a small quantity of cocaine and a pair of crack pipes for personal use are not major drug offenses, Easton chief of police John Solomon decided to call in the Southwest Emergency Response Team (SWERT) to spearhead the Sunday afternoon raid of Terebesi's house. A multijurisdictional force, part-time SWERT officers were drawn from police departments in the Fairfield County towns of Easton, Trumbull, Monroe, Darien, Wilton, and Westport. At 2 P.M. that afternoon, 21 heavily armed SWERT officers wearing ski masks rolled down Dogwood Drive toward Ter-ebesi's house.

Following two flashbang explosions, officers simultaneously crashed through the front and back doors of the little gray house. Amid the sound and fury of the intrusion, officer Michael Sweeney of Monroe shot Gonzalo Guizan six times. In the confusion, one of the SWERT officers was shot and wounded by another member of the team. Guizan and an injured Terebesi were taken to the hospital. They pronounced Guizan dead. Terebesi was treated and released.

The next day, a spokesperson for the Connecticut State Police, the agency responsible for investigating the death, revealed almost nothing about the circumstances surrounding the shooting except to say that Guizan had physically confronted the SWERT officer who had shot him. He offered no information regarding the friendly fire incident. According to the spokes-person, officers who searched Terebesi's house had found a Ziploc bag of

cocaine, three glass crack pipes, a small tin containing cocaine, and a Deer-
ing precision instrument scale. Since they didn't find a gun, it was obvious
that Guizan had been unarmed.

A few days after the deadly raid, Gary Mastronardi, Terebesi's attorney, in
an interview with an online correspondent, said, "This guy [Terebesi] is not
a terrorist, he's not a drug dealer, he's not a gun runner. These two guys were
at the house that Sunday planning to open a business together, a personnel employment business. And the police go in there like it was Iraq. It's
outrageous . . . Nothing justified those police going in there the way they
went in."[17]

On May 24, six days after the search of Terebesi's house, the police charged
him with felony possession of narcotics paraphernalia. Terebesi turned himself in. At a superior court hearing in Bridgeport, the prosecutor offered him
a deal: if he completed a drug rehabilitation program, the charges would be
dismissed. A few months later, after Terebesi completed such a program, the
prosecutor kept his promise.

In June, Jay Ruane, the attorney representing the Guizan family, told reporters he was drawing up wrongful death lawsuit against the 20 or so
SWERT officers and their respective police departments. Ruane said, "I certainly . . . am under the belief there was excessive force used in this case,
and I'm sure that will be the subject of [the forthcoming] litigation."[18] Five
months later, Ruane filed the civil rights action in federal court. According
to the complaint, at the time of the raid, Gonzalo Guizan was a "visitor at the
home . . . seated and watching television on this Sunday afternoon [when]
suddenly, without warning or justification, after hearing a concussion grenade explode near his face, [he] was shot at least eight times, in a manner
consistent with him being on the ground with his hands up in front of his
face." Attorney Ruane wrote that the police "dragged [Guizan] out the door
and onto the driveway [after he had been] shot in the chest, abdomen, legs,
hands, and face." Regarding the wisdom of the SWERT raid in this case,
Ruane said that "the police knew . . . that the occupant of this home [Ter-
ebesi] had just been a victim on May 7, 2008 of an unknown gunman who
had fired a shotgun at close range through several windows . . . while the
occupant was inside. It was obvious to the assaulting police, therefore, that
upon the sounds of their assault, with explosives, breaking glass, and doors
being burst open, the recently victimized occupants would immediately fear
that the unknown assailant had returned." To illustrate the gratuitous nature
of the raid, Ruane offered a reasonable law enforcement alternative. Instead
of the no-knock SWERT attack, why hadn't a few Easton police officers
simply gone up to the house, knocked on the door, and executed the search
warrant? If that approach would have been too dangerous, the SWERT team
could have waited "until the house was empty, or at least until it could be

confirmed that there were no visitors in the house." Perhaps, the attorney thought, the paramilitary unit could have held off "until the nonresident [Guizan] was secured outside." According to Ruane, "the police inexplicably decided to enter the house with the force of violence, all to secure the two crack pipes and a small tin of crack cocaine."[19]

Attorney Gary Mastronardi, representing Terebesi, filed suit against the SWERT officers and their police departments, charging "negligent and improper use of unreasonable and excessive force."[20] Although it had been six months since Guizan's death, a spokesperson for the Connecticut State Police informed the media that their investigation of the shooting had not been completed.

In April 2009, Fairfield County State's Attorney Jonathan C. Benedict made his eight-page report on the shooting of Gonzalo Guizan by Monroe patrol officer Michael Sweeney available to the media. According to the state's attorney, chief of police John Solomon had acted reasonably in calling out the SWERT team to conduct the no-knock raid. Officer Sweeney, holding a ballistics shield in one hand and a Glock semiautomatic pistol in the other, had entered the house first. The officer, when he heard the two flashbang grenades go off, thought he had been fired upon and hit. Upon encountering Guizan, the two men struggled for control of Sweeney's pistol, which led the officer to shoot Guizan six times. Based upon these facts, State's Attorney Benedict had decided not to charge officer Sweeney with criminal homicide.

The federal lawsuits against the SWERT team and the police departments involved are pending.

SHOTS IN THE DARK

From 2002 through June 2008, in the rural western Ohio town of Lima, population 38,000, the police department's SWAT team conducted 198 no-knock drug raids. In 25 percent of these invasions, the police found nothing incriminating—no drugs, no weapons, no cash—not even paraphernalia. In a third of the raids, the officers didn't find drugs or guns. These statistics suggest that Greg Garlock, the chief of the 74-member police force since 1998, had not implemented any kind of policy that limited SWAT raids to well-investigated major drug operations. Unfortunately, this is not an omission peculiar to the Lima Police Department.

In December 2007, an undercover narcotics officer in Lima purchased crack cocaine from 31-year-old Anthony Terry, a small-time drug dealer. The street buy did not result in Terry's arrest. On January 2, 2008, a Lima patrol officer stopped Terry for a traffic violation, gave him a ticket, and let him go. Suspecting that Terry was dealing drugs out of his girlfriend's house, narcotics officers watched the place for a week; during that time, they saw comings and goings that suggested drug dealing. According to their plan, when the narcotics officers watching the house were certain that Terry was inside, they'd call in the SWAT team to raid the place.

No one on the case seemed bothered by the fact that Terry wouldn't be the only person in the house when the SWAT team broke into it. Terry's girlfriend, 26-year-old Tarika Wilson, lived at 218 East Third Street with her six children, ages one to eight. Raiding a house full of young people was an obvious formula for disaster. That the Lima police considered Terry dangerous because he had once allegedly tried to disarm a police officer during a shuffle made the raid of this house, under the circumstances, even more reckless. One false move and the bullets could start flying.

At 8:15 on the evening of January 4, under cover of darkness, the 11-man SWAT team closed in on the house. Because officers noticed toys on the front porch, they decided not to toss flashbang grenades into the dwelling through the windows. Instead, before battering down the front door, they set off the devices on the front porch. Armed with a fully automatic rifle, 52-year-old Sergeant Joe Chavalia started up the stairway to the second floor. As he inched his way upward, Chavalia saw movement in a doorway above him and ordered the shadowy figure to the floor. At this moment, another SWAT officer in the kitchen shot two pit bulls. Thinking he was under attack, Sergeant Chavalia fired three shots at the form on the landing. That shadowy figure turned out to be Tarika Wilson. The sergeant found her huddled against the wall on her knees holding her one-year-old son. Chavalia had shot her twice through the neck. The little boy bled from a shoulder wound. He would survive, but his mother lay dead in her home.

Chief of police Garlock placed Chavalia on paid administrative leave pending the results of the investigation to be conducted by the state bureau of criminal identification and investigation. The Montgomery County Sheriff's Office in Dayton would also look into the killing. According to a state forensic toxicologist, Tarika Wilson, at the time of her death, had no traces of alcohol or drugs in her system. The police found crack cocaine in the house, and four months later, a judge sentenced Terry to seven years in prison.

Twenty-five percent of Lima's 38,000 residents are African American. Tarika Wilson, who was black, lived in a minority neighborhood adjacent to a railroad yard south of the city's downtown district. In the 1990s, the local clergy in Lima established a program called Study Circles, in which diverse groups of citizens met to discuss issues of race relations, crime, and problems related to youth. The program had played a significant role in keeping the lid on the community's racial tensions. In recent years, however, owing to aggressive drug enforcement, the relationship between the police and the minority community had deteriorated. Young black men complained of police harassment in the form of racial profiling by patrol officers. Following the shootings of Tarika Wilson and her son, pastors in the black neighborhoods, worried about the potential for civil unrest, particularly if the authorities didn't charge officer Chavalia with some degree of homicide, called for restraint and calm.

On July 28, 2008, some 6½ months after the raid, Sergeant Chavalia, charged with negligent homicide and negligent assault, went on trial in Allen County, Ohio. His attorney, Bill Kluge, argued that the defendant had acted pursuant to a reasonable fear of being shot by the shadowy figure in the upstairs doorway. In his opening remarks to the jury, referring to Tarika Wilson's death, he said, "It's tragic, but it's that simple."[21] Officer Chavalia took the stand four days into the trial. He described the interior of the house as dark, and said that as he ascended the stairs, he saw the silhouette of a person standing on the landing. As he shouted "police department!" he heard three gunshots that he didn't realize had been fired in the kitchen. "There was absolutely, positively no doubt in my mind, right then and there, whoever this was, was shooting at me. They were trying to kill me. I fired one three-round burst."[22] When asked on cross-examination if he had seen a muzzle blast coming from the shadowy figure, the witness said he hadn't.

Following Sergeant Chavalia's testimony, the defense put Urey Patrick on the stand. Patrick, a former FBI agent and expert on the use of deadly force in law enforcement, testified that under the circumstances, the defendant's actions that night were appropriate. "All an officer can do is react to what he sees," Patrick said. "His decision [to use deadly force] was reasonable, therefore justifiable."[23]

On August 5, the jury of eight (the charges were misdemeanors, allowing less than 12 jurors to determine guilt or innocence), after deliberating three hours, found officer Chavalia not guilty. The verdict disappointed and angered a large segment of Lima's African American community. Jason Upthegrove, the president of the local NAACP chapter, said this to a reporter with the *Toledo Blade:* "We've got to do better. We've given people the license to kill." A protestor standing outside the courthouse, having predicted the verdict, held a sign that read: "Police Accountability Now," and "Liberty and Justice for Some?"[24]

A few days after the verdict, members of Tarika Wilson's family filed a civil rights lawsuit against Sergeant Chavalia and the City of Lima. Chavalia, awaiting the results of the internal investigations of the shooting, remained on paid administrative leave. On October 15, 2008, Chief Garlock announced that the internal reviews of the incident revealed that Sergeant Chavalia, in shooting Tarika Wilson and her child, did not violate the department's use of force policy. Officer Chavalia, before returning to work, would undergo a fitness for duty evaluation to determine if he were emotionally prepared to go back on the job. The chief didn't say whether the officer would be re-assigned to the SWAT team. NAACP's Upthegrove, in speaking to local reporters, said he wasn't surprised that other law enforcement agencies had cleared Chavalia of wrongdoing. "I mean that's like Lucifer investigating Satan," he said. "These agencies have to protect one another and they look at it through one prism . . . It takes moral courage to go against the grain and go against the system that supports you."[25]

In November, following his job fitness evaluation, Sergeant Chavalia returned to work, but not as a member of the SWAT team. The chief assigned him to organize the department's evidence room as well as other projects that kept him out of public view. Although he was seeking ways to improve his department's relationship with the community, Chief Garlock had no plans to rewrite the agency's SWAT deployment policy.

It is not surprising that the jury gave Sergeant Chavalia the benefit of the doubt. He thought the person on the landing was shooting at him, and he acted accordingly. The wrongdoing in this case involves the decision to use a SWAT team to raid the house in the first place. Who made that call, and why? Putting a SWAT team in the hands of the wrong leader is like handing a machine gun to a child.

At a luncheon speech on March 6, 2009, municipal court judge William Lauber told the audience that the police in Lima had charged 3,000 fewer people with crimes in 2008 than the year before. He attributed this decline in arrests to the Tarika Wilson case. Tarika's death had apparently put an end to zero-tolerance law enforcement in Lima, Ohio. The police were cutting people breaks, using their discretion in dealing with minor offenders.

In January 2010, attorneys for Tarika Wilson's family and the city of Lima announced that the wrongful death suit against the municipality and others had been settled for $2.5 million. The city law director explained that the money would be set aside in a fund for the six Wilson children.

THE MYSTERY KILLING

At 7:30 on the evening of September 17, 2008, 44-year-old Darryl Ross, after working his shift as a production supervisor, entered his apartment on 34th Street NE in Canton, Ohio. Forty minutes later, six members of the Canton Police Department's SWAT team broke into his apartment. In the bedroom, two of the officers shot Ross five times. He had just gotten out of the shower, and the towel around him was still wet. At 8:30, Darryl Ross was dead.

The next day, chief of police Dean McKimm, in response to reporters' questions about the killing, said there had been complaints about drug activity at the apartment. Two of the officers had shot Ross when he picked up a handgun, and refused to put it down, the chief said. As an 18-year-old in 1991, Ross had been convicted of carrying a concealed weapon. Six years later, he returned to prison on another gun possession offense. The chief didn't identify the handgun Ross had allegedly pointed at the officers and didn't say whether it had been fired. Moreover, Chief McKimm didn't identify the SWAT team shooters or indicate if the police had found drugs in Ross's apartment. When a reporter asked if Ross had been alone in the apartment, the chief didn't respond. He also failed to reveal details regarding the probable cause behind the search warrant, including whether the police had staked out the place or had made an undercover drug buy. The Stark County coroner also had little to say about the case regarding the dead man's bullet wounds and his gun.

Members of Ross's family, calling his killing a murder, insisted that he had not been selling drugs out of his apartment or anywhere else. His sister, Ida Ross-Freeman, as reported in the *Canton Repository*, said this: "Darryl had no one coming and going out [of his apartment] except for his one lady friend and his kids. He was not a person that hung around with a whole bunch of people. He had one or two good friends and that was it. If you're selling drugs, you're going to have some activity, and there was no activity. He worked every day. He took care of his children, he was a good father that way. How's he going to do all that and sell drugs? That doesn't make any sense to me."[26]

The idea that the shooting would be investigated by the Canton Police Department's Internal Affairs Office, as well as the Stark County Grand Jury, didn't sit well with Darryl's friends and relatives. Veronica Earley, another sister, in an appearance before the Canton City Council on September 22, said, "We do not believe the police can police themselves. We are going to do what it takes for justice to be brought."[27] Two days later, a Canton municipal judge ordered the police documents in the case sealed. This included the affidavit containing the search warrant's probable cause and the inventory sheet listing the items seized by the police that night. Frank Forchione, the city attorney who had requested the sealing of these records, justified his decision this way: "The main reason that the state is requesting that [the search warrant affidavit] be sealed is to protect the identity of the confidential informant. Obviously, we needed to use the confidential informant to get the information that was represented to the judge before the search warrant was signed."[28]

On November 14, 2008, Stark County Prosecutor John Ferrero, after announcing that the grand jury had declined to indict the SWAT team members who had shot Darryl Ross, refused to comment on whether the vice officers had found drugs in Ross's apartment. The prosecutor didn't say why this important piece of information had to remain a secret. He also didn't explain why the identities of the exonerated SWAT officers still had to be protected.

The authorities in Canton were not telling their citizens if Ross had actually been dealing in drugs or exactly how he had died or who had killed him. The officials in control of the criminal justice system were telling citizens that these details were none of their business. Members of the dead man's family and others in the community were furious over this governmental withholding of information in such an important case. They were convinced that these officials had something to hide. The case had dropped out of the news and the general public had lost interest, but members of Darryl's family were still asking questions and seeking the truth regarding the raid and his death.

Darryl Ross's son, on August 18, 2009, filed suit in federal court against the city of Canton and the still unidentified SWAT officers who shot him, defendants referred to in the suit as John Doe. Still insisting that Ross had not been selling drugs out of his house, the plaintiff accused the police of having made false statements to acquire the search warrant and that they had conducted the search in a reckless manner. According to the suit, Ross had not been armed and had posed no threat to the police.

Chapter 9

NEGLIGENT HOMICIDE: FATAL WRONG-HOUSE RAIDS

Because so many things can go wrong in a no-knock drug raid, no two SWAT disasters are alike. Although some botched raids cause more harm than others, they all create fear and distrust of the police. The worst mistake a SWAT team can make is to break into the wrong residence. Perhaps the informant directed them to the wrong place, the address on the search warrant was incorrect or vague, or the SWAT team simply missed the house or apartment they intended to enter.

The worst result of a wrong-house raid is the death of an occupant. Elderly residents have died of heart attacks created by the stress and exertion. SWAT officers have shot and killed residents trying to defend themselves against home invaders. Although victims of wrong-house raids have been killed by police negligence, the vast majority of SWAT officers directly involved in these kinds of deaths are not charged with criminal homicide. This is because, in most of the cases, the officers who used deadly force were simply following orders and fired their guns believing that they were defending themselves. Moreover, grand juries are reluctant to start police officers on the road to prison. The victims of these raids, however—victims of criminal homicide or not—are still dead.

Of the five wrong-house, no-knock deadly drug raids featured below, four involved big-city SWAT units. Four of the victims were black and one was Hispanic, which prompted charges of racism and discrimination. One of the bungled raids resulted in the homicide convictions of two police officers. In the other cases, a mayor fired a police chief, a police chief fired a supervisor, and a SWAT commander was transferred to another unit. No police officers suffered injuries in any of the raids. All of these law enforcement fiascos cost taxpayers large monetary court settlements paid to the victims' families. None of tragedies resulted in the serious reevaluation of how search warrants are acquired or new policies regarding the use of SWAT teams in the war on drugs. This is war, and war is hell.

THE SCANDALOUS DEATH OF REVEREND WILLIAMS

Reverend Accelynne Williams, a religious scholar and retired Methodist minister from the Caribbean island of Antigua, moved with his wife to Boston in 1984 to be closer to their daughter. In 1991, they took up residence in a second-floor apartment in the inner-city neighborhood of Dorchester. In the Caribbean, Reverend Williams had spent 40 years serving the congregations on the islands of St. Martin, Antigua, and St. Croix. He had urged his congregants not to indulge in illegal drugs, a social problem that had concerned him for decades.

On Friday afternoon, March 25, 1994, officers with the Boston Police Drug Control Unit, accompanied by 13 members of the department's SWAT team, entered the building at 118 Whitfield Street. The search warrant to be executed had been issued five months earlier and didn't specify the number of the second-floor apartment where the informant said he had purchased drugs and had seen guns. Working off a floor plan provided by the snitch, the narcotics officer in charge of the case sent the SWAT team into the wrong apartment.

After a battering ram had destroyed the door, three officers in black combat fatigues followed a flashbang explosion into the room, where they came upon Reverend Williams, whom they ordered to the floor. When the stunned 75-year-old hesitated, they forced him to the ground, where he struggled until, with two officers holding his legs, they put him into handcuffs. Breathing heavily, Reverend Williams began to vomit and then lost consciousness. EMS officers from the standby ambulance tried to resuscitate Williams with CPR. They rushed him to a nearby hospital where, at 4 o'clock that afternoon, he died. According to the medical examiner, his death had been caused by an acute myocardial infarction brought on by the struggle with the SWAT officers.

Reverend Williams had died violently at the hands of the police, but the prosecutor's officer didn't charge any members of the SWAT team for causing his death. His killing not only scandalized the Boston Police Department, it created lasting bad feeling with the African American community. An unnamed police source, quoted in the *Boston Globe* shortly after the raid, said the following:

The drug detective who was with the entry team was so sure of the apartment that he literally pointed at the door and said, "This is it." Then they burst right in. You'd be surprised at how easily this can happen. An informant can tell you it is the apartment on the left at the top of the stairs and there could be two apartments on the left at the top of the stairs. Or people could rent rooms within an apartment that the informant doesn't know about. You are supposed to verify it, and I'm not making excuses, but mistakes can be made.

The reporter asked this police source why SWAT team raiders wear ski masks. "On 'hits' or raids," he said, "members of the entry team generally wear black knit masks that are designed to psychologically freeze people where they stand."[1]

In speaking about the death of Reverend Williams, Reverend Albert J. D. Aymer of the Parkway United Methodist Church said, "They [the police] should be able to know the difference between decent, God-fearing people and criminals."[2] Boston's mayor and the city police commissioner, a week after the killing, appeared at a neighborhood council meeting to apologize for the mistake. The mayor promised a thorough investigation into the tragedy, an inquiry that ultimately led to disciplinary action against the narcotics officer who sent the SWAT team into the wrong apartment. In April 1996, Reverend Williams's wife, who was out shopping when the police broke into their apartment, received a $1 million settlement from the city. The Williams case has not been forgotten. Reporters often cite it when police officers break into the wrong place and kill someone.

A BAD WARRANT, A TROUBLED COP, AND AN UNNECESSARY DEATH

Ismael Mena, a 43-year-old Mexican farmer and former small-town police officer, entered the United States illegally in August 1997. He left behind a wife and nine children. Mena found a job in Idaho at a meat processing plant; then, a year later, he moved to Denver to work nights at a Coca-Cola bottling facility where he repaired pallets and loaded trucks. He sent most of his earnings, $300 a week, back to Mexico.

Mena lived with several other Mexican workers in a tough, rundown north Denver neighborhood two blocks from the Coca-Cola plant. During the day he tried to sleep in his rented eight-by-eight room on the second floor of a dilapidated house at 3738 High Street. His plant supervisors, about to promote him to jitney driver, considered him a reliable, hardworking employee. Mena had never been in trouble with the police in Mexico or the United States.

In Denver in the late 1990s, like today, whenever narcotics officers caught people in possession of crack cocaine, they turned the arrestees into informants. The deal in those days was this: if the crack user made three undercover buys, he would not be charged with a crime. Early in 1998, Joseph Bini, an aggressive and ambitious 35-year-old narcotics officer, started working with a semiprofessional snitch who, over the next 18 months, made more than a hundred undercover buys. Bini paid his informant $40 for every drug purchase. After the transaction, Bini would secure a warrant to search the house where the drug transfer had taken place. In most of these cases, Bini would call in the SWAT team to lead the no-knock entry. Quite often Bini would wait a week before having the warrant served. As a result, many of these raids produced nothing. Using the SWAT team this way was unnecessary and dangerous, but the Denver Police Department didn't have a policy limiting its use to high-risk situations. (In 1998, Colorado Senator Jim Gongrove, a former narcotics detective, had proposed legislation to place restrictions on the acquisition of no-knock search warrants. Lobbyists for the District Attorneys Association killed the bill.)

On September 21, 1999, officer Bini, driving an unmarked van, followed his snitch as he rode his bicycle to the 3700 block of High Street in search of a street dealer. The street dealer wasn't around, but in the alley behind a row of High Street houses the informant encountered a Hispanic man wearing a T-shirt and jeans, a man he knew only as Joe. After the snitch said he wanted to buy crack, Joe led him down the alley to a spot behind the house at 3742 High Street. Joe told the informant to wait there while he entered the house to get the drug. Upon Joe's return, the snitch paid Joe $20 for the crack. Bini didn't know exactly what High Street dwelling Joe had entered to secure the contraband. He asked his informant to identify the place, but the snitch, not being sure, guessed. He designated the house where Ismael Mena and the other Mexicans resided. This was not the dwelling Joe had entered to acquire the crack.

In the affidavit setting out the probable cause in support of the warrant to search the house at 3738 High Street, Mena's address, officer Bini implied that he and the informant had seen Joe enter this residence. Bini also swore that he had witnessed activity in front of that very house, which to him suggested drug trafficking activity. This was not true. Because he had no idea who lived at that address and neither he nor his informant had been inside, Bini didn't know if the occupants were armed. Nevertheless, to persuade the magistrate to issue an "immediate entry" search warrant, Bini said that in crack house raids, the police almost always found guns. The judge issued the no-knock warrant.

At 1:47 in the afternoon of September 29, 1999, a week after the magistrate had issued the warrant, SWAT officers from the Denver Police Department hit the house. Three minutes later, Ismael Mena, shot nine times by two SWAT officers, lay dead on the floor of his rented room. As reported by Alan Prendergast in the journal *Westword,* the initial law enforcement account of Mena's death differed from their later narration of the events.[3] According to both accounts, the officers, before breaking into the house, yelled, "Police!" and "Policia!" In the first report, two SWAT officers encountered Mena on the first floor in a crouched position with a .22-caliber revolver pointed at them. In the second version, the officers came upon Mena on the second floor, standing on his bed. Seeing the gun in his hand, they retreated. From his bed, Mena moved toward the officers and took up a position behind his partially opened door. At the sight of three muzzle flashes coming from Mena's handgun, the SWAT officers returned fire, killing him on the spot. Shooting scene investigators recovered two .22-caliber bullets from the hallway and one that had been lodged in the stairwell wall. A gunpowder residue test on Mena's right hand indicated he had recently fired a handgun. Searchers found no drugs in the house. According the coroner's office, Mena's body contained no trace of drugs or alcohol.

Because the media initially reported that the police had killed an illegal alien who had fired at them during a crack-house raid, Ismael Mena's death didn't generate much outrage or public pressure for a full scale, independent investigation. As time passed, however, unidentified whistleblowers surfaced, alleging a police cover-up. This included a veteran female police officer who claimed she had been pressured to falsify documents showing previous drug activity at 3738 High Street. There were also rumors that the "Saturday night special" Mena had supposedly fired at the SWAT officers—a German made, six-shot Burgo revolver that in the late 1960s retailed at $9.95—had been "dropped" by the police. (The gun didn't have a paper trail that connected it to either Mena or the police.) Alan Prendergast published a second article in *Westword* based on his interview of officer Bini's informant, a man who remained anonymous. According to the informant, neither he or Bini knew where Joe had obtained the crack.[4]

In November, almost two months after Mena's death, a Denver television station reported that the SWAT team may have raided the wrong house. Two weeks later, Denver mayor Wellington Webb appointed David Thomas, the district attorney of nearby Jefferson County, as special prosecutor in charge of investigating the raid. The mayor said he would assemble a panel of experts to review the police department's policy regarding no-knock search warrants. It was about this time that Denver police chief Tom Sanchez decided to retire to spend more time with his family.

At a news conference in February 2000, Mayor Webb announced that special prosecutor David Thomas's investigation revealed that the SWAT officers who had killed Ismael Mena had done so in self defense. "If Mr. Mena didn't have a gun and wasn't pointing it at [notice that he didn't say "shooting it at"] police officers, he'd be alive today."[5] LeRoy Lemos, a community activist with the Justice for Mena Committee, responded with, "If the police hadn't gotten the wrong house, Mena would be alive. No matter what the misconduct is, the police are always exonerated."[6]

Unlike the unidentified SWAT officers who would not be brought before a grand jury on charges of criminal homicide, officer Joseph Bini was not so lucky. That February, the Denver County district attorney charged him with perjury for swearing to the truthfulness of his affidavit in support of the no-knock search warrant. The chief of police also suspended Bini without pay. Claiming that he was being made the scapegoat, Bini denied any wrongdoing. Seven months later, while still maintaining that he had not committed perjury, Bini agreed to plead guilty to the misdemeanor offense of "official misconduct." In December, the judge sentenced him to a year of probation and 150 hours of community service. Two months after that, supporters of the Justice for Mena movement were outraged when Bini, assigned to a desk job, returned to police duty. Mayor Webb, in justifying Bini's reinstatement, said the police chief, pursuant to civil service regulations, had no choice but to keep Bini on the force. The mayor said he wanted to revise the civil service rules so that police officers could be more easily fired. This did not sit well with Denver's finest.

In January 2003, as a result of a settled defamation suit that had been brought by the SWAT officers who had shot Ismael Mena, a crime lab report surfaced that raised questions regarding the circumstances surrounding Mena's death. According to this document, the traces of gunpowder on Mena's right hand did not come from the Burgo .22-caliber revolver. However, the residue was consistent with the gunpowder inside cartridges used as submachine gun ammunition. David Thomas, the special prosecutor who had cleared the SWAT officers of criminal wrongdoing, said this revelation didn't change his mind about the shooting. Whether Mena had fired at the officers or just pointed his gun at them, they had reason to fear for their lives, and that alone justified the deadly force. The city of Denver, notwithstanding the absence of criminal culpability in the case, paid the Mena family $400,000 in settlement of the wrongful death lawsuit.

The Ismael Mena case dropped out of public view following the wrongful death settlement. But four years later, officer Joseph Bini bounced back into the news. In April 2007, the Denver County district attorney's office charged him with retail theft. According to the complaint, Bini had been caught by a shopping mall surveillance camera taking a three-by-ten foot floor mat valued at $88. Because he was a police officer who had played a prominent role in the Mena case, Bini was somewhat of a public figure, which made this particular theft case more newsworthy than most. A few months later, the district attorney, unable to prove Bini's intent to steal the mat, dropped the charges.

Shortly after the theft accusation, Bini retired from the police department on medical disability. He had been diagnosed with cancer. Bini and his wife divorced, he recovered from his illness, took up bodybuilding, and married a professional bodybuilder who owned a pair of CNC nutrition store franchises. Bini, when not working in one of the stores, gave motivational speeches to audiences made up of people trying to recover from cancer.

In the Mena case, the authorities, and to a lesser extent the media, portrayed Bini as the bad guy. His informant had given him flawed information and he had stretched the truth to get a no-knock search warrant, but this doesn't make him an evil person, and it doesn't make him unique among his fellow narcotics officers. In the history of American law enforcement, there have been countless search warrants based entirely on snitches who didn't even exist. Officer Bini, as a soldier in the war on drugs, was doing what his supervisors, local politicians, and a majority of Denver's citizens wanted him to do. If there is villainy in this case, it's the overheated drug war and the Denver Police Department's lack of restraint in the deployment of SWAT teams to execute no-knock search warrants.

KNOCK KNOCK—WHO'S THERE?

Sixty-four-year-old John Adams and his wife, Loraine, lived in Lebanon, Tennessee, a town of 20,000, 14 miles east of Nashville. John, suffering from arthritis, had retired after working 37 years for the Precision Rubber Company. With his lump-sum disability payment, John had purchased a new Cadillac and a double-wide trailer on Joseph Street, a short dead-end road on the eastern side of town. His place and the house next door were the only dwellings on the block.

At 10 o'clock Wednesday night, October 4, 2000, John and Loraine were watching television in their living room when someone pounded loudly on their front door. Loraine got out of her chair, "Who is it?" she asked. Whoever it was didn't respond. The pounding grew more intense. Realizing that someone was breaking down the door, Loraine, thinking that criminals were invading their house, yelled to John, "Baby, get your gun!" Adams grabbed the cane next to his easy chair and hobbled out of the room. Seconds later, five men, wearing helmets and ski masks and dressed in black combat fatigues, burst into the house. They shoved Loraine against a wall and forced her to her knees. Handcuffed and terrified, she said, "Y'all have got the wrong place! What are you looking for?"[7]

Officers Greg Day and Kyle Shedron, rookies in their mid-twenties, encountered John standing in the hallway holding a sawed-off shotgun. They shot him three times. Mr. Adams died four hours later on the operating table at Vanderbilt University Medical Center in Nashville.

At a news conference the following day, Lebanon chief of police Billy Weeks admitted that his officers had raided the wrong house. He acknowledged that—because there were only two residences on that block and one was a house trailer—people had a right to know how this could have happened. Chief Weeks said that the narcotics officer in charge of the case, a person he would not identify, had written the correct address on the search warrant. This address belonged to the drug suspect's house, next door to the Adams's place. But for some reason the search warrant bore the *description* of the Adams's dwelling. The narcotics officer, in directing the SWAT team to the place to be entered, relied on the description rather than the address.

According to the chief, the narcotics officer who had acquired the search warrant had been watching the drug suspect's house for weeks. The judge had issued the warrant after this officer had sworn to him that an informant had purchased drugs at this house. The drug suspect's car had been parked in the Adams's driveway, which may have caused the mix-up. Although this explained how the narcotics investigator might have incorrectly assigned the drug suspect's address to the Adams trailer, it also suggested that the officer had not actually witnessed the snitch enter the suspect's place to make the buy. If he had, the wrong description would not have ended up on the search warrant. Nevertheless, Chief Weeks said, "We did the best surveillance we could do, and a mistake was made. It's a very sincere mistake, a costly mistake. They [Mr. and Mrs. Adams] were not the target of our investigation. It makes us look at our own policies and procedures to make sure this never occurs again."[8] Mr. Adams had been shot, the chief said, because he had fired a shotgun at officers Shedron and Day. The matter was being looked into by the Tennessee Bureau of Investigation (TBI).

Chief of Police Weeks called a second news conference on October 19 to update the media on the status of the case. Having earlier assured the public that "We did the best surveillance we could do," he now revealed that "We lost sight of our informant and that should never occur." It seemed the head of the narcotics unit, who had watched the suspect's house and had acquired the search warrant, had not actually witnessed him enter the dwelling for drugs. "What we think happened is that we have a particular [narcotics] supervisor who made a very unwise decision." The "unwise decision," presumably, was to lie to the magistrate who had issued the search warrant. The chief had placed this officer on paid administrative leave pending the outcome of the TBI investigation. "We are not trying to make excuses for what happened. But I can tell you that we did identify ourselves [before breaking into the house], and maybe they got confused. And I know we were reacting to him [Mr. Adams] shooting at us. But obviously, this wouldn't have happened if we had not been in the man's house."[9]

John Fox, the mayor of Lebanon, also appearing before reporters that day, made the point that, wrong house or not, Mr. Adams would be alive had the SWAT team not been deployed in the first place. "We're going to back off this knocking down doors," he said. "There's going to have to be some really strong evidence that something life-threatening is actually there. I told him [Chief Weeks] to get rid of the damn black uniforms, get rid of them! [The Lebanon SWAT team had been trained by DEA agents, who recommend that officers dress in the "narco ninja" style, which consists of all-black outfits and ski masks.] When we go up to knock on a door, we're gong to have our suit and tie, or our [regular] police uniform, and that's it. And when they open the door, a citizen is going to be a citizen until there is actually proof of guilt."[10]

Mayor Fox also provided information that possibly explained how the narcotics supervisor had confused the suspect's residence with the Adams trailer. According to the mayor, the confidential informant was merely an anonymous tipster. Moreover, the so-called surveillance was nothing more than a "drive-by" scan of the neighborhood. If this were true, it's hard to imagine how the narcotics officer could have acquired the search warrant without fudging the facts.

The TBI completed its investigation, and on November 3, 2000, a Wilson County grand jury indicted Lieutenant Steve Nokes, the head of the Lebanon narcotics unit. Lieutenant Nokes stood accused of criminal responsibility for reckless homicide, tampering or fabricating evidence, and aggravated perjury, all felony offenses. A week later, Chief Weeks fired this 10-year veteran of the force. At his trial, Nokes pleaded not guilty, and in June 2001, the jury acquitted him of all charges.

The city of Lebanon, in May 2002, agreed to pay Loraine Adams the lump sum of $200,000. Pursuant to the court settlement, she would also receive $1,675 a month for the rest of her life. The city also paid Mr. Adams's $45,000 hospital bill and his $5,804 funeral expenses.

DEATH BY SWAT RAID: NO CRIME

On two occasions within a period of six weeks in 2003, members of the New York City's elite Emergency Services Unit (ESU) broke into the wrong apartments looking for drugs. Both raids took place in Harlem and involved unverified information from police informants. The second intrusion—which angered the public, aroused politicians and even led to mild police reform—involved the loss of a citizen's life.

The first police fiasco occurred on April 2 at 6 A.M. at the Jefferson Houses apartment complex at 114th Street and First Avenue in East Harlem. Cynthia Chapman's husband had just left for work, she was about to take a shower, and her 15-year-old son was getting dressed for school when the police broke down their door and rolled a flashbang grenade into the apartment which hit her son in the ankle. The next thing Cynthia knew, a police officer had her pinned to the floor. "Where is it?" he asked.

"I don't know what you're talking about!"[11] she screamed.

"Don't get smart with me or I'll kill you!"[12] he said. Meanwhile, the other intruders, while ransacking the apartment, broke the television set and a fish tank. The police, after allowing Cynthia and her son to get dressed, took her and the boy to the police station in the housing complex, where they were held until the officers realized they had raided the wrong dwelling. The drug suspect lived in the apartment next door. The officer in charge admitted the mistake and apologized to the family. As a result of the manhandling, Cynthia and her son were left with back and shoulder pains. In May they sued the city in federal court.

On May 16, 2003, six policemen assigned to the 25th Precinct, accompanied by a half-dozen ESU officers, raided Alberta Spruill's sixth-floor apartment at 310 West 143rd Street. The drug suspect they were after lived on the ninth floor of the building. Spruill, a 57-year-old city employee, had just gotten dressed for work when her door banged open and a flashbang grenade exploded in her living room. Startled and disoriented by the concussion device, Alberta could only scream as the police officer forced her to the floor. "I can't breathe, I can't breathe!"[13] she pleaded while being placed into handcuffs. When she complained of chest pains and started coughing, the officer removed the cuffs and called for medical personnel. In the ambulance en route to the hospital, Spruill went into cardiac arrest. At 7:15 that morning, less than two hours after the raid, she was pronounced dead.

At a news conference later that morning, Mayor Michael Bloomberg acknowledged that the police had raided the wrong apartment. On behalf of the city, he apologized for the mistake and promised a full investigation into the matter. Police Commissioner Raymond Kelly said there would be a review of the department's policy regarding the use of flashbang grenades. He admitted that the wrong-address raid had raised serious questions pertaining to the police work behind this no-knock search warrant. As it turned out, the target of this raid had been arrested four days earlier by officers with another unit. Until these problems were fixed, the commissioner had temporarily banned the use of flashbang grenades. The ESU lieutenant who had authorized the device in this case had been reassigned to a desk job.

Later that afternoon, the police department, in full damage-control mode, issued a press release announcing the formation of a database that would track search warrants from issuance to execution. This centralized repository would contain the address of the place to be searched; the identities of the supervisory officer who had approved the warrant application, the prosecutor who reviewed the affidavit, and the judge who issued the warrant; the date of its issuance; the date and time of its execution; and the results of the search. The database would also earmark no-knock warrants and include notations regarding forced entry and the utilization of flashbang grenades. Assuming that police personnel actively collected and maintained this information, and supervisors reviewed it, patterns of abuse could be identified and the people responsible held accountable. The idea looked good on paper; but in reality, holding police officers and their immediate supervisors responsible for their actions is easier said than done. Still, in a public relations crisis, public officials have to do something that at least appears remedial.

The medical examiner's report didn't help the police commissioner's public relations problem. Spruill, suffering from hypertensive heart disease, had died from the "stress and fear she experienced" during the SWAT intrusion into her apartment. Under "manner of death," the forensic pathologist who performed the autopsy wrote: "sudden death following police raid." The medical examiner ruled Spruill's death a homicide. A prosecutor, based upon an investigation of the case, would have to decide whether to purse the matter as a *criminal* homicide.[14]

Toward the end of May, Police Commissioner Kelly, no doubt aware that the Spruill family had filed a federal lawsuit against the city for $500 million, transferred the 25th Precinct commander to another station. Commissioner Kelly also moved the assistant police chief in charge of the ESU to the housing bureau. Since neither of these administrators had been directly responsible for the ill-fated raid, this bureaucratic action was more show than remedy. The commissioner, in a more substantive move, temporarily banned the use of flashbang grenades pending an internal study and analysis of this measure.

On May 28, 2003, picking up on the frustration and anger of the residents of New York, particularly the citizens of Harlem, a pair of city council members held a news conference on the steps of City Hall to announce a public hearing on the police department's policies and procedures regarding no-knock drug raids. According to councilman Peter Vallone, Jr., "We want to assure the public that there is judicial review over the issuance of warrants. We also want to look at what went wrong with that process to ensure that these mistakes never happen again."[15]

Philip Reed, the other councilman holding forth on the steps of City Hall, said, "Officers break down a door to a residence, storm in with their guns, and it turns out to be a completely innocent person, minding his or her own business. It is difficult to imagine how traumatic that must be for Mrs. Spruill. This shocked the entire city not just the African-American community."[16]

On June 5, the public hearing at the courthouse, occasioned by the botched raid, lasted four hours. The proceeding featured heated exchanges between a few council members and Police Commissioner Kelly who, in response to the question as to why so many no-knock drug raids take place in Hispanic and black neighborhoods, said that these happened to be the sections of the city where drugs were being sold. After several council members thanked the commissioner for the excellent job he had done for the city, Councilman Charles Barron said, "Commissioner, excuse me if I don't join your fan club this morning. I'm not impressed . . . with you and the mayor coming forth and saying, 'It's a mistake, we're being held accountable, we're sorry, this shouldn't happen again.' We have been so Giuliani-ized [referring to former Mayor Rudy Giuliani] that anything that comes that's supposed to be normal seems like it's something special. I'm getting tired of what I feel are crimes being considered mistakes and tragedies."[17]

In her testimony before the council, Susan L. Hendricks, the deputy attorney in charge of the criminal defense division of the Legal Aid Society, called for a state law requiring police officers seeking no-knock warrants to provide judges with lists of the people who might be inside the places to be raided. Under this proposed statute, officers would have to record the ages of these occupants as well as other pertinent data. This kind of oversight legislation, requiring considerably more investigation and paperwork, drives law enforcement personnel crazy. As far as they are concerned, proposals like this, offered up by people so high in their ivory towers that they're unaware of the chaos beneath them, makes effective crime fighting almost impossible. Forcing narcotics officers to gather such information in advance of a no-knock raid, if not discouraging the acquisition of search warrants, would eliminate the element of surprise. No serious supporter of the drug war would back such a law. Anticipating the charge that her proposal would risk officer safety, Hendricks said, "There has always been—and there should be—concerns about the dangers police face when executing search and arrest warrants. But it is clearly time to examine the dangers that [no-knock] warrants pose to innocent members of the public."[18]

The testimony of several New York City victims of wrong-address, no-knock drug raids filled the remainder of the council hearing. All of these stories involved broken doors, flashbang grenades, and serious manhandling by heavily armed officers in combat dress and attitude. It was not a good day for the New York City Police Department.

Police Commissioner Kelly told William Rashbaum of the New York Times, in an article published on July 17, 2003, that although he had lifted the ban on flashbang devices 10 days after the Spruill raid, no flashbang grenades had been used since the woman's death. The previous year, New York City police were detonating these little bombs on an average of three times a week. According to the commissioner, flashbang use now required the approval of high-ranking uniformed officers. This new policy didn't sit well with Patrick J. Lynch, the president of the Patrolmen's Benevolent Association.

Quoted in the *Times* article, the labor leader said, "How is it that we went from using it [the stun device] fairly often to not at all? What my members are concerned with is that because we're not using these grenades when they should be used, the number of shootings [of police officers] will go up."[19] Tom Scotto, president of the Detective Endowment Association, said that the drop-off in grenade use had not endangered his members, including 300 ESU officers.

On October 29, just 5½ months after the raid, attorneys for the city, without dragging the Spruill family through preliminary court proceedings, depositions, and the like, agreed to settle the lawsuit for $1.6 million. In March 2004, Cynthia Chapman, the victim of the botched raid in East Harlem, settled with the city for $100,000. Because the city would have lost these cases in court, it was good to get them off the books and out of the public consciousness.

Although the medical examiner had classified Spruill's death as a homicide, none of the officers involved in the raid were charged with crimes. Most people killed by the police have been shot because they either possessed a weapon or the officers thought they were armed. They are killed in self-defense, which justifies the homicide. The police, in the Accelynne Williams and Alberta Spruill cases, scared these unarmed victims to death. In both instances the deaths were unintentional. In an unintentional killing, unless the killer has acted in an highly reckless manner in total disregard for human life, the death will not be handled as a criminal homicide. In the Spruill case, who could be appropriately charged with criminal homicide? The informant? The officer who broke down the door? The SWAT member who rolled in the flashbang grenade? The officer who manhandled Mrs. Spruill, thinking she was somehow related to the drug bust? Or no one? In the end, lacking the requisite criminal intent, it was no one. Alberta Spruill's death, while unjustified, violent, and unnecessary, was not a criminal homicide. It was simply stupid and tragic.

DEATH BY ILLEGAL WARRANT

Every month, narcotics officers with the Atlanta Police Department, in order to receive favorable job performance ratings, had to serve at least two search warrants and to arrest nine drug suspects. Under the pressure of this quota, certain narcotics officers cut corners, lied under oath, and planted evidence. It was just a matter of time before this absurd policy would lead to the injury or death of an innocent person.

In the early afternoon of November 21, 2006, in a crime-ridden northwest Atlanta neighborhood, Jason R. Smith, a 35-year-old member of the narcotics unit, arrested a low-level street dealer named Fabian Sheats. A couple of hours later, Officer Smith, in the process of obtaining a no-knock warrant to raid and search a house in that neighborhood, told magistrate Kimberly Warden that Sheats had identified a crack-cocaine dealer named Sam doing business out of that dwelling. Officer Smith swore that he had sent a highly reliable informant, Alex White, into that house, where he had purchased $50 worth of crack. The 25-year old informant had been earning $30,000 a year as an Atlanta Police Department drug snitch, and, according to the narcotics officer, was a highly reliable source. As further evidence of drug dealing at that location, Officer Smith reported that Sam had installed several surveillance cameras around the place for security.

Judge Kimberly Warden, relying on officer Smith's sworn testimony, issued a no-knock warrant to search the house at 933 Neal Street. The magistrate didn't know it, but nothing in Smith's testimony was true. There was no Sam, no undercover drug purchase by Alex White, and no surveillance camera. Officer Smith had no idea who lived in that house but assumed that because of the nature of the neighborhood, a search would produce drugs. He didn't know that Kathryn Johnston lived in that place alone, that she was 92 years old, and that she lived in constant fear of home invaders. Officer Smith also didn't know that Johnston, for protection, had purchased a handgun.

At 6:40 P.M. November 21, Jason Smith and six other plainclothes narcotics officers arrived at 933 Neal Street to execute their (illegal) search warrant. Nine minutes later, Officer Maurice Geurrin, Jr., without a knock or an announcement of the raiding team's presence, climbed the porch steps and battered down Johnston's front door. She must have seen them coming, because the first thing Geurrin saw when he stepped into the house was an old woman with a gun in her hand. Instead of shooting her, officer Geurrin backed out of the doorway and vaulted off the porch over the railing as the terrified woman fired a shot that missed everyone. Jason Smith and Officer Gregg Junnier fired back 39 times. Struck by six bullets, the old woman backed into her house and collapsed. As she lay gasping for air, officer Smith placed her in handcuffs. She died on the floor from the bullet wound in her chest.

Because the killing took place in a major media center, Johnston's death made national news. In an effort to claim some control over how the story would be narrated, the department's assistant chief of police, the day after the raid, assured the public that the officers involved in the death had played it "by the book." As constructed by the police, the story was simple enough: Narcotics officers bearing a search warrant, after knocking on the door and announcing themselves, had to force their way into the suspected crack house, whereupon they encountered a woman who shot at them with a .38-caliber revolver. Under these circumstances, the two officers under fire had no choice but to defend themselves. The search that followed this unfortunate shooting produced an undisclosed amount of illegal drugs. This case was one more example of the tragic consequences of America's drug culture and the dedication and bravery of the officers on the front line in this ongoing war on drugs.

A few days later, the police cover-up started to unravel when informant Alex White told a reporter that he had not purchased drugs from the Johnston residence. White said officers Smith and Junnier, after the shooting, told him to go along with their story. If he didn't, there would be hell to pay. After White's revelations became public, sources within the police department, to destroy his credibility, identified him as a drug dealer. But it was the police department's credibility that came under question, and it became obvious to Chief Richard Pennington that the media were just warming up to the task of uncovering something sinister. Having lost control of the story, Chief Pennington turned the matter over to the FBI for investigation. He also announced that police supervisors would now have to sign off on no-knock drug raids. The chief did not mention the monthly departmental quotas on drug searches and arrests.

In April 2007, a few days after the Fulton County grand jury indicted Smith and Junnier on charges of felony murder and voluntary manslaughter, respectively, as well as numerous false swearing offenses related to the search warrant and lying to the FBI, they pleaded guilty to voluntary manslaughter. Smith was sent away for 12 years and Junnier received a 10-year sentence. The grand jurors also indicted Arthur Tesler, a third member of the raiding party. The 40-year-old officer, just eight months on the job, had been guarding the back door when his partners shot Johnston. Tesler's charges related to false statements he had allegedly made in furtherance of the police cover-up.

Arthur Tesler went on trial in March 2008 for his role in the cover-up. Fabian Sheats, the man Jason Smith had arrested earlier on the day of the raid, testified that Smith, Junnier, and the defendant were corrupt police officers not above planting evidence. Junnier took the stand and revealed that officers on the narcotics squad routinely lied under oath to obtain search warrants. Testifying on his own behalf, Tesler admitted that he had lied to the FBI. He said he participated in the cover-up out of fear of what would happen if he didn't go along. He denied any involvement in the acquisition of the no-knock search warrant that led to Johnston's death.

The Fulton County Superior Court jury, on May 20, 2008, after deliberating on and off for four days, found Tesler guilty of lying to the FBI agents investigating the fatal shooting. The jury, however, acquitted him of two other charges related to the illegal drug raid. At the sentencing hearing a few days later, Tesler's wife asked the judge to give the father of four a light sentence. The judge, apparently in no mood for leniency, sent Tesler to the state penitentiary for 4½ years, the maximum penalty for his crime. In October, against the advice of his attorney, Tesler pleaded guilty in federal court of violating Johnston's civil rights. That judge sentenced him to 10 years in federal prison, time to be served after he completed his state penalty.

Following Tesler's trial, Chief Pennington created an internal task force to determine what role, if any, police supervisors had played in the illegal search warrant and drug-planting scandal. According to a story by Bill Torry in the *Atlanta Journal-Constitution,* William McKenney, Tesler's attorney, expressed his disappointment that the FBI investigation didn't reach beyond the three narcotics officers involved in the Johnston raid. Regarding Johnston's killing, he said, "There were thoughts this would uncover a huge ring of corruption in the police department. It never did." McKenney criticized the police department's drug-arrest and search quotes this way: "It's difficult to stay within a quota and abide by the rules. The [FBI] never addressed the question of where they [police department supervisors] came up with these numbers and why there was no accountability in that unit. That's the real failure. This investigation addressed the symptoms, not the cause. It's difficult to believe this corrupt unit could be functioning at the rate it did without [anyone] over the rank of sergeant knowing about it."[20]

In January 2009, the Georgia Court of Appeals, on a procedural issue related to venue, overturned Tesler's false swearing conviction. According to the appellate judges, because Tesler had lied to FBI agents in De Kalb County, the Fulton County Superior Court didn't have jurisdiction in the case. Although Tesler could be retried in De Kalb County, that was not likely to happen. The ruling did not affect his civil rights conviction and the time he would have to serve in federal prison. For the Fulton County prosecutor, however, the reversal on those grounds was an embarrassment.

Chapter 10

OFFICER DOWN: NO EXCUSES, NO DEFENSES

Drug raids are dangerous events, particularly when they involve SWAT officers breaking into homes in the middle of the night. When guns go off, it's usually the suspect or a bystander who is shot. That's because SWAT officers have training, better weapons, flashbang grenades, body armor, and the element of surprise. Since the police are the good guys and drug suspects and the people who associate with them are not, the overriding priority in these raids involves officer safety. In the military, however, the priority is the mission. Moreover, in real war, enemy combatants are also well trained, highly motivated, and heavily armed. In other words, a drug raid is nothing like military combat.

SWAT-raid shootings of civilians almost always follow the same procedural route. A police spokesperson, shortly after the incident, announces that the officer or officers involved have been placed on paid administrative leave pending the results of a thorough investigation. Occasionally, the local prosecutor presents the case to a grand jury, which almost always results in no bill. Most of the time the prosecutor simply announces that no assault or homicide charges will be filed. In cases referred to the FBI for investigation, the officers are usually cleared of federal civil rights violations as well. This is how it goes even when the police shoot people who were not armed. Absent gross negligence or extreme recklessness, honest law enforcement mistakes made under trying conditions are not considered crimes by prosecutors and grand jurors. If there are remedies for families of citizens killed by the police, they involve wrongful death damages from civil litigation. Even then, police officers, because of their qualified immunity protection, are rarely held personally liable for these deaths.

Although the deadly mistakes of police officers are generally not crimes, the injury or killing of SWAT officers by civilians who are reacting to middle-of-the-night home invasions are almost always treated as criminal acts. In America, if the police are involved, who has been shot by whom is more important than where the shooting took place or why it occurred. Even when a citizen shoots a SWAT officer who has raided the wrong house, the shooter, in the vast majority of cases, will be convicted of a crime and sent to prison. Regardless of the circumstances, jurors in trials involving downed police officers are generally not sympathetic to the shooters. They are in no mood for excuses and defenses. In realization of this fact, many police shooting defendants plead guilty and hope for the best.

Whenever the police invade a home for drugs, they not only risk their own lives and the lives of everyone in the dwelling but also create the opportunity, in the event of an officer's injury or death, for a much greater crime than the one warranting the raid. This is particularly true when the raid is unnecessary and excessive. Suddenly a person guilty of possessing a small amount of marijuana finds himself charged with assaulting a police officer—or worse, criminal homicide. Since these greater crimes would not have been committed had the police found some other way to achieve their mission, they have, in essence, entrapped these defendants. Because the legal doctrine of entrapment (the police are not supposed to go beyond merely giving suspects the opportunity to commit a crime) doesn't apply in these cases as a bar to prosecution, defendants who assault or kill police officers have very little available to them in the way of defense.

CASES OF ASSAULTING A POLICE OFFICER

The drug cases in this section feature civilians who have shot and wounded police officers amid the confusion of no-knock SWAT raids. Depending upon the state, these defendants are either charged with aggravated assault, felonious assault, or assault with a deadly weapon. In some instances the prosecutor will change the defendant with attempted murder. If tried and convicted, shooters of officers of the law can be sentenced to as much as 20 years in prison.

The Wrong Place at the Wrong Time

A no-knock raid of a suspected crack house on the east side of Columbus, Ohio, damaged the life of a hard-working family man who had never been in trouble with the law. Up until 9:45 on the night of April 30, 2008, 38-year-old Derrick Foster had been a respected member of society. Shortly after 9:45 on that terrible night, he was a man who had done the unthinkable. He had shot a police officer. Even though he was the same person before and after the shooting, his life would never be the same.

Officers with the Columbus Police Department's Drug Investigation and Tactical Unit (IN/TAC) were applying a battering ram to the barricaded back entrance of the house at 1781 East Rich Street when a person or persons inside fired several bullets through the door. IN/TAC officer Anthony Gillis, a 13-year veteran of the paramilitary unit, took two slugs in the arm and one in the hip. A bullet struck his partner and long-time friend, John Garrison, also a member of the team since 1995, in the leg. As a fire department paramedic and a police officer at the scene stanched the bleeding, other members of the unit stormed into the house and arrested eight men, including Derrick Foster and the other shooter, 19-year-old Michael T. Gravely. A standby ambulance rushed the wounded officers to the Grant Medical Center, and they all later recovered fully.

The Franklin County prosecutor charged Foster and Gravely with two counts of felonious assault and two counts of attempted murder. The prosecutor also charged Gravely with possession of cocaine and for having a concealed weapon as a convicted felon. Both men were held without bail at the county jail. A few days later, the prosecutor dropped the attempted murder charges. Still, Foster and Gravely could face sentences up to a maximum of 13 years on each count.

Whenever a police officer is shot in the line of duty, it is usually a big story in the local media. In the case of officers Gillis and Garrison, there was more media coverage than usual owing to the identity of one of the shooters, Derrick Foster. An Ohio State University football standout from 1988 to 1992, Foster was a local sports celebrity. With a degree in sociology, Foster had taken a job with the city of Columbus. At the time of his arrest, he held the position of supervisor in the city code enforcement office, a job that paid $60,000 a year. The father of two daughters, he lived in a medium-priced house in a quiet suburban neighborhood. He possessed a county-issued concealed weapons permit to carry the firearm he had used in the shootings. Shortly after the police took him into custody, Foster resigned from his city job and postponed his upcoming wedding to a Columbus woman.

Three weeks after the raid, Derrick Foster, in an interview with a local television reporter, said he had gone to the East Rich Street house that night to gamble with dice. He was carrying a lot of cash and had the handgun to prevent being robbed. If the IN/TAC officers had announced themselves before attacking the back door, Foster didn't hear them. Thinking they were intended victims of an armed robbery attempt, someone in the house fired the first shot. "Whoever was outside," Foster said, "fired back in, and that's when

I unholstered my gun and I fired two shots. Basically, I was firing two shots, like a warning shot. My whole mentality was, if they were robbers, I want them to know somebody's in here with a gun. Go away. They [the authorities] feel like, hey, this guy's a criminal. I'm not that."[1]

The television correspondent also interviewed Anthony Garrison, one of the officers who had been wounded. "I think any person that has a firearm and is willing to shoot at any person is a dangerous person,"[2] he said. Apparently Garrison didn't mean to include his fellow officers, who had fired their guns blindly into the house. Their bullets could easily have wounded or killed an unarmed person in the dwelling. Moreover, apparently officer Garrison does not think that citizens have the right to use deadly force when they believe their lives are in danger, or to protect themselves from being robbed.

Derrick Foster's attorney, at a hearing on May 22, asked the judge to allow his client to await his trial at home under house arrest. To convince the judge that Foster was not a flight risk, Attorney Samuel Weiner produced 14 letters of support from people in the community who knew Foster. One of the letters came from Michael McGuire, a local businessman who had known Foster since his football days at OSU. Another had been written by Scott Reeves, the principal of Pickering High School in Columbus. Despite these expressions of support and endorsement, the judge denied attorney Weiner's request.

The letters in support of Derrick Foster from prominent citizens of the community angered Jim Gilbert, the president of the local Fraternal Order of the Police. Gilbert sent copies of McGuire's and Reeve's letters to 4,100 members of the organization. Gilbert wanted all of these officers to know who in the community supported a man who had shot two of the city's finest. Questioned by a reporter with the *Columbus Dispatch*, Gilbert, in speaking about Foster, said, "I still believe he's a threat to society." In reference to McGuire, Reeves, and others who had come forward on Foster's behalf, Gilbert said, "The minute you put your thoughts on a letterhead, you open yourself and your business to criticism."[3] The president of the Fraternal Order of the Police wanted his members to contact these people and tell them how they felt about citizens who supported a man who had wounded two police officers. According to the *Columbus Dispatch* article, McGuire had felt threatened when a police officer telephoned and criticized him for writing the following sentence in his letter of support: "Derrick Foster is a tremendous role model to his children and other teens in the community."[4]

Ten days after Principal Reeves had written his letter, the school superintendent reprimanded him for writing such a personal message under the school district's letterhead. Attorney Samuel Weiner, in speaking about Gilbert's actions to the local newspaper reporter, said, "This is witness intimidation. I might be calling some of these people as character witnesses for the defense."[5]

On January 9, 2009, seven months after the shootings, Foster, in exchange for a five-year prison sentence, pleaded guilty to two counts of felonious assault. He also agreed to testify for the prosecution at Gravely's upcoming trial. Officers Garrison and Gillis made public statements supporting Foster's plea-bargained sentence.

After a week-long trial, on February 4, 2009, the jury found Gravely guilty of two counts of felonious assault. Gravely, arguing that he had tried to defend himself against people he thought were out to rob him, could not overcome the testimony of Foster and the two IN/TAC officers. Given the fact that this defendant had a criminal record and the reluctance of jurors to let shootings like this go unpunished, the verdict in this case didn't surprise anyone. On April 2, Gravely must have regretted his decision to turn down a plea-bargained sentence of 20 years when common pleas judge David W. Fais sentenced him to 36 years in prison. Because Gravely had also been convicted of the drug charge, the judge declared him a major drug dealer and fined him $17,500.

How to Make a Low-Risk Raid a Risky Operation

An officer with the Combined Ozark Multi-Jurisdictional Enforcement Team (COMET), a drug task force covering several counties in southwest Missouri, had acquired a warrant to search the house at 997 East 394th Road outside the town of Bolivar. According to the affidavit supporting the warrant, a criminal informant and later an undercover narcotics officer had purchased marijuana at the house occupied by David and Barbara Smith and their two daughters, 19-year-old Alyssa and 17-year-old Chelsey. The snitch said he had spotted a handgun sitting on the coffee table in the living room, and the undercover officer reported seeing Chelsey, seven months pregnant, smoking a marijuana cigarette. The narcotics officer in charge of the case, knowing that a pregnant woman lived in the house, still asked a Missouri State Police SWAT team to spearhead the raid.

On the day of the assault, December 13, 2008, six people—Mr. and Mrs. Smith, the two girls, and their boyfriends—were asleep in the house. At 4:30 on that Saturday morning, SWAT officers with Troop D of the state police broke down the side door near Alyssa's bedroom, and lobbed in a flashbang grenade. Alyssa Smith pulled the 12-gauge shotgun she used for hunting and trap shooting and kept for self-protection out from under her bed and fired one shot through her bedroom door. The pellets didn't hit anyone, but debris from the door struck trooper Kevin Morris, ripping his uniform. The moment she realized the intruders were police officers, Alyssa laid the gun on her bed and surrendered. To their credit and restraint, the SWAT officers did not return fire.

The big question in this case is whether or not Alyssa Smith knew she was firing at a police officer. She and the other members of the family insisted they had no warning of the police intrusion. The officers, on the other hand, claimed to have pulled up to the house with their emergency lights flashing and had announced their presence before breaking down the door. (The flashing-lights scenario doesn't seem consistent with the rationale behind a no-knock drug raid.) The account of what took place in the Smith house after the officers seized Alyssa's shotgun is based on statements made by members of the family, claims that were not disputed or contradicted by the police officers involved in the action.

SWAT officers pulled Chelsey and her boyfriend, who were both naked, out of bed and dragged them into the living room. When Chelsey refused to drop to the floor, a SWAT officer grabbed her by the throat and slammed her against the wall. The boyfriend, who was not allowed to get himself dressed, was thrown a blanket by an officer who called him "naked guy." He handed Chelsey a pair of coveralls, which she had to put on in front of the police. David and Barbara Smith had been forced to the floor and handcuffed. They both received scratches and bruises from the manhandling.

Alyssa, the only person taken into custody that morning, ended up in the Polk County Jail under $250,000 bond. Although narcotics officers said they had found four pounds of marijuana, two guns, and $2,500 in cash, David and Barbara Smith, pending a crime lab analysis of the pot, were not charged with any crime. A week later, the county prosecutor charged them with felony distribution of a controlled substance. The Smiths denied being involved in the drug trade and accused the police of stealing $6,000 in cash. The authorities charged Chelsey Smith with endangering the welfare of her unborn child by smoking a marijuana cigarette.

A couple of weeks after the SWAT action, the *Springfield News-Leader* published an article by Matt McSpadden, who wondered if the seizure of marijuana had been worth the consequences of the raid. Noting that it was a miracle that no one had been injured or worse, McSpadden wrote:

> A nineteen-year-old girl could potentially go to prison for the best years of her life, so that four pounds of marijuana, an herb, is taken out of circulation. At the end of this raid, did the police congratulate themselves in serving "justice"? How about if the worst possible scenario had played out? Had the girl accidentally killed the policeman, and I do believe that she had no idea what was going on in the house for her to have shot

through that door (what do we think, that this girl was planning on taking out an entire SWAT team but stopped at the one shot?), and then the police responded by shooting her, would it still have been worth it? Had the other policemen decided to be rougher on the remaining suspects in the house, after seeing two people shot and killed, and a policeman decided to sit on the young pregnant girl, as officers do to stop a struggling suspect, and the baby had been killed, would it still have been worth it?[6]

In February 2009, a circuit court judge dismissed the child endangerment charges against Chelsey Smith. According to Missouri case law, a pregnant woman smoking marijuana does not constitute endangerment under the state's criminal statute. At her May 11 arraignment, Alyssa Smith entered a plea of guilty to the charge of assault on a police officer. The drug case against her parents remained unresolved.

Forcing the Action, Inviting Disaster

Undercover officers with the Las Vegas Metro Police Department, according to the sworn affidavit behind the warrant authorizing the search of Emmanuel Dozier's house in Henderson, Nevada, had purchased small amounts of cocaine from Dozier on December 7, 9, and 21, 2008. If these officers were to be believed, the 32-year-old Dozier was a full-time cocaine dealer and pimp for his live-in girlfriend, who worked as a Las Vegas prostitute. Because this alleged criminal kingpin associated with dangerous underworld figures and kept guns in his upscale house in Henderson's Seven Hills community, the narcotics officer in charge of the case asked the Las Vegas Metro SWAT team to execute the warrant.

At 9:30 P.M. on Sunday, December 28, four hours after nightfall, narcotics detectives accompanied by a dozen SWAT officers outfitted in black, approached the house on Panorama Ridge Drive. Using special ammunition designed to destroy door locks, a SWAT officer discharged three slugs into the metal security barrier. Before the officers could enter the house, someone inside returned fire, hitting three officers in the legs. One of the SWAT-team members took a bullet in the arm. None of the officers shot back.

The moment Dozier realized that the men at his door were police officers, he laid down his handgun and surrendered. The wounded men were taken to the University Medical Center, where two of them were treated and released. The third officer required surgery on his arm. They all recovered fully.

Dozier's girlfriend, Belinda Saavedra, her 13-year-old daughter, and the couple's 3-month-old son were in the house with him that night. Sitting in a police car outside his house, Dozier spoke to one of the narcotic officers. He said, "I want you to know something in your heart. I did not mean to shoot any cops."[7]

Although the search warrant identified the narcotics being sought as cocaine, the police found only a small amount of marijuana and some drug paraphernalia. In dealing with Dozier, the prosecutor, holding nothing back, charged him with three counts of attempted murder of a police officer, three counts of battery with a deadly weapon, three counts of selling a controlled substance, and one count of discharging a firearm inside a structure. With his bond set at $3.5 million, Dozier wouldn't be getting out of the Clark County Detention Center on bail.

The next day, one of Dozier's Panorama Ridge Drive neighbors, in speaking with a reporter with the *Las Vegas Review-Journal*, expressed shock over the SWAT raid. Noting that Dozier was a sheet metal worker by trade, this man said, "There's been some kind of huge mistake from the get-go. The bottom line is, the guy isn't a drug dealer, and he doesn't do drugs. It just doesn't make sense. No way. There's something just plain wrong."[8]

The police did not take Saavedra into custody that night, but child protection agents took her 13-year-old daughter and her infant son and placed them in the custody of Saavedra's mother, who resided in California but happened to be visiting Las Vegas at the time of the raid. Saavedra's attorney, Vicki Greco, petitioned a family court judge for a hearing in which her client could attempt to regain custody of her children.

An editorial published in the *Las Vegas Review-Journal*, after pointing out that narcotics officers hadn't found cocaine at Dozier's house, went on to say that "The raid itself instigated a crime more serious than that cited in the warrant." It then continued as follows: "Some neighbors allege he [Dozier] was treated roughly during the arrest; his arraignment photographs show a man with a bruised and swollen eye. Indeed, assertions that a surrendering suspect 'resisted arrest' seem odd."[9]

Clark County prosecutor Ron Cordes, appearing on January 6, 2009, before the family court magistrate, argued that Saavedra should not be granted custody of her children. In making his case, Cordes cited her three prostitution arrests in 2003 and claimed that Dozier functioned as her pimp. According to the prosecutor, Saavedra either knew or should have known that Dozier was selling cocaine out of the house. Cordes informed Thomas Leeds, the family court hearing master, that he had just filed criminal abuse and neglect charges against the couple.

In her testimony, Saavedra said her five-year-old prostitution arrests reflected a past life that had nothing to do with the present. She insisted that Dozier had not been selling narcotics out of their residence, noting that she had passed a drug test after his arrest. Asked by her attorney to describe that night's SWAT raid, Saavedra said her daughter, in a state of panic, ran into the kitchen screaming that people were breaking into the house. Dozier, who had been asleep, woke up in a haze, grabbed his handgun, and rushed to the front door. Saavedra gathered up the children and fled to a closet, where she called 911 from her cell phone to report a home invasion. When she realized the intruders were police officers, she called 911 back to announce Dozier's surrender to the police.

Addressing hearing master Leeds, Vicki Greco, Saavedra's attorney, said, "If anybody put the children in harm's way, it was the police."[10] After Leeds declared his decision to release the children back to their mother, prosecutor Cordes said he would appeal this ruling to the family court judge. Under Nevada law, decisions of hearing masters must be approved by family court judges. Therefore Saavedra would not be getting her children back anytime soon.

At Dozier's January 20 preliminary hearing before Justice of the Peace David Gibson, Las Vegas Police Sergeant James Causey testified that he and his fellow SWAT officers shouted "Police, search warrant!"[11] before breaking down the front door. Dozier, represented by a deputy public defender, testified that because he didn't hear the police announce themselves, he believed his home was under attack by criminal invaders. Justice Gibson then reduced Dozier's bail from $3.5 million to $75,000. He also dismissed one of the attempted murder counts as well as the charge involving the firing of a gun inside a building. Apparently convinced that Dozier thought he was shooting at criminals, Gibson said, "This case cries out for a lot of things. The policy used by the [police] department in how to get people out of a house needs to be re-evaluated . . . This is a scary, scary situation and the whole thing was handled in an unusual way."[12]

At his arraignment on February 1, 2009, Dozier posted his $75,000 bail and pleaded not guilty on all counts. Eleven days later, on KLAS-TV, Dana Gentry, the producer and host of a Las Vegas interview program called *Face to Face*, revealed that Dozier had in fact been employed as a sheet metal worker. Moreover, the police inventory of items seized from Dozier's house that night did not include marijuana or drug paraphernalia. Officials with the metro police department declined comment on these revelations.

The authorities moved Dozier's trial, originally scheduled for November 9, 2009, to May 2010.

KILLING A POLICE OFFICER: MANSLAUGHTER TO CAPITAL MURDER

In the following cases, the defendants, like those in the nonfatal police shootings, believed they were firing at criminals invading their homes. In these cases, however, the police officers died. Although the police, by breaking into the homes of drug suspects at night, create the fear and panic that can lead to their deaths, the people who kill them must be punished. And when they are, the sentence can be death. Regardless of the circumstances, someone has to pay dearly for these tragedies, and it's never the people responsible for the raids.

Mississippi v. Cory Maye

On the day after Christmas 2001, 29-year-old Ron Jones, a respected and well-liked sergeant with the Prentiss, Mississippi Police Department, received information from a paid confidential informant that a man named Jamie Smith was in possession of a large stash of marijuana. Smith lived in half of a duplex on Mary Street. According to the snitch, the occupants of the other apartment in the duplex, people he didn't know, also possessed marijuana.

Sergeant Jones, a Prentiss K-9 officer (an officer who patrols with a police dog) in the economically depressed town of 1,000, normally would have passed the informant's tip to the Pearl River Narcotics Task Force, a multijurisdictional agency that could have investigated the matter further and then, if appropriate, launched a SWAT raid. Because of the holiday season and his eagerness to act quickly on this information, Sergeant Jones decided to round up an ad hoc raiding party and hit the duplex that night.

At 11 P.M., Jones and another Prentiss officer, along with one member of the Pearl River SWAT team and three officers recruited from neighboring police departments, split into two groups in order to hit both apartments at the same time. Sergeant Jones led the raid into the apartment occupied by the unidentified suspects, who happened to be 21-year-old Cory Maye and his 18-month-old daughter Ta'Corriana.

Two hours before the raid, Chenteal, Maye's girlfriend and the mother of their child, had left the duplex en route to her night-shift job at a chemical plant in Hattiesburg. At 11 P.M., as Maye dozed in front of the television, sounds of violent pounding on his front door startled him awake. Believing that criminals were invading his apartment, Maye fled into his bedroom. Lying on the floor next to his bed holding his .380-caliber pistol, Maye waited and, when someone kicked open the bedroom door, fired three shots into the darkness. Two of the bullets hit Ron Jones's bulletproof vest. The third slug entered his stomach just below his protective gear. When Maye realized that he had shot a police officer, he laid down his gun, which still held four unfired rounds. Sergeant Jones died before the ambulance reached the hospital.

Sergeant Jones's informant, an unemployed self-described racist with a criminal record, had been wrong about the large stash of marijuana. In Jamie Smith's apartment, the police found a small amount of pot and a scale containing traces of crack cocaine. The search of Maye's place produced less than a gram of dried-out marijuana. Although the police took Smith into custody that night, they didn't charge him with a drug violation and released him shortly thereafter. After giving Maye a bruised and swollen eye and a bleeding ear, the police hauled him off to the Forest County Jail in Hattiesburg, where he was held without bail. Six weeks later, a Jefferson Davis County grand jury indicted Maye for capital murder.

The local magistrate appointed Bob Evans to represent Maye. A 56-year-old attorney from Monticello, Mississippi, Evans served as the public defender for Jefferson Davis County. Following the indictment, Maye's family decided it would be better to replace Evans, an experienced criminal defense attorney, with Rhonda Cooper, a private practice attorney from Jackson with no experience representing clients facing the death penalty.

As the murder trial unfolded in January 2004, it became apparent that attorney Cooper was in over her head. She had met with her client only three times and had not deposed many of the key prosecution witnesses. The prosecutor put Dr. Steven Hayne on the stand, intending to challenge the defense assertion that when officer Jones entered the bedroom, Maye was on the floor in a defensive posture. Hayne, a private contract forensic pathologist who had been accused of tailoring his findings to the needs of prosecutors, testified that the trajectory of the fatal bullet, as evidenced by officer Jones's wound, contradicted Maye's account of the shooting. Although Hayne was not certified by the American Board of Pathology and had a history of controversial findings, the jurors found his testimony, which painted the defendant as a liar, impressive. (A posttrial reexamination of the firearms evidence by a qualified forensic pathologist discredited Hayne's analysis. In August 2008, members of the state medical examiner's commission removed Hayne from its list of accredited forensic pathologists.)

On January 24, 2004, after deliberating a little over an hour, the jury found Maye guilty of capital murder. At the penalty phase of the trial, attorney Cooper, because she never thought her client would be found guilty, informed the judge that she had not prepared a set of proposed sentencing instructions for the judge to give to the jury. The process went forward and the jurors sentenced Maye, a convicted cop killer, to death.

In January 2006, after Jefferson Davis County public defender Evans helped Cooper prepare Maye's appeal, the authorities in Prentiss fired him as the public defender. About this time, Maye received help from a pair of lawyers from Washington, D.C. Attorneys Abe Pafford and Drin Kerr, after reading what Radley Balko of the CATO Institute had written about the case, took over his appeal. Based on their efforts and the work of Evans, on September 21, 2006, a Pearl River circuit judge ruled that Maye, during the sentencing phase of his trial, had not received competent legal representation. In 2007, the judge reduced his sentence to life. In November 2008, Maye's legal team filed a new appeal with the Mississippi appellate court. At present, Maye is serving his life sentence in the high-security wing of Mississippi's Parchman Penitentiary.

On November 17, 2009, the Mississippi Appeals Court, sitting en-banc, overturned Maye's murder conviction on the ground that the state had denied the defendant's right to be tried in Jefferson Davis County. The judges remanded the case for a new trial.

Qualifying for the Death Penalty in Georgia

At 1:15 A.M. on March 23, 2006, 10 members of the Middle Georgia Task Force, comprising mostly officers with the Macon Police Department and deputies with the Bibb County Sheriff's Office, raided a house on Atherton Street in Macon. The no-knock warrant, based upon information from a "concerned citizen" and a pair of informants who claimed to have witnessed persons selling drugs out of the place, had been acquired by deputy sheriff Joseph Whitehead, the officer in charge of the operation. In the rather vague but not atypical affidavit setting out the probable cause for the no-knock intrusion, the snitches said they had seen guns in the house. The occupants also kept two pit bulls in the backyard, and someone had installed an outdoor surveillance camera. As for the evidence the officers expected to find in the house, the warrant listed marijuana, cash, and records of illegal drug transactions.

Seconds after entering the house, Deputy Whitehead encountered gunfire from the rear of the dwelling. Hit several times, he didn't survive the assault. In one of the back bedrooms, officers arrested the shooters, Antron Fair, age 23, and 22-year-old Damen Jolly. The suspects had fired an Uzi-type machine pistol and a chrome-plated .38-caliber revolver; they said they didn't know the house was being raided by police officers. Searchers found pieces of crack cocaine on the floor; they seized 21 packages of marijuana and an undisclosed amount of cash. The officers also arrested three other occupants of the house.

Shortly after the arrests, the Bibb County prosecutor announced his intention to seek indictments against Jolly and Fair on charges of murder with malice (in most states called first-degree or capital murder), and to seek the death penalty. In April 2006, while the defendants were incarcerated without bond at the Bibb County Law Enforcement Center in Macon, a grand jury handed down the murder indictments. In Georgia, killing a police officer in the line of duty constitutes one of the 11 aggravating circumstances that qualifies a murder defendant for the death sentence. Although this part of the statute does not specifically require that the defendant must have *know-*

ingly killed a police officer, the attorneys for Fair and Jolly argued that because their clients did not know they were firing at a law enforcement officer, they should not be eligible for the death penalty. The defense attorneys filed a motion requesting that this legal issue be resolved before the defendants went to trial. The question was this: did the state, before a jury could impose the death sentences, have to prove that the defendants knew they were shooting at a police officer? The judge denied this defense motion. The attorneys appealed this decision to the state supreme court, which agreed to address the issue.

On July 14, 2008, the Georgia Supreme Court ruled, in a five-to-three decision, that under the state's death penalty provision, prosecutors *do not* have to prove that a defendant accused of shooting a police officer had prior knowledge of the victim's law enforcement status. According to the majority opinion, had the state legislators intended to require this mental element, they would have included the word "knowingly" in the language of the statute. One of the three dissenting justices, in a 10-page dissent, wrote: "A defendant who knowingly murders a police officer . . . is more culpable than one who does not know the status of his victim. Without such knowledge, there is nothing to distinguish the defendant who murders a victim who by happenstance was a public servant from a defendant who murders any other victim, and thus has done nothing to specifically justify the imposition of the ultimate penalty."[13]

Jolly, scheduled to be tried separately from Fair, asked for and was granted a change of venue to Savannah in Chatham County. Defendant Fair had not asked to be tried outside of Bibb County. Both men are awaiting their murder trials.

Cops without Badges: The Drug-War Snitch

Ryan Frederick, a 28-year-old soft drink deliveryman, lived with his two dogs in a modest, well-kept house with a manicured lawn on the 900 block of Redstart Avenue in Chesapeake, Virginia. On January 15, 2008, a day after someone had broken into his detached garage behind the house, this small, quiet man with a steady work record and no history with the police purchased three dead-bolt locks to secure the garage and his house against burglary. Frederick didn't report the break-in because the thief had taken a couple of marijuana plants he had grown for personal use. Moreover, he believed that Steven Wright, his fiancée's brother, had broken into his garage.

At 8:40 P.M. on January 17, three days after the burglary, Ryan, asleep in his bedroom at the rear of the house, was awakened by his barking dogs. He grabbed his handgun and, as he walked down the hall toward the front of the house, saw someone breaking through the bottom panel of his door. Thinking that the intruder or intruders had returned and fearing for his life, Frederick got off two shots before his gun jammed. He ran back into his bedroom to call 911 and then heard men yelling, "Police!" He immediately dropped his gun and surrendered.

Ryan Frederick had killed 34-year-old Jarrod Shivers, an eight-year veteran of the Chesapeake Police Department. Shivers and his narcotics crew were serving a no-knock warrant to search for evidence of a major marijuana growing operation based solely upon information provided by a pair of snitches. In the garage, officers confiscated grow lights, a fan, several tub containers, magazines entitled *Marijuana Horticulture, Buds for Less,* and *Growing Great Marijuana,* a smoking bong, and a small amount of pot.

When interrogated, Frederick denied that he grew marijuana for profit. He said he was an avid gardener who cultivated tropical plants such as banana trees and Japanese maples. He had landscaped his backyard, which included a Koi pond he had installed himself. Frederick expressed his grief over officer Shivers's death, which he believed had been caused by a terrible law enforcement mistake. Had he known that his door was being battered down by a police officer, he would not have fired his gun. He was not a criminal and certainly not an intentional cop killer.

A police spokesperson insisted that the officers, prior to forcing their way into Frederick's house, had announced their presence. They had no way of knowing, however, whether Frederick, asleep in a back bedroom, had heard them. Fearing that the evidence they sought was in danger of being destroyed, the officers broke into the house.

A local television reporter, in May 2008, interviewed Frederick at the Chesapeake City Jail where he was being held without bail on the charge of capital murder. Frederick told this correspondent that he believed his fiancée's brother, Steven Wright, was one of the snitches behind the no-knock warrant. Frederick also suspected that Wright and another man had broken into his garage three days before the raid. Reporters with the television station had obtained court documents that revealed Steven Wright's arrest, on January 8, for grand larceny and fraud in connection with the theft of a Chesapeake woman's credit cards. Nine days later, officers Shivers and his narcotics unit raided Ryan Frederick's house.

At a preliminary hearing concerning the defense's request for a change of venue, Paul Ebert, the special prosecutor from Prince William County brought in to handle the case, stated that two men had broken into Frederick's garage on January 14. According to Ebert, these men had stolen Frederick's marijuana plants. Following this clever way of explaining away a search that had produced very little evidence and perhaps unwittingly revealing the sources behind the no-knock warrant, the special prosecutor asserted that Frederick had been involved in a "significant if not lucrative marijuana growing operation"[14] out of his garage. Frederick's attorney, James Broccoletti, reminded the court that the police had seized only one-third of an ounce of marijuana.

On September 25, 2008, Radley Balko, in *Reason Magazine Online,* reported that a journalist with the *Virginia-Pilot* named John Hopkins had, in February, spoken to an inmate at the Chesapeake Jail who said he had worked with Steven Wright as a paid Chesapeake police informant. According to Hopkins, the inmate, Renaldo Turnbull, told him that the deal was this: if he and Wright brought the police evidence of a major marijuana operation, the cops would drop the larceny, credit card, and fraud charges against Wright. Turnbull said the police had encouraged Wright to break into Frederick's garage for evidence. Because Turnbull's story seemed a bit farfetched at that time, reporter Hopkins didn't publish it until September.

On December 15, 2008, James Broccoletti, Frederick's attorney, filed a motion in the Chesapeake Circuit Court to have officer Whitehead's no-knock search warrant declared invalid because the probable cause supporting it had been illegally acquired by informants working for the police. That would, in turn, invalidate the raid, rendering the evidence seized from it inadmissible in court. To bolster his contention that the informants who had broken into the garage for evidence of a major drug operation were working at the behest of the police, Broccoletti played part of an audio recording of Frederick's conversation with a narcotics detective as the two men sat in a police vehicle shortly after his arrest. After Frederick told the detective about the January 14 break-in, the officer said, "We know that." This is important, because Frederick had not reported the burglary to the police. Later in the tape, the detective said, "First off, we know your house had been broken into. Okay?"[15]

The circuit court judge denied attorney Broccoletti's motion to suppress the evidence produced by the raid. The murder case went to trial in January 2009. Despite prosecutor Ebert's efforts to win a capital murder conviction, the jury, on February 4, found Frederick guilty of voluntary manslaughter. The judge, relying on the jury's recommendation, sentenced Frederick to 10 years in prison.

At his April 2009 trial for grand larceny, credit card theft, and fraud, Steven Wright, Frederick's fiancée's brother, and one of the informants behind the raid that led to officer Shivers's death, acknowledged that the Chesapeake police had promised to take care of him in return for his testimony against Frederick. Wright's attorney argued that the police had broken their word and that the defendant should now reap the benefit of that promise. The prosecutor countered the defense's assertion by denying that any deal had been made between Wright and the Chesapeake police. Later that month, the jury found Wright guilty as charged.

Very few defendants found guilty of killing police officers get off as lightly as Ryan Frederick. But in his case, the jurors realized that the police had no business, given the nature of the evidence and the way they had acquired it, conducting a no-knock raid on his house. In the war on drugs, the police turn half the users into snitches and the rest into subjects. And worse, they often let informants do the work they should be doing more professionally themselves. Turning a militarized criminal justice system over to flipped drug arrestees, jailhouse snitches, and paid informants is dangerous. It also leads to a lot of injustice. In the Ryan Frederick case, it led to both.

CONCLUSION:
NO EASY SOLUTION

As noted in an article about police militarism by North Carolina State University professor James R. Brunet, modern policing has its roots in the military tradition. Patrol officers have always worn uniforms, carried guns, and followed orders pursuant to a rigid chain of command staffed by officers holding the ranks of major, captain, lieutenant, and sergeant. Officers who distinguish themselves in service are awarded medals, and when they die in the line of duty, receive military-like burial ceremonies. At the police academy, recruits undergo militaristic boot camp–style training before graduating to the streets to do battle with lawbreakers. Although Professor Brunet doesn't believe that increased SWAT-team usage has had much effect on overall policing (I obviously disagree), he suggests three measures to help rein in paramilitary operations:

1. Institute stronger internal controls. (Specialized police units have been difficult to manage because of a tendency to defer to their expertise. This makes controlling them difficult.)
2. Intensify external oversight. Elected officials and citizens should ask questions about how paramilitary units are used and what tactics they employ. (Police agencies tend to be secretive organizations that resist external oversight.)
3. Convene commissions to oversee these specialized tactical units. (A few states, like California, have created blue-ribbon panels to investigate ways to standardize SWAT training; but on the whole,

commissions and civilian review boards have had little influence over SWAT-team use.)

Because increased SWAT-team deployment reflects how the police view their role in society and look upon the people they deal with every day, the above measures, while possibly leading to improved SWAT-team performance, will not demilitarize law enforcement. As long as police officers think they are fighting a war against crime and that criminal suspects are their enemies, nothing will change. The American public, in order to be more open to the idea of the police officer as a public servant, will have to be disabused of the notion that the police stand between us and chaos. The police cannot prevent crime. The decision to obey or disobey the law is a personal decision that has nothing to do with law enforcement. Crime rates in the 1960s, 1970s, and 1980s were much higher than they are today—a reality that has nothing to do with the increased militarism of our law enforcement agencies. Demilitarizing the police in significant ways is a hard sell because of traditional police fear mongering and the politicians' fear of being perceived as soft on crime. In bad economic times, crime rates go up, and when that happens, policing tends to becomes more aggressive and militaristic.

For now, the best chance of demilitarizing law enforcement involves eliminating, or at least seriously reducing, the use of no-knock SWAT raids against nonviolent criminal suspects. Ideally, hundreds of SWAT teams, particularly in the smaller agencies where they aren't really needed, should be disbanded. A few SWAT units have been dismantled, but not because of a change in law enforcement philosophy. Because of bad economic times, the smaller departments cannot afford the training, equipment, and costs of liability insurance associated with paramilitary units.

ELIMINATING LOW-RISK SWAT RAIDS

After the catastrophic SWAT attack at the Davidian headquarters in Waco, a reasonable person might expect that the police in Texas, or anywhere else, would never again use paramilitary tactics to raid a religious compound occupied by innocent women and children. But in April 2008, state and local SWAT units invaded the Latter Day Saints complex in Eldorado, Texas. The place didn't burn to the ground, but the removal of hundreds of children from their families created a nightmare for their parents in an operation that turned out to be a law enforcement fiasco. In that heavy-handed operation, the police disrupted families and put lives at risk.

As a part of everyday law enforcement, SWAT officers should not be assigned to street patrol. Sending men in combat dress—with their faces hidden behind masks, who are armed with fully automatic rifles—to patrol inner-city neighborhoods in armored personnel carriers is not only unnecessary but also makes positive police–community relations extremely difficult. The use of SWAT units to help detectives execute warrants involving suspects charged with nonviolent crimes constitutes another form of militaristic law enforcement overkill. SWAT teams have no business raiding gambling sites such as private clubs and home poker gatherings, brothels, musical events, and fraternity houses. Massive roundups of illegal aliens (in some cases legal workers as well) at work sites, churches, and homes, particularly when conducted by county and city police officers, is a waste of local law enforcement resources. And finally, SWAT raids of places where people are gathered peacefully and lawfully to plan and coordinate political protests is a dangerous form of police harassment that challenges the constitutional right of assembly.

Low-Risk Drug Raids: Pursuing Michael Phelps

On February 1, 2009, a British newspaper published a photograph of Michael Phelps, the star of the 2008 Olympics, smoking a marijuana pipe at a party in Columbia, South Carolina. Although the photograph had been taken three months earlier, Leon Lott, the television-friendly sheriff of Richland County, known for his aggressive approach to drug enforcement, opened a narcotics investigation of the famous gold medalist swimmer. Sheriff Lott, in September 2008, had overseen the purchase of an army surplus armored personnel carrier equipped with a .50-caliber belt-fed machine gun used to transport his SWAT team to drug raids. Six days after he had launched the Phelps investigation, a 12-man Richland County SWAT team, guns drawn, broke into a Lake Murray house rented by four University of South Carolina students believed to have attended the November 2008 party. After confiscating less than a gram of marijuana, Lott's deputies arrested the students for drug possession and grilled them about Michael Phelps. As it turned out, none of the arrestees had attended the party and were no help in the Phelps investigation. From Lake Murray, Lott's SWAT officers traveled to Columbia and raided the party house, where they seized six grams of marijuana and the bong depicted in the photograph. The deputies arrested four more students and charged them with the misdemeanor possession of marijuana.

At a news conference on February 15, 2009, Sheriff Lott announced that his officers had not gathered enough evidence to charge Michael Phelps with a crime. "We had a photo," he said, "and we had him saying he was sorry for his inappropriate behavior. That behavior could have been going to a party . . . He never said, 'I smoked marijuana.' He never confessed to that. We don't have enough we could go arrest him." When asked why he, in an effort to make a case out of a three-month-old photograph of an Olympic swimmer smoking pot, had deployed his SWAT team to raid houses occupied by college students suspected of attending the party, Sheriff Lott, either missing or ignoring the point, said, "As a cop, my responsibility is to enforce the law, not to create it or ignore it. Marijuana in the State of South Carolina is illegal."[1]

In response to Sheriff Lott's assessment of his responsibilities as a law enforcement officer, Suzanne Smalley and Weston Kosova of *Newsweek*, wrote: "If cops chased down every kid who took a bong hit at a frat party, the jails would be full and the lecture halls empty. Half the professors would wind up in the clink, too."[2] But the media's most popular narrative of the Olympic swimmer and the bong story had nothing to do with law enforcement. It focused on Michael Phelps's fall from grace and his loss of millions of dollars worth of product endorsements. The news narrative would have been different, however, if one of the students, believing the house was being invaded by criminals, had picked up a gun.

Shooting Derek Copp

The West Michigan Enforcement Team (WEMET) is a multijurisdictional, militarized drug enforcement task force that covers the counties of Ottawa, Muskegon, and Allegan on the western border of the state. The 25 officers on the squad are drawn from the three sheriff's offices, six police departments, and the Michigan State Police, the agency in control of the unit. WEMET officers conduct narcotics investigations, handle informants, make undercover buys, and raid the homes of suspected drug users and dealers. In 2007, WEMET officers seized $244,700 worth of drugs and drug-related assets including cars and television sets. The vast majority of confiscations involved marijuana. For example, in 2008, the unit, in 66 raids, recovered 639 pounds of marijuana, compared with 12.4 pounds of cocaine, 44 ounces of crack, 22 ounces of heroin, and only 6½ ounces of methamphetamine. From these statistics, it is obvious that WEMET was not in the business of arresting big-time drug lords.

At 9 P.M. on March 11, 2009, in Allendale Township, 15 miles west of Grand Rapids, six WEMET officers raided an apartment occupied by a Grand View State University (GVSU) student named Derek Copp. The 20-year-old lived with his roommate at Campus View Apartments, a 372-unit complex on 42nd Avenue. Copp, from Spring Arbor, Michigan, after graduating from Jackson Community College, had enrolled at GVSU in the fall of 2007 as a film and video major. Describing himself on his Facebook page as a "left-wing hippie peace-keeping liberal," he worked part-time at a local restaurant making pizza.

On the night of March 11, the raid went wrong when one of the officers, a 12-year veteran of the Ottawa Sheriff's Office who had been on the WEMET team for two years, shot Derek Copp. The officer's .40-caliber bullet, fired from his Glock pistol, entered Copp's right upper chest, traveled down and hit his lung and liver, and lodged in his back. Emergency medical personnel rushed him to a Grand Rapids hospital, where doctors removed the slug and saved his life. However, with the chance of infection and other complications, the young man's condition remained precarious.

Michigan State Police spokesman Lieutenant Cameron Henke, the day after the shooting, had little to say about the raid other than that the student had not been armed or confrontational and had not tried to run from the police. This, of course, begged the question as to why the student had been shot. Lieutenant Henke did not release Copp's name or the identity of the officer who had shot him other than to say he was a deputy with the Ottawa County Sheriff's Office. The spokesman did not reveal what evidence had brought the WEMET officers to Copp's apartment or what the search of the place had produced. Upon completion of the investigation by the Michigan State Police, the case would be turned over to Ron Frantz, the Ottawa County prosecutor.

At a March 14 news conference, Derek Copp's father, George, shed some light on the shooting. He had spoken with his son, who told him that it all started when someone pounded on the apartment's back door. When he pulled open the curtain to the sliding glass door, a flashlight beam blinded him. As he raised his arm to shield his eyes from the light, one of the officers on the other side of the door shot him. Mr. Copp said he had hired Grand Rapids attorney Frederick Dilley to represent his son.

At the university, students were organizing a protest march through town that would wind up as a sit-down outside the Ottawa County Sheriff's Office. Thomas Haas, the president of GVSU, called for the Michigan State Police to reveal more information about the nearly fatal incident.

Attorney Dilley, on March 18, issued a statement in which he disclosed that WEMET officers had recovered a few tablespoons of marijuana from Derek Copp's apartment. How, he asked, did this minor drug raid justify the use of deadly force? Ron Frantz, the local prosecutor, to avoid the appearance of a cover-up, had asked the state attorney general to assign the Copp investigation to a special prosecutor outside Ottawa County.

After nine days in the hospital, Derek Copp returned to his family's home in Spring Arbor to recuperate. A week later, at a news conference, he said he was experiencing breathing difficulties and that his fractured ribs caused him pain. He declined to discuss the shooting. Two days following the news conference, after a CT scan showed problems in Copp's right lung, doctors reinserted a chest tube to drain fluid and flush out the clotted blood. On March 30, Copp left the hospital, but he still wasn't feeling well.

On April 2, Jeffery Fink, the special prosecutor from Kalamazoo County, received the investigative report from the Michigan State Police. Four days later, Fink announced that Ottawa County deputy sheriff Ryan Huizenga had been charged with careless discharge of a weapon, causing injury, a high misdemeanor that carried a maximum sentence of two years in prison. The sheriff had placed the 37-year-old WEMET officer on unpaid administrative leave, a move that angered members of the sheriff's office and Huizenga's fellow WEMET officers. The magistrate allowed Huizenga to stay out of jail on a $10,000 personal recognizance bond. According to prosecutor Fink, the WEMET officers were at Derek Copp's back door to execute a valid search warrant when Copp made a sudden move to shield his eyes from a flashlight beam. This prompted officer Huizenga, whose finger was on the trigger instead of the trigger guard, to shoot him accidentally.

Huizenga had been on unpaid administrative leave one week when the sheriff, feeling the heat from his rank and file, removed him from leave status. The sheriff assigned the deputy to a desk job. On April 15, special prosecutor Fink charged Derek Copp with the crime of delivery or manufacture of marijuana. According to the prosecutor, Copp had sold $60 worth of marijuana, or 3.3 grams, to an undercover WEMET officer earlier on the day of the raid. A week after the felony charge, which could have sent him to prison for up to four years, Copp attended his arraignment hearing. At the proceeding, Copp admitted to the judge that he had smoked marijuana as recently as a week earlier. He also said, in a bit of a twist, that he wanted to write a letter of apology to officer Huizenga. The defendant pleaded not guilty to the drug dealing/manufacture charge, paid the standard 10 percent of his $3,000 bail, and was bound over for trial.

A week before Derek Copp's arraignment, support for officer Huizenga, which had been building in the community since the shooting, culminated in a rally on his behalf attended by some 300 supporters (many of whom were police officers and their families) outside the sheriff's office. One of Huizenga's supporters, a friend who had known him since grade school, had set up a Web site devoted to Huizenga's cause. Some of the rally participants held signs that read: "Support the ones who risk their safety for ours." Deputy Huizenga did not speak to his supporters, but the president of the local police union addressed the crowd.

On April 24, Derek Copp's roommate, Conor Bardallis, accused of selling three grams of marijuana to a WEMET undercover officer in February 2009, pleaded not guilty to the same charge facing Copp. According to the complaint, the officer had purchased the pot for $50 at the apartment on 42nd Avenue. Bardallis remained free on $3,000 bail. That afternoon, a small group of participants held a fourth rally in support of Derek Copp at Rosa Parks Circle in downtown Grand Rapids. The turnout was much smaller than before. Perhaps some of his supporters didn't like the idea of his apologizing to the police officer who had shot him, or maybe students were simply losing interest in the case.

Two attorneys who had represented suspects arrested by WEMET officers were quoted in an April 26 piece in the *Grand Rapids Press* about the small-time nature of most WEMET drug cases. Don Hann said, "Most of the things they [WEMET] do are with low-level people and very seldom do they net a major player. If they have done their investigation enough to get a search warrant, they know what they're dealing with inside [the place being raided] and should adjust [their tactics]."[3] David Hall, the other attorney questioning the tactics in the Copp case, said, "Why don't you send [Copp] a letter and say 'You're charged?' I wouldn't think they would necessarily need to do a raid under those circumstances."[4]

Derek Copp, on June 25, 2009, pleaded guilty before Ottawa County Judge Edward Post to a felony count of delivery of or manufacturing marijuana. He admitted selling marijuana to an undercover narcotics officer. In anticipation of Copp's sentencing hearing scheduled for August, his attorney petitioned the court to allow his client to be sentenced under the Holmes Youthful Training Act which allows criminal records to be expunged after first-time offenders complete their sentences. Copp could receive, at the maximum, a four-year prison term. On August 10, 2009, the judge, under the youthful training law, sentenced Copp to 18 months probation and 80 hours of community service. He also fined the student $400.

Trenton Drug Sweeps

At least once a week in Trenton, New Jersey, a convoy of police vehicles—squad cars, white vans, a paddy wagon, and a massive brown SWAT tank known as the "ice cream truck"—rolls into neighborhoods carrying 20 to 25 members of a multijurisdictional paramilitary unit called the Narcotics Quick Response Team (QRT). Between 6 and 9 P.M. on the evening of "Impact Thursday," February 26, 2009, these black-clad, knee-padded, helmeted men carrying automatic rifles battered down six doors and arrested five people. They didn't recover any weapons and found only small quantities of drugs in three of the houses.

The previous week, QRT officers broke into Michael and Tierra Hill's house. They slammed the couple's 14-year-old son, an honor student who had never been in trouble with the law, to the floor and took his mother away in handcuffs after finding a marijuana roach in an ashtray. Michael came home from work to find his house torn apart, his front door bashed in, and his wife in jail. The officer in charge of the search refused to show him a copy of the search warrant. Because he couldn't lock his front door, Michael Hill stayed up all night to protect his ransacked house. His son, speaking to a newspaper reporter about the weekly drug sweeps, said, "It was scary, I just think it's going to happen again."[5]

Trenton's special operations commander, Captain Michael Flaherty, said this to a local reporter regarding these drug enforcement tactics: "We'll make a search and see what we come up with."[6] Perhaps Captain Flaherty should be reminded that the Fourth Amendment, protecting citizens from unreasonable searches and seizures, requires that the police acquire probable cause justifying the search before, not after their entry. It's hard to imagine how these home intrusions in the name of drug enforcement have improved the quality of life in Trenton, New Jersey. Living in constant fear of a home invasion prompted by nameless, faceless drug informants is not how Americans are supposed to live.

Absent exigent circumstances, before any kind of home invasion, officers should make every effort to determine who is in the dwelling and where they might be in order to protect children and other innocent occupants. Moreover, although acquiring a search warrant, even a no-knock warrant, is not a rigorous procedure legally, drug enforcement officers should not raid homes solely on the words of flipped or paid informants. Snitch information, because it is so unreliable, should always be corroborated by at least one undercover buy and police surveillance of the site. Drug enforcement in general should be more of an investigative function than a combat operation.

Jack Cole, a former New Jersey narcotics officer who heads an organization dedicated to reforming drug laws, advocates a more thoughtful approach to drug enforcement: "It's better to use stealth and imagination, wait until you get people out of the house."[7] Once suspects are taken into custody outside their houses, the police won't have to enter these places forcibly in the middle of the night to search for drugs. Although this much safer approach might take a little more time and effort and might be less satisfying to the officers involved, from the public's point of view it represents a more responsible form of law enforcement.

DISBANDING PARAMILITARY POLICE UNITS

Sheriffs, police chiefs, and the heads of federal law enforcement agencies love their paramilitary teams, as do the men (there are very few female SWAT officers) assigned to these elite units. Despite the high costs of these operations, the legal liability problems they create, and the fact that many of them are simply unnecessary, police administrators as well as police union leaders are extremely reluctant to give them up. Whenever an agency disbands its

SWAT unit, it is usually because of bad publicity related to a string of botched raids, scandals involving SWAT team members, big lawsuit settlements, and/or reduced police budgets. They are rarely disbanded because they are a bad idea.

Albuquerque, New Mexico

Late one night in October 1996, Larry Harper told his wife he was going to the park to kill himself. The 33-year-old plumber had been in drug treatment but had slid back into crack cocaine addiction. As he left the dwelling armed with a handgun, he muttered that his life wasn't worth living. The Albuquerque Police Department responded to his wife's call for help by dispatching to the park a police sniper and a nine-man SWAT team with a history of controversial shootings. Upon arrival at the scene, one of the officers, as he alighted from the van, said, "Let's go get the bad guy."[8]

After wandering around in the cold for two hours, Larry Harper decided not to commit suicide. As he walked back to his pickup truck, members of the SWAT team started shooting at him. They chased Larry through the woods and found him standing behind a juniper tree. The police sniper took aim at a range of 43 feet, then shot Harper through the head. The authorities didn't charge the police marksman with a crime, and the chief of police didn't remove him from the SWAT team.

The killing of Larry Harper created public outrage, which caused the mayor of Albuquerque to hire Sam Walker, a criminal justice professor at the University of Nebraska to study the police department's SWAT practices and policies regarding the use of deadly force. In his report, professor Walker wrote: "The rate of killings by the [Albuquerque] police was just off the charts . . . They had an organizational culture that led them to escalate situations rather than de-escalating."[9]

Following the Harper shooting, the Albuquerque police started videotaping SWAT-team encounters with suicidal people. Because SWAT-team members had been accused of planting guns on persons they had killed, weapons would be linked to these dead subjects through their latent fingerprints. Since latent fingerprints can also be planted, this measure wasn't particularly reassuring. The city also developed a program that provided the families of police shootings with free counseling.

In the fall of 1998, the city paid Larry Harper's wife an out-of-court wrongful death settlement of $200,000. The following year, the new chief of police, convinced that a city of 400,000 didn't need a full-time SWAT team, assigned its members to routine law enforcement duties. The chief did, however, maintain the unit as a part-time force to be deployed in high-risk situations.

Easton, Pennsylvania

In 2003 and 2004, the town of Easton, located in the eastern part of the state, paid out $5 million in settlements to the families of two men killed, in separate incidents, by Easton police officers. In March 2005, a SWAT officer accidentally shot and killed a fellow member of the unit while they were cleaning their guns inside the station following a training exercise. Although the earlier lawsuit settlements didn't involve SWAT officers and the accidental killing in 2005 concerned the issue of gun safety, the mayor decided to reevaluate the town's need for a SWAT unit. One of the mayor's concerns, especially after the million-dollar settlements, pertained to the $191,000 annual cost of maintaining the SWAT operation—and this didn't include the $50,000 annual liability insurance premium.

Two months after the SWAT officer's accidental death, the mayor hired three independent consulting groups to study the department and make recommendations regarding how the city, through better policing, could reduce the chances of future excessive force lawsuits. The expert with Keystone Municipal Services found that the department was at odds with itself over whether the overall law enforcement approach should be oriented to community service or to aggressive, zero-tolerance crime control. All of the consulting groups suggested a revision of the department's policies regarding the use of deadly force, and they all recommended the transfer of city SWAT duties to the Pennsylvania State Police. Consultants with the Pennsylvania Chiefs of Police Association. In their 127-page report, they characterized the Easton Police Department as an "agency in crisis."[10]

In July 2005, Easton mayor Phil Mitman held a news conference to announce the results of the police studies. "We don't need to study and analyze this anymore to start the department on the road to high quality," he said. "We cannot have the risks of $2 and $3 million lawsuits anymore. We will be headed toward zero-tolerance for lawsuits." The editor of the *Allentown Morning Call*, writing that Easton SWAT team members had been "rude, arrogant, and disrespectful" and had "lost the confidence of the civilians who supervise them and pay their paychecks,"[11] praised the mayor's decision to disband the SWAT team.

As is often the case whenever law enforcement units are disbanded, leaders of police unions complain bitterly. Charles McMonagle, vice president of the local Fraternal Order of the Police lodge, warned that the elimination of the SWAT team would probably be followed by the dismantling of the K-9 and accident investigation units. Because of the chief's backing of the mayor's decision, McMonagle called for the chief's resignation: "The chief will never have the confidence or the backing of the majority of his men. At this point, the city police department needs a change. Any change would be better than what we know now."[12] The mayor followed through on his promise to disband the SWAT team, and the chief of police stood by that decision.

Wrong House in Temecula

In Temecula, California, a town of 100,000 midway between Los Angeles and San Diego, the police department's Street Enforcement Team (SET) raided the wrong house on Ranch California Road. At 9:30 P.M., August 24, 2007, eight officers broke into David and Lillian Scott's living room and threw them face-down onto the floor. In the garage, officers handcuffed the couple's 15-year-old daughter and her visiting friend. The Scott's 16-year-old son, who had been feeding the couple's 5-month-old baby in a bedroom, ended up on the floor in handcuffs. When Mrs. Scott asked to leave the living room to check on the infant, one of the officers threatened to shoot her if she moved. The target of the raid, a fugitive parolee, lived down the street.

A week after this fiasco, chief of police Jerry Williams, in office less than a month, temporarily disbanded the SET unit pending the results of an internal inquiry. To his credit, he, along with the mayor, visited the Scotts at their ransacked house to apologize for the mistake. The chief also reassigned the eight SET members to routine police duty.

Those who had hoped this wrong-house raid would lead to the permanent elimination of the Temecula SET unit were disappointed when Chief Williams, on September 13, 2007, announced that he was forming a new tactical unit staffed by different officers. Speaking to a local newspaper reporter, he said, "They are my front-line team. It is critical we keep them out there."[13] Perhaps the chief, new to his position, felt he couldn't risk alienating his force by eliminating the department's most prestigious crime-fighting unit.

The Hoboken SWAT Scandal

It all started in November 2007 when dozens of photographs surfaced in the New Jersey media showing members of the Hoboken Police Department's SWAT team partying with Hooter waitresses in Tuscaloosa, Alabama. Some of the shots were mildly racy and others featured the Hooter girls handling various SWAT weapons and clowning around with the officers. The photographs had been taken in the fall of 2006 when the officers, during one of several trips to Kenner, Louisiana, on Hurricane Katrina humanitarian missions, stopped over in Tuscaloosa. No one explained exactly how Louisiana's hurricane victims were served by a New Jersey SWAT team.

One of the more disturbing photographs featured the commander of the SWAT squad, Lieutenant Angelo Andriani, wearing a napkin with eye holes cut out, meant to look like a Ku Klux Klan hood. A month before the photographs became public, five Hispanic Hoboken police officers had filed a lawsuit against Andriani accusing him of creating a racist and hostile work environment. In November 2007, public safety director Bill Bergin permanently disbanded the SWAT team.

The *Jersey Journal,* in February 2008, obtained a videotape showing Lieutenant Andriani's gun being passed around at a party in New Orleans hosted by a Louisiana developer and his wife. When the weapon came back around to Andriani, he slipped the magazine out of the gun and distributed the bullets to partygoers. Chief of police Carmen La Bruno can be seen laughing as the Lieutenant's gun is being passed around.

The *New York Times,* in March 2008, ran a story based on an internal police report leaked to the media. According to the Hoboken Police Department's internal affairs investigators, SWAT-team members had each been contributing $20 a month to an equipment and gear fund controlled by Lieutenant Andriani and that these monies that had been diverted and misused. The report also included allegations that Andriani had forced off-duty police officers to work at his home in Verona, New Jersey. Regarding the Hoboken paramilitary unit, the author of the report had written that the "SWAT team had provided virtually no meaningful service to the city."[14] A few days after the article appeared, the public safety director placed Lieutenant Andriani on paid administrative leave. Nine other members of the former SWAT squad, while kept on regular duty, received a variety of "behavior unbecoming" citations.

Hoboken police chief Carmen La Bruno, after 37 years on the job, retired on July 1, 2008. A year later the safety director officially placed Andriani on an $11,000 per month, two-year suspension, a paid vacation mandated by his employment contract. The lieutenant, insisting that he had done nothing wrong, accused his accusers of being politically motivated. In January 2010, Andriani was back in the news after reportedly creating a disturbance at Tampa International Airport (TIA) by allegedly flashing his badge and berating TIA employees for allowing a flight crew to move ahead of him in a screening line.

Budget Constraints

The police department in Escondido, California, a town of 125,000 just north of San Diego, had been spending $180,000 a year to fund its 22-member SWAT team. The mayor, facing a budget deficit, asked his department heads to cut costs. Chief of police Jim Maher floated the idea of disbanding the SWAT team, a unit that responded to an average of only 17 calls a year. The chief had discussed the idea with the sheriff of San Diego County, who had offered, at no expense, to make his tactical unit available to the city. The Escondido police rank and file caught wind of the proposal and let the chief know it was not acceptable. In February 2009, the chief, instead of disbanding the unit, announced that he had cut the annual SWAT budget in half by reducing the team's training regimen from 20 to 16 hours a month. In addition, SWAT officers would no longer be paid overtime during training sessions. These measures and cuts in other police services made it possible to save the SWAT unit, even though it wasn't needed. In explaining how the city of Escondido benefited from a poorly trained, rarely used SWAT team, the chief cited officer morale. So, in the end, saving the SWAT unit was more about the police department than the citizens it served.

In Lacey, Washington, a suburb of 38,000 outside of Olympia, the chief of police, in February 2009, disbanded the Special Response Team (SRT). Chief Dusty Pierpoint said he had no choice, the department simply couldn't afford the 10-man unit. In making the announcement, the chief assured the public that the slack would be picked up by the Thurston County tactical unit and by SWAT teams in Olympia and other nearby towns. Resistance to the elimination of the Lacey SRT unit didn't come from citizens but from the local police union. Police guild vice president Ken Kollman called the dismantling arbitrary because it had not been the subject of a labor negotiation. The union leader threatened to file an unfair labor practice complaint against the city. Once again, it was all about the police, not the public.

Once SWAT teams are established, regardless of whether or not they are needed, effective, and affordable, chiefs of police find it difficult to disband them. In modern law enforcement, a police agency without a paramilitary unit is considered unprepared and weak. Such an agency is like an army without a fleet of tanks. But domestic law enforcement isn't war, and if two thirds of the 3,500 or so SWAT teams were eliminated, the country would not be overrun by criminals, and citizens would not be exposed to nearly as much violence by the police.

Recommendations for Less Militarized Policing

Although militarized policing doesn't provide added protection from crime and domestic terrorism, it alienates innocent people; costs money the country can't afford; turns public servants into combat warriors; and, in a free nation, is inappropriately oppressive. The first step toward demilitarization would include a de-escalation of the war on drugs; the disbanding of the SWAT teams that exist primarily to serve predawn, no-knock search warrants; and the termination of the special forces training of ordinary police officers. Step two would involve replacing zero-tolerance, no-discretion law enforcement with the less aggressive community model of policing where officers function more as public servants than as occupiers of enemy territory. Less fear mongering from politicians and police administrators would also improve police–community relations. And finally, reducing the role of the federal government in dealing with criminal offenses that can be adequately handled on the local level would further enhance police–community relations.

In the larger jurisdictions where SWAT teams are occasionally needed, training should be standardized and intense. Officers assigned to routine patrol should not receive SWAT training or be issued paramilitary weapons. SWAT operations should be subjected to enhanced civilian oversight and, if there are too many botched or low-risk raids, disbanded. Legislators, in cases where victims of wrong-house SWAT raids sue the government, might consider a kind of tort law reform that would make the recovery of damages less difficult.

NOTES

CHAPTER 1: THE NATURE AND SCOPE OF MILITARIZED POLICING

1. John Wooley, "Memorandum to the House of Representatives Returning without Approval of the 'National Defense Authorization Act for Fiscal Year 2008,'" *American Report,* December 28, 2007.

2. Michael Levenson and Donald Slack. "Mayor Says No to Rifle Patrols," *Boston Globe,* May 30, 2009.

3. "David Kopel, "Smash-up Policing: When Law Enforcement Goes Military," *National Review,* May 22, 2000.

4. Erin Halasz, "With SWAT on the Streets, Residents Fear Harassment," *Windy Citizen,* April 25, 2008.

5. Peter Sachs, "Police Rush Ahead With Plan to Buy M 4 Rifles," *Chi-Town Daily News,* October 17, 2008.

6. Charlie Deitch, "Military-Style Police Tactics Reflect—and Arguably Worsen—Distrust Between Black Neighborhoods and Police," www.everyday-democracy.org, March 22, 2007.

7. David Kopel, "Smash-Up Policing: When Law Enforcement Goes Military," *National Review,* May 22, 2000.

8. Torsten Ove, "No Citations for Giving the Finger to Police, Judge Says," *Pittsburgh Post-Gazette,* March 24, 2009.

9. "Dash Cam Video Released by Oklahoma Public Safety Department." *Tulsa World,* June 13, 2009.

10. Ibid.

11. "Video: Witness: Trooper in the Wrong," *Tulsa World,* June 14, 2009.

12. "OHP/EMS Incident Dash Cam Released." KOKI-TV, June 13, 2009.

13. Mike Celizic, "Great-Grandma Dared Cop to Taser Her—So He Did." http://today.msnbc.msn.com/id/31202935/, June 10, 2009.

14. Paula Reed Ward, "High-Speed Pursuit Bad Idea, Experts Say," *Pittsburgh Post-Gazette,* September 24, 2008.

15. Steven Greenhut, "The Militarization of American Police," *Freeman,* March 2008.

16. Peter Kraska and Victor Kappeler, "Militarizing Police: The Rise and Normalization of Paramilitary Units," *Social Problems,* February 1997.

17. Nicholas Pastore, "SWAT Overkill," *Nation,* May 31, 1999.

18. "The Sniper" with correspondent Jim Stewart, *60 Minutes II* segment, January 25, 2001.

19. Nicholas Riccardi, "Man Charged in Artifact Theft Killed Self, Police Say," *Los Angeles Times,* June 13, 2009.

20. Mike Stark, "Feds Face Criticism over Arrests in Artifacts Case," Associated Press, June 17, 2009.

21. Lee Davidson, "Attorney General Defends Relics Raid," *Deseret News,* June 17, 2009.

CHAPTER 2: STRONG-ARMING GROUPS

1. Robin Wallace, "Danforth Disputes New Criticism of His Waco Report," www.foxnews.com, April 24, 200l.

2. "Affidavit: Teen Bride's Cry for Help Led to Raid," www.cnn.com, April 9, 2008.

3. Alex Tresniowski, Darla Atlas, Anne Lang, and Carry Cardwell, "This Is Home," *People Magazine,* March 23, 2009.

4. Ibid.

5. Rick Anderson, "U.S. Army Supplies Surveillance Support," *Seattle Weekly,* December 12, 1999.

6. Joe Garofoli, "250 Protestors Arrested, Including Amy Goodman," *San Francisco Chronicle,* September 2, 2008.

7. Jeff Wilford, "DanceSafe Condemns Racine Raid in Which Each Attendee Received $968 Fine," *Racine Journal Times,* November 5, 2002.

8. Knick Evol, "SWAT Raids Legal Utah Rave Scary!" http://raindanceheads.tribe.net, August 22, 2005.

9. Farhad Manjoo, "Mass Gathering," www.salon.com, September 26, 2005.

10. Syze, "The Utah Rave Raid," www.drizzten.com/blog, August 2005.

11. Sara Israelsen, "Police Heavy-Handed, Party Organizers Say," *Deseret News,* August 23, 2005.

12. "Community Rallies After Outrageous Raid," www.drugpolicy.org, September 1, 2005.

13. "ACLU Joins Lawsuit Challenging Raids of Concerts and Violations of Free Speech," www.acluutah.org, September 26, 2005.

14. "Charges Dropped in Raid on Detroit Art Gallery," www.detnews.com, September 22, 2008.

15. Chris Casey, "Report Rips ICE's Handling of 'Abuse' Raids," *Greeley Tribune,* June 19, 2009.

16. Ibid.

17. Norman Oder, "In Overnight Sweep, Janitors at Public Library in Mesa, Arizona, Arrested on Immigration Charges," *Library Journal,* October 17, 2008.

18. J. J. Hensley and Gary Nelson, "Deputies Sweep Mesa City Hall, Library Overnight," *Arizona Republic,* October 16, 2008.

19. Nick R. Martin, "Ex-Judges Stunned by Raid on Mesa Buildings," *East Valley Tribune,* October 17, 2008.

20. Nick R. Martin and John Leptich, "Mesa Mayor Rips Arpaio in City Buildings Raid," *East Valley Tribune,* October 16, 2008.

21. Douglas Rivlin, "Media-Hound Sheriff Arpaio Marches Immigrants Through Town Square for Fox News Cameras," *New America Media,* February 18, 2009.

22. Mike Sunnucks, "Sheriff Joe Arpaio Scoffs at Possibility of Broader Federal Probe," *Phoenix Business Journal,* June 18, 2009.

CHAPTER 3: BOOTS IN THE HOUSE

1. "Maricopa County School Chief Intends to Sue," Associated Press, September 26, 2008.

2. Michael Kiefer, "Dowling Sues Arpaio, County Supervisors Over SWAT Raid," *Arizona Republic,* June 4, 2009.

3. Renee Cardelli and John Paul, "Sheriff Defends Armed Escort at Amish Community," www.wtov9.com/news, September 21, 2007.

4. Attorney Felmet quote: Mark Law, "Hearing Set in Amish Raid," *Wheeling News-Register,* September 20, 2007.

5. Renee Cardelli and John Paul, "Sheriff Defends Armed Escort at Amish Community," www.wtov9.com/news, September 21, 2007.

6. Mark Law, "Sheriff Faces Amish Suit," *Wheeling News-Register,* September 19, 2008.

7. Bob Linrlih, "SWAT Team-Seized Boy Refuses Doc's Painkillers," www.worldnetdaily.com, January 8, 2008.

8. Sarah Foster, "Just an 'Uneventful Execution' of a Search Warrant," www.newswithviews.com, December 23, 2008.

9. "Raid on Family's Home and Organic Food Co-op Challenged," www.buckeyeinstitute.org, December 17, 2008.

10. Ibid.

11. Matt Loveless, "Police Play Down Frat House Raid," KLEW-TV, January 31, 2009.

12. Dan Herbeck, "Woman Hurt in Drug Raid Still Serious," *Buffalo News,* January 24, 2005.

13. Radley Balko, www.theagitator.com, February 10, 2008.

14. Carol Comegno, "Judge: 'Flash Bang' Grenade Unnecessary," *Courier Post* (New Jersey), August 28, 2008.

15. Ibid.

16. Ibid.

17. Kristina De Leon, "House Catches Fire During Police Drug Raid," WOAI-TV, February 4, 2009.

18. Alison Gendar and Corky Siemaszko, "NYPD Investigates Two Officers in Taser Death of Naked Brooklyn Man," *New York Daily News,* September 25, 2008.

19. Ruben Rosario, "Police Raid Wrong House," *St. Paul Pioneer-Press,* December 17, 2007.

20. Caroline Lowe, "Settlement Reached in Raid on Wrong House," *WCCO Crime Resources,* December 13, 2008.

21. Ibid.

22. Catherine Wilson, "Miami Officer's Corruption Trial Hinges on Toy Gun Presence," *Naples News,* May 5, 2004.

23. "Attorney General's Press Release," August 27, 2008.

24. "NH State Police Director: Review SWAT Teams," Associated Press, August 29, 2008.

CHAPTER 4: STOMPING ON SIN

1. Colleen Lutolf, "Police SWAT Raid on Retiree 'Unfortunate,'" *Sentinel* (Woodbridge, New Jersey), May 17, 2005.

2. Arielle Levin Becker, "State Police Search Targets Wrong Tenant," *Home News Tribune* (New Jersey), May 11, 2005.

3. Ibid.

4. Tim Davis, "Gretna Couple Angry Over Botched Child Porn Raid," *Star-Tribune* (Virginia), November 1, 2006.

5. Ibid.

6. Ibid.

7. Ibid.

8. Ibid.

9. "Do 'Computer Police' Have Too Much Power?" *Chatham Star-Tribune,* November 1, 2006.

10. Radley Balko, "SWAT Teams with Star Power," *Reason Magazine,* February 2007.

11. Jim Stingl, "Sometimes 'Sorry' Doesn't Cut It," *Journal Sentinel* (Milwaukee), November 24, 2007.

12. Ibid.

13. Ibid.

14. www.milwaukee.gov/attachments, March 10, 2008.

15. Paul Myerscough, "Diary," *London Review of Books,* January 29, 2009.

16. Bob Pajich, "Poker Players Fight the Law in South Carolina," *Card Player Magazine,* April 28, 2008.

17. Ibid.

18. Glenn Smith, "Some Implicated in Hanahan Poker Raid Also Charged in Mt. P," *Post and Courier* (Charleston, South Carolina), April 9, 2008.

19. Bob Ciaffone, "Nice and Nasty Poker Busts," *Card Player Magazine*, July 25, 2006.

20. Meg Kinnard, "Poker Aficionados Watching South Carolina Texas Hold'em Case," Associated Press, January 29, 2009.

21. Radley Balko, "San Mateo Police Raid Small-Stakes Poker Game," *Reason Magazine*, January 14, 2008.

22. Tom Jackson, "SWAT Tactics at Issue After Fairfax Shooting," *Washington Post*, January 27, 2006.

23. Tom Jackson, "Officer Won't Face Charges in Shooting Death," *Washington Post*, March 23, 2006.

24. Tom Jackson, "Va. Officer Might Be Suspended for Fatality," *Washington Post*, November 25, 2006.

25. Ibid.

26. "Federal Officials Close Investigation Into Fatal Shooting of Dr. Salvatore J. Culosi, Jr., by Fairfax County Police Officer," U.S. Department of Justice, June 1, 2007.

CHAPTER 5: PART-TIME WARRIORS

1. "Militarization of Police: No-Crime City Gets Its Own SWAT Team," www.tricities.com, October 25, 2007.

2. "S.C. Sheriff's Department Armored Vehicle With Belt-Fed Machine Gun," *Police Magazine*, March 6, 2008.

3. Derrick Mahone, "Cobb Police Add Tank to Arsenal," *Atlanta Journal-Constitution*, October 10, 2008.

4. Gina Snider, "City of Newnan Police Receives Armored Personnel Carrier," www.cinewnan.ga.us, July 2, 2008.

5. www.supremecorp.com, December 18, 2008.

6. "Armored Police Vehicle Worth Its Weight," *Cedar Rapids Gazette*, October 9, 2008.

7. Mike Lee, "Concerns on SWAT Aired Year Before Raid," *Fort Worth Star-Telegram*, April 13, 2003.

8. *Estate of Davis v. City of North Richland Hills*, 406 F. 3d 375 (2005).

9. Ibid.

10. Ibid.

11. "Police, School District Defend Drug Raid," CNN, November 7, 2003.

12. Ibid.

13. Ibid.

14. "High School Drug Sweep Investigated," www.about.com, November 9, 2003.

15. "Goose Creek School Raid," *USA Today*, July 19, 2006.

16. Brian Huber, "Police Broke Through Wrong Door on House, Man Says," *Waukesha Freeman,* January 4, 2006.

17. Ibid.

18. Ibid.

19. Gwen Albers, "Police Raid Targets Wrong Address," *Bonner County Daily Bee,* May 2, 2007.

20. Shane Benjamin, "Drug Raid Nabs Wrong Woman," *Durango Herald,* June 15, 2007.

21. Ibid.

CHAPTER 6: LEGAL POT

1. Warren P. Strobel, "Clinton Says U.S. Shares Responsibility for Mexico's Drug Violence," *Christian Science Monitor,* March 27, 2009.

2. August Vollmer, *Crime, Crooks, and Cops,* New York: Funk & Wagnalls, 1937.

3. Bob Egelko, "U.S. to Yield Marijuana Jurisdiction to States," *San Francisco Chronicle,* February 27, 2009.

4. Jason Blevins, "Marijuana, a Growing Battle," *Denver Post,* September 14, 2008.

5. Ibid.

6. Ibid.

7. Karen Romer, "Film Shoot Nixed by SWAT Team," *Greeley Tribune,* June 19, 2006.

8. Jason Blevins, "Marijuana, a Growing Battle," *Denver Post,* September 14, 2008.

9. Ibid.

10. Ibid.

CHAPTER 7: COLLATERAL DAMAGE

1. Radley Balko, "Little Oversight, Bad Information a Deadly Mix," *Reason Magazine,* December 6, 2006.

2. "APD Seeks Snitches in Want Ads," www.kob.com, November 26, 2006.

3. "Family Angry After SWAT Team Mistakenly Raids Home," www.wlky.com, August 10, 2007.

4. "Shot in the Dark," *Arkansas Times,* April 24, 2008.

5. Ibid.

6. "NLR Chief Defends SWAT Unit," *Arkansas Times,* April 24, 2008.

7. James V. Franco, "Troy Cops Faulted for 'No-Knock' Raid," *Record,* September 17, 2008.

8. Ibid.

9. Ibid.

10. Geoffrey Fattah, "Suit Filed in SWAT Team's Home Raid," *Deseret News* (Salt Lake City), July 27, 2005.

11. Ibid.

12. Holly Hollman, "Man Shot by Officers Had Guns in Home, Sheriff Says," *Decatur Daily News,* June 29, 2006.

13. Rosalind S. Helderman and Aaron C. Davis, "Pr. George's Police Arrest 2 in Marijuana Shipping Plot," *Washington Post,* August 7, 2008.

14. Aaron C. Davis, "Prince George's Police Clear Mayor, Family," *Washington Post,* August 9, 2008.

15. Ibid.

16. Rosalind S. Helderman and Aaron C. Davis, "Killing of Mayor's 2 Dogs Justified, Pr. George's Finds," *Washington Post,* September 5, 2008.

17. "SWAT Officer Defends Calvo Raid," *National Review,* September 1, 2008.

18. April Witt, "Deadly Force," *Washington Post* February l, 2009.

19. Rosalind S. Helderman, "Bill Calls for More Scrutiny of SWAT Teams by Police," *Washington Post,* February 5, 2009.

20. Jonah Schuman, "Calvo Joins Legislators Calling for SWAT Reports," *Washington Post,* February 5, 2009.

21. Don Markus, "Md. Panel Hears Testimony on Police Raids," *Baltimore Sun,* March 4, 2009.

22. Ibid.

23. www.stopthedrugwar.org., April 9, 2009.

24. Aaron C. Davis, "Sheriff Says Deputies 'Did Their Job,'" *Washington Post,* June 20, 2009.

25. Ibid.

26. Nafeesa Syeed, "Mayor Sues Over Dog-Killing Raid," Associated Press, June 23, 2009.

27. Peter Hermann, "Numbers Paint Portrait of SWAT Team Use." *Baltimore Sun.* February 24, 2010.

28. April Witt, "Deadly Force," *Washington Post,* February 1, 2009.

29. Kevin Rowson, "Gwinnett Police Raid Wrong House," www.11alive.com, December 11, 2008.

30. Ibid.

CHAPTER 8: UNJUSTIFIABLE HOMICIDE

1. Luke Broadwater, "Family of Slain Dundalk Woman Sues Baltimore County Police," *Baltimore Examiner,* August 10, 2009.

2. Ibid.

3. "Brenden Kearney, "Trial Opens Over Fatal Police Raid in Dundalk," *Daily Record,* March 16, 2009.

4. Ibid.

5. "SWAT Team Found Not Liable in 2005 Death of Dundalk Woman," Associated Press, March 31, 2009.

6. "'Excitable' Tag Haunts Deputy," *St. Petersburg Times,* May 6, 2005.

7. Jose Cardenas, "Family Sues in Shooting Death," *St. Petersburg Times,* July 7, 2007.

8. Brian Haas, "Man Killed Had Gun Permit," *South Florida Sun-Sentinel*, August 13, 2005.

9. David Hunt, "For a Family, Drug Raid Went Terribly Wrong," *Florida Times-Union*, November 5, 2006.

10. Ibid.

11. Ibid.

12. Ibid.

13. Barry Halvorson, "Officer Won't Be Charged on Teen's Killing," *Victoria Advocate*, March 15, 2007.

14. Tom McGhee, "Denver SWAT Officers Cleared in Shooting," *Denver Post*, April 21, 2008.

15. Kirk Mitchell, "Police: Suspect Sold Crack Before Fatal Raid," *Denver Post*, April 10, 2008.

16. Daniel Tepfer and Joel C. Thompson, "Raid Sought Drugs From Easton Home," *Connecticut Post*, May 21, 2008.

17. Brigid Quinn, "Police Raid Ends in Death," fairfieldminuteman.com, May 22, 2008.

18. Maggie Caldwell, "Not Guilty Plea in Case That Killed Ex-Ridgefielder," *Easton Courier*, June 26, 2008.

19. Jarret Liotta, "Easton Deadly Raid Prompts Lawsuit," www.fairfieldminuteman.com, November 20, 2008. Also: Susan Silvers, "Former Ridgefield Man's Estate Plans Action Against 6 Towns," www.newstimelive.com, November 20, 2008.

20. "Deadly Police Raid May Lead to Wrongful Death Lawsuits," *Easton Courier*, November 20, 2008.

21. Jennifer Feehan, "Prosecutor Questions Justification for Lima Shooting," *Toledo Blade*, July 30, 2008.

22. Greg Sowinski, "Chavalia Said He Fired to Defend His Life," www.limaohio.com, July 31, 2008.

23. Ibid.

24. Jennifer Feehan, "Lima Police Officer Not Guilty in Deadly Raid," *Toledo Blade*, August 5, 2008.

25. Jennifer Feehan, "Review Clears Lima Officer in Slaying," *Toledo Blade*, October 16, 2008.

26. Lori Monsewicz, "SWAT Team Kills Mom," *Canton Repository*, September 19, 2008.

27. Melissa Griffy Seeton, "Family Defends Independent Investigation of Fatal Shooting," *Canton Repository*, September 23, 2008.

28. Lori Monsewicz, "Warrants, Records Sealed in Fatal SWAT Shooting," *Canton Repository*, September 24, 2008.

CHAPTER 9: NEGLIGENT HOMICIDE

1. Joseph Mallia and Maggie Mulvihill, "Minister Dies as Cops Raid Wrong Apartment," *Boston Globe*, March 28, 1994.

2. "Sorry, Wrong Apartment," *Time Magazine*, April 11, 1994.

3. Prendergast reporting, Alan Prendergast, "Unlawful Entry: The High Price of Denver's Drug War," *Westword,* February 24, 2000.

4. Ibid.

5. Ibid.

6. Ibid.

7. "Man Killed in Police Raid of Wrong House" www.cnn.com, October 6, 2000.

8. Ibid.

9. Ashley Fantz, "Fatal Mistake," www.salon.com, October 19, 2000.

10. Ibid.

11. Robert Gearty and Owen Moritz, "Suit in Another Grenade Goof," *New York Daily News,* May 28, 2003.

12. Ibid.

13. William K. Rashbaum, "Woman's Death After Raid Is Officially Ruled Homicide," *New York Times,* May 28, 2003.

14. Ibid.

15. Donna Lamb, "Alberta Spruill Murder Taken Seriously by City Council," *Caribbean Life,* June 3, 2003.

16. Ibid.

17. William K. Rashbaum, "Lawyers Urge Council to Increase Oversight of Police Raids," *New York Times,* June 5, 2003.

18. Ibid.

19. William K. Rashbaum, "No Stun Grenades Since Death in Raid, as Debate Continues," *New York Times,* July 17, 2003.

20. Bill Torry, "Elderly Woman's Killing Casts Shadow on ATL Cops," *Atlanta Journal-Constitution,* November 9, 2008.

CHAPTER 10: OFFICER DOWN

1. "Officers, Ex-OSU Player Discuss Shooting," www.wbns10tv.com, May 21, 2008.

2. Ibid.

3. Bruce Cadwallader, "Ex-OSU Player's Support Criticized," *Columbus Dispatch,* June 2, 2008.

4. Ibid.

5. Ibid.

6. Matt McSpadden, "Effort to Get Marijuana Raises Question of Worth," *Springfield News-Leader,* December 31, 2008.

7. Lawrence Mower, "Suspect Says He Thought Officers With Warrant Were Trying to Break In," *Las Vegas Review-Journal,* December 31, 2008.

8. Ibid.

9. "No Deaths, This Time," *Las Vegas Review-Journal,* January 4, 2009.

10. Brian Haynes, "Girlfriend of Suspect in SWAT Shooting Awarded Custody of Children," *Las Vegas Review-Journal,* January 7, 2009.

11. Jeff O'Brien, "Two Charges Dismissed in Police Shooting Case," *Las Vegas Review-Journal,* January 20, 2009.

12. Ibid.

13. *Jolly v. Georgia,* 284 Ga. 165 (2008).

14. John Hopkins, "Prosecutors Say Frederick Knew Police Were Coming to Door," *Virginia-Pilot,* September 9, 2008.

15. Radley Balko, "Did Police Misconduct Lead to Another Fatal Marijuana Raid?" *Reason Magazine,* September 25, 2008.

CONCLUSION: NO EASY SOLUTION

1. "Not Enough Evidence to Charge Phelps, Sheriff Says," www.cnn.com, February 26, 2009.

2. Suzanne Smalley and Weston Kosova, "Reefer Madness," *Newsweek,* March 2, 2009.

3. John Tunison and John Agar, "Drug Critics Sometimes Fault Tactics, Say Enforcement Teams Uncover Few Major Dealers," *Grand Rapids Press,* April 26, 2009.

4. Ibid.

5. "Beefed-Up Presence on the Streets: Police Increase Visibility in City," *Central Jersey News,* March 1, 2009.

6. Ibid.

7. Cole quote: Michael Mayo, "Overzealous Drug War Claims Another Casualty," *Sun-Sentinel* (Florida), June 15, 2008.

8. Timothy Egan, "Soldiers of the Drug War Remain on Duty," *New York Times,* March 1, 1999.

9. Ibid.

10. Tracy Jordan, "City Awaits Third Set of Recommendations from Consultants," *Newsday,* July 9, 2005.

11. "Easton SWAT Team's Behavior: Further Evidence It Deserves Dismantling," *Allentown Morning Call,* July 29, 2005.

12. Tracy Jordan, "Mitman Hopes to End Lawsuits Against City, Police Union Calls for Mazzeo's Resignation," *Newsday,* July 22, 2005.

13. John Hall and John Hunneman, "Team of Temecula Officers Disbanded, Under Investigation," *North County Times,* September 2, 2007.

14. Jonathan Miller, "Police Scandal Grows to Include Possible Misuse of Money," *New York Times,* March 1, 2008.

BIBLIOGRAPHY

CHAPTER 1: THE NATURE AND SCOPE OF MILITARIZED POLICING

Alden, Diane. "Worrywarts, Black Helicopters and Trust." www.newsmax.com. September 12, 2000.

Balko, Radley. "Overkill: The Rise of Paramilitary Police Raids in America." CATO Institute white paper. February 2006.

Brezezinski, Piotr C. "SWAT State." *Harvard Crimson.* March 2, 2007.

Ericson, Edward Jr. "Commando Cop." *Orlando Weekly.* May 7, 1998.

Kopel, David B., and Paul H. Blackman. *No More Wacos.* Amherst, NY: Prometheus Books, 1997.

Kraska, Peter B. "Enjoying Militarism: Political/Personal Dilemmas in Studying U.S. Police Paramilitary Units." *Justice Quarterly.* Fall 1996.

Murphy, Chuck, and Sydney P. Feedberg. "Fort Florida." *St. Petersburg Times.* March 2, 2003.

Reynolds, Glenn Harlan. "SWAT Overkill: The Danger of a Paramilitary Police Force." *Popular Mechanics,* November 28, 2006.

Ryan, Rob. "Police Develop Military Mind Set." *Baltimore Sun.* September 12, 1999.

The Insurrection and Posse Comitatus Acts

Camire, Dennis. "Governors Poised to Regain More Control Over National Guard." *Shreveport Times.* January 2, 2008.

Moore, Richter Jr. "Posse Comitatus Revisited: The Use of the Military as Civil Law Enforcement." *Journal of Criminal Justice.* 15: 1987.

Wittes, Benjamin. "A Posse Comitatus Crusade." *Legal Times.* September 1, 12, 1997.
Woolley, John. "Memorandum to the House of Representatives Returning Without Approval of the 'National Defense Authorization Act for Fiscal Year 2008.'" *The American Presidency Project.* December 28, 2007.

Los Angeles and the Birth of SWAT Policing

Dunphy, Jack. "Is a SWAT Team the Place to Get PC?" www.pajamasmedia.com/blog. March 26, 2008.
"LAPD SWAT." www.specwarnet.net/taclink/Police/LAPD_SWAT.

Bombs Away in Philadelphia

Linder, Brad. "Philadelphia Still Feels Effects of MOVE Bombing." NPR. May 13, 2005.
McQuiston, James. "A Basic History of the 1985 MOVE Bombing." www.associated content.com. October 23, 2006.
Moore, Martha T. "1985 Bombing in Philadelphia Still Unsettled. *USA Today.* May 11, 2005.
Sullivan, Laura. "Philadelphia MOVE Bombing Still Haunts Survivors." "All Things Considered." NPR. May 13, 2005.

The Columbine Effect

Banda, Solomon. "Teacher Tackles Gunman Suspected in School Shooting." Associated Press. February 24, 2010.
Bovard, James. "They Couldn't SWAT a Fly." *American Spectator.* August 1999.
Bulwa, Damian. "Woman Says She Pointed Police to Oakland Killer." *San Francisco Chronicle.* March 24, 2009.
"Columbine Altered Police Procedures." Associated Press. April 20, 2009.
James, Susan Donaldson. "Surviving Columbine: What We Got Wrong." www.abc news.com. April 20, 2009.
Jonsson, Patrik. "Surprise Winner of Obama Stimulus Spending: Gun Industry." *Christian Science Monitor,* September 11, 2009.
O'Brien, Jeff. "Police and SWAT." *Police Magazine.* January 2008.

Bucking the Trend in Boston

Levenson, Michael, and Donovan Slack. "Mayor Says No to Rifle Patrols." *Boston Globe.* May 30, 2009.
Slack, Donovan, and Maria Cramer. "Police Getting More Firepower." *Boston Globe.* May 29, 2009.

More Firepower in Western Pennsylvania

Ballngit, Moriah. "McKeesport Seeks Funds to Start Special Response Unit." *Pittsburgh Post-Gazette*. May 7, 2009.

Lord, Rich. "City Police to Carry More Firepower." *Pittsburgh Post-Gazette*. April 28, 2009.

Micco, Lisa. "High Risk." *New Castle News*. June 3, 2009.

Sherman, Jerome L. "SWAT Deployments on Swift Pace This Year." *Pittsburgh Post-Gazette*. May 1, 2009.

"Shooter Wearing Bulletproof Vest Guns Down 3 Pittsburgh Officers, Upset Over Losing Job." Associated Press. April 4, 2009.

Saturation Patrols and Crowd Control

Chicago's "Summer Safety" Plan

Cassidy, Peter. "Operation Ghetto Storm: The Rise of Paramilitary Policing." *Covert Action Quarterly*. Fall 1997.

Deitch, Charlie. "Military-Style Police Tactics Reflect—and Arguably Worsen—Distrust Between Black Neighborhoods and Police." www.everyday-democracy.org. March 22, 2007.

Halasz, Erin. "With SWAT in the Streets, Residents Fear Harassment." *Windy Citizen*. April 25, 2008.

Kahn, Jeremy. "Culture of Silence in Minority Communities." *Atlantic*. April 2007.

Michels, Scott, and Theresa Cook. "Some Big Cities See Homicides Drop in 2008." www.abcnews.go.com. January 2, 2009.

Muhammad, Ashahed M. "SWAT Teams and Helicopter Patrols in Chicago." www.Finalcall.com. May 6, 2008.

Pastore, Nicholas. "SWAT Overkill." *Nation*. May 3, 1999.

Sachs, Peter. "Police Pushing Ahead with Plan to Buy M4 Rifles." *Chi-Town Daily News*. October 17, 2008.

Making Chattanooga Safer

LaSalle, Renee. "Chattanooga Police Have a New Weapon to Fight Crime." www.wdef.com. July 23, 2008.

The War on Drugs

Carpenter, Ted Galen, and R. Channing Rouse. "Perilous Panacea: The Military in The Drug War." CATO Institute, Washington, D.C. February 15, 1990.

Kopel, David. "Smash-Up Policing: When Law Enforcement Goes Military." *National Review*. May 22, 2000.

The SWAT Team Explosion

Booth, William. "Exploding Number of SWAT Teams Sets Off Alarms." *Washington Post.* June 17, 1997.

Fraser, Ronald. "SWAT Teams Are Out of Control." *Roanoke Times.* October 3, 2006.

Leona, Vera. "Paramilitary Police Raids Must Be Reined In." *Hartford Courant.* September 8, 2008.

Weber, Diane Cecilia. "Warrior Cops: The Ominous Growth of Paramilitarism in American Police Departments." CATO Institute, Washington, D.C. August 26, 1999.

Shock-and-Awe Policing

Carroll, Rick. "Drug Raid Arrestee Gets Two Years." *Aspen Daily News.* July 3, 2006.

Becker, Maki. "How Effective Is the Drug War?" *Buffalo News.* May 24, 2006.

Levine, Jay. "NW Side Club Members Sue Cops Over Raid." www.cbs.com. June 11, 2008.

Miller, Ellen. "Drug Raid in Aspen Stirs Pot." *Rocky Mountain News.* December 8, 2005.

Thomas, Vanessa, and T. J. Pignataro. "3 Days of Secret Police Drug Raids Bring 78 Arrests Throughout City." *Buffalo News.* April 21, 2006.

Zero-Tolerance Policing

Ove, Torsten. "No Citation for Giving the Finger to Police, Judge Says." *Pittsburgh Post-Gazette.* March 24, 2009.

Ward, Paula Reed. "Cops Challenged on Citations." *Pittsburgh Post-Gazette.* September 2, 2008.

"Woman Angered by Police Treatment." *Trenton Times.* September 3, 2008.

Welcome Home Maurice White

Maxwell, Sally. "EMT, Cop Face-Off Under Investigation." *Sequoyah County Times.* June 15, 2009.

Murphy, Sean. "Attorney Defends Trooper in Okla. Ambulance Stop." Associated Press. June 16, 2009.

"Video: Witness: Trooper in the Wrong." *Tulsa World.* June 14, 2009.

Shocking Older Women: What Ever Happened to Helping Them Cross the Street?

Celizic, Mike. "Great-Grandma Dared Cop to Taser Her—So He Did." www.msnbc.com. June 10, 2009.

Cusac, Anne-Marie. "The Trouble with Tasers." *Progressive.* May 2005.

Mitchell, Mary. "Chicago Police Taser 82-Year-Old Grandma After Forced Entry for 'Wellness' Check." *Chicago Sun-Times.* November 6, 2007.

Rubin, Joel. "Federal Court Restricts Taser Use by Police." *Los Angeles Times.* December 30, 2009.

Schorn, Daniel. "Tasered Granny Suing Police." www.cbsnews.com. December 8, 2005.

"Tasered Mo. Grandmother Gets Probation." Associated Press. July 28, 2005.

"Tasered Woman Takes Texas County's Settlement Bid. Associated Press. October 6, 2009.

Cracking Down on Kids

Bonham, Nick. "Deputy Zaps Boy, 10, with Taser." *Pueblo Chieftain.* December 3, 2009.

Boyle, Patrick. "Stunning Decisions: After Deaths and Cautions, Still No Consensus for Stun Gun Use on Youths." www.youthtoday.org. January 1, 2010.

Chen, Stephanie. "Girl's Arrest for Doodling Raises Concerns About Zero Tolerance." www.cnn.com. February 18, 2010.

"Cop Fired After Girl Tasered." Associated Press. November 20, 2009.

"Dozens of Kids Picked Up in Truancy Sweep." www.nbc.com. February 24, 2005.

Egan, Paul. "Excessive Force Charge in Taser Death of Teen." *Detroit News.* December 17, 2009.

Epstein, Victor, and Rachel Monahan. "Don't Blame Me, Says Principal Who Called for the Arrest of Queens Girl, 12, for Doodling on Desk." *New York Daily News.* February 5, 2010.

Espinosa, Juan. "Using Tasers on Kids Should Be Scrutinized." *Pueblo Chieftain.* December 5, 2009.

Fitzpatrick, Michael C. "9-Year-Old Arrested for Waving Toy Gun." *Morning Journal* (Lorain, Ohio). October 28, 2003.

Gordy, Cynthia. "Extreme Lockup: Why Are So Many of Our Young Children Being Treated Like Criminals?" www.essence.com. ND

Kelly, Cathal. "Cop Tasers Girl for Resisting Bedtime." www.thestar.com. November 20, 2009.

Krueger, Curtis. "Under 12, Under Arrest." *St. Petersburg Times.* December 17, 2000.

Mangino, Matthew T. "PA Leads Nation in Juvenile Lifers." *Vindicator* (Youngstown, Ohio). March 1, 2009.

"Mother of 'Tasered' Girl Defends Cop." www.radaronline.com. November 30, 2009.

Peterson, Lindsay. "Handcuffing Children Not the Answer, Experts Say." *Tampa Tribune.* April 6, 2003.

"Police Probe Handcuffing of Children." Associated Press. February 20, 2005.

"Students Arrested over 'Violent' Stick Figure Drawings." Associated Press. January 26, 2005.

Ward, Paula Reed. "Boy 11, Leads State Police on High Speed Chase." *Pittsburgh Post-Gazette.* September 22, 2008.

Ward, Paula Reed. "High-Speed Pursuit Bad Idea, Experts Say." *Pittsburgh Post-Gazette.* September 24, 2008.

Wilson, Michael, and Al Baker. "Police Criticized for Student Arrests." *New York Times.* October 9, 2008.

Win, Hanna Ingber. "Civil Rights Lawyer Sues City Over Handcuffing of Girl, 10." *New York Sun.* August 8, 2008.

The Emergence of "Dirty Harry" Policing

Greenhut, Steven. "The Militarization of American Police." *Freeman,* March 2008.

Kraska, Peter B., and Victor Kappeler. "Militarizing American Police: The Rise and Normalization of Paramilitary Units." *Social Problems.* February 1997.

McNamara, Joseph. "Officer Safety." *Wall-Street Journal.* November 29, 2006.

Police Snipers

Bartlett, Derrick D. "Tools of the Visual Intruder: The Virtues of the High Power Scope for Law Enforcement." *SWAT Digest.* February 2008.

Sherman, Jerome L. "City SWAT Team Takes First in One Sniper Contest Event." *Pittsburgh Post-Gazette.* March 22, 2009.

"The Sniper," with correspondent Jim Stewart. *60 Minutes II* segment. January 25, 2001.

The Federalization of Law Enforcement

"Feds Create One New Law Each Week." www.digitaljournal.com. July 13, 2008.

Hulse, Carol. "House Votes to Expand Hate Crimes Definition." *New York Times,* October 9, 2009.

Meese, Edwin III. "Federalization in Law Enforcement." *Criminal Law & Procedure Practice Group Newsletter.* Spring 1998.

Pershing, Ben. "Senate Passes Measure That Would Protect Gays." *Washington Post,* October 23, 2009.

Walsh, Brian W. "Heritage Foundation: One New Crime a Week." www.foxnews.com. July 3, 2008.

FBI Agents on the Warpath

Application/affidavit for search warrant filed in U.S. District Court, District of Utah, Central Division. June 8, 2009.

Davidson, Lee. "Attorney General Defends Relics Raid." *Deseret News.* June 17, 2009.

Foy, Paul. "Utahan Accuses Feds of Misconduct in Artifact Case." Associated Press. February 24, 2010.

Foy, Paul, and Mike Stark. "Prosecutor: Artifacts Informant Clean." *Durango Herald.* February 2, 2010.

Gonzales, Jason. "Suspected Trafficker Found Dead." *Durango Herald.* June 20, 2009.

Henetz, Patty. "Death of 'Source' Puts Videos in Jeopardy." *Salt Lake Tribune.* March 21, 2010.

Henetz, Patty. "Affidavits Describe Vast American Indian Artifacts Stash." *Salt Lake Tribune.* June 17, 2009.

Henetz, Patty. "Artifacts Cases Proceed Despite Source's Death." *Salt Lake Tribune.* March 9, 2010.

Henetz, Patty. "Artifact Raids: Feds' Relics 'Source' Has Deep Utah Business Roots." *Salt Lake City Tribune.* October 6, 2009.

Henetz, Patty, and Brandon Loomis. "Another Suicide in American Indian Artifacts Looting Case." *Salt Lake Tribune.* June 20, 2009.

"Indian Artifact Informant Ted Gardiner Commits Suicide." *Deseret News.* March 2, 2010.

Johnson, Kirk. "Suicide Raises Legal Issues in Indian Artifacts Cases." *New York Times.* March 8, 2010.

Maffly, Brian. "Many Artifacts Remain in Alleged Looters' Custody." *Salt Lake Tribune.* June 13, 2009.

O'Neill, Helen. "A Town's Love of Indian Artifacts Backfires." Associated Press. October 4, 2009.

Riccardi, Nicholas. "Man Charged in Artifact Theft Killed Himself, Police Say." *Los Angeles Times.* June 13, 2009.

Riccardi, Nicholas, and Jim Tankersley. "24 Charged in Crackdown on Native American Looting." *Los Angeles Times.* June 11, 2009.

Stark, Mike. "Feds Face Criticism Over Arrests in Artifacts Case." Associated Press. June 17, 2009.

Botched Drug Raids

Balko, Radley. "Overkill: The Rise of Paramilitary Police Raids in America." CATO Institute White Paper, February 2006.

Balko, Radley. "Little Oversight, Bad Information a Deadly Mix." www.reason.com. December 6, 2006.

Brezezinski, Piotr C. "SWAT State: When They Kick at Your Front Door, How You Gonna Come?" *Harvard Crimson.* March 2, 2007.

Trounson, Rebecca. "Deaths Raise Questions About SWAT Teams." *Los Angeles Times.* November 1, 2000.

Pop Culture and SWAT Team Acceptance

McGrory, Kathleen. "SWAT School Teaches Kids About Law Enforcement." *Miami Herald.* October 14, 2008.

Sanzenbach, Erik. "Slidell Teens Go to Camp to Learn About Police Work." www.thesttammanynews.com. July 30, 2008.

Schoon, Lindsay. "Little Cop Lesion: Students Participate in Mock Raid." www.qconline.com June 28, 2007.

Wilson, Lynne. "Selling SWAT." *Covert Action Quarterly.* Fall 1997.

CHAPTER 2: STRONG-ARMING GROUPS

Saving the Children

Disaster at Waco

Boyer, Peter J. "The Children of Waco." *New Yorker.* May 15, 1995.

Dougherty, Jon. "Expert Supports Waco Video Conclusions." www.WorldNetDaily. com. June 6, 2001.

Labaton, Stephen, and Sam Howe Verhovek. "Missteps in Waco: A Raid Re- examined—A Special Report; U.S. Agents Say Fatal Flaws Doomed Raid on Waco Cult." *New York Times.* March 28, 1993.

Larson, Erik. "How a Cascade of Errors Led ATF to Disaster at Waco." *Time Maga- zine.* July 24, 1995.

Wallace, Robin. "Danforth Disputes New Criticism of His Waco Report." Associated Press. April 24, 2001.

Williams, David, and Glenn F. Bunting. "Agent Disputes Boss on Waco Warning." *Los Angeles Times.* July 25, 1995.

The Eldorado Raid

Anthony, Paul A. "FLDS Custody Case Has Cost Texas $12 Million." www.gosanan gelo.com. November 26, 2008.

"Children at Polygamist Sect May Have Been Pregnant as Young as 13—Source." As- sociated Press. April 18, 2008.

Dobner, Jennifer. "Armored Officers, Personnel Carrier Led Raid on Ranch." Associ- ated Press. April 16, 2008.

Dobner, Jennifer, and Michael Graczyk. "What Happened to 416 Kids in Polygamy Raid?" Associated Press. April 15, 2008.

Elkins, Keith. "False Abuse Claim Investigated in Texas Polygamist Raid." www. keyetv.com. April 20, 2008.

Johnson, Kirk, and Gretel C. Kovach. "Dispute on Treatment of Children After Raid." *New York Times.* April 17, 2008.

Lavandera, Ed. "Affidavit: Teen Bride's Cry for Help Led to Raid." www.cnn.com. April 9, 2008.

MacLaggan, Corrie. "Raid, Aftermath's Early Cost: $75 million." *American States- man.* May 16, 2008.

Roberts, Michelle. "Texas Officials Seek Custody of Polygamists' Kids." Associated Press. August 18, 2008.

Roberts, Michelle. "Appeals Court Says Officials Failed to Show Seized Children in Imminent Danger." Associated Press. May 23, 2008.

Skovsen, Joel. "FLDS Raid—A Dangerous Legal Precedent." www.rense.com. April 26 2008.

"Texas Judge Orders Return of Polygamist Group's Children." Associated Press. June 2, 2008.

"Texas Polygamist Sect Member Found Guilty of Sexual Assault." www.cnn.com. November 5, 2009.

"Texas Seizure of Sect Kids Thrown Out." Associated Press. May 23, 2008.

Tresniowski, Alex, Darla Atlas, Anne Lang, and Cary Caldwell. "This Is Home." *People Magazine*. March 23, 2009.

A War on Terror or a War on Dissent?

Seattle WTO Protests

Anderson, Rick. "Delta's Down With It." *Seattle Weekly*. December 22, 1999.

Brunner, Jim. "3 WTO Lawsuits Settled by City." *Seattle Times*. May 4, 2001.

De Mause, Neil. "Pepper Spray Gets in Their Eyes." *Fairness & Accuracy in Reporting*. March/April 2000.

"$25,000 Award in WTO Pepper Spraying." *Seattle Times*. June 1, 2001.Wilson, Kimberly A.C., and Elaine Porterfield. "Brutal Police Behavior Was Recorded on Video." *Seattle Post-Intelligencer*. December 9, 1999.

Young, Bob, and Jim Brunner. "City to Pay Protestors $250,000 to Settle WTO Suit." *Seattle Times*. January 17, 2004.

The Preemptive Raid

Clancy, Eileen. "I-Witness Video Emergency Press Statement From the RNC." www.iwitnessvideo.org. August 30, 2008.

Garofoli, Joe. "250 Protestors Arrested, Including Amy Goodman." *San Francisco Chronicle*. September 2, 2008.

McGovern, Roy. "Storm Troopers at the RNC." www.consortiumnews.com. September 8, 2008.

Moynihan, Colin. "Dozens Detained Ahead of Convention." *New York Times*. August 30, 2008.

Pheifer, Pat. "St. Paul Activist to Sue City Over Police Raid Before RNC." *Star Tribune* (Minneapolis–St. Paul). October 10, 2008.

Operation Stop the Music

Raiding a "Disorderly House" in Racine

Keil, Jeremy. "Don't Sweep Racine Rave Under the Rug." www.1pwi.org. November, 10, 2002.

Mauriello, Tracie. "Sober Tailgating Promoted: Too Much Alcohol, Coarse Language, Announcements Say." *Pittsburgh Post-Gazette*. October 24, 2008.

"Racine Rave-Goers Appear in Court." www.channel3000.com. December 9, 2002.

"Stories From the Racine 'Rave Raid.'" www.aclu.org. January 17, 2003.

Wilford, Jeff. "Partygoers, Organizers Say Police Overreacted With Mass Citations." *Racine Journal Times*. November 5, 2002.

An Illegal Assembly in Utah County

"ACLU Joins Lawsuit Challenging Raids of Concerts and Violations of Free Speech." www.acluutah.org. September 26, 2008.

Gadette, Jamie. "Utah County Enforced Its Permit, Even if Time Was on the Side of Dance Party Promoters." www.slweekly.com. September 1, 2005.

Israelsen, Sara. "Police Heavy-Handed, Party Organizers Say." *Deseret Morning News.* August 23, 2005.

"Judge Dismisses Rave-Bust Lawsuit. www.ksl.com. June 28, 2001.

Pinette, Parker. "Police Raid Outdoor Music Event." www.utahmedia.org. August 22, 2005.

Toth, Heidi. "ACLU Joins Suit by Rave Organizers." www.usmjparty.blogspot.com. September 27, 2005.

"SWAT Raids Legal Utah Rave—Scary!" www.raindanceheads.tribe.net. August 22, 2005.

"The Utah Rave Raid." www.drizzten.com. August 20, 2008.

A Public Nuisance in Detroit

Ashenfelter, David. "Charges Dropped in Art Gallery Raid." *Free Press* (Detroit). September 22, 2008.

Hunter, George. "Charges Dropped in Raid on Detroit Art Gallery." *Detroit News.* September 22, 2008.

McGraw, Bill. "Towed Cars Sticking Point of Raid Deal." *Free Press* (Detroit). October 17, 2008.

McGraw, Bill. "Raid at Detroit Art Gallery Sows the Seeds of Rebellion." *Free Press* (Detroit). September 22, 2008.

Rounding Up Illegal Immigrants

Alexander, Ames, and Franco Ordoquel. "Immigration Authorities Raid Chicken Processing Plant." *Rome News-Tribune* (Georgia). October 8, 2008.

Almada, Jorge Morales. "ICE Conducts 1,172 Raids in 11 Months." www.11news.newamericamedia.org. October 17, 2008.

Casey, Chris. "Report Rips ICE's Handling of 'Abusive' Raids." *Greeley Tribune.* June 19, 2009.

Henry, Samantha. "Senators Push for Immigration Raid Guidelines." Associated Press. October 10, 2008.

"Immigration Enforcement Must Always Be Humane." www.dailyrecord.com. October 5, 2008.

"Immigration Raid Costs Taxpayers $6.1 million." www.gazetteoneline.com. October 15, 2008.

"Judge: Hearings to Be Held on Illegal Alien Raids." www.courant.com. October 7, 2008.

Petroski, William. "Taxpayers' Costs Top $5 Million for May Raid at Postville." *Des Moines Register.* October 14, 2008.

Theriault, Denis C. "More Than 1,000 Arrested Throughout California in Immigration Raids." *Mercury News.* September 29, 2008.

Sheriff Joe's War on Illegal Immigration

Hensley, J. J., and Gary Nelson. "Deputies Sweep Mesa City Hall, Library Overnight." *Arizona Republic.* October 16, 2008.

Martin, Nick R. "Ex-Judges Stunned by Raid on Mesa Buildings." www.eastvalleytribune.com. October 17, 2008.

Martin, Nick R., and John Leptich. "Mesa Mayor Rips Arpaio on City Buildings Raid." www.eastvalleytribune.com. October 16, 2008.

Nelson, Gary, Michael Kiefer, and J. J. Hensley. "Arpaio Raids Mesa City Hall; Mayor Outraged." *Arizona Republic.* October 17, 2008.

Oder, Norman. "In Overnight Sweep, Janitors at Public Library in Mesa, AZ, Arrested on Immigration Charges." *Library Journal.* October 17, 2008.

Rivlin, Douglas. "Media-Hound Sheriff Arpaio Marches Immigrants Through Town Square for Fox 'News' Cameras." www.alternet.org. February 18, 2009.

Sunnucks, Mike. "Sheriff Joe Arpaio Scoffs at Possibility of Broader Federal Probe." *Phoenix Business Journal.* June 18, 2009.

CHAPTER 3: BOOTS IN THE HOUSE

High-Risk Tactics in Low-Risk Cases

Sheriff Joe's White-Collar Bust: The SWAT Raid as Political Theater

"Dowling's Ordeal." *Arizona Republic.* August 28, 2008.

Kiefer, Michael. "Dowling Files Intent to Sue County, Arpaio for $1.75 Million." *Arizona Republic.* September 26, 2008.

Kiefer, Michael. "Dowling Sues Arpaio, County Supervisors Over SWAT Raid." *Arizona Republic.* June 4, 2009.

Kiefer, Michael. "Probation Ends Probe of County School Chief." *Arizona Republic.* August 26, 2008.

"Maricopa County Schools Chief Intends to Sue." Associated Press. September 26, 2008.

"She Walks Away, Head Held High." *Arizona Republic.* November 20, 2009.

Paramilitary Presence in New Hampshire

Gorenstein, Dan. "Policing the Police." http://www.nhpr.org/node/21816. February 17, 2009.

Friendly Persuasion versus Show of Force

Elias, Dave. "Amish Woman Drops Charges Against Jefferson County Sheriff." www.statejournal.com. May 15, 2008.

Elias, Dave. "High Profile Case Heard in Jefferson County." www.wtrf.com. July 9, 2008.

Elias, Dave. "Sheriff Explains Why He Took Amish Children Out of Their Bergholz Community." www.wtrf.com. November 18, 2008.

Elias, Dave. "Shrouded in Secrecy: An In Depth Look at Amish Community." www.statejournal.com. November 19, 2008.

Gossett, Dave. "Bergholz Man Enters Plea to Sexual Conduct With Minors." www.haconnect.com. September 11, 2008.

Law, Mark. "Amish Woman Dismisses Lawsuit." *Wheeling News-Register.* May 14, 2008.

Law, Mark. "Hearing Set in Amish Raid." *Wheeling News-Register.* September 20, 2008.

Law, Mark. "Sheriff Faces Amish Suit." *Wheeling News-Register.* September 19, 2008.

Excessive Force in Colorado: The SWAT Seizure of John Shiflett

Unruh, Bob. "Colorado SWAT Team Invades Home, Brutalizes Family." www.WorldNetDaily.com. January 10, 2008.

Unruh, Bob. "Mother Warns Community About 'Nazi' Home Invasion." www.WorldNetDaily.com. January 10, 2008.

Unruh, Bob. "SWAT Officers Invade Home, Take 11-Year-Old at Gunpoint." www.WorldNetDaily.com. January 7, 2008.

Unruh, Bob. "SWAT Team-Seized Boy Refuses Painkillers." www.WorldNetDaily.com. January 8, 2008.

In the Name of Property: Busting Burglars

Donaghue, Erin. "Charges Dropped Against Home Burglary Suspects." www.gazette.net. November 19, 2008.

Donaghue, Erin. "Police Launch Internal Investigation After Gang-Related Raid." www.gazette.net. October 16, 2008.

Donaghue, Erin. "Scotland Community Members Form Action Group." www.gazette.net. October 22, 2008.

Stern, Aaron. "Police Analyzing Scotland Raid." *Potomac Almanac.* October 14, 2008.

Stern, Aaron. "Residents Question Motives of Police Raid." *Potomac Almanac.* October 28, 2008.

Stern, Aaron. "Two Burglary Suspects Cleared." *Potomac Almanac.* November 4, 2008.

Suderman, Alan. "Family Sues After SWAT Team Raids Their Apartment by Mistake." *Washington Examiner.* June 21, 2009.

Knuckle Under or Be Raided

Fogarty, Steve. "Couple Sue Over Raid on Organic Food Co-op." *Chronicle-Telegram* (Lorain, Ohio). December 18, 2008.
Foster, Sarah. "Just an 'Uneventful Execution' of a Search Warrant." www.NewsWith Views.com. December 23, 2008.
"Local Food Cooperative Searched by State." *Morning Journal* (Lorain, Ohio). December 3, 2008.
"Raid on Family's Home and Organic Food Co-op Challenged." www.buckeyein stutute.org. December 17, 2008.
Stowers v. Ohio Attorney General. Ct. of Common Pleas, Lorain County (2008).
Unruh, Bob. "SWAT Raid on Food Co-op Called 'Entrapment.'" www.NewsWith Views.com. December 26, 2008.

The Frat House Sweep

Loveless, Mott. "Police Play Down Frat House Raid." www.klewtv.com. January 31, 2009.
"Police Raid Fraternity For Drugs, Alcohol." *Daily Evergreen* (Pullman, Washington). January 22, 2009.
"Pullman: SWAT Team Called in to Search WSU Fraternity." www.ar15.com. January 22, 2008.
"WSU Fraternity Suspended After SWAT Raid." Associated Press. January 28, 2009.

Flashbang Grenade Fires

Ijames, Steve. "Less Lethal Options for Today's Law Enforcement Challenges." www. policeone.com. October 21, 2005.
Knapp, Louise. "A Stunning New Flash-Bang." www.wired.com. April 20, 2002.

Niagara Falls, New York

Herbeck, Dan, and Bill Michelmore. "Niagara Falls Police Burn 18-Year-Old Girl With Flashbang, U.S. Customs Was There Too." *Buffalo News.* January 22, 2005.
"Niagara Falls Drug Raid Arrests Suspect; Injures Woman." www.wgrz.com. January 21, 2005.
"Police Use Flash Bang Grenade in Marijuana Raid, Injure Innocent Woman." www. stopthedrugwar.com. January 21, 2005.

San Bernadino County, California

Balko, Radley. "Police Militarization Roundup." www.theagitator.com. February 10, 2008.

Gary, Indiana

"Gary Man Gets Break on Sentence for Drugs." *Post-Tribune* (Gary). August 30, 2008.

Corvallis, Oregon

Boyd v. City of Corvallis, F. 3d 374 (2004).
"9th Circuit: 'Flash-Bang' Device Is Legitimate for Police." *Crime Control Digest.* July 2, 2004.

Burlington Township, New Jersey

Comengo, Carol. "Judge: 'Flash Bang' Grenade Unnecessary." *Courier Post.* August 28, 2008.

Sheriff Joe Arpaio's Incendiary Raid

Dougherty, John. "Dog Day Afternoon." *Phoenix News-Times.* August 5, 2004.

San Antonio, Texas

De Leon, Kristina. "House Catches Fire During Police Drug Raid." www.woai.com. February 4, 2009.

The Killing of Peyton Strickland

Carlson, Kelcey. "Autopsy Shows Deputies Shot Durham Teen in Head." www.wial.com. December 5, 2006.
Carlson, Kelcey. "Ex-Deputy Charged with Murder in Durham Teen's Death." www.wial.com. December 11, 2006.
Coleman, Erin. "3 Deputies on Pail Leave Following Student's Shooting Death." www.wial.com. December 3, 2006.
Coleman, Erin. "Pathologist: 'Tumbling' Bullet Killed Durham Teen." www.wial.com. December 7, 2006.
Gannon, Patrick. "Strickland Case Turned Over to N.C. Attorney General." www.starnewsonline.com. February 12, 2007.
Lamb, Amanda. "Bullets May Have Gone Through Door Before Killing Durham Teen." www.wial.com. December 6, 2006.
Lamb, Amanda. "DA: Case 'Still Open' Against Deputy in Durham Teen's Shooting." www.wial.com. December 14, 2006.

Locke, Mandy. "Family Sues UNCW in Son's Death." *News & Observer.* November 1, 2008.

Locke, Mandy. "Stricklands Settle After Death of Son." *News & Observer.* February 28, 2008.

Mims, Bryan. "Father of Slain Teen Speaks to Grand Jury." www.wial.news.com. July 10, 2007.

Mims, Bryan. "No Indictment for Ex-Deputy in Fatal Teen Shooting." www.wial. news.com. July 11, 2007.

The Deadly Use of a Nonlethal Weapon

Gendar, Allison. "NYPD Lt. Michael Pigott, Who Ordered Fatal Tasering of Naked Man, Left Suicide Note: It's My Fault." *New York Daily News.* October 2, 2008.

Gendar, Allison, and Corky Siemaszko. "NYPD Investigates Two Officers in Taser Death of Naked Brooklyn Man." *New York Daily News.* September 25, 2008.

Hauser, Christine. "Taser Use in Man's Death Breaks Rules, Police Say." *New York Times.* September 26, 2008.

"Lieutenant Found Dead After NYC Taser Killing." *USA Today.* October 2, 2008.

McFadden, Robert D., and Christine Hauser. "2nd Victim of Taser Fire: Officer Who Gave Order." *New York Times.* October 3, 2008.

"Statement From the New York City Police Department." *New York Times.* September 25, 2008.

The High Cost of Police Mistakes in High-Risk Raids

Dodging Bullets in Minneapolis: The Vang Khang Case

Aamot, Gregg, and Steve Karnowski. "Botched Raid Terrorizes Minn. Family." Associated Press. December 18, 2007.

Cochran, Lee. "Cops Given Medals for Shootout With Innocent Family." www.abc news.com. July 31, 2008.

Lowe, Caroline. "Settlement Reached in Raid on Wrong House." www.wcco.com. December 13, 2008.

Lowe, Caroline. "SWAT Team Honored For Raid on Wrong House." www.wcco. com. July 29, 2008.

"Police Raid Wrong House, Trade Gunfire." Associated Press. December 17, 2007.

Rosario, Ruben. "The Police Are in Prime CYA Form on the Khang Raid." *St. Paul Pioneer-Press.* December 17, 2007.

No Bullets, No Story

"Grandfather Says Police Stormed Home, Pointed Gun at Head." www.wftv.com. October 17, 2008.

Sudden Death: Fatal Endings to Standoff Dramas

"4 Miami Police Officers Guilty of Corruption." *Seattle Times.* April 10, 2003.
"Officer Not Guilty in Miami Police Corruption Trial." www.officer.com. July 8, 2008.
"SWAT Officer Goes to Trial in Fatal Shooting." *St Petersburg Times.* May 3, 2004.
Wilson, Catherine. "Miami Officer's Corruption Trial Hinges on Toy Gun's Presence." *Naples News.* May 5, 2004.
Wilson, Catherine. "Miami SWAT Officer's Obstruction Trial Goes to Jury." *Naples News.* May 19, 2004.

Killing Cheri Lyn Moore

Greenson, Thadeus. "Attorneys Ask for Douglas-Zanotti Dismissal." *Eureka Times-Standard.* June 20, 2008.
Greenson, Thadeus. "DA Opposes Motions to Dismiss Douglas-Zanotti Charges." *Eureka Times-Standard.* August 1, 2008.
Greenson, Thadeus. "EPD Officers to Join SWAT Team." *Eureka Times-Standard.* August 7, 2008.
Greenson, Thadeus, and John Driscoll. "Calif. Commanding Officers May Be Indicted for Other Officer's Shooting." *Eureka Times-Standard.* December 7, 2007.
Sims, Hank. "Cause of Death: Questions Answered and Questions Raised in the Cheri Lyn Moore Inquest." *North Coast Journal Weekly.* September 21, 2006.
"Timeline of Cheri Lyn Moore Case." *Eureka Times-Standard.* April 14, 2006.
Wear, Kimberly. "Douglas, Zanotti Set to Be Arraigned Today in Moore Shooting." *Eureka Times-Standard.* February 21, 2008.
Wilson, Emily. "Grand Jury Papers Unsealed in Moore Case." *Eureka Reporter.* February 20, 2008.
Wohlsen, Marcus. "Eureka Officers Indicted in Fatal Shooting Didn't Fire a Shot." Associated Press. December 25, 2007.

SWAT Raid Consequences: The Killing of Anthony Jarvis

Attorney General Kelly A. Ayotte press release. www.unionleader.com. August 27, 2008.
Davis, Mark. "Man Arrested After Shootout Indicted." *Valley News* (Concord, NH). August 14, 2008.
"Investigators Say Shooting was Justified." www.wmur.com. August 27, 2008.
"NH State Police Director: Review SWAT Teams." www.boston.com. August 29, 2008.
Senz, Kristen. "N.H. Police Shooting 'Legally Justified.'" *New Hampshire Union Leader.* August 30, 2008.
Senz, Kristen. "Son of Man Shot by Police Indicted." *New Hampshire Union Leader.* August 13, 2008.

Tirrell-Wysocki, David. "A G Says Trooper, Police Justified in Fatal Shooting." *Nashua Telegraph*. August 28, 2008.

Touhy, Dan. "State Panel to Review Police Raid." *New Hampshire Union Leader*. August 28, 2008.

CHAPTER 4: STOMPING ON SIN

Prostitution Raids

Cat House or Wrong House: Ask Philip Petronella

Becker, Arielle Levin. "State Police Search Targets Wrong Tenant." *Home News Tribune*. May 11, 2005.

Lutolf, Colleen. "Police SWAT Raid on Retiree 'Unfortunate.'" *Woodbridge Sentinel*. May 17, 2005.

Lutolf, Colleen. "Retiree Can't Sleep at Night." *Woodbridge Sentinel*. May 24, 2005.

Rounding Up the Lap Dancers

Alvarado, Francisco. "Hallandale Vice Gets Busy in the Champagne Room." *Miami Times*. March 27, 2009.

"Hallandale Beach Strip Bar Closed After Police Raid." *South Florida Sun-Sentinel*. March 10, 2009.

Jean-Francois, Macollvie. "19 Arrested in Prostitution Sting: Hallandale Beach Strip Shut." *Palm Beach Post*. March 10, 2009.

Wrong-House Pornography Possession Raids

Deputy Shaquille O'Neal: The Missed Slam Dunk in Gretna, Virginia

Balko, Radley. "SWAT Team With Star Power." *Reason Magazine*. February 2007.

Bangeman, Eric. "Faulty I P Address Data Leads to Shaq Attack on Innocent Family." www.arstechnica.com. October 24, 2006.

Davis, Tim. "Gretna Couple Angry Over Botched Child Porn Raid." *Star-Tribune* (Virginia). November 1, 2006.

"Deputy Shaq Helps Child Porn Raid in Virginia." www.sfgate.com. October 4, 2006.

Nuckols, A. J. "Do 'Computer Police' Have Too Much Power?" *Star-Tribune* (Virginia). October 19, 2006.

Reed, Travis. "'Shaq' Part of Botched Porn Raid." Associated Press. October 25, 2006.

Milwaukee SWAT: A Dollar Short and Six Weeks Late

City Attorney Langley letter to Milwaukee City Council. www.milwaukee.gov. February 12, 2008.

Schweitzer, Nick. "Botched SWAT Raid Closer to Home." www.nickschweitzer.net. November 25, 2007.

Stingl, Jim. "Sometimes 'Sorry' Doesn't Cut It." *Milwaukee Journal Sentinel.* November 24, 2007.

Rush to Judgment: The Walmart "Porn" Cases

Charles Town, West Virginia

Bailey, Cara. "Jefferson Man Says He Was Wrongly Accused of Child Pornography." *West Virginia Record.* June 13, 2008.

Briscoe, Nance. "SOPs for SWAT Team." www.watchjeffersoncounty.net. July 7, 2007.

Unger, Morgan. "Man Sues Wal-Mart." *Journal* (Charles Town). June 17, 2008.

Gridley, Indiana

Brady-Lunny, Edith. "Man Whose Porn Conviction Was Reversed Awaits Release." www.pjstar.com. August 7, 2008.

"Former CDM Store Manager Pleads Innocent." www.pantagraph.com. July 15, 2008.

Guetersloh, M. K. "Supreme Court Won't Revisit Overturned Child Porn Conviction." www.pantagraph.com. September 24, 2008.

Gaming Yes, Gambling No: Raiding the Bad Bettors

The Charleston County Poker Wars

Ciaffone, Bob. "Nice and Nasty Poker Busts." *Card Player Magazine.* July 25, 2006.

Kinnard, Meg. "Poker Aficionados Watching SC Texas Hold'em Case." Associated Press. January 29, 2009.

Kropf, Schuyler. "Defendants in Gambling Sting Determined to Go to Trial." *Post and Courier* (Charleston). March 10, 2008.

Kropf, Schuyler. "Judge Refuses to Dismiss Case Against Poker Players." *Post and Courier* (Charleston). August 22, 2008.

Kropf, Schuyler. "Poker Players to Get Hearing." *Post and Courier* (Charleston). August 21, 2008.

Kropf, Schuyler. "Poker Players 'Legal Saga' to Go On." *Post and Courier* (Charleston). August 23, 2008.

Pajich, Bob. "Poker Players Fight the Law in South Carolina." www.cardplayer.com. April 28, 2008.

Smith, Glenn. "19 Poker Players Plead Guilty; One Requests Jury Trial." *Post and Courier* (Charleston).April 14, 2008.

Smith, Glenn. "Some Implicated in Hanahan Poker Raid Also Charged in Mt. P." *Post and Courier* (Charleston). April 9, 2008.

"Will SC Texas Hold'em Trial Rule Poker Is a Game of Skill, Not Chance?" www.
    pokerpages.com. January 30, 2009.

Crashing the Party in San Mateo, California

Aparton, Tamara Barak. "Poker Players Say Police Dealt Them Bad Hand." www.
    examiner.com. January 15, 2008.
Oremus, Will. "County Authorities Defend Poker Bust." *Oakland Tribune.* January
    17, 2008.
Yates, Dana. "Cops Shut Down Poker Party." *San Mateo Daily Journal.* January 14,
    2008.

The Fight against Poker in North Carolina

"North Carolina Poker Raid Charges 40, Seizes Money." *Poker News Daily.* October 6,
    2008.
McCleary, Nancy. "Police Raid Yadkin Road Poker House." *Fayetteville Observer.*
    October 7, 2008.

The Atlanta Area Crackdown

Cunningham, Craig. "Atlanta Poker Games Raided." www.pokerworks.com. April 12,
    2007.
Mac Donald, Mary. "Affluent Neighborhood Rocked by Gambling Arrests." *Atlanta
    Journal-Constitution.* February 6, 2009.
Mac Donald, Mary. "Sandy Springs: Raid Surprises Neighbors." *Atlanta Journal-
    Constitution.* February 7, 2009.
Morris, Mike. "27 Arrests in Roswell Poker Raid." *Atlanta Journal-Constitution.*
    April 10, 2007.

Ruthless in Virginia: The Death of a Sports Bettor

Davis, Matthew. "Death Raises Concern at Police Tactics." BBC News, Washington.
    March 21, 2006.
Diamond, Richard. "Demilitarizing Local Police." *Washington Times.* February 26,
    2010.
Jackman, Tom. "FBI Is Asked to Investigate Fatal Police Shooting." *Washington Post.*
    March 25, 2006.
Jackman, Tom. "Officer Won't Face Charges in Shooting Death." *Washington Post.*
    March 23, 2006.
Jackman, Tom. "SWAT Tactics at Issue After Fairfax Shooting." *Washington Post.*
    January 27, 2006.
Jackman, Tom. "Va. Officer Might be Suspended for Fatality." *Washington Post.* No-
    vember 25, 2006.

Smith, Amy M. "Fairfax County, Virginia Faces $12 million Lawsuit for SWAT Shooting Death of Local Optometrist Dr. Salvatore J. Culosi. www.business wire.com. March 20, 2007.

"A Tragedy of Errors." *Washington Post.* January 20, 2007.

CHAPTER 5: PART-TIME WARRIORS

Elbow, Steven. "Military Muscle Comes to Mayberry." *Capital Times.* August 18, 200l.

Kraska, Peter B., and Louis J. Cubellis. "Militarizing Mayberry and Beyond: Making Sense of American Paramilitary Policing." *Justice Quarterly.* Fall, 1997.

La Salle, Renee. "Chattanooga Police Have a New Weapon to Fight Crime." www. wdef.com. July 23, 2008.

Miller, Joel. "The Drug War and the Militarization of Mayberry." *Oldspeak, The Rutherford Institute.* December 30, 2002.

Call to Arms

SWAT Vehicles

"Armored Police Vehicle Worth Its Weight." *Cedar Rapids Gazette.* October 9, 2008.

Balint, Ed. "Police Request Money for SWAT Vehicle." *Canton Repository.* July 18, 2008.

"Cop's Newest Arsenal: M113A2 Armored Personnel Carrier." www.deathby1000pa percuts.com. February 21, 2008.

Grigg, William Norman. "From Local Police to Occupying Army, or LESO: The Greater of Many Evils." www.lewrockwell.clickability.com. January 31, 2007.

"Look What Seized Drug Money Can Buy." www.kjct8.com. July 18, 2008.

Mahone, Derrick. "Cobb Police Add Tank to Arsenal." *Atlanta Journal-Constitution.* October 10, 2008.

Snider, Gina. "City of Newnan Police Receives Armored Personnel Carrier." www. ci.newnan.ga.us. July 2, 2008.

Tumgoren, Serdar. "N.J. Police Stockpile Assault Weapons." www.policeone.com. August 20, 2008.

Qualified Police Immunity in Wrongful Death Suits

Jensen v. City of Oxnard

Jensen v. City of Oxnard, 145 F3d 1078 (1998).

Killing Troy Davis

Estate of Davis v. City of North Richland Hills, 406 F. 3d 375 (2005).

Grimes, Andrea. "COP Out: Former North Richland Hills Officer Allen Hill Claims He Killed a Man in Self-Defense." *Dallas Observer.* July 6, 2006.

Hawes, Chris. "Author Continues Search for Answers in Son's Death." www.author
    barbaradavis.com. August 19, 2008.
Lee, Mike. "Concerns on SWAT Aired Year Before Raid." *Fort Worth Star-Telegram.*
    April 13, 2003.
Lieber, Dave. "Davis Wrongful-Death Suit." *Fort Worth Star-Telegram.* December 16,
    2005.
Lieber, Dave. "It's Time to Answer Troubling Questions to Drug-Raid Death." *Fort
    Worth Star-Telegram.* December 15, 2002.
Ramirez, Domingo Jr. "Police Lacked Cause for Fatal Drug Raid, Court Says." *Fort
    Worth Star-Telegram.* July 22, 2004.

Hudson v. Michigan *and the Helriggle Case*

Budd, Lawrence. "Father Denies That Dead Man Held Pistol." *Dayton Daily News.*
    October 11, 2002.
Gambrell, Jon. "A Son Dead, Couple Looks for Answers." *Cincinnati Enquirer.* April 8,
    2004.
McCarty, Mary. "Helriggles Question Convict's Lie." *Dayton Daily News.* October 27,
    2003.
Mon, Cathy. "Dozens Protest Preble County Police Station." *Dayton Daily News.* Oc-
    tober 1, 2002.
Mon, Cathy. "No Indictments Returned in Helriggle Death." *Dayton Daily News.*
    February 5, 2003.
Mon, Cathy. "The Death of Clayton Helriggle." *Dayton Daily News.* June 29, 2003.
Mon, Cathy. "Slain Man's Family Gets Settlement, Not Closure." *Dayton Daily News.*
    September 27, 2006.

Did William Bing Have to Die?

"Civil Liability for SWAT Operations." 2007 (7) AELE Mo. L. J. 101. July 2007.
Estate of William J. Bing v. City of Whitehall, Ohio. Sixth Circuit Ct. of Appeals. www.
    caselaw.findlaw.com. April 2006.

The Goose Creek Fiasco

"Drug Raid at S.C. High School." www.cbs.newscom. November 7, 2003.
"Goose Creek School Raid." *USA Today.* July 19, 2006.
Lewin, Jamar. "Raid at School Leads to Radical Divide, Not Drugs." *New York Times.*
    December 9, 2003.
"Police, School District Defend Drug Raid." www.cnn.com. November 10, 2003.
"Raid Might Have Broken Drug-Dog Rules." Associated Press. December 8, 2003.
Sage, Mark. "Armed Police Storm School in Drug Raid." *Scotsman.* November 7
    2003.
Smith, Bruce. "Police Respond to Federal Lawsuit in Drug Sweep." Associated Press.
    February 11, 2004.

Small Town, Wrong Address

Valid Warrant, Wrong House in Pewaukee

Huber, Brian. "Police Broke Through Wrong Door on House, Man Says." *Waukesha Freeman.* January 4, 2006.

You Weren't Home, So We Let Ourselves In

Albers, Gwen. "Police Raid Targets Wrong Address." *Bonner County Daily Bee.* May 2, 2007.

Who Were Those Masked Men?

Benjamin, Shane. "Drug Raid Nabs Wrong Woman." *Durango Herald.* June 15, 2007.
"Officers Try to Arrest 77-Year-old; Intended Target was Next Door." www.realrap talk.com. June 24, 2007.

CHAPTER 6: LEGAL POT

Nightingale, Jon. "U.S. Drug Policy Under Obama." www.dailynexus.com. May 5, 2009.
Peters, Jeremy W. "Deal on State's Drug Law Means Re-sentencing Pleas." *New York Times.* March 28, 2009.
Strobel, Warren P. "Clinton Says U.S. Shares Responsibility for Mexico's Drug Violence." *Christian Science Monitor.* March 27, 2009.
Webb, Jim. "Why We Must Fix Our Prisons." *Parade Magazine.* March 29, 2009.

The Federal War on Legal Marijuana

Abodollah, Tami. "DEA Agents Raid Culver City Medical Marijuana Dispensary." *Los Angeles Times.* August 1, 2008.
"DPA Press Release: As Feds Raid Medical Marijuana Dispensaries in CA, Congress Rejects Proposal to Protect Ill Patients." www.stopthedrugwar.org. July 30, 2007.
Egelko, Bob. "366-Day Sentence for Pot Dispensary Owner." *San Francisco Chronicle.* June 12, 2009.
Egelko, Bob. "U.S. to Yield Marijuana Jurisdiction to States." *San Francisco Chronicle.* February 27, 2009.
Garmon, Ron. "Bad Memories of the DEA's Wild Day in L.A." www.lacitybeat.com. August 2, 2007.
Lane, Charles. "A Defeat for Users of Medical Marijuana." *Washington Post.* June 7 2005.

Manekin, Michael. "San Mateo Pot Shop Raided." *Oakland Tribune.* August 30, 2007.

"Medical Marijuana Crackdown." *Santa Barbara Independent.* February 25, 2010.

Moore, Solomon. "Dispensers of Marijuana Find Relief in Policy Shift." *New York Times.* March 20, 2009.

Moore, Solomon. "Prison Term for a Seller of Medical Marijuana." *New York Times.* June 12, 2009.

Stout, David, and Solomon Moore. "U.S. Won't Prosecute in States That Allow Medical Marijuana." *New York Times,* October 20, 2009.

Medical Marijuana: Use It, Sell It, But Don't Grow It in Colorado

Spellman, Jim. "Colorado's Green Rush: Medical Marijuana." www.cnn.com. December 14, 2009.

Don't Grow Pot in Huerfano County

Batuello, Jonathan. "Pot Suspect Claims Medical Permission." *Summit Daily News* (Colorado). August 30, 2008.

Blevins, Jason. "Marijuana a Growing Battle." *Denver Post.* September 14, 2008.

Caregiver Troubles in Larimer County

Romer, Karen. "Film Shoot Nixed by SWAT Team." *Greeley Tribune.* June 19, 2006.

Zaffos, Joshua. "Sheriff Jim Alderden Says He Needs Money Now to Keep Gang Activity in Larimer County From Busting Out of Control. *Rocky Mountain Chronicle.* March 7, 2007.

Larimer County's Embarrassing SWAT Team Sugar Bust

Dickman, Pamela. "All Charges Dropped in Sugar Factory Meth Case." *Loveland Reporter-Herald.* November 15, 2007.

Dickman, Pamela. "CBI Report Casts Doubt on Meth Find." *Loveland Reporter-Herald.* November 6, 2007.

Looby, Katie. "Loveland Man Files Lawsuit for Raid." www.coloradoan.com. November 28, 2009.

More Trouble for the Crumblisses

"Larimer Crime Unit Arrests Two in Major Drug Bust." *Greeley Tribune.* June 1 2007.

"Two Arrested for Marijuana Cultivation." Larimer County Press Release. www.co.larimer.co.us. August 14, 2008.

CHAPTER 7: COLLATERAL DAMAGE

Snitch-Based Drug-Raid Fiascos

"APD Seeks Snitches in Want Ads." www.kob.com. November 21, 2008.
Weiser, Benjamin. "Payments to Informants in Columbia Revealed." *New York Times*.
    November 4, 2008.

Louisville, Kentucky: Calvin Roach

"Family Angry After SWAT Team Mistakenly Raids Home." www.wlky.com. Au-
    gust 10, 2007.

North Little Rock, Arkansas: Tracy Ingle

Balko, Radley. "Tracy Ingle: Another Drug War Outrage." www.reason.com. May 7,
    2008.
Balko, Radley. "Tracy Ingle Gets a Lawyer." www.reason.com. May 14, 2008.
"Filing in Ingle Case Questions NLR Police Affidavit." *Arkansas Times*. Septem-
    ber 18, 2008.
"Jury Convicts After No-Knock Police Search." www.wxut.com. April 15, 2009.
"NLR Chief Defends SWAT Unit." *Arkansas Times*. April 24, 2008.
"Shot in the Dark." *Arkansas Times*. April 25, 2008.

Troy, New York: Ronita McColley

Franco, James V. "Troy Cops Faulted for 'No-Knock' Raid." *Troy Record*. Septem-
    ber 17, 2008.
"Troy Raid Fallout." www.wten.com. September 18, 2008.

Boots in the House—The Wrong House

Neutralizing the Chidesters

Chidester v. Utah County. Tenth Circuit Ct. of Appeals. March 6, 2008.
Fattah, Geoffrey. "Family Can Sue SWAT, Judge Says." *Deseret News* (Salt Lake City).
    August 11, 2006.
Fattah, Geoffrey. "Suit Filed in SWAT Team's Home Raid." *Deseret News* (Salt Lake
    City). July 27, 2005.
Fattah, Geoffrey. "Trial Date Set Over Springville SWAT Raid." *Deseret News* (Salt
    Lake City). June 14, 2008.

Here We Come, Ready or Not

Balko, Radley. "Kenneth Jamar Update." www.theagitator.com. January 7, 2008.

Clines, Keith. "Officers Return to Regular Duty, Victim Improves." *Huntsville Times.* June 30, 2006.

Hollman, Holly. "Officers Allegedly Shoot Man at Wrong Address." *Decatur News.* June 28, 2008.

Hollman, Holly. "Man Shot by Officers Had Guns in Home, Sheriff Says." *Decatur News.* June 29, 2008.

Middleton, Karen. "Limestone Man Shot in Drug Raid." *News Courier* (Athens, Alabama). June 27, 2006.

Mindless and Trigger-Happy in Prince George's County

Balko, Radley. "Failing His Way to Higher Office." www.reason.com. October 12, 2009.

Castaneda, Ruben. "Lawyers Find Fault with Pr. George's Drug Arrests." *Washington Post.* October 14, 2008.

Davis, Aaron C. "Prince George's Police Clear Mayor, Family." *Washington Post.* August 9, 2008.

Davis, Aaron C. "Sheriff Says Deputies 'Did Their Job.'" *Washington Post.* June 20, 2009.

"Feds Investigating Drug Raid on Small-Town Mayor's Home." www.cnn.com. August 9, 2008.

Helderman, Rosalind S. "Bill Calls for More Scrutiny of SWAT Teams by Police." *Washington Post.* February 5, 2009.

Helderman, Rosalind S. "Pr. George's Officers Lacked 'No-Knock' Warrant in Raid." *Washington Post.* August 6, 2008.

Helderman, Rosalind S., and Aaron C. Davis. "FBI to Review Raid That Killed Mayor's Dogs." *Washington Post.* August 8, 2008.

Helderman, Rosalind S., and Aaron C. Davis. "Killing of Mayor's 2 Dogs Justified, Pr. George's Finds." *Washington Post.* September 5, 2008.

Helderman, Rosalind S., and Aaron C. Davis. "Pr. George's Police Arrest 2 in Marijuana-Shipping Plot." *Washington Post.* August 7, 2008.

Hermann, Peter. "Numbers Paint Portrait of SWAT Team Use." *Baltimore Sun.* February 24, 2010.

Markus, Don. "Md. Panel Hears Testimony on Police Raids." *Baltimore Sun.* March 4, 2009.

McCabe, Scott. "FBI Opens Probe of SWAT Team Raid That Led to Death of Mayor's Dogs." www.examiner.com. August 8, 2008.

"Md. Senate Passes Bill Requiring SWAT Team Reports." *Washington Post.* March 19, 2009.

"New Questions About SWAT Raid on Berwyn Heights Mayor's Home." www.news-8net. August 5, 2008.

Norman, Nancy. "Lawsuit Can Proceed Over Deaths of Two Dogs in Raid." www.nbcwashington.com. February 24, 2010.

Schuman, Jonah. "Bill Would Require Information on Operation Deployments." www.gazette.net. February 5, 2009.

Suderman, Alan. "Md. Lawmaker Wants More Oversight of SWAT Teams." *Examiner* (Washington). December 27, 2009.

Syeed, Nafeesa. "Mayor Sues Over Dog-Killing Raid." Associated Press. June 23, 2009.

Witt, April. "Deadly Force." *Washington Post*. February 1, 2009.

Keep Your Dogs out of Maryland

"Another Maryland SWAT Team Kills a Dog." www.ohmidog.com. February 7, 2009.

Hager, Jeff. "Police Kill Family Dog During Raid." www.abc2news.com. February 7, 2009.

McPherson, Kelly. "Dog Killed in Home Search, Owner Files Complaint." www.wjz.com. February 5, 2009.

Rita, Mike Santa. "Home Raid Leads to Complaint." *Howard County Times*. February 5, 2009.

Gwinnett County Malfeasance

Bothwell, Trevor. "Oops…Our Bad." www.examiner.com. December 12, 2008.

Hamacher, Heath. "Investigator Transferred for Botched Drug Raid." www.gwinnettdailypost.com. December 13, 2008.

"Police Mistakenly Raid Wrong Gwinnett Co. House." www.mvfoxatlanta.com. December 10, 2008.

Rowson, Kevin. "Gwinnett Police Raid Wrong House." www.11alive.com. December 11, 2008.

Simmons, Andria. "Gwinnett Police Break Down Wrong Door." *Atlanta Journal-Constitution*. December 10, 2008.

Tuccille, J. D. "Another Dog Shot When Police Screw Up." www.examiner.com. December 18, 2008.

Young, Camie. "Libertarians Condemn Raid at Wrong House, War on Drugs." *Gwinnett Daily Post*. December 14, 2008.

CHAPTER 8: UNJUSTIFIABLE HOMICIDE

License to Kill in Baltimore County

Broadwater, Luke. "Family of Slain Dundalk Woman Sues Baltimore County Police." www.examiner.com. August 10, 2008.

Broadwater, Luke. "Study: Slain Dundalk Mother Part of Troubling SWAT Team Trend." www.examiner.com. August 18, 2006.

Giordano, Joseph M. "Woman Is Shot, Killed by Police in Drug Raid." *Dundalk Eagle*. January 27, 2005.

Giordano, Joseph M. "Petition Reflects Anguish." *Dundalk Eagle*. March 31, 2005.

Hermann, Peter. "Lawsuit Brings Dissection of Fatal SWAT Raid." *Baltimore Sun*. March 18, 2009.

Kearney, Brendan. "Trial Opens Over Fatal Police Raid in Dundalk." *Daily Record* (Maryland). March 16, 2009.

Noel v. Artson et al. Fourth Circuit Ct. of Appeals. October 22, 2008.

"SWAT Team Found Not Liable in 2005 Death of Dundalk Woman." Associated Press. March 31, 2009.

Excitable and Confrontational in Pinellas County

Brink, Graham. "Deputy Mayor Responds to Critic." *St. Petersburg Times.* May 26, 2005.

Brink, Graham. "National Drug Bust Snares 33 Locally." *St. Petersburg Times.* November 18, 2005.

Cardenas, Jose. "Family Sues in Shooting Death." *St. Petersburg Times.* July 7, 2007.

Girardi, Steven. "Uhurus Seek Reparations for Teens Shot by Law Enforcement." *Tampa Tribune.* August 16, 2008.

"Jarrell Walker Case Now a National Investigation." www.baynews9.com. May 25, 2005.

Leary, Alex. "'Excitable' Tag Haunts Deputy." *St. Petersburg Times.* May 6, 2005.

Maxam, June. "Pinellas County Deaths: Justified or Covered Up?" *North Country Gazette.* May 3, 2008.

Tisch, Chris. "Family of Man Killed in Controversial Raid Arrested." *St. Petersburg Times.* October 15, 2005.

The Predawn Raid in Sunrise, Florida

Ashe, Suzanne. "SWAT Officer Cleared in Shooting Death." *Courthouse News Service.* September 1, 2009.

Haas, Brian. "Dead Man's Family Says Sunrise Broke Law on Records." *South Florida Sun-Sentinel.* January 12, 2006.

Haas, Brian. "Man Killed Had Gun Permit." *South Florida Sun-Sentinel.* August 13, 2005.

Haas, Brian. "Relatives of Slain Man Hire Lawyer." *South Florida Sun-Sentinel.* August 11, 2005.

Haas, Brian, and Kevin Smith. "Man Killed by Sunrise Police in Drug Raid Had 2 Ounces of Marijuana." *South Florida Sun-Sentinel.* August 10, 2005.

Mayo, Michael. "An Ounce of Pot, 10 Bullets, and One Failed Drug War." *South Florida Sun-Sentinel.* August 16, 2005.

Neuwahl, Janette. "Relatives, Friends Criticize Death of Man in Sunrise Police Raid." *South Florida Sun-Sentinel.* August 10, 2005.

Justified Killing, Unjustified Raid

Hunt, David. "Another Isolated Incident." *Florida Times-Union.* November 6, 2006.

Hunt, David. "For a Family, Drug Raid Went Terribly Wrong." *Florida Times-Union.* November 5, 2006.

Malcom, Shannon. "Deputy Shoots Woman Dead." *News-Leader* (Florida). December 23, 2005.

The Predawn Raid on Sunset Street

"As a Wharton Teen is Buried, the Investigation Continues." www.abc13.com. February 16, 2007.
Balko, Radley. "Daniel Castillo Buried." www.theagitator.com. February 17, 2007.
Halvorson, Barry. "Family: Wharton Teen Shot by Police was Unarmed." *Victoria Advocate* (Texas). February 16, 2007.
Halvorson, Barry. "FBI Investigation is Next Step in Wharton Killing: Agency Will Forward Its Review of the Case to Washington, D.C." *Victoria Advocate* (Texas). March 16, 2007.
Halvorson, Barry. "Officer Won't Be Charged in Killing." *Victoria Advocate* (Texas). March 15, 2007.
Villafranca, Armando. "Dad Seeks Answers in Killing by Wharton Police." *Houston Chronicle*. February 15, 2007.

One Killing: Two Stories

Brennan, Charlie. "Lawsuit Looms in Fatal Police Shooting." www.myfoxcolorado. com. July 17, 2008.
Chacon, Daniel J. "Families Seek $10 Million in Police Shootings Deaths." *Rocky Mountain News*. October 25, 2008.
District Attorney Morrissey Letter to Chief Whitman. "Re: Investigation of the Shooting Death of Nathan Paul Aguillard, Jr." www.denverda.org. April 21, 2008.
"Man Identified After Police Shooting." *Denver Post*. April 7, 2008.
McGhee, Tom. "Denver SWAT Officers Cleared in Shooting." *Denver Post*. April 21, 2008.
Mitchell, Kirk. "Judge Seals Warrant in Cop Shooting Case." *Denver Post*. April 9, 2008.
Mitchell, Kirk. "Police: Suspect Sold Crack Before Fatal Raid." *Denver Post*. April 10, 2008.
Mitchell, Kirk. "'Red Flags' in Denver Cop Shooting, Kin Say." *Denver Post*. April 9, 2008.
"Public Statement of the Manager of Safety Regarding an Officer-Involved Shooting by Technician Thomas McKibben and Technician Ronald Fox." City and County of Denver. October 2, 2008.

Death by Association

Adade, Audrey. "'No plea' For Terebisi." www.FairfieldMinteman.com. June 26, 2008.

Balko, Radley. "Gonzalo Guizan: Another Death by Drug War." www.theagitator. com. June 9, 2008.

Caldwell, Maggie. "Not Guilty Plea in Case that Killed Ex-Ridgefielder." *Easton Courier.* June 26, 2008.

Caldwell, Maggie. "Woman's Report Triggered Police Raid." *Easton Courier.* June 6, 2008.

Grosso, Meg Larson. "Officer Cleared in Easton Shooting." www.FairfieldMinute man.com. April 2, 2009.

Liotta, Jarret. "Easton Deadly Raid Prompts Lawsuit." www.FairfieldMinuteman. com. November 20, 2008.

Quinn, Brigid. "Police Raid Ends in Death." www.FairfieldMinuteman.com. May 22, 2008.

Silvers, Susan. "Former Ridgefield Man's Estate Plans Action Against 6 Towns." www. newstimes.com. November 20, 2008.

Tepfer, Daniel, and Joel C. Thompson. "Raid Sought Drugs From Easton Home." www.hcc.commnet.edu. May 21, 2008.

Weisberg, Julie. "Deadly Police Raid May Lead to Wrongful Death Lawsuits." *Easton Courier.* November 20, 2008.

Weisberg, Julie. "State Police Continue to Investigate Dogwood Drive Police Raid." *Easton Courier.* August 28, 2008.

Weisberg, Julie, and Macklin Reid. "Estate of Former Ridgefielder Sues Six Towns Over Police Shooting Death." *Easton Courier.* November 9, 2008.

Shots in the Dark

Barr, Meghan. "Ohio City Settles for $2.5 M with Children of Black Woman Killed by White Officer in Drug Raid." www.latimes.com. January 1, 2010.

Freehan, Jennifer. "Target of Raid Receives Sentence." *Toledo Blade.* May 20, 2008.

Freehan, Jennifer. "Lima Police Officer to Begin Trial in Deadly Drug Raid." *Toledo Blade.* July 28, 2008.

Freehan, Jennifer. "Jury Chosen for Officer in Lima Shooting." *Toledo Blade.* July 29, 2008.

Freehan, Jennifer. "Prosecutor Questions Justification for Lima Shooting." *Toledo Blade.* July 30, 2008.

Freehan, Jennifer. "Doctor Tells Allen County Jury Wilson Wasn't Standing When Shot in Drug Raid." *Toledo Blade.* July 31, 2008.

Freehan, Jennifer. "Lima Police Officer Not Guilty in Deadly Raid." *Toledo Blade.* August 5, 2008.

Freehan, Jennifer. "Review Clears Lima Police Officer in Slaying." *Toledo Blade.* October 16, 2008.

Messina, Ignazio, and Erica Blake. "Lima on Edge After Police Kill Woman, Wound 1-Year-Old Child in Drug Raid." *Toledo Blade.* January 6, 2008.

Sowinski, Greg. "Chavalia Said He Fired to Defend His Life." *Lima News.* July 31, 2008.

Sowinski, Greg. "The Numbers Behind SWAT Raids." *Lima News.* August 9, 2008.

Sowinski, Greg. "Tarika Wilson Shooting: One Year Later, What Have We Learned?" *Lima News.* January 3, 2009.

The Mystery Killing

Duer, Benjamin. "Officers Won't Be Charged in Shooting Death of Man During Raid." *Canton Repository.* November 15, 2008.
Hoover, Shane. "Canton Man's 2008 Shooting Death at Hands of Police Prompts Lawsuit." *Canton Repository.* September 4, 2009.
Monsewicz, Lori. "SWAT Team Kills Man." *Canton Repository.* September 19, 2008.
Monsewicz, Lori. "Warrant, Records Sealed in Fatal SWAT Shooting." *Canton Repository.* September 24, 2008.
Seeton, Melissa Griffy. "Family Demands Independent Investigation of Fatal Shooting." *Canton Repository.* September 23, 2008.

CHAPTER 9: NEGLIGENT HOMICIDE

The Scandalous Death of Reverend Williams

Mallia, Joseph, and Maggie Mulvihill. "Minister Dies as Cops Raid Wrong Apartment." *Boston Globe.* March 28, 1994.
Rimer, Sara. "Minister Who Sought Peace Dies in a Botched Drug Raid." *New York Times.* March 28, 1994.
"Sorry, Wrong Apartment." *Time Magazine.* April 11, 1994.

A Bad Warrant, a Troubled Cop, and an Unnecessary Death

Duran, Marcelo. "Denver Police's No-Knock Raid Cost Mena His Life." *Rocky Mountain Collegian.* February 11, 2000.
Finley, Bruce. "Talks Begin in No-Knock Raid." *Denver Post.* March 16, 2000.
Imse, Ann. "He Quietly Retires Eight Years After Deadly Raid." *Rocky Mountain News.* April 22, 2008.
Kopel, David B. "Supreme Court Paved Way for Mena Killing." www.davekopel.com. February 15, 2000.
Lindsay, Sue. "Deal May Allow Bini to Keep His Badge in Failed Drug Bust That Led to Shooting Death." *Rocky Mountain News.* October 2, 2000.
Maass, Brian. "Controversial Denver Officer Under Investigation." www.cbs4denver.com. April 2, 2007.
Prendergast, Alan. "Officer Bini's Informant: An Interview From the Shadows." www.westword.com. February 24, 2000.
Prendergast, Alan. "The High Price of Denver's Drug War: Lies, Bad Busts, Cops in Harm's Way—And the Death of an Innocent Man." www.westword.com. February 24,2000.
"Two Cleared in No-Knock Raid Killing." Associated Press. February 5, 2000.

Knock Knock—Who's There?

Frantz, Ashley. "Fatal Mistake." www.salon.com. October 19, 2000.

"Innocent Man Dies in Police Blunder." *Tennessean*. October 6, 2000.

"Man Killed in Police Raid on Wrong House." Associated Press, October 6, 2000.

Miller, Joel. "DOA: Take a Bite Out of Life." www.WorldNet.Daily.Com. October 7, 2000.

Peet, Preston. "DEA 'Ninja Narc' Tactics Kill Another Innocent Man." www.high times.com. October 20, 2000.

Death by SWAT Raid: No Crime

Dewan, Shailak. "City to Pay $1.6 Million in Fatal, Mistaken Raid." *New York Times*. October 29, 2003.

Fine, Larry. "New York Police Raid Wrong Apartment; Woman Dies." www.news mine.org. May 16, 2003.

Gearty, Robert, and Owen Moritz. "Suit in Another Grenade Goof." *New York Times*. May 28, 2003.

Lamb, Donna. "Alberta Spruill Murder Taken Seriously by City Council." *Caribbean Life*. June 3, 2003.

Polygreen, Lydia. "Wider Inquiry Sought in Woman's Death." *New York Times*. June 2, 2003.

Rashbaum, William K. "Lawyers Urge Council to Increase Oversight of Police Raids." *New York Times*. June 5, 2003.

Rashbaum, William K. "No Stun Grenades Since Death in Raid, As Debate Continues." *New York Times*. June 17, 2003.

Rashbaum, William K. "Police Transfer a Commander In Response to Deadly Raid." *New York Times*. May 29, 2003.

Rashbaum, William K. "Woman's Death After Raid Is Officially Ruled Homicide." *New York Times*. May 28, 2003.

Saulny, Susan. "Judge Keeps Raid Papers Sealed." *New York Times*. June 11, 2003.

"Two Deaths and No Excuses." *New York Times*. May 29, 2003.

Death by Illegal Warrant

Bluestein, Greg. "Jury Convicts Atlanta Cop of Lying After Raid." Associated Press. May 20, 2008.

Boone, Christian, and Marcus K. Garner. "Kathryn Johnston's Family Wants City to Pay $18 million. *Atlanta Journal-Constitution*. July 17, 2008.

Goodman, Brenda. "3 Officers Indicted in Drug Raid Death." *New York Times*. April 26, 2007.

Rankin, Bill. "Atlanta Cop in Botched Drug Raid Pleads Guilty." *Atlanta Journal-Constitution*. October 30, 2008.

Rankin, Bill. "Fulton Conviction Overturned for Cop in 92-Year-Old's Killing." *Atlanta Journal-Constitution*. January 15, 2009.

Reid, S. A. "Tesler Foes Want More Charges." *Atlanta Journal-Constitution.* May 22, 2008.

Rowson, Kevin. "Two Cops Plead Guilty to Manslaughter." www.11alive.com. April 27, 2007.

Scott, Jeffry, and S. A. Reid. "5 Years for Officer in Botched Raid." *Atlanta Journal-Constitution.* May 23, 2008.

"3 Police Officers Charged in Drug Raid Death." Associated Press. April 26, 2007.

Torpy, Bill. "Elderly Woman's Killing Casts Shadow on ATL Cops." *Atlanta Journal-Constitution.* November 9, 2008.

Visser, Steve. "Ex-Cop Not Guilty in Fatal Shooting." *Atlanta Journal-Constitution.* May 20, 2008.

Visser, Steve. "Lawyer: Turf War Led to Cop's Botched Prosecution." *Atlanta Journal-Constitution.* January 16, 2009.

Visser, Steve. "Witness: 'I'm Not a Snitch' in Killing." *Atlanta Journal-Constitution.* May 8, 2008.

Wagner, Andrew. "'No-Knock' Policy Risky." *Badger Herald* (Wisconsin). December 1, 2006.

Weber, Harry R. "Cops Admit to Planting Marijuana on 92-Year-Old Woman Killed In Botched Drug Raid." Associated Press. April 30, 2007.

Weber, Harry R. "2 Officers Plead Guilty in Drug-Related Death." Associated Press. April 27, 2007.

CHAPTER 10: OFFICER DOWN

Cases of Assaulting a Police Officer

The Wrong Place at the Wrong Time

Andes, Jodi, and Theodore Decker. "Former OSU Football Player Charged With Shooting 2 Columbus Police Officers." *Columbus Dispatch.* May 1, 2008.

Andes, Jodi, and Theodore Decker. "Ex-OSU Foster to Take Plea Deal in Shootings of 2 Police Officers." *Columbus Dispatch.* January 7, 2009.

Andes, Jodi, and Theodore Decker. "Ex-OSU Player's Support Criticized." *Columbus Dispatch.* June 2, 2008.

Andes, Jodi, and Theodore Decker. "Police Shootings Get Man 36 Years." *Columbus Dispatch.* April 2, 2008.

Gray, Kathy. "Ex-OSU Player's Testimony Attacked." *Columbus Dispatch.* January 30, 2009.

"Officers, Ex-OSU Player Discuss Shooting." www.wbns10tv.com. May 21, 2008.

"2 Charged with Shooting Police Officers." www.wbns10tv.com. May 1, 2008.

How to Make a Low-Risk Raid a Risky Operation

McSpadden, Matt. "Effort to Get Marijuana Raises Questions of Worth." *Springfield News-Leader.* December 31, 2008.

Trotter, Gregory. "Alyssa Kaye Smith Could Enter Plea May 11." *Springfield News-Leader.* April 10, 2009.

Trotter, Gregory. "'She Really is a Good Shot,' Teenager Charged After Shooting Gun During Drug Raid." *Springfield News-Leader.* December 17, 2008.

Trotter, Gregory. "Teenager Arraigned in Shooting." *Springfield News-Leader.* December 18, 2008.

Trotter, Gregory. "Woman Accused of Firing at Patrol Officer." *Springfield News-Leader.* December 16, 2008.

West, Sara. "Child Endangerment Charge Against Pregnant Teen Dismissed." www.bolivarmonews.com. February 11, 2009.

Forcing the Action, Inviting Disaster

"Editorial: No Deaths, This Time." *Las Vegas Review-Journal.* January 4, 2009.

Gentry, Dana. "Face to Face: The Final Take." *Las Vegas Sun.* February 12, 2009.

Haynes, Brian. "Girlfriend of Suspect in SWAT Shooting Awarded Custody of Children." *Las Vegas Journal-Review.* January 7, 2009.

Mower, Lawrence. "'I'm Not a Vendetta Cop-Killer,' Suspect Says He Thought Officers With Warrant Were Trying to Break In." *Las Vegas Review-Journal.* December 31, 2008.

O'Brien, Jeff. "Man Pleads Not Guilty in Henderson Police Shooting." *Las Vegas Sun.* February 2, 2009.

O'Brien, Jeff. "Trial Delayed in Police Shooting Case." *Las Vegas Sun.* March 4, 2009.

O'Brien, Jeff. "Two Charges Dismissed in Police Shooting Case." *Las Vegas Sun.* January 20, 2009.

"Trial in Henderson Shooting Case Postponed." Associated Press. November 12, 2009.

Killing a Police Officer: Manslaughter to Capital Murder

Mississippi v. Cory Maye

Anderson, William L. "Death, the Drug War, and Cory Maye." www.lewrockwell.com. August 4, 2008.

Balko, Radley. "The Case of Cory Maye." *Reason Magazine.* October 2006.

Balko, Radley. "Drug War Casualties Left Behind." www.cato.org. October 16, 2006.

Gillespie, Nick. "At Reason TV: 'Mississippi Drug War Blues' Takes Honors at Oxford Film Festival!" www.reason.com. February 9, 2009.

Mott, Ronni. "Capital Murder Conviction Reversed." *Jackson Free Press.* November 18, 2009.

Qualifying for the Death Penalty in Georgia

Hansen, Jane. "Summaries of Opinions." Supreme Court of Georgia. July 14, 2008.

Jolly v. State, 284 Ga. 165 (2008).

Ramati, Phillip, and Joe Kovac Jr. "'It Just Went Wrong,' Sheriff Says of Slaying." *Macon Telegraph.* April 5, 2006.

Rankin, Bill. "Ga. Court Rules Killing Deputy Is Capital Offense." *Atlanta Journal-Constitution.* July 16, 2008.

Womack, Amy Leigh. "Attorneys Attack Warrant in Bibb Deputy Shooting Case." *Macon Telegraph.* April 15, 2008.

Womack, Amy Leigh. "Jolly to Be Tried in Savannah, Judge Rules." *Macon Telegraph.* September 5, 2008.

Womack, Amy Leigh. "Trial of Man Accused of Killing Bibb County Deputy to Be in Albany or Savannah." *Macon Telegraph.* August 14, 2008.

Cops without Badges: The Drug War Snitch

Balko, Radley. "The Railroading of Ryan Frederick." www.reason.com. March 18, 2008.

Balko, Radley. "Did Police Misconduct Lead to Another Fatal Marijuana Raid?" www.reason.com. September 25, 2008.

Davis, Stacy. "Police Misconduct in Fatal Pot Raid Revealed." www.wtkr.com. September 24, 2008.

Hopkins, John. "Frederick Informant: Police Implied He'd Receive Leniency." *Virginia-Pilot.* April 12, 2009.

Hopkins, John. "Frederick's Lawyer: Police May Have Known of Break In." *Virginia-Pilot.* December 16, 2008.

Hopkins, John. "'I'm Not the Murderer They Make Me Out to Be,' Frederick Says." *Virginia-Pilot.* August 10, 2008.

Hopkins, John. "Prosecutors Say Frederick Knew Police Were Coming to Door." *Virginia-Pilot.* September 9, 2008.

CONCLUSION: NO EASY SOLUTION

Eliminating Low-Risk SWAT Raids

Brunet, James R. "Police History Has Plenty of Military Fingerprints." *News & Observer.* January 7, 2007.

California Department of Justice. "Attorney General's Commission of Special Weapons and Tactics Final Report." September 10, 2002.

Gabor, Tom. "Re-thinking SWAT: Police Special Weapons and Tactics Units." *FBI Law Enforcement Bulletin.* April 1993.

Low-Risk Drug Raids: Pursuing Michael Phelps

Collins, Jeffrey. "Lawyer: Is Sheriff Too Aggressive in Phelps Case?" Associated Press. February 12, 2009.

"Michael Phelps 'Bong-Gate' Latest." www.radaronline.com. February 4, 2009.

"Not Enough Evidence to Charge Phelps, Sheriff Says." www.cnn.com. February 16, 2009.

Smalley, Suzanne, and Weston Kosova. "Reefer Madness." *Newsweek.* March 22, 2009.

Shooting Derek Copp

Agar, John. "Attorney Representing GVSU Student Derek Copp Has Won Cases for Others Shot by Police." *Grand Rapids Press.* March 16, 2009.

Agar, John. "Derek Copp Family Hires Lawyer; Fred Dilly Questions Police Tactics." *Grand Rapids Press.* March 16, 2009.

Agar, John and John Tunison. "Supporters of Deputy Ryan Huizenga Rally at the Sheriff's Department in West Olive." *Grand Rapids Press.* April 16, 2009.

Bickel, Nardy Baeza. "GVSU Students Plan Sit-In, March, to Fight for Change in Drug Policies After Unarmed Student Derek Copp Shot by Police." *Grand Rapids Press.* March 15, 2009.

Deiters, Barton, and Nate Reens. "Police Say Deputy's Shooting of Unarmed GVSU Student Will by Handled Like Any Other Shooting Investigation." *Grand Rapids Press.* March 13, 2009.

"Derek Copp is Name of Grand Valley Student Shot, Injured by Police During Raid." *Grand Rapids Press.* March 12, 2009.

"Derek Copp Pleads Guilty to Felony Marijuana Charge." *Grand Rapids Press.* June 26, 2009.

"Editorial: Public Needs More Information About Shooting of GVSU Student During Drug Raid." *Grand Rapids Press.* March 21, 2009.

Murray, Dave. "Derek Copp's Dad Says GVSU Student is Not a Drug Dealer; Family Wants Information From Cops." *Grand Rapids Press.* March 14, 2009.

Murray, Dave. "GVSU Classmates Can't Fathom Why Derek Copp, Described as 'Relaxed Guy,' Would be Shot by Deputy." *Grand Rapids Press.* March 15, 2009.

Schmidt, Megan. "Deputy Shouldn't Have Had Finger on Trigger When Entering Student's Apartment." *Holland Sentinel.* April 7, 2009.

Schmidt, Megan. "OCSD Deputy Charged in GVSU Shooting." *Holland Sentinel.* April 7, 2009.

"Shot That Hit Grand Valley State University Student Was Fired by Ottawa Deputy, State Police Say." *Grand Rapids Press.* March 12, 2009.

Tunison, John. "Ottawa County Sheriff's Office Reverses Decision: Deputy Ryan Huizenga, Accused of Shooting GVSU Student Derek Copp, Will Return to Work." *Grand Rapids Press.* April 13, 2009.

Tunison, John. "Police Shooting Victim Derek Copp is Eager to Get Back to His Routine on GVSU Campus." *Grand Rapids Press.* March 26, 2009.

Tunison, John. "Prosecutor Ron Frantz Asks Attorney General to Reassign Review of Derek Copp Case." *Grand Rapids Press.* March 18, 2009.

Tunison, John, and John Agar. "Drug Raid Critics Sometimes Fault Tactics, Say Enforcement Teams Uncover Few Major Dealers." *Grand Rapids Press.* April 26, 2009.

Tunison, John, and Nate Reens. "Friends of Grand Valley Student Derek Copp, Shot by Police in Campus View Apartments, Accuse Officers of Overreacting." *Grand Rapids Press*. March 12, 2009.

Trenton Drug Sweeps

"Beefed-Up Presence on The Streets: Police Increase Visibility in City." *Central Jersey News*. March 1, 2009.
Mayo, Michael. "Overzealous Drug War Claims Another Casualty." *South Florida Sun-Sentinel*. June 15, 2008.

Disbanding Paramilitary Police Units

Albuquerque, New Mexico

Egan, Timothy. "Soldiers of the Drug War Remain on Duty." *New York Times*. March 1, 1999.
Harper v. The Albuquerque Police Department. U.S. District Ct. for NM. Cause No. CIV 96-1048 (1996).
Weber, Diane Cecilia. "Warrior Cops: The Ominous Growth of Paramilitarism in American Police Departments." *Issues & Views*. Summer/Fall, 1999.

Easton, Pennsylvania

"Easton SWAT Team's Behavior: Further Evidence it Deserves Dismantling." *Morning Call* (Allentown). May 25, 2005.
Jordan, Tracy. "Consultants to Study Easton SWAT Team." *Morning Call* (Allentown). July 29, 2005.
Jordan, Tracy. "Easton SWAT Team Out, Advisor In." *Morning Call* (Allentown). July 22, 2005.
Jordan, Tracy. "Report: Dissolve Easton's SWAT Unit." *Morning Call* (Allentown). July 9, 2005.

Wrong House in Temecula

Hall, John. "New Enforcement Replaces One Disbanded." *North Country Times*. September 13, 2007.
Hall, John, and John Hunneman. "Team of Temecula Officers Disbanded, Under Investigation." *North County Times*. August 31, 2007.

The Hoboken SWAT Scandal

Balko, Radley. "Bad Hoboken Cop Punished with $132,000/Year Vacation." www.reason.com. January 31, 2010.
Clark, Amy Sara. "Disciplinary Charges in SWAT Scandal." *Jersey Journal*. February 28, 2008.

Clark, Amy Sara. "11-Month Paid Leave." *Jersey Journal.* October 13, 2008.

Hack, Charles. "Lawyer for Hoboken SWAT Cop Denies Wrongdoing." *Jersey Journal.* January 2, 2008.

"Hoboken Councilman Wants Investigation into 'Hooter Cops.'" *Jersey Journal.* November 16, 2007.

"Hoboken Lt. Angelo Andriani: Abuse of (Suspended) Powers." *Star-Ledger* (New Jersey). January 31, 2010.

Judd, N. Clark, and Paul Koepp. "Hoboken SWAT Team Disbanded in the Wake of Raunchy Photos." *Jersey Journal.* November 16, 2007.

Miller, Jonathan. "Police Scandal Grows to Include Possible Misuse of Money." *New York Times.* March 1, 2008.

Zeitlinger, Ron. "Hoboken Public Safety Director's Job Threatened." *Jersey Journal.* June 5, 2008.

Budget Constraints

"Budget Crisis May Take Out SWAT, K-9 Cops." www.mantecabulletin.com. March 6, 2009.

Garrick, David. "Escondido: City Cancels Plan to Disband Police SWAT Team." *North Country Times.* February 12, 2009.

Pawloski, Jeremy. "Police Unit Disbanding Decried." *Olympian* (Washington). February 21, 2009.

INDEX

ABOUT THE AUTHOR

A graduate of Westminster College (Pennsylvania) and Vanderbilt University Law School, **Jim Fisher** conducted criminal investigations as a special agent for the FBI from 1966 to 1972. He spent the next 30 years teaching criminal investigation, criminal law, and forensic science at Edinboro University of Pennsylvania. Two of his eight books have been nominated for Edgar Allan Poe Awards in the Best Fact Crime category. His work has been featured three times on *NBC Dateline* as well as on *Current Affair,* the Learning Channel, *Inside Edition,* PBS, CBS, the Discovery Channel, and Fox News. He has spoken at national law enforcement conferences and has guest-lectured at numerous colleges and universities on the subjects of criminal justice and policing. You can reach Jim Fisher at jfisher@edinboro.edu and keep up with developments in police militarization through his Web site, http://jimfisher. edinboro.edu/.